THE MOST TRUSTED NAME IN TRAVEL: **FROMMER'S**

FROMMER'S EasyGuide to
NEW ORLEANS
2019

6th Edition

By Diana K. Schwam

P9-DZO-656

The sugar-mounded beignets of Café du Monde are a classic treat (p. 129).

CONTENTS

Football is hugely popular in New Orleans, meaning tickets to the Superdome (pictured) can be hard to come by.

A LOOK AT NEW ORLEANS

Tennessee Williams famously wrote "America has only three cities: New York, San Francisco, and New Orleans. Everything else is Cleveland." And while that may be an extreme viewpoint (and one that reflects an outdated view of Cleveland!), it's undeniable that NOLA, Crescent City, Nawlins, The Big Easy, or whatever other nickname you want to give it has a *joie de vivre* that's unmatched in the United States, if not the world. This is a city that raises the pursuit of pleasure to an art form—in its food, its music scene, its festivals, its embrace of culture, and the exquisite architecture that graces its streets. What follows in this section is a brief peek at just some of the scintillating sights and experiences that await you on your own trip.

—*Pauline Frommer*

Since the mid–19th century, black New Orleans residents have been marching in "Indian" krewes for Mardi Gras, their costumes inspired by Native American ceremonial wear.

FRENCH QUARTER

Jackson Square is the heart of the French Quarter. It is flanked by the oldest continuously operating cathedral in the United States, St. Louis Cathedral (p. 139); the Cabildo, where the Louisiana Purchase transfer was signed (p. 142); and other important buildings.

Maison Bourbon (p. 193) is one of the French Quarter's top spots for traditional jazz and Dixieland music.

The cutting-edge Audubon Aquarium of the Americas (p. 136) houses marine life from across the globe, with an emphasis on the Gulf of Mexico and the Mississippi River.

Butterflies and moths at the exceptionally well-curated Audubon Insectarium.

Voodoo dolls and gris-gris bags are on display in the Voodoo Museum (p. 145).

The Hurricane cocktail was invented at Pat O'Brien's, which is also famous for its dueling pianos.

Definitely the oldest bar, and possibly the oldest building, in the French Quarter, the always-crowded Lafitte's Blacksmith Shop (p. 204) is a swell place to down a brewskie and make new friends.

Some love it, some find it unrelentingly sleazy, but almost everyone winds up on Bourbon Street at some point during a NOLA vacay—it has that kind of magnetic pull.

The soaring ceiling of St. Louis Cathedral (p. 139).

Arnaud's flaming Café Brûlot coffee cocktail, made with brandy, cinnamon, cloves, and citrus peel (p. 84).

Begun in 1849, the Pontalba Buildings (pictured; more on p. 140) originally were owned by Baroness Micaela Almonester de Pontalba. Look up: You can see her initials in the elaborate iron-work balconies.

BEYOND THE QUARTER

Designated a National Historic Landmark, the St. Charles streetcars (p. 270) are a wonderfully atmospheric, and convenient, way to get between the French Quarter and Uptown.

A walking tour of the Garden District (in front of the house used in the film *Benjamin Button*). See p. 174 and 236.

There's no better place to while away an evening than on Frenchman Street, especially at the always-hopping Spotted Cat (p. 198).

There's a flavor for everyone at the Creole Creamery (p. 131).

A monument in Greenwood Cemetery (p. 165).

Aboveground tombs at Lafayette Cemetery No. 1 (p. 165).

The renowned Commander's Palace (p. 118).

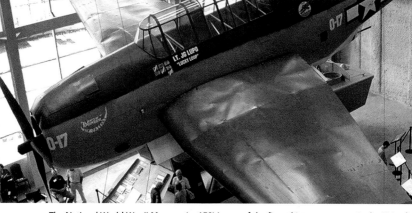

The National World War II Museum (p. 150) is one of the finest history museums in the United States. Talk with a docent; some are veterans.

A proper high tea is served at the swank Le Salon of the equally posh Windsor Court hotel (p. 71).

Some 40,000 works are owned by the New Orleans Museum of Art (p. 151), everything from pre-Columbian sculptures to paintings by European masters to the biggest collection of decorative glass on the planet.

At the Creole restaurant Jacques-Imo's (p. 120), the most coveted table in the house is actually the one set in the truck parked outside.

Strollers in Audubon Park (p. 158).

Hometown team the Big Easy Rollergirls have made roller derby popular once more (p. 185).

Mardi Gras Indians costumes are displayed at the fabulous Backstreet Cultural Museum (p. 149).

A Carnival float from the Zulu Aid and Pleasure Club.

Rain or shine, the New Orleans Jazz & Heritage Festival (p. 52) presented by Shell packs the fairgrounds.

The hipster Lobby Bar of the Ace Hotel (p. 69).

Loyola University is just one of several celebrated universities in the city.

Meals are an event in Crescent City, and that's certainly the case at Compère Lapin (p. 109), which is helmed by Nina Compton, a runner-up on TV's *Top Chef*.

Named for the trees that flank its grand entrance, Oak Alley Plantation (p. 253) is an easy drive from the city.

The traditional celebrations of Mardi Gras in the Cajun countryside involve bands of masked revelers dressed in patchwork costumes, bringing music to all parts of the community. See chapter 4 for more.

A tour of Atachfalaya Swamp, by kayak or motorboat, is a must (p. 263).

Randol's is the place for traditional Cajun food (fab crab), dancing, and music (p. 262).

The fanciful "steamboat Gothic" San Francisco Plantation (p. 252).

THE BEST OF NEW ORLEANS

New Orleans should come with a warning label. No, no, not about hurricanes. That's like solely identifying Hawaii with erupting volcanoes. No, this is about the city itself. See, there's this group of residents known as the "never lefts." They are the people who come to New Orleans as tourists, and the city worked its magic on them.

They become spellbound by the beauty of the French Quarter and the Garden District and marvel that history is alive right beneath their feet. They listen to music flowing from random doorways and street corners—jazz, soul, blues, whatever—and find themselves moving to a languorous rhythm. They kiss beneath flickering gas lamps and groove to a brass band in a crowded club long past their usual bedtimes. They eat sumptuous, indulgent meals and scandalously indulge yet again hours later, with 3am beignets at Café du Monde, where they watch the passing human parade. They'll catch the scent of jasmine and sweet olive (with a whiff of the Caribbean, and a garlic top note, perhaps) wafting through the moist, honeyed air.

The air...aah, the New Orleans air. People say romance is in the air here. It's true, of course, because the air is dreamy. It's the dewy ingénue who grows up fast in the first act, softly whispering your name. And if you're meant to be together, you'll feel that undeniable flutter, the high-voltage spark that says *you're in my heart forever.*

That's what happens to the never lefts. They came for Mardi Gras, for a festival, a conference, a tryst, wedding, reunion—just came—and fell hard. New Orleans does that to people.

What is it about this place? Well, for one thing, New Orleans is where centuries commingle, perhaps not effortlessly but nowhere more fruitfully, as if nothing essential has passed between them. It's where a barstool or a park bench becomes the opening salvo in a conversation you may never forget—for raconteurship thrives here. It's where a masquerade party of old masters, modernists, and bohemian street artists fill the city's stunning mélange of museums and galleries. It's a city that actually has an *official cocktail*—which speaks volumes to its state of mind. It's where gumbo—the savory Creole stew that is often (over) used in describing the city's multicultural tableau—is actually an apt metaphor: It speaks of a place that's deep and mysterious, rich with flavor and spiked with spice, and so much more than the sum of its many disparate parts.

New Orleans, the most unique city in the United States (hold your fire, grammarians), works its charms like a spell. But don't take our word for it. Go. See, hear, and taste for yourself. The best way to get inside New Orleans is to plunge right in. Don't just go for the obvious. Sure, we've met people who never left Bourbon Street and had a terrific time, but the city has so much more to offer. Look over the advice that follows, and see if New Orleans casts its seductive spell on you. Perhaps you'll come to understand the never lefts. Perhaps you'll even become one.

THE most authentic NEW ORLEANS EXPERIENCES

o **Do Festivals, Big or Small:** Yes to Jazz Fest, Mardi Gras, or French Quarter Fest, but also the smaller fests in New Orleans and nearby towns. If one is on while you're visiting, seek it out. See p. 24.

o **Dress Up. Or Down:** At better restaurants, men wear jackets—including seersucker when in season—and un-ironic hats. Women can and do wear dresses (not just LBDs) and heels. It's required at the finest spots, optional but common at more moderate bistros (where jeans are also okay). Dressing down might mean wacky wigs, cosplay, whatever. You can get away with it here, where every day is Halloween.

o **Frequent Dive Bars,** if that's your thang. For those whose thang it is, this town is siiick with good ones. See p. 202.

o **Tour the Swamps:** Don't discount this because you think it's too touristy (New Yorkers still go to Broadway, right?). It's an absolutely authentic, ecologically and historically fascinating, unique-to-the-region experience. See p. 175.

o **Ride a Bike:** New Orleans is flat and compact, and you can see a lot on two wheels that you might otherwise miss. See p. 268 for rentals and p. 180 for tours.

o **Cheer the Saints:** In the Dome, if possible—ain't nothing like it, nowhere. Or at least from a barstool, like everyone who ain't in the Dome. See p. 157.

o **Eat Takeout from Corner-Grocery Back Counters:** Traditionally done while leaning against a building or sitting on the curb (or on someone's stoop, which we probably shouldn't encourage). See p. 95.

o **Argue about the Best Po' Boy:** Which requires trying a few. See p. 95.

o **Go to Church:** Despite the reputation for decadence, this is a pretty pious city. Going to church is a wonderful way to get some faith on, hear some astounding gospel, and mingle with the welcoming locals. See p. 154.

o **Check Out Freebie Concerts:** Spring through autumn, free shows bring the locals to **Armstrong Park** near the French Quarter (Thurs; www.pufap. org); **City Park** in Mid-City (Thurs; p. 160); and **Lafayette Square** in the CBD (www.wednesdayatthesquare.com).

- **Stroll the Galleries:** Look for openings with wine and low-key revelry the first Saturday evening of each month on Julia Street, and second Saturdays on St. Claude Avenue. (http://secondsaturdaystclaude.com). But any time will do. See p. 214.
- **Eat Indulgent, Unhurried, Fancy Lunches:** Especially on Friday.
- **Chat:** Discuss. Debate. Banter. In restaurants, bars, or shops. With people you've just met. We'll give you locals' topics: football and city politics/ineptitude. Barring your expertise in those arenas, trading anecdotes about your observations as a tourist, discussing a recent meal, or asking for recommendations for your next meal (or next activity) gets the convo started.
- **Eat with Your Hands:** Specifically, peel shrimp and crawfish (in season), best done outdoors; and slurp oysters, best done standing at a bar and jiving with the shucker.
- **Loosen Up:** If a wailing trumpet catches your ear, follow the sound 'til you find it. If the swing band playing in the middle of Royal Street moves you, give your partner a whirl (and drop a few bucks in their hat). If you track every calorie and swear by the FitBit, lose count for a few days. And if you're lucky enough to happen upon a second-line parade passing by, don't even think of watching from the sidewalk. Jump in, and high-step it down the street. In other words, if there's something you wouldn't dare do, now might be your opportunity (assuming it's legal). You needn't lose *all* sense of propriety—just a little. It's New Orleans—it's what you do.

THE best PLACES TO EAT IN NEW ORLEANS

- **Best All-Around Dining Experience You Can Have in New Orleans:** No surprises here, they're world-famous for good reason: **Commander's Palace** (p. 118), hands down. At the other end of the spectrum, **Café du Monde** (p. 130). Somewhere in the middle: **Brigtsen's** (p. 116) and **Lilette** (p. 121)
- **Best Classic New Orleans Restaurant:** Of the three old-line, fine-dining mainstays that have been enjoyed for generations, **Arnaud's** (p. 84) is our choice for food; **Galatoire's** (p. 88) for the overall experience; **Antoine's** (p. 81) for room after amazing room full of history.
- **Best Contemporary Creole:** Our long-standing, well-deserved favorites are still the lovely **Coquette** (p. 119) and **Herbsaint** (p. 110).
- **Best Contemporary Cajun:** Popular vote goes to pork-centric **Cochon** (p. 113), where you won't find yo mama's Cajun, but we're keen on **Sac-a-Lait**'s (p. 112) refined rustic fare. **K-Paul's** (p. 90), the one that started it all, is still a standard-bearer despite Paul Prudhomme's 2015 passing.
- **Best Italian: Irene's Cuisine** (p. 89) and **Marcello's** (p. 110) represent New Orleans' traditional Creole Italian; **Domenica** (p. 113) carries the contemporary banner; and we fell hard for the *nuovo* take by sexy Uptown newcomer **Avo** (p. 116).

o **Best Neighborhood Restaurants:** New Orleans tucks away some shock-ingly good restaurants on unassuming residential streets. **Clancy's** (p. 118), **Elizabeth's** (p. 101), **Gautreau's** (p. 120), and **Liuzza's by the Track** (p. 107) show the range.

o **Best Neighbahood Restaurants:** In contrast to those above, these are old-school joints, where locals still ask, "Hey, dahwlin', wheah y'at?" We've gotta go wit da Creole Italian oldies at **Mandina's** (p. 105) and **Liuzza's** (p. 104).

o **Most Innovative Restaurants: Maypop** (p. 114) combines superb local ingredients with Southeast Asian concepts that work beautifully. **Compère Lapin** (p. 109) is up there for blending heretofore uncommon Caribbean flavors and ingredients with local traditions. **Killer PoBoys** (p. 204) pushes the sammie boundaries.

o **Best Expense- or Savings-Account Blowouts: Restaurant R'evolution** (p. 92), **Emeril's** (p. 109), or **August** (p. 111) will do the job.

o **Best Bistro:** Tough choice given the richness of this category, but **La Petite Grocery** (p. 120), **Meauxbar** (p. 90), and **Sylvain** (p. 95) figure highly.

o **Best Outdoor Dining:** Start with the pretty courtyards at **Bayona** (p. 84), and **Café Amelie** (p. 93) on starry nights or balmy afternoons; **Bacchanal**'s (p. 99) funky backyard vibe, and **Avo**'s romantic patio (p. 116). The second-floor galleries at **Tableau** (p. 92) and **Dat Dog** (p. 127) overlook the two entertaining extremes of Jackson Square and Frenchmen Street, respectively.

o **Best Rooftop Bars:** They've sprung up nearly everywhere, but we're par-tial to **Hot Tin,** at the Pontchartrain Hotel (p. 205), and **Alto,** atop the Ace Hotel (p. 69).

o **Best for Kids:** The no-brainers are **Café du Monde** (p. 130), for powdered-sugar mess and mania; the counter at **Camellia Grill** (p. 126); and a **sno-ball** (p. 129). **Antoine's** (p. 81) offers a good intro to fine-dining.

o **Best Slightly Offbeat but Utterly New Orleanian Restaurants:** Defi-nitely **Jacques-Imo's** (p. 120) and **Bacchanal** (p. 99). The fancier **Upper-line** (p. 122) and decidedly unfancy deli **Cochon Butcher** (p. 113) also fit the category.

o **Best Seafood:** Upscale **GW Fins** sets a high bar (p. 88), though **Peche** (p. 111) is a strong contender; Mid-City's **Bevi** (p. 106) covers the low-key, boiled-seafood angle. For oysters, hit **Felix** (p. 96) or **Casamento's** (p. 127).

o **Best Desserts:** A meal at **Emeril's** (p. 109) is incomplete without banana cream pie; ditto **Commander's Palace**'s (p. 118) bread pudding soufflé or bananas Foster. The pastry chefs at **Lilette** (p. 121), **La Petite Grocery** (p. 120), and **Coquette** (p. 118) excel. Or head to a specialist at **Sucré** (p. 132), **Bywater Bakery** (p. 102), or **Angelo Brocato's** (p. 130).

o **Best Brunch:** Yay! **Brennan**'s is back (p. 86). **Ralph's on the Park** (p. 103) or **Dante's Kitchen** (p. 123) can't miss, while the jazz brunch at **Antoine's** (p. 81), **Arnaud's** (p. 84), and **Commander's Palace** (p. 118) are great fun. Gotta give love to the drag brunch at **Country Club** (p. 100) and to eclectic newbie **Bywater Americana Bistro** (p. 99).

- **Restaurants with the Best Cocktail Programs:** From a looong list, we'll go with **Latitude 29** (p. 94), **High Hat** (p. 124), **Compère Lapin** (p. 109), and **Brennan's** (p. 86), with a nod to wacky **Turkey & the Wolf** (p. 129).
- **Best Wine Lists:** The extensive collections at **Emeril's** (p. 109), **Arnaud's** (p. 84), **Commander's Palace** (p. 118), and **Antoine's** (p. 81) cover every base. The lists are smaller but smart at **Bayona** (p. 84), **La Petite Grocery** (p. 120), and **Gautreau's** (p. 120), and well-curated at **Bacchanal** (p. 99) and **Saffron** (p. 122).

THE best PLACES TO STAY IN NEW ORLEANS

This is a little like deciding on a scoop of ice cream—so many tasty options to choose from, and different people like different flavors. We've tried to narrow down the selections based on specific criteria.

- **Best Moderately Priced Lodging:** In general, you'll get the biggest bang in the **off-season** (including the heat of summer), when even luxury properties feature enticingly lower rates. In the CBD, the **Drury Inn** (p. 72) is surprisingly reasonable and an easy hop to the Quarter, and same goes for the spiffily redone **Fairfield Inn & Suites** (p. 72). In the B&B category, the **Chimes** (p. 77), a delightful family-owned guesthouse in the Garden District, has generated legions of loyal return guests.
- **Best Luxury Hotel:** At the intimate **Audubon Cottages** (p. 54), luxury commences when your 24-hour butler greets you at the private, unmarked entrance. For sheer opulence, attention to your every need, and vast expanses of room, it's the **Windsor Court** (p. 71). A Club Level suite, of course. The **Pontchartrain Hotel** (p. 76) is slightly less soignée but still worthy.
- **Best Service:** All those in the "Luxury" category above excel in the service category. We're also continually impressed by the attentive **Loews** (p. 69). Of the more modest accommodations, congeniality and overall graciousness awards go to Uptown's **Maison Perrier** (p. 76); the Bywater's **Maison de Macarty** (p. 65); the **Chimes** (p. 77) in the Garden District; and Mid-City's **1896 O'Malley House** (p. 67).
- **Most Romantic:** Romance is wherever you make it, but **Ashton's** (p. 66) encourages long, languid mornings. The **Saint,** particularly its outlandish, fiery Lucifer Suite, was made for misbehavior (931 Canal St.; www.thesainthotelneworleans.com). No one will find you in the secluded **Audubon Cottages** (p. 54).
- **Best for Families:** It's not fancy, but we like both **Homewood Suites** (p. 72) locations for the spacious two-room suites, amenities, and freebie meals. The **Richelieu** (p. 61) offers easy comfort, topnotch service, and a pool.

- **Best Faaaabulous B&B:** A lot of B&Bs are crammed with over-the-top antiques, but at the **Antebellum** (p. 67), they all come with a story. We love the tawdry over-the-topness, hidden hot tub, and actual bordello bed.
- **Best for Hipness:** The **Ace** is the place du jour (p. 69), and we like the sexy, worn-leather steampunk vibe at the **Q&C** (p. 70). The **Renaissance Arts** (p. 70) is film-crew central, for what that's worth. The **Catahoula** (p. 69) is giving them all a quiet run for their money; the **Troubadour** (p. 74) brings high style and a fizzy rooftop-bar scene. **The Drifter** (p. 67), though not for everyone, is on a whole 'nother hipness plane.
- **Best Funky Spots:** We're fond of the sweetly eccentric **B&W Courtyards** (p. 65), a Marigny gem; the Frenchmen-adjacent **Royal Street Inn** (p. 65); and the hodge-podgey but well-located ex-brothel now called the **Dauphine Orleans** (p. 55).
- **Best Hidden Gem:** The uneventful location of the **Henry Howard** (p. 74) belies its stunningly renovated interior and comfortable, hip vibe. The **Claiborne Mansion**'s two superb suites and splendid pool are a serene oasis a block from the Frenchmen Street mayhem (p. 63).

THE best TRIP MEMENTOS

Nothing wrong with T-shirts, caps, Mardi Gras beads, and snow globes (except that you can get those anywhere). We offer some alternate ideas.

- **A Book from Faulkner House:** Many an author has tried, with varying success, to capture New Orleans on the page. Their efforts may help you know what it means to miss New Orleans. Pick up some reading material from this charming jewel on little Pirate's Alley, crammed with Louisiana-related tomes (p. 218). Check out our reading list in chapter 2.
- **A Photo or Art Book from A Gallery for Fine Photography:** The owner calls his impressive shop "the only museum where you can buy the art." A photograph from one of the many famed photographers represented here is a souvenir to relish every day, not to mention a wise investment. If an original isn't feasible, consider a fine photo book. See p. 216.
- **A Southern Scent from Hové:** This classic perfumery creates its own perfumes and soaps. We got hooked on sachet-favorite Vetivert, described as "smelling like the South." Locals also adore the scents made from the indigenous sweet olive, and the fine gentlemanly scents. See p. 223.
- **Local art:** Take home a singular treasure from one of the many excellent galleries and art markets including Palmer Park (p. 212) and the Palace Market on Frenchmen Street (p. 212)
- **Tunes:** New Orleans' soundtrack is as essential to your experience as her sights and tastes. A few CDs purchased (yes, bought) at gigs or some record-shop vinyl (p. 224) will keep the good times rolling back home. See our recorded-music recommendations in chapter 2.
- **A Hat from Meyer:** We're mad about **Meyer the Hatter** for the selection, the service, and the 100-year-plus history. You're in the South, *darlin';* you can rock some class headgear. See p. 221.

- **A "be nice or leave" Sign:** Dr. Bob's colorful, bottle-cap-edged signs may have proliferated around the city, but they're still true, local works of folk art, handmade with found materials. Available in a variety of sizes, materials, and sentiments at **Pop City,** 940 Decatur St. (☎ **504/528-8559**) and **Funrock'n,** 3109 Magazine St. (☎ **504/895-4102**)—but it's more fun to visit **Dr. Bob's Bywater studio,** 3027 Chartres St. (http://drbobart.net; ☎ **504/945-2225**), open 10am to 5pm daily.

- **Fleur-de-lis Jewelry:** Gold, silver, glass, cufflink, nose ring, pendant—the selection is unending. Wear it with pride; share it with a smile. Consider something from **Mignon Faget** (p. 223) or an inexpensive bauble from the flea-market stands at the **French Market** (p. 213).

- **Sazerac Glasses:** If you've taken a shine to the city's official cocktail, the **Roosevelt Hotel** (p. 71) has perfect reproductions of their original glasses.

- **Pralines:** The choice for office gifts. And for home. Maybe one for the plane or car on the way there. (And remember it's *prah*, not *pray*.) See p. 219.

THE best OF OUTDOOR NEW ORLEANS

Not exactly what you think of when you think Big Easy—it's not Yellowstone, after all. But there are some surprisingly wonderful outdoorsy things to do here that will only enhance the vacation you envisioned. Besides, it can't all be about dark bars and decadent meals. Oh wait, it's New Orleans. Yes, it can. Still…these experiences provide a fine counterpoint and a different perspective.

- **Kayak Bayou St. John:** A guided kayak tour of placid, pretty Bayou St. John is an entrancing way to see this historically significant waterway—and maybe work off a few bites of fried shrimp po' boy. See p. 147.

- **City Park It:** Whatever your outdoor thing, it's probably doable somewhere in the glorious, 1,300-acre **City Park** (p. 160), from pedal-boating to picnicking, birding to bicycling, golfing (mini or big) to art-gazing. It's great for a morning run, as is Uptown's **Audubon Park** (p. 158). **Lafitte Greenway** (p. 161) and **Crescent Park** (p. 161), two new, smaller parks, offer interesting and different perspectives of the city.

- **Tour the Swamps:** The swamps are eerie, serene, and fascinating. The gators are spellbinding, and most guides are knowledgeable naturalists who will open your eyes to this unique ecoculture. See p. 175.

- **Ferry Cross the Mississippi:** It's not quite Huck Finn, but a brief "cruise" on the ferry to the historic Algiers neighborhood is an easy way to roll on the river and take in a different view. See p. 269.

- **See the City from Two Wheels (or Three):** Whether you rent a bike (p. 268), take a guided bike tour (p. 180), or roll through on a Segway (p. 181), seeing the flat, compact city via two wheels makes for a sweet ride.

- **Dine Alfresco:** We didn't say the best of *active* outdoor New Orleans, did we? A languid, courtyard dinner under the Southern stars (or lunch under an umbrella) at **Bayona, Café Amelie, Bacchanal, Green Goddess, Avo, Brennan's, Tableau, Sucré in the Quarter,** or **Napoleon House** is an experience to be savored.

- **Yoga in the Besthoff Sculpture Garden:** We can't think of a more sublime way to start a Saturday—especially when it's followed by beignets and coffee (just steps away at **Morning Call** cafe). A little yin, a little yang. It's Saturdays at 8am in City Park (© **504/482-4888**; p. 152).

- **Walk. Walk. And Walk Some More:** This city is made for walking. It's truly the best way to take in the captivating sights, appreciate the silken air, and ogle (or join) the goings-on you will undoubtedly encounter. We won't bring up the c-word benefits (calories—oops, drat…sorry). No texting while walking, though—these buckling old sidewalks require your full attention.

THE best MUSEUMS IN NEW ORLEANS

New York, Chicago, Paris, Rome…great museum cities, all. New Orleans isn't included in that list, but it's a surprisingly excellent museum city. Museums also make stellar retreats when the elements become overbearing.

- **Backstreet Cultural Museum:** To truly appreciate them, you really must see the Mardi Gras Indians' astounding beaded suits up close (if not in action, then in this collection) and learn about this unique tradition. See p. 149.

- **The Cabildo:** Louisiana and New Orleans history, including terrific Mardi Gras exhibits. And Napoleon's death mask. See p. 142.

- **The Insectarium:** Yes, it is what it sounds like. It's especially good for families, but unexpectedly captivating even for the bug-averse. See p. 138.

- **Louisiana Children's Museum:** So much hands-on, interactive fun (for all ages) you don't even realize you're also learning. See p. 184.

- **National World War II Museum:** It's the best museum of its kind. Period. Do not miss its world-class collection and interactive displays. See p. 150.

- **New Orleans Museum of Art:** Consistently well-curated exhibits and an excellent permanent collection of all forms of fine art, housed in a stunning, neoclassical-meets-modernist building in beautiful City Park. See p. 151.

- **Ogden Museum of Southern Art:** A splendid collection of the art of the American South in a modern atrium between historic buildings. See p. 152.

- **Pharmacy Museum:** Leeches and opium and Voodoo spells, oh my. A mightily worthwhile, off-the-wall diversion. See p. 144.

- **The Presbytère:** The excellent exhibit on hurricanes captures their impact from all aspects; other rotating exhibits are consistently good. See p. 145.

NEW ORLEANS IN CONTEXT

Throughout this book, we talk about the mystique of New Orleans and its intoxicating, ineffable essence. But first, it's time for some stats. The largest city in Louisiana (pop. 389,000) and one of the chief cities of the South, New Orleans is nearly 100 miles above the mouth of the Mississippi River system and stretches along a strip of land 5 to 8 miles wide between the Mississippi and Lake Pontchartrain. Surrounded by a river and a lake, the city is largely under sea level. The highest natural point is in City Park, a whopping 35 feet above sea level.

New Orleans has always been known for its jazz-infused joie de vivre, a place where antebellum meets bohemia in a high-stepping dance of life, lived fully and out loud. Its recent history, however, is marked by two horrific, well-known events: the Deepwater Horizon oil spill in the nearby Gulf of Mexico, and the failure of the levee system following Hurricane Katrina. But more than a decade following that devastation—with the city's 2018 tricentennial in the rearview—it is rebounding so palpably that the air fairly prickles with energy.

In this chapter, we briefly recount the area's rich history, starting at present and reaching back to its foundation, to help explain how New Orleanians got their resilient, life-affirming "yatitude" (from "Where y'at?"—the local version of "How ya doin'?").

NEW ORLEANS TODAY

Happy 300th birthday indeed, New Orleans. The city celebrated its tricentennial in 2018, and the party continues apace. A new entre-preneurial drive and creative spirit engulfed the city after Katrina, and the results are palpable. The annual number of visitors to Loui-siana has set records for the past 4 years running. The hotel market is growing like kudzu, with the opening of more than 20 new or renovated properties since 2015, with still more in the works. The Rampart Street streetcar line hums along from the Marigny to the CBD, and the sprawling, ambitious biodistrict along Tulane Avenue is buzzing. Louis Armstrong Airport recently welcomed its first international flights in nearly 3 decades, and its enormous North Terminal addition should be complete by the time you read this.

Off-the-beaten-path streets like Oak, Freret, St. Claude Avenue, and Oretha Castle Haley Boulevard have blossomed with activity. The number of restaurants in the city (1,500+) is nearly *double* the pre-Katrina. The hopping Frenchmen Street club scene continues to boom. Sure, some say it's jumped the shark, but we say good luck finding a better street in the U.S.A. for music, people-watching, and sheer exhilaration. HBO's series *Tremé* portrayed authentic New Orleans with a (mostly) spot-on eye and a killer soundtrack, focusing a new fascination on the local culture.

It's a thrilling time in the city that time forgot—and with the countless travel-press accolades being reigned upon New Orleans, the buzz is about as loud as Rebirth Brass Band playing the tin-ceilinged Maple Leaf bar.

Still, all is not rosy. While the tourist zones show few signs of ill wind, folks venturing into certain neighborhoods will still find pristine, rebuilt homes next to abandoned blight. In the decimated Lower 9th Ward, redevelopment chugs along slowly, but proudly, with small but significant new developments and the architecturally curious "Make It Right" homes (Brad Pitt's foundation). Other areas are repopulating and redeveloping radically, gentrifying rapidly, and threatening, some believe, the very authenticity that attracted the gentrifiers (and tourists) in the first place. The sociological, economic, and cultural impact of the city's shifting demographics is a source of much concern and debate, as exemplified by the displacement of long-term renters by speculators and profiteering **Airbnb** landlords (see p. 62). Crime and the hobbled criminal-justice system remain complicated, vexing problems, and more water woes plague the city in its struggle to maintain and update an ancient pumping system and prevent (too-common) street flooding. More recently, as with so many American cities, New Orleans' persistent and persistently unresolved struggle with the racial divide flared up in the eye of the world, as four confederate monuments were removed from their long-held positions of reverence. Even more recently, markers are going up all over New Orleans memorializing the city's sorry history as a major slave-trading hub, and recognizing the influence of enslaved people on the region's development.

The grim images that focused the eyes of the world on New Orleans in August 2005 are not easily erased, nor should they be. The category 5 storm was downgraded to a category 3 when it hit New Orleans, but the surge was too much for the city's federal levee system. Its failure flooded 80% of the city, causing 1,836 recorded deaths and all forms of astounding, horrifying loss. Some 28,000 people took refuge in the Superdome, the ill-prepared refuge of last resort.

Four and a half years later, the Dome's home football team, the New Orleans Saints, at long last came marching in with their first-ever Super Bowl victory. The long-derided 'Aints restored what billions in rebuilding funds couldn't: civic pride. It may seem trivial, even disrespectful, to cite a football game as a turning point in the city's rebirth—but it isn't. The effects of this

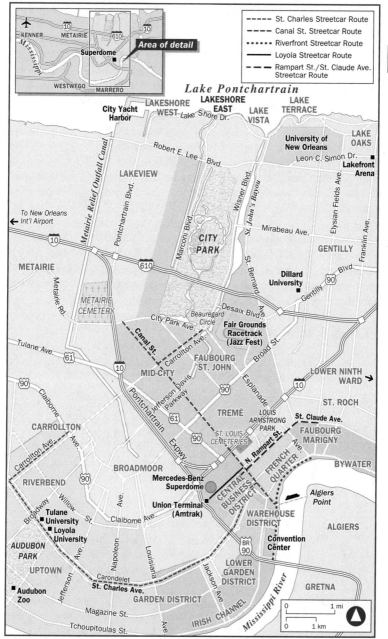

real and symbolic victory reached far beyond the ecstatic, extended celebrations—and they cannot be overstated.

That same year saw more high points: Mitch Landrieu won the mayoral race with 66% of the vote, marking the end to the previous administration's fumbling, inertia, and corruption; and massive crowds poured into the city for Mardi Gras and French Quarter Fest. The good times were rolling once again, at full speed.

And then, the whammy. One. More. Time. (Eye roll, headshake.)

The 2010 Deepwater Horizon oil spill hit, with potent imagery again tainting New Orleans with a wide, crude brush. In reality, New Orleans is some 150 miles from the spill, and those images were far worse than the reality (though state-mates in the affected areas were hard-hit).

Although locals will forever mark time as B.K. or A.K. (Before Katrina or After Katrina), New Orleanians just did what they do: proclaim their undying love for their city, mix a cocktail, and set to tidying up. Oh, and throw a few parties for half a million people, and earn top awards on umpteen "Best of" travel polls.

The indomitable spirit is intact. The oysters are still sweet, the jasmine-infused air still sultry. Bands still play in Jackson Square, and parades erupt at random. New Orleans is still the best city in America, and the *bons temps*—like those beloved Saints of field and song—go marching in and on. We're right there with them. You should be, too. Go, and be in that number.

HISTORY 101

In 1682, explorer René-Robert Cavelier, Sieur de la Salle, claimed the region for France. Just 5 years later, his navigational and leadership failures in later explorations resulted in his mutinous murder by his own party.

At the turn of the 18th century, French-Canadian brothers Pierre Le Moyne, Sieur d'Iberville, and 18-year-old Jean Baptiste Le Moyne, Sieur de Bienville, staked a claim at a dramatic bend in the Mississippi river, near where La Salle had stopped almost 2 decades earlier. Iberville also established a fort at Biloxi. Brother Bienville stayed on there, becoming commanding officer of the territory while harboring thoughts of returning to the spot up the river to establish a new capital city.

Right about 300 years ago Bienville got his chance. In 1718 the French monarch, eager to develop, populate, and garner the riches that Louisiana promised, charged Bienville with finding a suitable location for a settlement, one that would also protect France's New World holdings from British expansion. Bienville chose the easily defensible high ground at the bend in the river. Although it was some 100 miles inland along the river from the Gulf of Mexico, the site was near St. John's Bayou, a waterway into Lake Pontchartrain. This "back door" was convenient for a military defense or escape, and as a trade route (as the Choctaw Indians had long known)—allowing relatively easy access to the Gulf while bypassing a perilous section of the Mississippi.

The new town was named La Nouvelle-Orléans in honor of the duc d'Orléans, then the regent of France. The "property development" was entrusted to John Law's Company of the West. Following the plan of a late French medieval town, a central square (the Place d'Armes) was laid out with streets forming a grid around it. A church, government office, priest's house, and official residences fronted the square, and earthen ramparts dotted with forts were built around the perimeter. A tiny wooden levee was raised against the river, which still periodically turned the streets into rivers of mud. Today this area of original settlement is known as the Vieux Carré (old square) and the Place d'Armes as Jackson Square.

A Melting Pot

In its first few years, New Orleans was a community of French officials, adventurers, merchants, soldiers, the enslaved, and convicts from French prisons, all living in crude huts of cypress, moss, and clay. These were the first ingredients of New Orleans' population gumbo. The city's commerce was mainly limited to trade with native tribes and to instituting agricultural production.

To supply people and capital, John Law's company marketed the territory and the city as Heaven on Earth, full of boundless opportunities for wealth and luxury. Real estate values soared, and wealthy Europeans, merchants, exiles, soldiers, and a large contingent of German farmers arrived—to find only mosquitoes, a raw frontier existence, and swampy land. The scheme nearly bankrupted the French nation, but New Orleans' population grew, and in 1723 it replaced Biloxi as the capital of the Louisiana territory.

In 1724, Bienville approved the Code Noir, which set forth laws under which African slaves were to be treated and established Catholicism as the territory's official religion. While it codified slavery and banished Jews from Louisiana, the code did give enslaved people recognition and a very slight degree of legal protection, unusual in the South at that time.

A lack of potential wives created a significant barrier to population and societal development. In 1727, a small contingent of Ursuline nuns was sent over and established a convent. While the nuns weren't exactly eligible, they did provide a temporary home and education to many subsequent shiploads of *les filles à la cassette.* The "cassette girls" or "casket girls"—named for the government-issue *cassettes* or casketlike trunks in which they carried their possessions—were young women of appropriate character sent to Louisiana by the French government to be courted and married by the colonists. (If we're to believe the current residents of the city, the plan was remarkably successful: Nearly everyone in New Orleans claims descent from the virtuous casket girls or from Spanish or French nobility. By insinuation, then, the colony's motley initial population of convicts and "fallen women" was wholly infertile. Hmm....)

John Law's company relinquished its governance of Louisiana in 1731, and the French monarch regained control of the territory. In the following decades, planters established estates up and down the river. In the city, wealthier society began to develop a courtly atmosphere on the French model. Alongside their rough-and-tumble plantation existence, families competed to see who could throw the most opulent parties in their city townhouses.

During the 18th century, colonization of a different sort began along the Gulf of Mexico. There, many French colonists, displaced by British rule from Acadia, Nova Scotia, made their way south from Canada and formed a rural outpost, where their descendants still live, farm, trap, and speak their unique brand of French to this day. The Acadians' name has been Anglicized, and we know them today as Cajuns.

Meanwhile, New Orleans' commercial development was stymied by French restrictions requiring the colony to trade only with the mother country. To subvert the restrictions, smugglers and pirates provided alternative markets and transportation for local crops, furs, bricks, and tar.

As the French saw it, this colonial development's return on investment wasn't paying off. In 1762, Louis XV traded the city and all of Louisiana west of the Mississippi to his cousin Charles III of Spain in the secret Treaty of Fontainebleau. It took 2 years for the news to reach a shocked New Orleans, and 2 more for Spain to send a governor, Don Antonio de Ulloa—who made few friends among local residents and was eventually sent packing. Some proposed the formation of a Louisiana republic. For a time, New Orleans and Louisiana were effectively independent of any foreign power. That came to a crashing end in 1769 when the Spanish sent forth Don Alexander "Bloody" O'Reilly and 3,000 soldiers. Local leaders of the relatively peaceful rebellion were executed, and Spanish rule was imposed again. With a Gallic shrug, French aristocracy mingled with Spanish nobility, intermarried, and helped to create a new "Creole" culture.

A devastating fire struck in 1788, destroying more than 850 buildings; another in 1794 amidst the rebuilding. From the ashes emerged a new architecture dominated by the proud Spanish style of brick-and-plaster buildings replete with arches, courtyards, balconies with their famed cast-iron railings, and, of course, attached slave quarters. Today you'll still see tile markers giving Spanish street names on French Quarter street corners.

This was a period of intense imperial conflict and maneuvering among the Spanish, French, English, and Americans. There were more trade restrictions, and more good times for pirates like the infamous brothers Pierre and Jean Lafitte. Spain allowed some American revolutionaries to trade through the city in support of the colonists' fight against Britain, but France rallied and regained possession of the territory in 1800 with a surprisingly quiet transfer of ownership. The French held on for 3 years while Napoleon negotiated the Louisiana Purchase with the United States for the paltry sum of $15 million. For Creole society, a return to financially-strapped French rule was unpleasant enough. But a sale to uncouth America was anathema. To their minds, it meant the end of a European lifestyle in the Vieux Carré. Feeling the burn, the American upper classes installed their showy new settlements across Canal

Street (so named because a drainage canal was once planned along its route)—away from the old city and its insulated Creole society.

So it was that New Orleans came to be two parallel cities. The American Sector spread outward from Canal Street along St. Charles Avenue; business and cultural institutions centered in the Central Business District; and mansions rose in what is now the Garden District, which was a separate, incorporated city until 1852. French and Creole society dominated the Quarter for the rest of the 19th century, extending toward Lake Pontchartrain along Esplanade Avenue. Soon, however, the Americans (crass though they may have seemed) brought commercial success to the city, which quickly warmed relations. The Americans sought the vitality of downtown society, and the Creoles sought the profit of American business. They also had occasion to join forces against hurricanes, yellow-fever epidemics, and floods.

From the Battle of New Orleans to the Civil War

The great turning point in Creole-American relations was the Battle of New Orleans during the War of 1812. To save the city, Andrew Jackson set aside his disdain for the pirate Jean Lafitte (and Choctaw Indians, and black soldiers) to create a ragtag army, and Lafitte supplied the Americans with cannons and ammunition that helped swing the battle in their favor. When Jackson called for volunteers, some 5,000 citizens from both sides of Canal Street responded. During the battle on January 8, 1815, at Chalmette Battlefield (p. 159), a few miles downriver from the city, approximately 2,000 British troops and 20 Americans were killed or wounded. The course of history was changed, Louisiana was incorporated into the Union, and Jackson became a hero—despite the treaty concluding the war having been signed a full 2 weeks before. Who knew? Naturally, the recent 200th anniversary of this milestone was cause for massive celebration.

In this boom period, colonial trade restrictions had evaporated with the Louisiana Purchase, and steam-powered river travel arrived in 1812. River commerce exploded, and by the 1840s New Orleans' port was on par with New York's. Cotton and sugar made many local fortunes (on the backs of slave labor); wealthy planters joined the city merchants in building luxurious townhouses and attending festivals, opera, theater, banquets, parades, and spectacular balls (including "Quadroon Balls," where beautiful mulatto girls were peddled to the male gentry as possible mistresses). As always, politics and gambling were dominant pastimes of citizens and visitors.

By the middle of the century, cotton-related business was responsible for nearly half of the total commerce in New Orleans, and the city housed a large and ruthless slave market to support it. Paradoxically, New Orleans also had an extensive, established population of "free men (and women) of color," uncommon in the American South. Furthermore, racial distinctions within the city became increasingly difficult to determine; people could often trace their ancestry back to two or even three different continents. Adding to the diversity were waves of Irish and German immigrants, vital labor sources supporting the city's growth.

The only major impediments to the development of the city in these decades were occasional mosquito-borne yellow fever epidemics, which killed thousands of residents and visitors, and persisted until late in the 19th century.

Reconstruction & Beyond

The boom era ended rather abruptly with the Civil War and Louisiana's secession from the United States in 1861. Federal troops marched into the city in 1862 and stayed until 1877, through the bitter Reconstruction period. All over the South, this period saw violent clashes between armed white groups and the state's Reconstruction forces.

After the war, the city went about the business of rebuilding its economic life—without slavery. Without a free labor base, some fortunes crashed, but the city persevered. By 1880, annexations had fleshed out the city limits, port activity had picked up, and railroads were establishing their economic importance. A new group of immigrants, Sicilians, came to put their unique mark on the city. Through it all, an undiminished enthusiasm for fun survived. Gambling thrived; there were hundreds of saloons and scores of "bawdy houses" engaged in prostitution (illegal, but largely unenforced). New Orleans was earning an international reputation for open vice, much to the chagrin of the city's polite society.

In 1897, Alderman Sidney Story moved all illegal (but highly profitable) activities into a restricted district along Basin Street next to the French Quarter, in an effort to improve the city's tarnished image. Quickly nicknamed Storyville, the district boasted fancy "sporting palaces" with elaborate decor, entertainment, and all variety of ladies of pleasure. The *Blue Book* directory listed the names, addresses, and races of more than 700 prostitutes working the swanky "palaces" down to the decrepit "cribs." Black musicians such as Jelly Roll Morton played in the more ornate bordellos, popularizing early forms of jazz. When the Secretary of the Navy decreed in 1917 that armed forces should not be exposed to such open vice, Storyville closed down and disappeared—with nary a trace beyond its immense cultural impact.

The 20th Century

In the 20th century, the city's port become the largest in the United States and the second-busiest in the world (after Amsterdam), with goods coming in by barge and rail. Electrification and other modern technology kept the port whirring. Drainage problems were conquered by means of high levees, canals, pumping stations, and great spillways, which direct floodwater away from the city. Bridges were built across the Mississippi River, including the Huey P. Long Bridge, named after Louisiana's infamous politician and demagogue. New Orleans' emergence as a regional financial center, with more than 50 commercial banks, led to the construction of soaring office buildings, mostly in the Central Business District. World War II spawned a thriving shipbuilding industry, which was replaced by the expansion of oil, gas, and petrochemical businesses after the war. Later in the 20th century, tourism became another primary economic driver.

Like that of most other American cities, the city's population spread outward, filling suburbs and nearby municipalities. A thriving community in New Orleans East was developed by Vietnamese refugees, who immigrated here in the 1970s. Unlike other cities, however, New Orleans has been able to preserve its original town center and much of its historic architecture.

NEW ORLEANS IN POPULAR CULTURE

Books

You can fill many bookcases with New Orleans literature and authors, so consider the following list as just a jumping-off point. Get more recommendations at the fine bookshops listed in chapter 9.

GENERAL FICTION

Many early fiction works provide a taste of old-time New Orleans life. George Washington Cable's stories are revealing and colorful, as in *Old Creole Days* (1879). Kate Chopin, whose late-1800s works include the revered *The Awakening,* are set in Louisiana and discuss the earliest Creoles. Frances Parkinson Keyes lived on Chartres Street from 1945 to 1970. Her most famous work, *Dinner at Antoine's,* has curious descriptions of life in the city at that time and excellent descriptions of food.

Ellen Gilchrist's contemporary short-story collection *In the Land of Dreamy Dreams,* portrays life in wealthy uptown New Orleans. Sheila Bosworth's wonderful tragicomedies perfectly sum up the city and its collection of characters—check out all-time favorites *Almost Innocent* or *Slow Poison.* Michael Ondaatje's controversial *Coming Through Slaughter* is a wonderful, fictionalized account of Buddy Bolden and the early New Orleans jazz era.

Newer favorites include Moira Crone's sci-fi thriller *The Not Yet,* set in a future even stranger than the present; Michael Zell's challenging but satisfying thriller *Errata;* and *King Xeno* by Nathaniel Rich, in which a serial ax murderer meets a Mafia kingpin in the early jazz age, and fiction meets fact. In the perennially popular, well-crafted series by James Lee Burke, misfit Cajun detective Dave Robicheaux keeps the bad guys running and the pages turning.

And then there is the cottage industry known as Anne Rice, who undeniably ignited the current era of pop vampire culture (bow to the master, *True Blood, Twilight,* and *Vampire Diaries*). Her now-classic *Vampire Chronicles* books expertly capture the city's elegant, otherworldly essence.

HISTORY

Lyle Saxon, director of the writer's program under the WPA, wrote *Fabulous New Orleans*—a charming place to start learning about the city's past—and coauthored the folk-tale collection *Gumbo Ya-Ya*. Mark Twain visited the city often in his riverboat days, and his *Life on the Mississippi* has a number of tales about New Orleans and its riverfront life. *The WPA Guide to New Orleans* also contains excellent social and historical background and provides a fascinating picture of the city in 1938. *Beautiful Crescent,* by Joan Garvey and Mary Lou Widmer, is a solid reference book on the city's history. *Gangs of New York*'s author Herbert Asbury gave the same highly entertaining—if not terribly factual—treatment to New Orleans in *The French Quarter: An Informal History of the New Orleans Underworld.* New Orleans's favorite patroness, the Baroness de Pontalba, gets the biography treatment in Christina Vella's *Intimate Enemies.* In *The Last Madam: A Life in the New Orleans Underworld,* Christine Wiltz reveals a bawdy bygone era, conveyed through the words of Norma Wallace. The brothel owner recorded her memoirs before her 1974 suicide. Before there was *Frommer's,* there was *The Bachelor in New Orleans,* a guide for the coolest of visiting cats. The 2017 reissue of the 1942 guide is positively retro-charming and surprisingly informative.

Three newer, eminently readable histories are Ned Sublette's *The World That Made New Orleans,* which focuses on the cultural influences of European, African, and Caribbean settlers; Lawrence Powell's *Accidental City,* a look back at the city's scrappy evolution; and the elegantly entangled *Unfathomable City,* a coffee-table atlas with essays by Rebecca Solnit and Rebecca Snedecker.

Of the many guides to Mardi Gras, Henri Schindler's *Mardi Gras New Orleans* account is that of a historian and a long-term producer of balls and parades. *Mardi Gras in New Orleans: An Illustrated History*, by *Mardi Gras Guide* publisher Arthur Hardy, describes the celebration's evolution.

Lovers of the lurid will enjoy *Madame LaLaurie,* a well-researched biography of the notorious high-society murderess. Sara Roahen's charming *Gumbo Tales: Finding My Place at the New Orleans Table* leaves readers hungry for more of her uproarious insights, as the recent transplant to New Orleans discovers the culture through its distinctive food and drink.

In *The Fish That Ate the Whale: The Life and Times of America's Banana King,* Rich Cohen recounts the rags-to-riches-to-revolution tale of local fruit magnate Sam Zemurray. Finally, *In the Shadow of Statues: A White Southerner Confronts History*, is ex-Mayor Mitch Landrieu's provocatively reflective 2017 memoir.

LITERATURE

William Faulkner came to New Orleans, lived on Pirate's Alley, and penned *Soldiers' Pay.* Several other Faulkner novels and short stories are set in New Orleans. Tennessee Williams became a devoted New Orleans fan, living in the city on and off for many years. It inspired him to write *A Streetcar Named Desire,* one of the best-known New Orleans tales. He also set *The Rose Tattoo* in the city.

Other notable New Orleans writers include Walker Percy and Shirley Ann Grau. Percy's novels, notably *The Moviegoer,* are classic portrayals of the idiosyncrasies of New Orleans and its residents. Grau's *The Keepers of the House* won the Pulitzer Prize in 1964. John Kennedy Toole also received a Pulitzer; however, at the time of his suicide, none of his works had even been published. His *A Confederacy of Dunces* is a timeless New Orleans tragicomedy and probably the city's most beloved novel.

Robert Penn Warren's classic novel *All the King's Men,* an exceedingly loose telling of the story of Huey P. Long, portrays the performance art known as Louisiana politics. New Orleans' Vietnamese community is the setting for Robert Olen Butler's 1993 Pulitzer Prize–winning collection, *A Good Scent from a Strange Mountain.*

POST-KATRINA LITERATURE

From great tragedy comes great art, and the following help shape an image of pre- and post-flood New Orleans. Tom Piazza's *Why New Orleans Matters* is a love letter to and about the city and the number-one choice for people trying to "get" New Orleans. His novel *City of Refuge* bisects Katrina through the experiences of two families. Rosemary James of Faulkner House Books (p. 218) edited *My New Orleans,* essays by locals from writers to restaurateurs and raconteurs, attempting to pin down what it is about this place that keeps them here, come hell or high water. Historian Douglas Brinkley's meticulous *The Great Deluge* may be the definitive postmortem examination of Katrina. *Times-Picayune* columnist Chris Rose (p. 171) collected his heartbreaking personal essays, written as he and his colleagues covered their flooded city, in *1 Dead in Attic,* while Pulitzer Prize–winning journalist Sherri Fink recounts the complexities of the tragic, harrowing *Five Days at Memorial.* For young kids, Janet Wyman Coleman's *Eight Dolphins of Katrina* (set in Gulfport, Mississippi) is a relatable, pictorial tale of disaster and survival.

Zeitoun, Dave Eggers' gripping narrative nonfiction, recounts the tale of one man's horror and a nation's injustice (look up Zeitoun's even more shocking personal epilogue for a completely divergent take), while *New Yorker* columnist Dan Baum weaves together differing perspectives to illustrate how the multihued city unifies nine diverse narratives in *Nine Lives.*

Finally, fans of football and motivational memoirs may enjoy *Home Team* by Saints coach Sean Payton or Drew Brees' *Coming Back Stronger.*

BOOKS ABOUT MUSIC

Ann Allen Savoy's *Cajun Music Vol. 1* is a combination songbook and oral history featuring previously untranscribed Cajun music with lyrics in French and English. A labor of many years, it's a definitive work and an invaluable resource.

For a look at specific time periods, people, and places in the history of New Orleans jazz, you have a number of choices. They include William Carter's *Preservation Hall;* John Chilton's *Sidney Bechet: The Wizard of Jazz;* Gunther Schuller's *Early Jazz: Its Roots and Musical Development;* the excellent *A Trumpet Around the Corner: The Story of New Orleans Jazz,* by Samuel Charters; *New Orleans Jazz: Images of America,* by Edward Branley; and *New Orleans Style,* by Bill Russell. Al Rose's *Storyville, New Orleans* is an excellent source of information about the very beginnings of jazz; while *Up From the Cradle of Jazz* tells its story post-WWII. *Songs of My Fathers* is Tom Sancton's fine retelling of his boyhood at the feet of the great Preservation Hall musicians.

If you prefer primary sources, read Louis Armstrong's *Satchmo: My Life in New Orleans,* or *Satchmo: The Wonderful World and Art of Louis Armstrong,* a bio by way of his own artworks. Sidney Bechet's *Treat It Gentle,* and the story of Mac Rebennack's (aka Dr. John) wild life is reflected in *Under a Hoodoo Moon.* Ben Sandmel's exhaustively researched *Ernie K-Doe: the R&B Emperor of New Orleans* can't help but be entertaining, given the subject.

Film & Television

With atmosphere and mystery to spare, all forms of water and roadways, new and old architecture, and, until recently, attractive tax incentives—film and TV production abound here in "Hollywood South." The city isn't a character in all of them, but it's the heart of the highly authentic HBO series *Tremé.* Don't miss the stellar, hard-to-find series *Frank's Place* (1987–88). *True Blood* was filmed mostly in Baton Rouge, but important scenes were set in the gorgeous Marigny Opera House, among other New Orleans locations. The popular *NCIS New Orleans* is filmed on location and tries to catch the city's lightning-in-a-bottle aura. The creepy FX series *American Horror Story: Coven* filmed in some of the city's oldest mansions, a notorious haunted house, and a possible fountain of youth in City Park. The most affecting recent filmwork came from Beyoncé, in her thought- (and tweet-) provoking, long-form video "Lemonade."

Consider these for some pre- or post-visit flavor: classics like Brando in *A Streetcar Named Desire* (1951); Betty Davis in *Jezebel* (1938); the certified best Elvis film *King Creole* (1958); and counterculture Mardi Gras freakout *Easy Rider.* Tom Waits bums around the city, the countryside, and jail in the indie *Down by Law* (1986); and a young Brooke Shields navigates a Storyville childhood in Louis Malle's *Pretty Baby* (1978). Then there's the steamy but flawed (and locally derided) *The Big Easy.* Brad Pitt ages backwards in *The Curious Case of Benjamin Button* (2008) and goes fang to fang with Tom Cruise in *Interview with the Vampire* (1994). Nic Cage just goes all Nic Cage in *Bad Lieutenant: Port of Call New Orleans* (2009). The Oscar-nominated *Beasts of the Southern Wild* (2012) set its powerful magic realism in the Louisiana bayous. Lastly, for kids of any age, when *Abbott & Costello Go to Mars* (1953), they end up at Mardi Gras—an altogether different universe.

All of the late, very great Les Blank's documentaries on Louisiana are worthy, but start with *Always for Pleasure* (1978). Bayou Maharajah, the excellent 2013 biodoc of noted pianist James Booker, also explains much about the New Orleans music scene in his day (and now). Documentaries about the Katrina experience cover every angle, notably in Spike Lee's *When the Levees Broke;* the remarkable, Oscar-nominated *Trouble the Water; and* the superb prize-winning *Faubourg Tremé: The Untold Story of Black New Orleans.*

Recordings

Oh, boy. Well, the selections listed below should give you a good start, though we could fill pages more (and we're barely even touching on the many fine pop, rock, or folky contributions, but I can't not mention the Revivalists, Lost Bayou Ramblers, and Hurray for the Riff Raff). Also check out the names listed in the Nightlife chapter (p. 188), and for more advice, consult the uber-helpful know-it-alls at **Louisiana Music Factory** and the other stores on p. 224.

CROSS-GENRE ANTHOLOGIES

There are many collections and anthologies of New Orleans and Louisiana music available, including the 1990s Alligator Stomp series by Rhino Records. The most comprehensive, critically acclaimed *Doctors, Professors, Kings & Queens: The Big Ol' Box of New Orleans* is a four-disc package released in 2004 by Shout! Factory and the one collection that touches all the bases of the diverse musical gumbo that is the Crescent City. The *Tremé, Season 1* soundtrack covers a bit of the same fertile, funky ground, albeit just from recent years.

JAZZ

A classic New Orleans jazz collection starts with the originators: King Oliver, Kid Ory, Sidney Bechet, Original Dixieland Jazz Band, and Jellyroll Morton. Add early Louis Armstrong, with his Hot Five and Hot Seven bands.

Ken Burns' Jazz box covers the originators and more from New Orleans and beyond, and the anthologies *New Orleans* (Atlantic Jazz), *Recorded in New Orleans Volumes 1 and 2* (Good Time Jazz), and *New Orleans Jazz* (Arhoolie) are good choices. Preservation Hall's *Preservation* covers the classics; Pete Fountain, Al Hirt (try *Honey in the Horn*), and Louis Prima (*The Wildest*) all swing things in a new direction.

Leaping forward, Wynton Marsalis, Terrance Blanchard, clarinetist Tim Laughlin, and Harry Connick, Jr., build on those traditions, and trumpeters Irvin Mayfield and Nicolas Payton push them forward. Terrific old-time revivalists like the New Orleans Jazz Vipers, Meschiya Lake (check out *Lucky Devil*), the Smoking Time Jazz Band, Tuba Skinny, Debbie Davies, and Aurora Nealand are well worth the cost of a disc or a download. These days (well, always) pianist Jon Cleary is killing it, as heard on his Grammy-winning *Go Go Juice. American Tunes,* Allen Toussaint's final collection, is not at all a sentimental choice. Okay it is. But it's also excellent.

BRASS BANDS

The age-old tradition of brass-oriented street bands underwent a spectacular revival in the 1980s and 1990s with the revitalization of such long-term presences as the Olympia Brass Band and the arrival of newcomers like the Dirty Dozen Brass Band (try their monster anthology, *This Is the Dirty Dozen Brass Band*). They inspired a younger and funkier generation, including Grammy winners Rebirth Brass Band, New Birth, the Hot 8, the Stooges, up-and-comers TBC, hybridists the Brass-a-Holics, the Soul Rebels, and the Soul Brass Band, among the best of the crowd. It's all better live, so get ye to the clubs or try *The Main Event: Live at the Maple Leaf*, or the loose, bumping *Rock with the Hot 8*. Alternatively, *I Am a Brass-a-Holic* is not live but is irresistibly bumping.

RHYTHM, BLUES & SOUL

First things first: Get your Fats on with *My Blue Heaven* or any "Best of" compilation. Then get Dr. John's *Gumbo* or *Mos Scocious: The Dr. John Anthology*. Round out your legends collection with Professor Longhair's *'Fess: The Professor Longhair Anthology* and fellow key wizard James Booker's *Classified: Remixed*. Go down funk road with the Meters' classic *Cissy Strut* and *The Wild Tchoupitoulas* for Mardi Gras Indian funk. Ivan Neville's Dumpstaphunk band is keeping the funk alive, while Galactic might be funk, might be jazz, could be rock or jam—but is never uninteresting. Start with *Ruckus*. Trombone Shorty rocks jazz, R&B, funk, and hip hop into his own thang, turning out monster hits like *Say That to Say This*. We're true to hometown heroes the Neville Brothers' *Yellow Moon* and *Treacherous: A History of the Neville Brothers, 1955–1985*. *Songbook* shows why producer/writer Allen Toussaint, who passed away in 2016 to tremendous shock and sadness, remains a true icon and son of the city. Also get some soul crooners in, like Soul Queen Irma Thomas's *Time Is on My Side* and Johnny Adams' *Heart & Soul*. Worthwhile anthologies include *The Best of New Orleans Rhythm & Blues Volumes 1 and 2; Sehorn's Soul Farm;* and *The Mardi Gras Indians Super Sunday Showdown*. Bring it all current with Tank and the Bangas' infectious *Big Bang Theory* (which could also fit in the next paragraph).

HIP HOP & BOUNCE

New Orleans's distinctive hip hop and rap scene produced numerous stars and a home-grown subgenre: booty-dropping, second-line-influenced, twerk-propagating bounce. It began with Big Freedia, who must be experienced live, but *Just Be Free* will do. Breakout dirty Southerner Juvenile's *400* is a classic, while rebounding hip hop star Lil Wayne's breakout flow on *Tha Carter III* still holds up massively (really, any Hot Boyz cuts will do). The risqué rhymes on Mystikal's eponymous debut broke musical ground before jail time sidelined his career; he's out and back now, big-time.

WHEN TO GO

With the possible exception of muggy July and August, just about any time is the right time to go to New Orleans. We love the jasmine-infused nights and warmer days of mid-fall and spring best, and even relish the occasional high drama of a good summer thunderstorm.

It's important to know *what's* going on *when*, since the city's landscape, hotel availability, and rates can change dramatically depending on what events are going on. Mardi Gras is, of course, the hardest time of year to get a hotel room, but it can also be difficult during major festivals (French Quarter Fest, Jazz & Heritage Festival, Essence) and sporting events (BCS, Sugar Bowl, Saints and LSU Superdome games). New Orleans isn't particularly known as a holiday destination, but in December it's gussied up with decorations, there are all kinds of holiday special events, and the weather is quite fine. Eager hotels often have good deals, and many restaurants offer special prix-fixe "Réveillon" deals.

The Weather

The average mean temperature in New Orleans is an inviting 70°F (21°C), but it can drop or rise considerably in a single day. (It can be 40°F/4°C and rain one day, 80°F/27°C and low humidity the next.) Conditions depend primarily on whether it rains and whether there is direct sunlight or cloud cover. Rain can provide slight and temporary relief on a hot day; it tends to hit in sudden (and sometimes dramatically heavy) showers, which disappear as quickly as they arrive. In unimpeded sun it gets much warmer. The high humidity can intensify even mild warms and colds. Still, the semitropical climate is part of New Orleans' appeal—the slight moistness makes for lush, sensual air.

New Orleans is pleasant most of the year. During the sweltering, bargain summer months, follow the natives' example: stay out of the midday sun, seek shade, and duck from one air-conditioned locale to another. June and September can still be humid and warm; early spring and mid-fall are glorious. Winter is mild by American standards—but don't expect Florida warmth—and punctuated by an occasional freeze-level cold snap. But *unpredictable* and *flexible* are the watchwords. The whims of the weather gods are at play, so be ready to adjust accordingly.

Hurricane season runs June 1 to November 30. There are no guarantees, but severe storms are fairly rare. In the height of summer, T-shirts, shorts, and tissue-weight fabrics are acceptable everywhere except the finest restaurants. In the spring and fall, something a little warmer is in order; in the winter, carry a mid-weight coat or jacket and pack a folding umbrella (though they're available everywhere, as are cheap rain ponchos for unexpected downpours). The biggest summertime climate problem can be the air-conditioning overcompensation that chills rooms—especially restaurants—to meat-locker-like temps, so bring those light wraps along even on warm nights.

New Orleans's Average Temperatures & Rainfall

	JAN	FEB	MAR	APR	MAY	JUNE	JULY	AUG	SEPT	OCT	NOV	DEC
High (°F)	62	65	71	78	85	89	91	90	87	80	71	65
High (°C)	17	18	22	26	29	32	33	32	31	27	22	18
Low (°F)	43	46	52	58	66	71	73	73	70	60	50	45
Low (°C)	6	8	11	14	19	22	23	23	21	16	10	7
Days of Rainfall	10	9	9	7	8	11	14	13	10	6	7	10

New Orleans Calendar of Events

There's lots more on **Mardi Gras** and **Jazz Fest** in chapter 4. For other Louisiana festivals, see www.laffnet.org. Times and dates are always subject to whim and change; check the event websites to be safe. For general information, contact the **New Orleans Convention & Visitors Bureau,** 2020 St. Charles Ave., New Orleans, LA 70130 (www.neworleanscvb.com, www.neworleansonline.com; ✆ **800/672-6124** or 504/566-5011).

JANUARY

Allstate Sugar Bowl Classic. New Orleans' oldest yearly sporting occasion dates to 1934. The football game in the Superdome is the main event, but in the preceding days look for a kickoff second-line parade and a massive Fan Fest in the French Quarter. https://allstatesugarbowl.org. ✆ **504/828-2440.** Jan 1, 2019.

MARCH

Lundi Gras. This tradition brings a free, outdoor music-and-food celebration to Spanish Plaza (Poydras St. at the river), with the big event at 6pm: the ceremonial, waterfront arrival of the Kings of Rex and Zulu, marking the start of Mardi Gras. They're welcomed by the mayor, fireworks, and much whoop-de-doo. www.lundigrasfestival.com. See p. 45. Monday before Mardi Gras (March 4, 2019; February 24, 2020).

Mardi Gras. The culmination of the 2-month-long carnival season, Mardi Gras is the centuries-old annual blowout. Each year the eyes of the world are on New Orleans, as the entire city stops working and starts partying, and the streets are taken over by awe-inspiring parades. See chapter 4. Day before Ash Wednesday (March 5, 2019; Feb 25, 2020).

St. Patrick's Day Parades. There are several, with dates (like the paraders) usually staggered. Instead of Mardi Gras beads, watchers are pelted with veggies, including the coveted cabbages. In 2019, a funky French Quarter parade kicks off at Molly's at the Market (1107 Decatur St.) on Friday, March 15, at 6pm. On Saturday, March 16, and on St. Patrick's Day, the party goes on all day between Tracey's and Parasol's bars in the Lower Garden District. On St. Patrick's Day (Sun, Mar 17, 2019), the downtown parade begins at 6pm at Burgundy and Piety in Bywater and stumbles to Bourbon Street. www.stpatricksdayneworleans.com. ✆ **504/525-5169.**

Buku Music + Art Project. This packed millennial party of hip hop, EDM, acrobats, and visual artists is New Orleans' answer to Electric Daisy or Movement. Sellout crowds of 35,000 anything-goes attendees fill the six stages overlooking the Mississippi River and floats at Mardi Gras World. Unsurprising, given artists like SZA, Migos, Kid Kudi, Flaming Lips, and Kendrick. Tickets for the 2018 Buku started around $100 per day; VIP packages were way more. www.thebukuproject.com. March 9–10, 2019.

St. Joseph's Day Parade. Another fascinating, little-known fete. Sicilians venerate St. Joseph, patron saint of families and working men, on his saint's day (March 19) with a parade and the creation of devotional altars. These moving, elaborate works of art feature food, candles, and statues. They can be viewed at various churches and private homes (where you might also get fed), and at the **American Italian Museum** (537 South Peters St.). Locations are listed in the *Times-Picayune* classifieds and on www.nola.com prior to the event. Also try http://american italianculturalcenter.com or ✆ **504/522-7294.** March 19.

Super Sunday. At these annual Mardi Gras Indians gatherings, tribes garbed in full, feathered regalia preen, parade, and engage in ritualized showdowns with traditional chants. The Uptown event take place on the Sunday nearest St. Joseph's Day (March 19) at A.L. Davis Park, Washington Avenue, and LaSalle Street, from noon till late afternoon, with music and food booths. The looser Downtown street meeting is usually a few weeks later on Bayou St. John at Orleans Avenue. For details, check with the **Backstreet Cultural Museum** (p. 149) or www.wwoz.org/inthestreet. Mid-March to mid-April. More on p. 46.

Tennessee Williams New Orleans Literary Festival. This 5-day series celebrates New

Orleans' rich literary heritage with theatrical performances, readings, discussions, master classes, musical events, walking tours, and the ever-popular Stella Shouting Contest. It's not exclusive to Williams, and the roster of writers and publishers participating is impressive. www.tennesseewilliams.net. ☏ **504/581-1144.** March 22–25, 2019.

Hogs for the Cause. If you go to Hogs, you can no longer say New Orleans isn't a BBQ town. Proceeds from this plethora of porky goodness support pediatric brain cancer research. Some 85 cleverly named teams of talented pitmasters + rootsy music = darn good times. *Tip:* Get tix early; Friday night is gloriously less crowded. Ticket options $25–$50. www.hogsforthecause.org. March 23–24, 2019.

APRIL

French Quarter Festival. The 4-day French Quarter Festival celebrates local music of the traditional jazz, brass band, Cajun/zydeco, or funk variety. The free event has become wildly popular, attracting more than 700,000 in 2017. Scores of outdoor concerts, food booths, art shows, children's activities, tours, and seminars are set throughout the Quarter, making it easy to return to your hotel for a rest, though some stages are at far-flung ends of the Quarter. Book travel early; this good time is becoming a victim of its own success. www.french quarterfest.org. ☏ **800/673-5725** or 504/5225730. April 11–14, 2019.

The Crescent City Classic. This scenic 10K race from the Superdome through the French Quarter to City Park brings in an international field of top (and lesser) runners. www.ccc10k.com. ☏ **504/861-8686.** March 31, 2019.

Festival International de Louisiane. Some people split their festing between Jazz Fest and the popular Festival International in Lafayette, which focuses on French music and culture. The free, 5-day street fair, held on the first weekend of Jazz Fest, dovetails nicely with the opening events of the bigger fest. See p. 50. www.festivalinternational. org. ☏ **337/232-8086.** April 25–29, 2019.

New Orleans Jazz & Heritage Festival presented by Shell (Jazz Fest). A 7-day event that draws musicians, cooks, and craftspeople and their fans to celebrate music and life, Jazz Fest rivals Mardi Gras in popularity. Get a full description in chapter 4. See www.nojazzfest.com or call ☏ **504/410-4100.** April 26-May 5, 2019.

MAY

Bayou Country Superfest. Country kings from classic to current (George Straight to Chris Stapleton to Kasey Musgraves) headline a Saturday concert in the Superdome, which anchors related events on the days before and after. Tickets $79–$395. www.bayoucountrysuperfest.com. ☏ **504/4123-4567.** Memorial Day weekend.

Mid-City Bayou Boogaloo. Another weekend, another laidback New Orleans music, art, and food fest. This one's themeless, with the pretty location along Bayou St. John (and the rubber-ducky derby) the draw for the largely local crowd. Bring a blanket, a parasol, and cash for snacks and brews, and go now before it gets too huge. www.the bayouboogaloo.com. ☏ **504/488-3865.** May 25–27, 2019.

New Orleans Wine & Food Experience. More than 10,000 people attend this 3-day gourmandistic pleasure, at which some 150 vintners, 75 restaurants, and myriad chefs feature wines and wares via tastings, seminars, and vintner dinners. The culmination is a grand tasting held at Mardi Gras World, but the party really hits its stride with the Royal Street Stroll, where revelers indulge their way from one tasting station to the next along the closed street. www.nowfe.com. ☏ **504/934-1474.** May 24–26, 2019.

JUNE

Oyster Festival. Aw shucks, it's a weekend dedicated to slurping delicious Gulf oysters and listening to live music while overlooking the Mississippi River at Woldenberg Park. Local restaurants serve up their best bivalve recipes and pro shuckers compete, all to promote the centuries-old local oyster fishing industry. It's still free and the crowd is mostly local. www.neworleansoysterfestival. org. ☏ **504/888-7608.** June 1–2, 2019.

Creole Tomato Festival. This sweet, smallish fest set in the French Market celebrates the humble tomato with cooking demos, tastings, a Tomato Parade, local music…and all manner of Bloody Marys. www.frenchmarket. org. ℂ **504/522-2621.** June 9–10, 2019.

Louisiana Cajun-Zydeco Festival. This growing free fest sponsored by Jazz Fest brings plenty of two-stepping, a few waltzes, and lessons for both at Armstrong Park in the Tremé. It also has art markets, kids' activities, and yes, food booths with a seafood focus. www.jazzandheritage.org/cajun-zydeco. ℂ **504/558-6100.** June 16–17, 2019.

JULY

Essence Music Festival. This massive 3-day event sponsored by *Essence* magazine consistently presents a stellar lineup of first-name-only R&B, soul, and hip hop musicians (like Mary J., Kendrick, Usher, Beyoncé, Kanye, Prince [RIP], and Janet) in evening concerts on a main stage and clublike "Super Lounges." During the day, this "party with a purpose" has educational and empowerment seminars featuring A-list speakers (Oprah! Deepak! Rev. Al!), plus crafts, merch, and trade fairs. In 2018 tickets ranged from $70 for a single day to $3,500 for a VIP weekend package. www.essence. com/festival. Tentatively June 28–July 1, 2018.

Go Fourth on the River. The Independence Day celebration culminates with a spectacular fireworks display from dueling barges in the Mississippi River at 9pm. www.go4thon theriver.com. ℂ **800/672-6124.** July 4th.

Running of the Bulls. In perfectly imperfect New Orleans logic, Bastille Day, the famed Pamplona event, and the city's mixed French-Spanish heritage are celebrated with a reenactment of the manic dash, except the bulls are roller-skating **Big Easy Rollergirls** (p. 185) and other roller derby clubs using plastic bats as horns. Pomp, parties, and hilarity accompany what is now the centerpiece of a 3-day **San Fermin in Nueva Orleans** fiesta. www.nolabulls.com. ℂ **800/672-6124.** July 12–14, 2019.

Tales of the Cocktail. This 6-day mixtravaganza celebrates all things liquor. Based at the Monteleone Hotel but pouring over into other venues, it's a serious, sometimes scholarly gathering of upwards of 20,000 professional mixologists, brand ambassadors, and admirers of cocktail culture. (If you make your own bitters and take 10 minutes to mix a drink, this might be for you.) The seminars, tastings, and popular "Spirited Dinners" (food and cocktail pairings at top restaurants) fill up fast. www.talesofthecocktail. com. ℂ **504/948-0511.** July 16–21, 2019.

AUGUST

Satchmo Summerfest. Louis Armstrong, hometown boy made very good, is celebrated with his own festival, held around his real birthday (he claimed to be born on July 4th, but records say Aug). There's food, music, kids' activities, and seminars, with the emphasis on jazz entertainment and education to ensure that Satchmo lives on. The token $5 admission is well worth it. www. satchmosummerfest.org. ℂ **504/522-5730.** August 3–5, 2019.

SEPTEMBER

Southern Decadence. This multiday, multinight dance/party/raunchfest attracts more

---

Hot Time in the City

If you can stand it, brave the city in summer. The tourist business slows down a tad, leading to hotel bargains. On a recent July visit, high-end hotels were offering rooms from $89 to $129 (way below regular rates), sometimes with additional perks. Plus, you can often get upgrades to fancy suites for a song—ask when you check in. In August, local restaurants run bargain, prix-fixe **"COOLinary"** specials (www. coolinaryneworleans.com). Yeah, it's hot and humid, bearable for some, miserable for others—but there are always plenty of air-conditioned respites.

than 100,000 gay men (and some women), and peaks during a frenzied, bar-studded parade. Book rooms early and get a weekend ticket in advance to save time; and even if *you're* not too hot for leather, September in New Orleans is. www.southern decadence.net. Labor Day weekend, August 31–September 2, 2019.

OCTOBER

Festivals Acadiens & Creoles. Much smaller than the nearby Francophone-focused Festival International (see April), this Lafayette event combines the Bayou Food Festival, the Festival de Musique Acadienne, and the Louisiana Native Crafts Festival. Players, bring your instruments—there's a jam tent. It's fun, easygoing, tasty, and free, so spend freely to help keep it going. www. festivalsacadiens.com. ℭ **800/346-1958** in the U.S., 800/543-5340 in Canada, or 337/232-3737. October 10–13, 2019 (exact dates subject to change).

Crescent City Blues & BBQ Festival. A recent rash of credible BBQ restaurants might finally be changing the city's low profile in the pantheon of great BBQ destinations. 'Cue teams strut their stuff at this free fest, located in Lafayette Park in the Central Business District. Add two stages for blues tunes, a good lineup, and consider our folding chairs strapped on; this one is set to blow up. www.jazzandheritage.org/blues-fest. ℭ **504/558-6100.** October 11–13, 2019.

Halloween. Halloween is celebrated especially grandly in this haunted city, rivaling Mardi Gras for costume outrageousness. The French Quarter is Halloween central (especially for the LGBT crowd), where the **Krewe of Boo** parade rolls a week or so before Halloween (www.kreweofboo.com); another parade leaves **Molly's at the Market** (p. 204) on Halloween Night. Other ghoulish action includes **Boo-at-the-Zoo** (last 2 weekends in Oct) for kids; and the truly scary **Mortuary Haunted House** in Mid-City (www.themortuary.net). October 31 and surrounding days.

Ponderosa Stomp. This biannual weekend celebration of early American rock is a mecca for fans and students of all things roots—blues, twang, swamp, thrash, or beyond—who attend scholarly conferences during the day and groove to concerts by seminal but largely unheralded performers at night. www.ponderosastomp.org. ℭ **504/810-9116.** Fall 2019; call or check website for exact dates.

Voodoo Music Experience. The monstrous 3-day Voodoo Fest draws close to 150,000 music fans to the City Park festival grounds, where more than 70 acts fill six live stages. The diverse lineup features major stars from Ozzy and Jason Isbell to the Killers Skrillex and Snoop Dogg, plus up-and-comers and a solid crop of locals. Eclectic art and exotic performances, a huge EDM space, Halloween-costumed people-watching, and food and drink round out the diversions. Tickets start at around $150 and go way up. www. worshipthemusic.com. October 25–27, 2019.

NOVEMBER

Words & Music: A Literary Fest. This highly ambitious conference offers round-table discussions with eminent authors with varying connections to the city, plus original drama, poetry readings, master classes, and writing competitions. https://faulknersociety. org. ℭ **504/586-1609.** Mid-November.

Po-Boy Festival. OkAU, you could just go to the participating restaurants any other day of the year and avoid the wait, but then you'd miss the blessing of the po' boy. This Oak Street fest is crazy crowded, but it's got some dang deelish sandwiches and a fun locals' scene. www.poboyfest.com. Late November.

DECEMBER

LUNA Fête. An immediate hit after its 2014 debut, this free, multi-day, multi-location "Light Up" festival uses lighting, music, and video projections to transform architecturally significant buildings around Lafayette Square, creating artistic awesomeness. www. artsneworleans.org/event/luna-fete. Early December.

Christmas, New Orleans Style. The ever-celebratory New Orleanians do Christmas really well. The town is decorated to a fare-thee-well, with nightly concerts in St. Louis Cathedral and candlelit caroling in Jackson Square (the Sunday before Christmas, Dec

16, 2018). Bonfires line the levees along the River Road on Christmas Eve (to guide Papa Noël, in his alligator-drawn sled), and house tours offer glimpses of stunningly turned-out residences. Reduced room rates and discounted "Réveillon" restaurant dinners also make this an economically attractive time to visit. The Running of the Santas adds hilarity whether you're a runner or watcher. www. neworleansonline.com/christmas. *C* **504/522-5730.** Throughout December.

Celebration in the Oaks. Thousands of lights illustrating holiday themes bedeck sections of City Park, and a walking and miniature-train tour lets you take in the charm and grandeur at your leisure. It's nostalgic winter wonderment for the whole family. Plus, there's ice skating and amusement-park rides. www.neworleanscitypark. com. *C* **504/482-4888.** Late November to early January.

New Year's Eve. The countdown party takes place in Jackson Square and, in the New Orleans equivalent of Times Square, revelers watch a lighted fleur-de-lis drop from the top of Jackson Brewery. Fantastic fireworks ensue. December 31.

RESPONSIBLE ECO-TOURISM

Responsible tourism in New Orleans may start as you leave the airport in a hybrid shuttle van or taxi. Mardi Gras revelers will probably watch biodiesel-powered floats and catch beads on biodegradable string to help the strands fall from the tree branches. Bicycle and kayak tours are terrific options (see p. 179), and many attractions are easily accessed by foot, streetcar, tour bus, or bike.

Caloric intake in New Orleans can (and should) be decidedly *ir*responsible. Vegetarian and vegan restaurants are around if you look, as are Middle Eastern and Asian fallback options. Fortunately, nearly every restaurant offers options or accommodates dietary preferences. Further, most fine and contemporary dining establishments (and many simpler ones) have long embraced the lake-, river-, Gulf-, bayou- and farm-to-table movement, sourcing from local ingredients and purveyors; some even have their own farms and gardens.

Infrastructure, fragility and regulations protecting historic construction can make green improvements difficult or prohibitive, especially in the French Quarter. Many that suffered damages in Katrina's flooding expended their rebuilding resources to get back on their feet, forsaking going green—an understandably missed opportunity. The city has no LEED- or Green Seal-certified hotels—yet, but nearly every property has instituted programs like recycling and on-demand linen replacement. Although our preferences lean away from major hotel chains, those with corporate-supported sustainability programs, like **Hyatt, Sheraton**, **Marriott,** and **Loews** (p. 69), are doing some of the better work in this arena. On the indie side, **Hotel Monteleone** leads the charge. An ironic environmental upside to Hurricane Katrina and the Deepwater oil spill is increased awareness of the need to support locally owned businesses as a means of economic rebuilding and cultural preservation. The Urban Conservancy's **Stay Local** program (www.staylocal.org) has a directory of locally owned businesses to patronize.

Voluntourism is still popular, especially with groups. **Habitat for Humanity** accepts volunteers for a day or a year. The respected organization has created the Musicians Village for artists who lost their homes in the flood (www.habitat-nola.org; © **504/861-2077**). Or try **Common Ground** (www. commongroundrelief.org; © **504/312-1729**) or the **United Saints Recovery Project** (www.unitedsaints.org; © **504/233-8883**). **Youth Rebuilding New Orleans,** which rehabs homes primarily for teachers, is geared towards teens and even younger kids—service hours, anyone? (www.yrno.com; © **504/264-3344**). **America's Wetland Foundation** focuses on vitally important wetlands restoration and sometimes has volunteer activities (www. americaswetland.com; © **504/293-2610**), as does **Groundwork New Orleans,** which builds rain gardens and other ecological improvements (www.face book.com/GroundworkNewOrleans; © **504/208-2771**).

Larger groups can also work through the **New Orleans Convention & Visitors Bureau** (www.neworleanscvb.com) or **Projects with Purpose** (www. projectswithpurpose.com; © **504/934-1000**). Allow 2 weeks to complete applications and paperwork. Volunteers may be responsible for certain expenses, equipment, and accommodations.

Given the tribulations that New Orleans and Louisiana have undergone, the most important act of responsible travel may simply be going, spending, enjoying, and encouraging others to do the same.

SUGGESTED ITINERARIES

t's easy to wander aimlessly through New Orleans with your eyes wide, your mouth agape, and your hand holding someone else's (or your *Frommer's* guide). It's truly unlike any place in the United States, so nearly everything you happen upon will be new and wondrous. It's equally easy to duck into a restaurant or watering hole, or take a meditative rest on a bench in Jackson Square or along the Mississippi River...and end up there for hours. Nothing wrong with that (we encourage it, in fact). But New Orleans has gobs of locales and historic sites that can't be missed and countless curious little nooks that shouldn't be.

The following itineraries are designed to help you make the most of your visit as you navigate the city. If you have the time, take our **walking tours** (p. 226) or sign up for a **guided tour**—see our recommendations for the best on p. 171.

ORIENTATION & NEIGHBORHOODS IN BRIEF

"Where y'at?" goes the traditional local greeting. "Where" is straightforward in the French Quarter, a 13-block-long grid between Canal Street and Esplanade Avenue, running from the Mississippi River to North Rampart Street.

After that, fuggedaboutit. Because of the bend in the river (the "crescent" in the "Crescent City" moniker), the streets are laid out at angles and curves that render directions useless. Readjust your thinking to New Orleans's compass points: *lakeside, riverside, uptown,* and *downtown.* You'll catch on quickly if you keep in mind that North Rampart Street is the *lakeside* boundary of the Quarter, and Canal Street is its *uptown* border. And by all means, use the maps provided—you'll need them.

Note that street names change when they cross Canal Street: Bourbon Street becomes Carondelet, and Royal becomes St. Charles Avenue, for example.

City Layout

The French Quarter Made up of about 90 square blocks with Jackson Square at its center, this section is also known as the Vieux Carré (Old Square) and is bordered by Canal Street, North Rampart Street, the Mississippi River, and Esplanade Avenue. Packed with hotels, restaurants, clubs, bars, stores, residences, and museums, the Quarter (or FQ) is the most historic and best-preserved area in the city, and the natural focal point for most first-time visitors. Use our French Quarter walking tour (p. 227) to explore the neighborhood in detail.

Faubourg Marigny Bordering the eastern edge of the French Quarter across Esplanade Avenue, the Marigny boasts the city's premier nightlife center: famed Frenchmen Street. Named for six rebellious French dudes who were hung here for promoting formation of a new government (in 1768—8 years before the Declaration of Independence), Frenchmen Street is a must-visit haunt for music lovers and anyone seeking a scene. This small Creole suburb is populated by old-time residents, young urban dwellers who've moved in recently, and a thriving LGBTQ community.

Bywater This riverside neighborhood downriver from the Faubourg Marigny, a hotbed of renovation and gentrification, still has its share of modest and rundown homes set amid sparkling renovations and artily rehabbed shotgun and double shotgun–style homes. Historically, the area was also home to immigrants, free people of color, tradesmen, and artisans. Today, studios and old-school corner groceries and watering holes still dot the area, along with new hipster bars, cafes, many, many moustaches, and the freshly minted **Crescent Park** (p. 161).

Mid-City/Esplanade Ridge Stretching north from the French Quarter to City Park, Esplanade Ridge hugs either side of Esplanade Avenue (once the grand avenue of New Orleans' Creole society, rivaling St. Charles Ave.). Crossing Esplanade is the historic **Bayou St. John** waterway, adjacent to the lovely **Faubourg St. John**

neighborhood. Booming, popular **Mid-City** also encompasses **City Park,** and its residential neighborhoods stretch upward toward Lake Pontchartrain and include the recently developed biodistrict along Tulane Avenue.

Faubourg Tremé Directly across Rampart Street from the French Quarter, this dense 19th-century Creole community is one of the oldest African-American neighborhoods in the country. Packed with fascinating history and home for generations to many of the city's best and best-known musicians, it remains a massively productive musical incubator. Today it is seeing creeping gentrification, especially closer to Rampart Street and Esplanade Avenue. Fortunately, it continues to be a dynamic, organic residential community and a remarkable keeper of cultural flames with a fierce heritage (as highlighted in the eponymous HBO series). Once considered unsafe for tourists, it's vastly improved, more populated, and welcoming. Still, as with many parts of the city, some sections have their share of crime. So do explore; just go with a pal and heed your Spidey sense.

Central Business District In the 19th century, **Canal Street** divided the French and American sections of the city. Historically New Orleans' main street, it's a far cry from the days of yore when white-gloved ladies and seersuckered men shopped this grand avenue. But several fine hotels, restaurants, and renovated theaters are evidence of Canal's ongoing renewal. Uptown of Canal Street is the **CBD,** also roughly bounded by the elevated Pontchartrain Expressway (Business Rte. U.S. I-90) between Loyola Avenue and the Mississippi River. This hotbed of hip houses New Orleans' major business and government offices, along with some of the city's coolest and most elegant hotels, best restaurants, and the **Mercedes-Benz Superdome.** Within the CBD is the **Warehouse District,** which was just a heap of abandoned warehouses 20-ish years ago. With the efforts of some dedicated individuals and institutions, it has evolved into a thriving

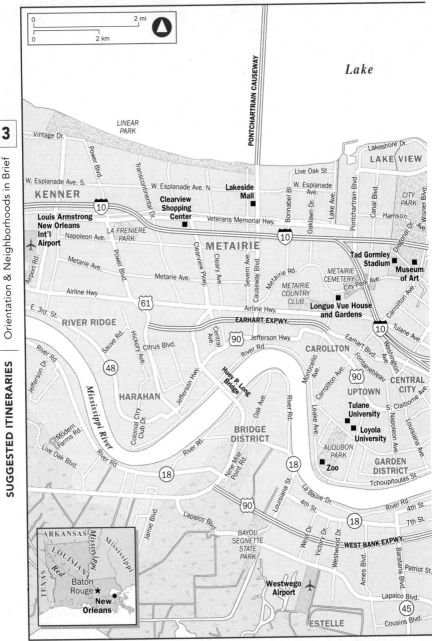

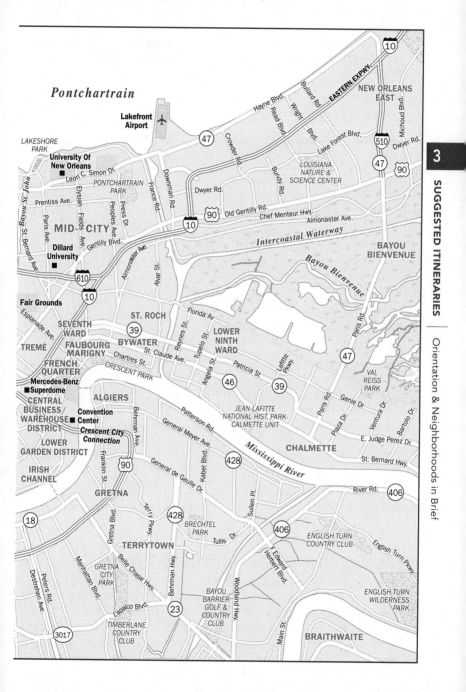

Pontchartrain

residential and commercial neighborhood. Besides cool loft conversions, terrific restaurants, and hot music clubs, the area also houses the city's lively **arts district,** with major museums and myriad galleries along **Julia Street** (see p. 213). The entire CBD is still growing madly; construction projects abound (before booking, ask your hotel if any nearby construction might impact your rest or view).

Uptown/The Garden District Bounded by St. Charles Avenue (lakeside) and Magazine Street (riverside) between Jackson and Louisiana avenues, the **Garden District (GD)** remains one of the most picturesque areas in the city. Originally the site of a plantation, it was subdivided and developed as a residential neighborhood for wealthy Americans who built elaborate homes and gardens, some still existing. See our Garden District walking tour on p. 236. The Garden District is *located* "uptown"; the neighborhood west of the Garden District is also *called* **Uptown** (the term is used for the *direction* and the *area,* just to confuse us). The **Lower Garden District (LGD)** refers to the segment between the Pontchartrain Expressway (I-90) and Jackson Avenue.

The Irish Channel The area bounded by Magazine Street and the Mississippi River, Louisiana Avenue, and the Central Business District got its name during the 1800s when more than 100,000 Irish immigrated to New Orleans and found (mostly blue-collar) work. Not much has changed. The quiet residential neighborhood, where the rundown mixes comfortably with the fixed-up, is dotted with some amazing churches, a few good restaurants, a "triangle" bordered with cute shops, a whole lotta good dive bars, and the occasional cobblestone street.

Algiers Point Directly across the Mississippi River and connected by ferry (p. 269), quaint Algiers Point is another original Creole suburb, largely unchanged if a little less lively than it was during the once-booming days of the railroad and dry-docking industries.

Central City This sleepy neighborhood of shotgun houses was the city center for a thriving population of Irish, German, and Jewish immigrants in the early 1800s, as well as working-class African-Americans (including jazz legends Jelly Roll Morton, Buddy Bolden, and Professor Longhair). But hard times fell, blight set in, and while it's still home to many, it's long been eschewed by tourists. That's changing with the recent blossoming of **Oretha Castle Haley Boulevard,** a renovated destination now dotted with worthy eateries and attractions (see p. 124). It's an easy walk from the St. Charles Streetcar (Euterpe St. stop), but other than that it's best not to stray far from OCH (as it's known) after dark, to play it safe.

Carrollton/Riverbend Once a resort destination for French Quarter denizens (a whopping 5 miles away—or an overnight train ride in the mid-1800s), this is now a charming, solidly middle- and upper-middle-class bedroom 'hood. The St. Charles streetcar makes the big turn here, as does the entire neighborhood, following the arching Mississippi River, after which the **Maple Street** and **Oak Street** stops both lead to sweet stretches for shopping, noshing, and hanging with the locals. Head riverside of St. Charles to stroll Maple Street; lakeside for Oak Street.

THE ICONIC QUARTER IN 1 DAY

You could spend days, weeks even, in the glorious, historic **French Quarter,** but even if you only have 1 day to explore, you can't go wrong here. This very full day includes all the requisites for an ideal New Orleans visit: eating, walking, drinking, soaking in some history, eating more, music, and dancing. *Tip:* As you stroll the neighborhood, check out te building exteriors: Apart from the ironwork (mostly slave-made, originally; and in the Spanish style, not French), they're actually on the plain side. The Creoles saved the embellishments for their indoor living quarters. Many current residents outfit their courtyards with lush landscaping, so do peek discreetly through gates and down alleyways. ***Start:*** *Along the riverfront at St. Louis Street.*

Hour 1: A Riverfront Stroll in Woldenberg Park ★

Rise with the riverboats, and take a walk along the **Moonwalk** pedestrian walkway (named for former Mayor Moon Landrieu, not a dance step), which parallels the river on one side and grassy, sculpture-dotted **Woldenberg Park** on the other. Stop to notice some of the curious public art installations and take in the sight of the vessels rounding the curving crescent in Ol' Man River, much as they have for centuries. **Washington Artillery Park**, the platform above the steps just across from **Jackson Square** (named for General/President Andrew, not Michael, King of Pop), provides a perfect picture-taking perch.

Hour 2: Café du Monde ★★★

Downing a cup of creamy, chicory-laced café au lait (coffee with milk) and savoring beignets heaped with powdered sugar is the ideal way to start a New Orleans day. Watch this city come to lazy life as carriage drivers queue up across the street, or get your order to go and enjoy it from a park bench in Jackson Square or along the river. ***Hint:*** Dark clothing and powdered sugar don't mix. More hints on p. 130.

Hour 3: St. Louis Cathedral ★

It's not the most inspiring ecclesiastical building, but it is the center of spiritual life for a town that is surprisingly devoutly Catholic (it's always a shock to note how many foreheads bear ashes the day after Mardi Gras' frantic antics). Legend has it that the serene garden in the back was a favorite haunt of good Catholic Marie Laveau—better known as the Voodoo Queen. Not even the infamous Pere Antoine, sent to New Orleans by the Office of the Inquisition, could convince Madame Laveau to forsake Voodoo. The imposing statue of Jesus lost a thumb to Katrina; at night its stunning shadow is otherworldly. See p. 139.

Hour 4: The Presbytère & the Cabildo ★★★

The former home of the priests who worked at St. Louis Cathedral has been turned into a museum housing a terrific "Living with Hurricanes" exhibit (p. 145). It's well worth an hour. If you still have time, the **Cabildo** museum (on the other side of St. Louis Cathedral; p. 139) is where the Louisiana Purchase was signed. Its exhibits illustrate New Orleans and Louisiana history and culture—including Mardi Gras and Napoleon Bonaparte's death mask. For real. See p. 142.

Hour 5: Muffuletta at Central Grocery ★★★

Ya gotta do it. Gotta get a muffuletta from **Central Grocery,** whose version of the celebrated Italian sandwich—filled with olive salad, Italian cold cuts, and cheese—is ginormous; half is more than enough for one

New Orleans Itineraries

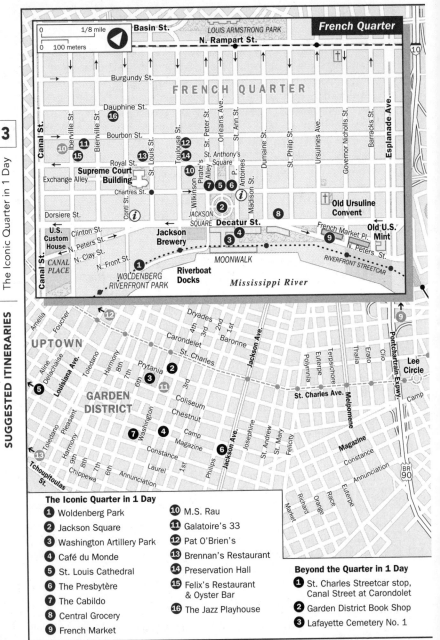

The Iconic Quarter in 1 Day

1. Woldenberg Park
2. Jackson Square
3. Washington Artillery Park
4. Café du Monde
5. St. Louis Cathedral
6. The Presbytère
7. The Cabildo
8. Central Grocery
9. French Market
10. M.S. Rau
11. Galatoire's 33
12. Pat O'Brien's
13. Brennan's Restaurant
14. Preservation Hall
15. Felix's Restaurant & Oyster Bar
16. The Jazz Playhouse

Beyond the Quarter in 1 Day

1. St. Charles Streetcar stop, Canal Street at Carondelet
2. Garden District Book Shop
3. Lafayette Cemetery No. 1

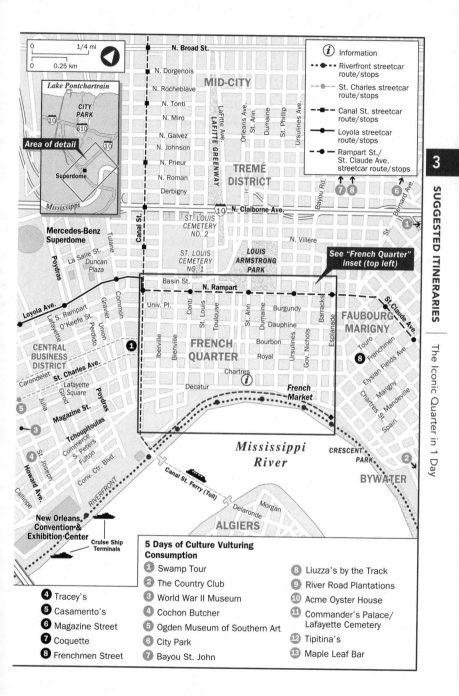

5 Days of Culture Vulturing Consumption

1. Swamp Tour
2. The Country Club
3. World War II Museum
4. Cochon Butcher
5. Ogden Museum of Southern Art
6. City Park
7. Bayou St. John
8. Liuzza's by the Track
9. River Road Plantations
10. Acme Oyster House
11. Commander's Palace/ Lafayette Cemetery
12. Tipitina's
13. Maple Leaf Bar

4. Tracey's
5. Casamento's
6. Magazine Street
7. Coquette
8. Frenchmen Street

hungry person. Eat in at the tiny tables in back or thread your way through the buildings across the street to chow down along the banks of the Mississippi (p. 96). *Option:* If you'd rather shop than stroll, take a detour to the **French Market** (p. 213), 2 blocks down and across the street.

Hour 6: Shops & Street Color on Royal Street ★★★

Royal Street is lined with swanky antiques, art, and clothing shops and has loads of antebellum eye candy, architecturally speaking. Be sure to browse the sublime and ridiculous collection at **M. S. Rau,** at 630 Royal (p. 214). The 100+-year-old antiques store welcomes gawkers. Several blocks of Royal are closed to vehicles from 11am to 4pm, and colorful street performers, from the talented to the tawdry, entertain for tips.

Hour 7: Bourbon Street ★

Sure, Bourbon Street is gaudy, loud, and sometimes even gross. For our money, the best time to do Bourbon is dusk, when it's not too tame and it's not too rowdy. Before the sleaziness gets serious and the obnoxiousness sets in, when music pours out the doors and dancers and barmen hawk their wares, it's also seductive and exhilarating. Everyone has to do it once; some do it often. Have a pre-dinner cocktail at **Galatoire's 33,** the newer bar next to the famed fine-dining restaurant (p. 88), or a legendary Hurricane on the always-lively patio at **Pat O'Brien's** (p. 203).

Hour 8: Brennan's Restaurant ★★★

Food is an intensely important part of your time in New Orleans, and you must dine well, several times daily. For your iconic French Quarter dinner, hit **Brennan's,** which is named for the famed first family of New Orleans restaurants and lives up to the mantle (p. 86). You've planned ahead and made reservations, right?

Hour 9: Let the Good Times Roll ★★★

Nightlife is essential to your day. Do not miss **Preservation Hall** (p. 193)—it's affordable, and it's the real, traditional jazz McCoy. Late-night munchies? Head for **Felix's Restaurant & Oyster Bar** (p. 97) for a dozen raw. Still going? Slink into the swanky **Jazz Playhouse** (p. 193), for the city's finest jazz and where burlesque performers take the late-night stage. When you finally must, collapse in your bed. If you're exhausted, full, smiling, and anticipating tomorrow, your day has been a success.

BEYOND THE QUARTER IN 1 DAY

You've had your day of exploring the Quarter. Now get out of the Quarter, *get out of the Quarter,* **get out of the Quarter!** Today you explore beyond the French Quarter, and we send you to the other side of the city for a completely different perspective. It's another full day, packed with great stuff to see and do. And eat. *Start: St. Charles Streetcar line, Canal Street stop.*

Hour 1: St. Charles Avenue Streetcar ★★★

Hop on the oldest continuously operating wooden streetcar in the country. Expect breezes through open windows, *not* air-conditioning, so doing this in the cool of the morning is a good idea. Admire the gorgeous homes and sprawling oaks along the way, and remember which side of the car you rode on so that you can sit on the other side on the ride back. (*Tip:* Get a **JazzyPass,** good for a full day of streetcar/bus transportation. See p. 269.)

Hours 2–3: The Garden District ★★★

Aside from its historical significance, this neighborhood of fabulous houses and lush greenery is just plain beautiful. Contrast the plain exteriors of the "French" Quarter with these grand, ornamented "American district" spectacles. Follow the walking tour on p. 236 or take a guided tour from **Historic New Orleans Tours** (p. 173). Start at the **Garden District Book Shop** (p. 218), 2727 Prytania St. at Washington Ave.

Hour 4: Lafayette Cemetery No. 1 ★★

The "little cities of the dead" are part of the iconic landscape of New Orleans. This pretty cemetery catered to Uptown folks, and has more foliage and room than others. Notice the tombs with French or German writing, and the four matching mausoleums in the far left corner. They belong to four boyhood friends (one a Civil War vet) who once played together here. Like many of the city's cemeteries, Lafayette No. 1 is in great need of maintenance and lacking funds to do so. See p. 165.

Hour 5: Magazine Street Lunch Break ★

Two surefire lunch options are on nearby Magazine Street. For a cold beer and a very respectable roast beef po' boy, hit up **Tracey's,** just 2 blocks away on 2604 Magazine St. **Casamento's** (p. 127), about a mile up at 4330 Magazine, is about as classic as an oyster bar gets, and its bivalves are sublime. A cab or the no. 11 bus will get you there. Call ahead to make sure they'll be open; lunch is served Thursday to Saturday.

Hour 6: Magazine Street Shopping ★★★

Explore the fab boutiques, antiques, and galleries along **Magazine Street** (p. 213), where even non-shoppers can enjoy the quirky mix of upscale-downscale, old-meets-new. The souvenir options trounce those of the Bourbon Street T-shirt shops. Use that JazzyPass to hop on and off the no. 11 bus (it runs about every 20 min.); cabs or feet also work.

Hour 7: Dinner at Coquette ★★★

Why are we so positively smitten with **Coquette?** Because it's perfect. Do make a reservation; don't skip dessert. See p. 119.

Hour 8: Frenchmen Street ★★★

Hit up the clubs and bars of **Frenchmen Street** in the Quarter-adjacent Faubourg Marigny. Wander, mingle, people-watch, heed the music pouring forth, and then pick a club or three in which to work your mojo. See p. 196.

5 DAYS OF CULTURE VULTURING

A trip to New Orleans is not just about eating, drinking, dancing, and admiring fancy houses (although that's a big part of it, *huge*). The city and environs are dripping with cultural coolness and historic eye-openers. Each of these five itineraries combines an enlightening or entertaining activity, plus suggestions for nearby dining (and maybe another suggestion or two that we can't resist planting)—leaving time to discover the city as it's meant to be discovered—in serendipitous fashion. Do them all, or choose a couple of faves.

Day 1: Swamp Tour ★★★

We scoff at those who scoff at swamp tours because they're too "touristy." Unless you're from Florida, you need to do this. Everyone knows about the gators, and they're cool enough. But the swamps themselves are mystical and otherworldly, and their ecological, cultural, historic, and economic relevance is fascinating. Get an early start so you have time for afternoon activities. Most tour companies can arrange round-trip transportation from your hotel. See p. 175.

After watching gators chow down on food unlikely to be part of their natural diet, you're probably ready to do the same. Since you're already out exploring far-flung waterways, we're sending you to the **Country Club** (p. 100) in Bywater, a wildly popular, under-the-tourist-radar spot in this artsy neighborhood. Newly renovated in eye-popping colors, this is the purview of talented chef Chris Barbato, last of Commander's Palace.

Day 2: National World War II Museum ★★★

This remarkable historical jewel sprawls across a complex of buildings, each jam-packed with thought-provoking exhibits. Make sure to listen to some of the potent, personal oral histories, and if you see a veteran, volunteering or visiting, say thank you for us, please.

You could spend hours here, and you should. But you could also split your time appreciating the premier collection of Southern art in the country, traditional and modern, at the stylish, airy **Ogden Museum of Southern Art,** just a block away (p. 152).

Have lunch at **Cochon Butcher** (p. 113), an upscale, Cajun-inflected deli 2 blocks from the museum. The cured meats stand out, but just about everything is stellar (including the marinated Brussels sprouts). If you liked the muffuletta from Central Grocery, you can taste-test the version here. It's debatable, but Butcher's might just be the best in town.

Day 3: City Park & Bayou St. John ★★★

The 1,300 acres here are as full of nature's glory as they are with activities, from the giant Spanish-moss-draped live oaks to the splendid **New Orleans Museum of Art** (p. 151) to the outstanding **Besthoff Sculpture**

Garden. If you have kids in tow, take a ride in a pedal boat in the lake, or visit the kids' amusement park and **Storybook Land.** The lush **Botanical Gardens** include the **Train Gardens,** a sort of melted Dr. Seuss replica of the city in miniature, complete with model trains (not to mention enormous lily pads). See p. 152.

Just outside the main entrance to City Park is **Bayou St. John,** a former bustling canal turned scenic body of water, and the site of the city's origins. If you're up for more footwork, a stroll here is one of the lesser-known, more peaceful delights of the city. Alternately, plan your timing to coincide with a kayak tour along this mellow waterway (p. 179). Or just point yourself down Esplanade Avenue and turn left on Lopez for shivering-cold schooners of Abita and one of the city's best gumbos at **Liuzza's by the Track** (p. 107). Also get the garlic oyster po' boy. You're welcome.

Day 4: River Road Plantation Homes ★★★

To see an altogether different, but vitally important side of the city's history, visit one or two of the **plantation homes along River Road** (p. 174). You'll need a car or tour company for this outing, a very worthwhile look at the pre– and post–Civil War eras, slavery, and Reconstruction. Afterwards, make a beeline for the French Quarter and get your slurp on at **Acme Oyster House** (p. 95). Don't neglect the charbroiled ones (gateway oysters for those who don't do them raw), and if it's in season get some boiled crawfish, too. Just for good measure.

Day 5: Do It Up & Get on Down ★★★

Your iconic cultural event today is a meal at **Commander's Palace** (p. 118). Choose a long, luxurious dinner or a languid, martini-laden lunch (perhaps preceded by the 10:30am tour of **Lafayette Cemetery**, across the street, see p. 165). *When* you fit this into your schedule is up to you; just do it in a leisurely fashion and savor the experience, one cocktail or course at a time. The world-famous establishment never rests on its laurels, but continues to push Creole cuisine in new and exciting directions—while honoring its origins. It's fine dining done the New Orleans way: with a side of fun. Later, check out **Tipitina's** (p. 201) or the **Maple Leaf Bar** (p. 200), both pillars of stellar NOLA tuneage (yes, you can wear your fancy-pants clothes to a club; you won't be alone and besides, no one cares). This represents our perfect day in New Orleans: mixing high-society dining with down-and-dirty dancing, going from an elegant manse to an everyman's dive. Great food. Great music. Great time.

MARDI GRAS & JAZZ FEST

For many people, what they know about New Orleans begins and ends with its parties: Mardi Gras—the biggest street blowout in America—or Jazz Fest, the grand-père of all other music fests and still the best music event in the country. In the place where anything is an excuse for a celebration (swamps, gumbo, crawfish, frogs, tomatoes, daiquiris, hexes, pork, cracklins, burlesque, and on it goes), all you need to bring is a rollicking, party-ready attitude. New Orleans pretty much does the rest.

While **French Quarter Fest** (p. 25) and **Essence Fest** (p. 26) attract nearly as many (or more) visitors, they're somewhat more straightforward to navigate. This chapter, therefore, gives you some background, foreground, and tips to get you on your good foot for the two other biggies: Mardi Gras and Jazz Fest.

MARDI GRAS

The granddaddy of all New Orleans celebrations is Mardi Gras. This massive, weeks-long street party rejoices in traditions new and old. It's a rare citywide event that's still remarkably and gloriously free of charge and sponsors.

Thanks to sensationalized media accounts that zero in on the salacious aspects of this Carnival, its rep as a Bourbon Street "Girls Gone Wild"–style spring break persists, drawing masses of wannabes for decadent, X-rated action rather than tradition. If that's your thang, by all means go forth and par-tay (just remember, the Internet is *eternal*).

But there is so much more to Carnival than media-hyped wanton action. Truth is, Mardi Gras remains one of the most exciting times to visit New Orleans, for people from all walks. Yes, you can hang in the Bourbon Street fratmosphere till you're falling down, but you can also spend days admiring and reveling in the city's rich traditions, or have a fun, memorable family vacation beyond what any mouse could offer.

Knowing some of its long and fascinating history helps put matters in perspective. First of all, Mardi Gras is just one day: French for "Fat Tuesday," Mardi Gras is the day before Ash Wednesday, when Lent begins. Though many people *call* it Mardi Gras, "Carnival" is the correct term for the 5- to 8-week "season" stretching from Twelfth Night (Jan 6) to Fat Tuesday. The idea was that good Christians would massively indulge in preparation for their impending self-denial during Lent.

The party's origins can be traced to the Roman **Lupercalia** festival: 2 days when all sexual and social order disappeared, cross-dressing was mandatory, and the population ran riot (sound familiar?). The early Christian church was naturally appalled by this, but unable to stop it. So Lupercalia was grafted onto the beginning of Lent, as a compromise to bribe everyone into observance.

Carnival (from a Latin word roughly meaning "farewell to flesh") and its lavish masked balls and other festivities became popular in Italy and France, and the tradition followed the French to New Orleans. The first Carnival balls occurred in 1743. By the mid-1800s, Mardi Gras mischief had grown so ugly (the harmless habit of tossing flour on partiers gradually turned into throwing bricks at them) that everyone predicted the end of the tradition.

The Birth of the Krewes

Everything changed in 1856. Tired of being left out of the Creoles' Mardi Gras, a group of Americans who belonged to a secret society called Cowbellians formed the Mystick Krewe of Comus (named after the hero of a John Milton poem). On Mardi Gras evening, they presented a breathtakingly imaginative, torch-lit parade. And so a new tradition was born, with new rituals established. Mardi Gras marked the height of the social season for **"krewes,"** groups comprised of prominent society and business types. After the Civil War put a temporary halt to things, two new enduring customs were added. Members threw trinkets to onlookers, and a queen reigned over their lavish balls.

As an elite Old South institution, Mardi Gras eschewed racial equality or harmony. African Americans participated in parades only by carrying torches to illuminate the route (the atmospheric if controversial *flambeaux,* as the torches are known). In 1909, a black man named William Storey mocked the elaborately garbed Rex (aka King of Carnival) by prancing after his float wearing a lard can for a crown. Storey was promptly dubbed "King Zulu." Thus begat the Krewe of Zulu, which parodied the high-minded Rex krewe while mockingly condemning racial stereotypes. The Zulu parade quickly became one of the most popular aspects of Mardi Gras, famously crowning Louis Armstrong as King Zulu in 1949.

Unfortunately, even as recently as the early 1990s many krewes still excluded blacks, Jews, and women. That was when anti-discrimination sentiment and laws (tied to parade permits) finally forced the issue. The mighty Comus, in a move that many old-liners still feel marked the beginning of the end of classic Mardi Gras, canceled its parade in 1992 rather than integrate. Proteus and Momus followed. Proteus later relented and now parades again; Momus parties but no longer parades.

Then as now, the krewes and traditions of Mardi Gras change. Today there are dozens of unofficial krewes and "sub-krewe" spinoffs, and more crop up like roadside wildflowers (or weeds), some with hilarious or subversive themes.

Spectacle, Beauty & Hilarity

Parades were always things of spectacle and beauty, but they grew bigger than the narrow Quarter streets could accommodate—and bigger yet. New "super-krewes" emerged, like Orpheus (founded by local musical royalty and lifelong Mardi Gras enthusiast Harry Connick, Jr.), Bacchus, and Endymion, with nonexclusive memberships and block-long floats. The largest parades can have dozens of floats, celebrity guests, marching bands, dance troupes, motorcycle or scooter squads, and thousands of participants.

The trinkets known as **throws** fly thick and fast from the floats, to the traditional cry of "Throw me something, Mister!" The ubiquitous plastic beads were originally glass, often from Czechoslovakia. **Doubloons,** the oversize aluminum coins stamped with the year and the krewe's coat of arms, are collector's items for locals. Other throws include toys, T-shirts, plastic krewe cups, stuffed animals, and blinky things. Many krewes have signature throws such as the cherished **Zulu coconuts** and glittery **Muses shoes.**

Hilarity, irony, political and social commentary, and New Orleans–based inside jokes are often on blatant display at the parades, on the floats, and among the spectator costumes. Also keep a watch out for offbeat homegrown and rogue krewes and marching clubs, like the sci-fi **Krewe of Chewbacchus;** the legume-adorned **Krewe of Red Beans;** or the severely spangled and sideburned, scooter-based **Krewe of Rolling Elvi.** These groups form among friends or neighbors or along any random theme. To track them down, check **WWOZ.org** or **Gambit** (www.bestofneworleans.com).

Kickin' Up Your Heels: Mardi Gras Activities

Mardi Gras can be whatever you want. The entire city shuts down (including schools and many businesses) so that every citizen can join in the celebrations. Families and friends gather on the streets, on their stoops, or on balconies. They barbecue on the neutral ground (median strip) along the route, and throw elaborate house parties. Bourbon Street is a parade of exhibitionism and drunkenness. Canal Street is a hotbed of bead lust. Royal and Frenchmen streets are a dance of costumed free spirits and fantasies come to life.

THE SEASON   The date of Fat Tuesday is different each year, but Carnival season always starts on **Twelfth Night,** January 6, when the Phunny Phorty Phellows kick things off with a streetcar party cruise. Over the following weeks, the city celebrates, often with round, purple, green, and gold **king cakes.** Each has a tiny plastic baby (representing the Baby Jesus) baked right in. Getting the slice with the baby is a good omen, and traditionally means you have to throw the next King Cake party. For the high-society crowd, the season brings parties and **masked balls,** where krewes introduce their royal courts.

Two or three weeks before Mardi Gras itself, the parading (and parodying) begins. Adorable canines parade in the **Mystick Krewe of Barkus,** often with their humans in matching costumes. The riotous **Krewe du Vieux** outrages with un-family-friendly decadence. Sweetly insubordinate '**tit Rǝx** features itsy-bitsy insurrectionary floats, shoebox-size stabs at the more established traditions (like those of *grande* Rex—'tit being an abbreviation of the French *petit,* meaning "wee"). To dip your toe into Mardi Gras, come for Mini Gras, the weekend 10 days before Fat Tuesday. You can count on at least 10 small-to-midsize parades, more manageable crowds, and better hotel rates.

The following weekend the parades (more than 15 of 'em) and the crowds are *way* bigger—the massive party is *on.* Saturday's biggie is **Endymion,** which parades through Mid-City; Sunday's Uptown route sees action all day, capped with the spectacular **Bacchus.**

LUNDI GRAS In a tradition going back to 1874, King Zulu arrives by boat (or train, sometimes) to meet King Rex on the Monday before Fat Tuesday. With the mayor presiding, this officially welcomes Mardi Gras day. Nowadays, there's (surprise!) an all-day music and food fest along the riverfront to celebrate the grand event (www.lundigrasfestival.com). Events start by noon (Mar 4, 2019; Feb 24, 2020); the kings meet around 5pm; major fireworks follow. That night, **Proteus** and the **Krewe of Orpheus** hold their parades, and a good portion of the city pulls an all-nighter.

MARDI GRAS DAY The two biggest parades, **Zulu** and **Rex,** run back to back to kick things off. Zulu starts near the Central Business District at 8:30am; Rex starts uptown at 10am. Across town, the bohemian **Societé of St. Anne** musters around 9am near Burgundy and Piety streets in the Bywater area. This fantastical walking club (no floats) is known for its incredibly creative, madcap, au courant, and occasionally risqué costumes.

In between the parades, you can see other elaborately costumed Mardi Gras **walking** or **marching clubs,** such as the Jefferson City Buzzards, the Pete Fountain Half-Fast, and Mondo Kayo (identifiable by their tropical/banana theme). They walk (or stumble), accompanied by marching bands, anywhere along St. Charles Avenue between Poydras Street and Washington Avenue.

By early afternoon, Rex spills into the CBD. Nearby, you may be able to find some of the elusive **Mardi Gras Indians,** small communities of African Americans and black Creoles (some of whom have Native American ancestors). The tribes have an established hierarchy and deep-seated traditions. They don enormous, elaborate beaded and feathered costumes made entirely by hand, each attempting to outlandish-do the next. The men work on them all year in preparation for rituals and parades on Mardi Gras and St. Joseph's Day; they're a great source of pride and the designs usually have deep personal meaning.

The timing and locations of Indian gatherings are intentionally discreet, but traditionally tribes converge throughout the day at St. Augustine Church in the Tremé, and at main intersections along the Claiborne Avenue median (underneath the interstate). Crowds of locals mill around to see the spectacle: When two tribes meet, they'll stage a mock confrontation, resettling their territory. After marching in various parades, they reconvene around mid-afternoon on Claiborne, where a party gets going. Play it cool, however—this is not your neighborhood, nor a sideshow act. It is a ritual deserving of respect. Also, Indian suits are copyrighted works of art; photos of them can't be sold without permission. To find the Indians, ask locals, check **www.wwoz.org/inthe street**, or head to Claiborne and Orleans avenues and listen for drums. You can also try to catch these fantastic cultural confrontations at **Super Sunday** near St. Joseph's Day, at parties, and at Jazz Fest.

As you make your way through the streets, keep your eyes peeled for members of the legendary **Krewe of Comus,** men dressed in tuxes with brooms over their shoulders, holding cowbells. Ask them if they are Comus, and they will deny it, insisting they are Cowbellians. But if they hand you a vintage Comus doubloon, the truth will be out.

The last parade each day (on both weekends) is loosely scheduled to end around 9:30pm but can run way later, and most krewes hold balls or parties after they parade. Some are members-only, but those of Bacchus, Endymion, Zulu, and Orpheus sell tickets to the public. Endymion's massive Extravaganza doubles as a concert; Rod Stewart and Jason Derulo played to around 20,000 people in 2018. At day's end (or the start of the next), expect exhaustion. If you're in the Quarter at midnight, you'll see another traditional marvel: The police come en masse, on foot and horseback, and efficiently, effectively, shoo the crowds off—officially ending Mardi Gras. If you're tucked in, tune in to WYES (Channel 12) for live coverage of the Rex Ball—it's serious pomp.

Doing Mardi Gras

LODGING During Mardi Gras, accommodations in the city and the nearby suburbs are booked solid, *so book a room as early as possible*—a year in advance is quite common. Price-spike, minimum-stay requirements, and "no cancellation" policies often apply. Some hotels along the parade routes offer popular but pricey packages that include bleacher or balcony seats.

CLOTHING For the parades before Mardi Gras day, dress comfortably (especially thy feets) and prepare for whatever weather is forecast (which can vary widely). You'll see lots of glitter, wigs, and masks, but most don't dress up. Fat Tuesday is a different story. A **costume** and **mask** automatically makes you a participant, which is absolutely the way to go. You needn't do anything fancy (though you certainly *can*); scan the thrift stores for something loud and it's all good. Anything goes, so fly your freak flag if you're so inclined.

If you've come unprepared, see p. 219 for costume shops, or try the secondhand stores along Magazine Street or Decatur Street, and in the Bywater.

Save the Date
Mardi Gras falls exactly 47 days before Easter: That's March 5, 2019; February 25, 2020; and February 16, 2021.

DINING   Many restaurants close on Mardi Gras day but are open the weekend prior. Make reservations as early as possible. Some (such as Emeril's, Herbsaint, and Palace Café) are right on the parade routes, which could be fun. *Pay attention to those parade routes,* because if there is one between you and your restaurant, you may not be able to drive or park nearby, or even cross the street, and you can kiss your dinner goodbye. Thus, restaurants often have a high no-show rate during Mardi Gras, so a well-timed drop-in may work to the nonplanner's advantage.

DRIVING & PARKING   Don't. Traffic and navigating during Mardi Gras is horrendous. Take a cab, walk, or pedal (arrange well in advance for bike-rental reservations; see p. 268). Parking along parade routes is not allowed 2 hours before and after the parade. Parking on the neutral ground (median strip) is illegal (despite what you may see), and you'll likely be towed. *Note:* Taxis and rideshares are hideously busy; and streetcar and bus schedules will be radically altered (none run on St. Charles Ave.). For more, go to the **Regional Transit Authority (RTA)** website (www.norta.com) or call ⓒ **504/248-3900.**

FACILITIES   Restrooms are notoriously scant along the parade routes. Entrepreneurs rent theirs, and the city brings in the ever-popular Porta Potties. Bring tissues and take advantage of any facilities you come across. The brilliant **airpnp** potty-locator app launched for Mardi Gras 2014 could be a life-saver, or at least a bladder saver, if you're willing to go the pay-to-pee route.

THE DAY PLAN   It's not necessary to make a plan for the big day, but it might help. Get your hands on the latest edition of *Arthur Hardy's Mardi Gras Guide* through **www.mardigrasguide.com** or at nearly any store. Download the app, since schedules and routes occasionally change at the last minute. Also download the real-time **parade-tracker app** from WWLTV. com. Resolve that you'll probably adjust the plan, or throw it out altogether—and that you'll chill and go with it. The fun is everywhere—but with limited transportation and facilities available (and until you've done it enough to determine a satisfying routine), you'll have to make some choices about what to do in advance *and* on the fly. Read the rest of this section and check the route maps. Then decide if you want to head uptown, downtown, to the Quarter, the Bywater, Claiborne Avenue, or some combination of the above, as your shoes and stamina dictate.

SAFETY   Many, many cops are out, making the walk from uptown to downtown safer than at other times of year. All in all it's a joyous occasion all around, but pickpockets come out at Mardi Gras and rowdy revelers are known to go too far. Stay ever-aware and reasonably cautious.

SEATING   Some visitors buy cheap folding chairs at local drugstores, which typically don't make it home; others just bring a blanket or tarp. You might find a spot to use them on the Uptown routes; downtown, you'll probably be standing. The longest parades can last 3-plus hours, so plan according to your staying power. A limited number of bleachers are erected along the downtown parade route and sold to the public. If you're crowd-averse or just prefer to have space pre-designated for your krewe, the privilege is actually not as pricey as you might expect (from $8 per person for the smaller, first-weekend parades; $60ish for Mardi Gras day). Bleacher seats sell out, so start checking **www.neworleansparadetickets.com** and **www.mardigras paradetickets.com** in September. Specific seats aren't assigned within the bleachers, so you still need to stake out your turf. But most of these reserved areas do come with designated Porta Potties.

KIDS   It may seem contrary to the common stereotype, but Mardi Gras *is* a family affair, and you can bring the kids (especially if you stick to the Uptown locales, where hundreds of local kids sit atop custom-rigged ladders…the better to catch throws). It's a long day, though, so make sure to bring supplies and diversions for between parades. There may be some schlepping involved, but their delight increases everyone's enjoyment considerably.

WHAT ELSE TO BRING   The usual dilemma applies: You'll want to stay unencumbered but well-supplied. Much depends on whether you plan to stay in one place or make tracks. A starter set of beverages and snacks is called for, or a full picnic if you desire (food trucks, barbecue rigs, not to mention enterprising homeowners-turned-delis, are often available along the routes). Toilet tissue and hand sanitizer are good ideas; don't forget a bag or backpack for those beads. Locals often stake a spot in or near a favorite bar along Magazine Street or St. Charles Avenue, where drinks and a potty are available.

How to Spend the Big Day

Despite the popular impression of Mardi Gras, the parades don't even go down Bourbon Street. Your Carnival experience will depend on where you go and whom you hang out with. Here are three ways to do it: nice, naughty, and nasty. Us? We prefer the first two, traversed on two wheels.

NICE   Hang out exclusively Uptown with the families. Find a spot on St. Charles Avenue (which is closed to traffic that day) between Napoleon Avenue and Lee Circle, and set up camp with a blanket and a picnic lunch for **Rex,** the walking clubs and truck parades. Dressed-up families are all around. One side of St. Charles is for the parades and the other is open only to foot traffic, so you can wander about, admire the scene, and angle for an invitation to a barbecue or balcony party. New Orleans kids consider Mardi Gras more fun than Halloween, and the reasons are obvious.

   Zulu's route starts at Jackson and goes downriver, so those farther uptown will miss out. Staking out a spot downtown is another option; the crowds are a bit thicker and rowdier.

   For an utterly different experience, head to Claiborne Avenue around 9am-ish and look for the **Mardi Gras Indian** tribes' meeting (p. 45). It's a hit-or-miss proposition; the Indians themselves may not know in advance when or where the gatherings occur. But running across them on their own turf is one of the great sights and experiences of Mardi Gras.

NAUGHTY Around mid-morning, track down the **Krewe of Kosmic Debris** and the **Societé of St. Anne:** no floats, just wildly creative, costumed revelers. At noon, try to be near the corner of Burgundy and St. Ann streets for the **Bourbon Street** awards. You may not get close enough to actually see the judging, but participants sporting all form of human expression (and sexuality) are everywhere, so you can gawk at their inventive, sometimes R- and X-rated costumes. It's boisterous and enthusiastic, but not (for the most part) obnoxious. Afterward, head to **Frenchmen Street,** where dancing and drum circles celebrate Carnival well into the night.

NASTY Stay on **Bourbon Street.** Yep, it's every bit as crowded, booze-soaked, and vulgar as you've heard. There are no fabulous floats. Instead, every square of street and overhanging balcony is packed with partiers. Those balcony dwellers pack piles of beads (some with X-rated anatomical features) ready to toss down in exchange for a glimpse of flesh (flashing is technically illegal). It's anything goes, which works for this crowd. (It can also grow old fast; try starting with semi-madness on the parade route in the Central Business District and migrating later to the full madness of Bourbon Street, or vice-versa.)

Parade Watch

A Mardi Gras parade works a spell on people. There's no other way to explain why thousands of otherwise rational men and women scream, plead, jostle, and sometimes expose themselves for a plastic trinket. Nobody goes home empty-handed (even the trees end up laden with glittery goods), so don't forget to actually look at the amazing floats. At night, when lit by flambeaux torchbearers, it is easy to envision a time when Mardi Gras meant mystery and magic. It still does, if you let it.

Below are just a few of the major parades of the last days of Carnival.

○ **Muses** (founded 2000): This popular all-gals krewe honors New Orleans' artistic community—and shoes. Its glittery, decorated pumps are highly sought throws. Thursday evening before Mardi Gras.

○ **Krewe d'Etat** (founded 1996): Social satire is its specialty. No current event is left unscathed, and its hilarious float designs can fuel water-cooler and barstool discussions for weeks. Friday evening before Mardi Gras.

○ **Iris** (founded 1917): This women's krewe follows traditional Carnival rules of costume and behavior. Saturday afternoon before Mardi Gras.

○ **Endymion** (founded 1967): One of the early 1970s "superkrewes," it features a glut of floats, 2,600 riders, and celebrity guests such as Alice Cooper, Tom Jones, Dolly Parton, and John Goodman. It runs in Mid-City, concluding with an enormous, black-tie party in the Superdome. Saturday evening.

○ **Bacchus** (founded 1968): The original "superkrewe," it was first to host international celebrities. Bacchus runs from Uptown to the Convention Center. Sunday before Mardi Gras.

- **Orpheus** (founded 1993): Another youngish krewe, it was founded by a group that includes Harry Connick, Jr., and adheres to classic krewe traditions. Popular for its many stunning floats and generous throws. Follows the Proteus route on Lundi Gras evening.
- **Zulu** (founded 1916): Lively Zulu's float riders are decked out in woolly wigs and blackface. Riders carry the most prized Mardi Gras souvenirs: glittery hand-painted coconuts. These status symbols must be placed in your hands, not tossed, so go right up to the float and do your best begging. Mardi Gras morning.
- **Rex** (founded 1872): Rex follows Zulu and various walking clubs down St. Charles. It features the King of Carnival and classic floats. Mardi Gras day.

CAJUN MARDI GRAS

For an entirely different experience, take the 2½- to 3-hour drive out to Cajun Country, where Mardi Gras traditions are just as strong but considerably more, er, traditional. **Lafayette** celebrates Carnival in a manner that reflects the Cajun heritage and spirit. The 3-day event is second in size only to New Orleans', with parades and floats and beads a-plenty, but the final pageant and ball are open to the general public. Don your formal wear and join right in!

MASKED MEN & A BIG GUMBO   In towns like Eunice and Mamou in the Cajun countryside, the Courir de Mardi Gras celebration is tied to the traditional French rural lifestyle. Bands of masked men (and women, now) dressed in raggedy patchwork costumes and peaked *capichon* hats set off on Mardi Gras morning on horseback, led by their *capitaine*. They ride from farm to farm, asking at each, *"Voulez-vous reçevoir le Mardi Gras?"* ("Will you receive the Mardi Gras?"). *"Oui,"* comes the invariable reply. Each farmyard then becomes a miniature festival of song, dance, antics, and much beer. As payment for their pageantry, they get "a fat little chicken to make a big gumbo" (or sometimes a bag of rice or other ingredients).

All meet back in town where cooking, dancing, storytelling, and general merriment continue into the wee hours, and yes, there is indeed a very big pot of gumbo. Some are private events, but your best bet for particulars comes from the **Lafayette Convention & Visitors Commission** (www.lafayette travel.com; ℂ **800/346-1958** in the U.S., 800/543-5340 in Canada, or 337/232-3737).

NEW ORLEANS JAZZ & HERITAGE FESTIVAL

What began in 1969 as a small gathering in Congo Square to celebrate the music of New Orleans now ranks as one of the best attended, most respected, and most musically comprehensive festivals in the world. Although people call it Jazz Fest (or just "Fest") the full name is **New Orleans Jazz & Heritage Festival.** The "Jazz" part hardly represents the scope of the musical fare.

Each of the 13 stages showcases a musical genre or three. The "Heritage" part is why this Fest rises above all those that have tried to claim its crown: they don't, can't, and will never be able to bring the NOLA.

Jazz Fest encompasses everything the city has to offer, in terms of music, food, and culture. That, and it's a hell of a party. In 2006, after Shell Oil sponsored Jazz Fest's uncertain return after Katrina, Bruce Springsteen's triumphant, emotionally stunning set sealed its eternal resurrection. Such musical and emotional epiphanies abound at Fest. While headliners like Stevie Wonder, Tom Petty, Foo Fighters, Arcade Fire, Ed Sheeran, Pearl Jam, The Who, Keith Urban, Pitbull, John Legend, Maroon 5, Janelle Monáe, Snoop Dogg, and Lady Gaga can draw huge crowds, serious Festers savor the lesser-known acts. They range from the avant-garde to old-time Delta bluesmen, African artists making rare U.S. appearances to bohemian street folkies, top zydeco players to gospel mass choirs. And, of course, jazz in its many forms.

Filling the infield of the Fair Grounds horse-racing track near City Park, the festival covers 2 long weekends, the last in April and the first in May (for 2019, that's April 2–28 and May 2–5; in 2020 it's April 24–26 and April 30–May 3). It's set up about as well as a large event can be. When the crowds get thick, though (especially on the popular second Sat), it can be tough to move around, more so if the grounds are muddy from rain (yet more so if Elton John is playing; he caused a massive human traffic jam in 2015). At peak times, lines at the most popular of the several dozen food booths can be frighteningly long, but it's all quite civil; most move quickly (and are invariably worth the wait).

Attending Jazz Fest means making some tough decisions. Hotels, restaurants, and flights fill up months (if not a year) in advance, but the schedule is not announced until a couple of months before the event. So reserving travel requires a leap of faith in the talent bookings. Truth be told, just about every day at Jazz Fest is a good day regardless of who is playing (avoid the dilemma by attending both weekends). The Thursday before the second weekend traditionally has more locals, on stage and in the audience, and smaller crowds. It's a great time to hit the most popular food booths and check out crafts areas.

Jazz Fest Pointers

"It's a marathon, not a sprint," as the saying goes. With music in every direction, you can plot out your day or just wander from stage to stage, catching a few songs by various acts—some of the best Jazz Fest experiences come from stumbling across an undiscovered musical gem. Or you can set up camp at one stage—from the big ones with famous headliners to the gospel tent, where musical miracles are pretty much a given. Everyone except perhaps serious Zen practitioners experience *some* FOMO (Fear of Missing Out), so stage-hopping is standard. The decision is akin to sit-down dining versus a buffet: Both have advantages, but the offerings are incredible so you really can't lose.

At your hotel, or as you're walking to Fest, grab a free *Offbeat* magazine (they're dispensed everywhere). You'll need the schedule "grids" and performer descriptions. Also download the Jazz Fest and Offbeat apps. For $6, the official Fest program (available on-site) also has the schedule, plus food coupons.

On a typical Jazz Fest day, arrive sometime after the gates open at 11am and stay until you are pooped or when they close at 7pm. The whole thing usually runs as efficiently as a Swiss train. After you leave, get some dinner and hit the clubs. Every club in the city has topnotch bookings—of note are **Piano Night** at the House of Blues; Tipitina's' **Instruments a Comin'** benefit; the **jam-heavy shows** produced by **NolaFunk** (nolafunk.com); **Fiyawerx** (fiyawerx.com); and Backbeat (backbeatfoundation.org). The **Jazz Fest Grids** (jazzfestgrids.com) is a very handy aggregate of the evening music options. Alternately, sleep.

The excellent nonmusical aspects of Jazz Fest are plentiful. Local craftspeople and juried artisans fill a sizable area with artwork and products for show, for demonstration, or for purchase. Most vendors will pack and ship goods to your home (and there's a U.S. Post Office on-site, too).

And as always in New Orleans, there is food. Expect the local standbys—not burgers and dogs but red beans and rice, jambalaya, étouffée, and gumbo. A few more interesting, favorite choices include *cochon de lait* (a mouthwatering roast-pig sandwich), a fried soft-shell crab po' boy, quail and pheasant gumbo, buttery, crab-topped trout Bacquet, and all manner of oyster and crawfish. And that's not even discussing the various ethnic or vegetarian dishes available, or the desserts…oooh, the desserts. Food ranges from about $6 to $12. The terrific kids' area has PB&J, mac and cheese, and other easy-pleasing faves. Try at least one new thing daily, and also share, so you can sample more variety and decide which booths to revisit. *Tip #1:* There's copious cold beer, but the lines can get long. Smaller stages = shorter lines, and it's often worth it to trek there. *Tip #2:* Many hours of sun + many beers = premature crash. Pace thyself, grasshopper.

Experienced Fest-goers also know to duck into the air-conditioned Grandstand for art and folklore exhibits, cooking demonstrations, and **real bathrooms.** The upstairs **Allison Miner Music Heritage Stage** features interviews and short performances by some of the top acts in a much more intimate setting. It's highly recommended.

Wear and bring as little as possible; you'll want to be comfy and unencumbered. Do bring sun protection, something that tells time, a poncho if rain is forecast (they sell them there, but at twice what you'll pay at a souvenir store), and moola (cash only for food; cards okay for crafts; there are ATMs but you'll want to be doing anything other than waiting in line for one). Wear comfy, supportive, well-broken-in shoes that you're willing to sacrifice to dirt or mud. If serious rain or mud is forecast, waterproof boots are your saviors (needless to say, this is *not* one of those fashion-forward fests). Flip-flops + mud = fail. No beverages (apart from 1 liter of unopened water) are allowed in.

There are seats in the tented stages. Outside, all stages have a small VIP pit area; behind that is a standing-only (no-chair) zone; then grass. The two largest stages have bleachers in the way back. Generally, people stand or sit on the ground, a blanket, or a folding chair where allowed. When left vacant, these become annoying space hogs. Kind Fest-goers invite others to use their space when they leave temporarily, but don't be shy about asking. VIPs also get covered, raised seating areas.

TICKETS   Purchase tickets when they go on sale in late fall or early winter, when they are the cheapest. Tickets are available through **Ticketmaster** (www. ticketmaster.com; *𝒞* **800/745-3000;** add their ample fees to the rates shown here) or at the gate. Daily admission for adults in 2018 was $65 plus service charges in advance, $80 at the gate, and $5 for children (ages 2–10, at gate only; kids must be present). Various VIP packages come with a range of swanky seating, access, and amenities, from the 2-weekend, $600 Brass Pass (which supports beloved local radio station WWOZ) to the single-weekend, $1,400 Big Chief VIP pass. All sell out, so order early. For details, contact **New Orleans Jazz & Heritage Festival** (www.nojazzfest.com; *𝒞* **504/410-4100**).

PARKING & TRANSPORTATION   The only parking *at* the Fair Grounds is for people with disabilities, at $50 a day, first-come, first-served. E-mail access@nojazzfest.com or contact *𝒞* **504/410-6104.** Enterprising neighbors, schools, and businesses provide parking in their driveways or lots at $25 a day and up. Most people take public transportation or a shuttle. The **Regional Transit Authority** operates bus routes to the Fair Grounds from various pickup points; for schedules, contact *𝒞* **504/248-3900** (www.norta.com). Taxis, though busy, charge a special-event rate of $7 per person or the meter reading if it's higher (see p. 267). Uber and Lyft are also in operation; expect surge rates, but if split it may even out. Gray Line's **Jazz Fest Express** (www. graylineneworleans.com; *𝒞* **800/233-2628** or 504/569-1401) operates shuttles from the steamboat *Natchez* dock in the French Quarter; the Sheraton at 500 Canal Street; and City Park. It's $20 round-trip and you must have a Jazz Fest ticket to ride (purchase shuttle tickets with your Ticketmaster ticket order). *Note:* The **Canal Street streetcar line** will be packed, but it's an option from the Quarter. Take cars destined for "City Park"—not "Cemeteries." Fare is $1.25 or use your multi-day **JazzyPass** (p. 269). All of these options have designated drop-off and pick-up locations outside the Fair Grounds.

PACKAGE DEALS   Check the "Travel" section of the Jazz Fest website for package deals that include airfare, hotel accommodations, Fest tickets, and shuttle tickets to get you there. If you're flying to New Orleans specifically for the festival, visit **www.nojazzfest.com** to get a Jazz Fest promotional code from a list of airlines that offer special Fest fares. **Festival Tours International** (www.gumbopages.com/festivaltours; *𝒞* **310/454-4080**) offers a tour that includes accommodations and tickets for Jazz Fest, plus a midweek visit to Cajun Country for unique personal encounters with leading local musicians. A crawfish boil with the Savoys (reigning first family of Cajun music) and a barbecue at zydeco master Geno Delafose's ranch are regular outings. The company has been around since 1982. Their "non-tours," which are filled with music lovers, are positively stellar.

WHERE TO STAY IN NEW ORLEANS

Accommodations in New Orleans range from your basic lodger to over-the-top luxurious: Like the city itself, there's something for every preference. Prices also vary widely. The rates shown here don't reflect spikes during high season or discounts during low season.

As a generality, in the New Orleans market, inexpensive hotels price most rooms $125 and under, moderate up to $199, and expensive, $200 and up.

Hotel taxes are 14.75% plus a per-night occupancy fee of $1 to $3. Parking rates shown may not reflect tax or rates for oversized vehicles. Be aware that parking can up your day rate considerably, and may not include ins-and-outs. By law, all hotels are now non-smoking, although some provide an outdoor smoking area.

FRENCH QUARTER & FAUBOURG TREMÉ

Called the Vieux Carré (old square), this is the picturesque soul of the city that most people envision—visitors walk out of their hotels and feel wholly transported to the late 17th and early 18th centuries, when the Quarter was built. In the French Quarter, you are ensconced in the total N.O. experience—from the serene to the sybaritic. The Tremé (just across Rampart Street; see p. 30) has a few lodging options, offering proximity at a (slightly) lower price point.

Best for: First-time visitors; short-term visitors; historians; architecture buffs; partiers; everyone in the entire world.

Drawbacks: During high season it can be bustling with tourists and goings-on. It's generally pricier than other areas, and valet parking can add to the wallop.

Expensive

Audubon Cottages ★★★ Liz Taylor stayed here, but it feels like you're staying at her place (if she lived in a sublime warren of 18th-century apartments). An unmarked gate and leaf-canopied pathway lead to seven ultra-private one- and two-bedroom cottages with a large courtyard (some private, some shared). Each is gracefully, but not overly, antiqued amid gorgeous brick walls and gleaming hardwood floors. The cottages surround a brick-lined, heated pool, and it's all attended to by a 24-hour butler. It's easy to imagine naturalist John James Audubon watching birds alight from his studio here (he did), inspiring him to capture their images in his historic paintings. If you have the means, by all means stay here.

509 Dauphine St. www.auduboncottages.com. *©* **504/586-1516.** 7 units. $279–$379 single; $369–$800 suite. Rates include welcome beverage, breakfast, bottled water. Valet parking at nearby Dauphine Orleans $36. **Amenities:** Butler service; fitness room; pool; Wi-Fi (free).

Bourbon Orleans Hotel ★★

Location, location, location—you really can't ask for a better one smack in the middle of the French Quarter. And a big pool. This large, bustling property has those, plus good service, and even better history (ask the concierge for some background). The formal lobby makes an impressive first impression. Room decor is reasonably fresh thanks to frequent updates (if still standard nouveau hotel); bathrooms are sexied-up in black marble. The smallest rooms are a tad tight; the bi-level loft suites with Bourbon-facing balconies are ideal for party people but may be too noisy for others. Long hallways mean you might be walking your muffuletta off—for some that's a plus (otherwise, request elevator proximity). **Bourbon O** bar has live jazz daily and a super cocktail list.

717 Orleans St. www.bourbonorleans.com. *©* **866/513-9744** or 504/523-2222. 218 units. $159–$429 double, $299–$579 suites. Rates include welcome beverage. Valet parking $36. **Amenities:** Restaurant (breakfast and dinner only); bar; concierge; fitness room; outdoor pool; room service (breakfast and dinner only); Wi-Fi (free).

Dauphine Orleans Hotel ★★

This labyrinth of vintage rooms, some with private courtyards, others surrounding the popular pool, is quite charming, if quirky. Avoid those overlooking the dour parking lot. Atmosphere and rooms are both friendly and relaxed—the former welcoming, the latter with comfortable but unremarkable furnishings, including Tempur-Pedic® beds. Inclusive breakfast and beverages are a bonus (the just-renovated bar, May Bailey's, displays authentication of its history as a former brothel). Easy access to—but a quiet respite from—Bourbon Street.

415 Dauphine St. www.dauphineorleans.com. *©* **800/521-7111** or 504/586-1800. 111 units. $139–$269 double, $229–$459 suite. Rates include continental breakfast and welcome beverage. Extra person $20. Children 17 and under free in parent's room. Valet parking $36. **Amenities:** Bar; coffee lounge; small fitness room; outdoor pool; Wi-Fi (free) and bottled water.

Hotel Monteleone ★★

There is almost nothing modest about the venerable Monteleone, family-owned since 1886. Not the ornate lobby, not the hallowed literary tradition (Faulkner, Hemingway, Capote, Tennessee Williams, and Eudora Welty slept, drank, and/or wrote here, among others), not the happy-hour scene or stellar view at the rooftop pool. And certainly not the fancifully sublime, legendary **Carousel Bar** (p. 203). Okay *maaay*be the

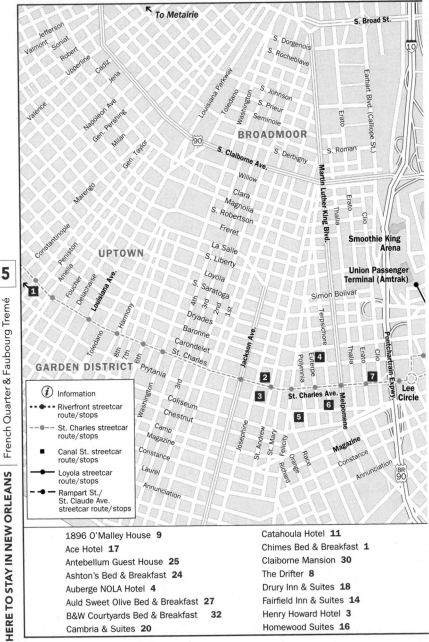

1896 O'Malley House 9
Ace Hotel 17
Antebellum Guest House 25
Ashton's Bed & Breakfast 24
Auberge NOLA Hotel 4
Auld Sweet Olive Bed & Breakfast 27
B&W Courtyards Bed & Breakfast 32
Cambria & Suites 20

Catahoula Hotel 11
Chimes Bed & Breakfast 1
Claiborne Mansion 30
The Drifter 8
Drury Inn & Suites 18
Fairfield Inn & Suites 14
Henry Howard Hotel 3
Homewood Suites 16

See also "French Quarter Hotels" map

NOPSI Hotel **15**
The Old No. 77 Hotel & Chandlery **21**
Olde Town Inn **31**
Parisian Courtyard Inn **6**
Park View Guest House **1**
Ponchartrain Hotel **2**
Q&C **19**
The Quisby **7**
Renaissance Arts Hotel **20**
The Roosevelt **13**
Royal Frenchmen **29**
Royal Street Inn & R Bar **28**
St. Charles Guest House **5**
Troubadour Hotel **12**
Windsor Court **22**

Hotel Storyville **26**
India House Hostel **8**
Jung Hotel **10**
Loews New Orleans Hotel **23**
Maison de Macarty **33**
Maison Perrier Bed & Breakfast **1**

traditional, gilt-y room decor, which leans toward the mumsie side of formal (but since that apparently extends to in-room fridges and robes, we'll take it). The larger suites offer roomy, classic gentility, but standard rooms can be, well, modest. Some are quite petite, in fact, and those ending in #27 have no windows (though #56 and #59 are bigger and high-ceilinged). The family ownership is reflected in gracious, accommodating service (gentlemen should spring for a proper hot-towel, straight-razor shave in the barbershop; everyone should spring for something from the pricy but so soothing full-service spa). The fitness equipment is notably good, and **Criollo Restaurant** is a big step up from standard hotel fare.

214 Royal St. www.hotelmonteleone.com. (C) **800/535-9595** or 504/523-3341. 483 units. $169–$499 double, $599 and up suite. Extra person $25. Children 17 and under stay free in parent's room. Valet parking $40. Pets allowed with fee and deposit. **Amenities:** 2 restaurants; coffee cafe; 5 bars; concierge; fitness center; heated rooftop pool; room service; spa; Wi-Fi (free).

Jazz Quarters ★★ An unexpected and unassuming enclave of entrancing private cottages (part of the original Tremé plantation) and a languid tropical garden lie hidden behind greenery and gates next to Armstrong Park. The one- and two-room parlor suites are well-decorated for comfort with contemporary wares, nods to the birthplace of jazz across the street, and a smattering of antiques (no more is needed—history seeps out from the very walls here). The rooms vary in size, and come with few amenities, but it's pretty, private, and convenient—making it especially inviting for reunions and romantics. Free parking, a rarity, is a substantive bonus for visitors driving in.

1129 St. Philip St. www.jazzquarters.com. (C) **800/523-1372** or 504/523-1372. 10 units. $325–$749 cottage. **Amenities:** Limited free secured parking; Wi-Fi (free).

Ritz-Carlton New Orleans ★★★ It may not be the ritziest of all Ritz-Carltons, but do expect Ritz-level luxury, service, and amenities, including a stellar spa and the soignée **Davenport Lounge.** It's all quite gracious and stately (as was its previous tenant, legendary department store Maison Blanche), though the hotel is a bit confusing to navigate. Room decor leans traditional, with posh purple and gold fabrics; bedding is superb even in the smaller rooms. Try for a larger room on the 12th, 14th, or 15th floor, or better yet, the updated Maison Orleans club level. With its plush lounge, handsome library, 24-hour concierge, and food and bev service, it's among the best VIP sleeps in town.

921 Canal St. www.ritzcarlton.com/neworleans. (C) **800/522-8780** or 504/524-1331. 527 units. $269–$599 double, $699 and up suites. Valet parking $52. Pets $150 fee. **Amenities:** Restaurant; bar; concierge; complimentary access to spa and fitness center; room service; shops; Wi-Fi (free in public areas; an annoying $13/day in rooms, waived for Ritz or Marriott members).

Royal Sonesta ★★★ You might forget you're right on Bourbon Street, what with all the graciousness inside. The Sonesta is large, busy, and classy, with outstanding service for the mix of tourists and business patrons. Rooms, redesigned in late 2016, are handsomely decorated in white and shimmery

Audubon Cottages **7**

Bourbon Orleans Hotel **9**

Chateau Hotel **13**

Dauphine Orleans Hotel **5**

Grenoble House **4**

Homewood Suites **3**

Hotel Monteleone **2**

Hotel Provincial **15**

Hotel St. Marie **8**

Jazz Quarters Bed & Breakfast **11**

Le Richelieu Hotel **16**

New Orleans Courtyard Hotel **12**

Place d'Armes Hotel **10**

Ritz-Carlton New Orleans **1**

Royal Sonesta **6**

Soniat House **14**

5

WHERE TO STAY IN NEW ORLEANS | French Quarter & Faubourg Tremé blue; bathrooms, on the smaller side, are white-on-white. Some of the better suite options are here, or opt for the added perks on the R Club floor. Rooms facing the inside courtyard avoid the Bourbon Street racket—unless that's what you're here for; some rooms open right onto the large courtyard pool, which is wonderfully welcoming but can get crowded. All amenity bases are covered; indeed, almost everything you could need is here, including the so-so **Desire Oyster Bar,** the terrific **Restaurant R'evolution** (p. 92), and the very good **Jazz Playhouse** (p. 193)—which adds to the luster and liveliness.

300 Bourbon St. www.sonesta.com/royalneworleans. © **800/766-3782** or 504/586-0300. 483 units. $199–$429 double, $400–$2,500 suite. Parking $41. **Amenities:** 3 restaurants; 5 bars; concierge; fitness center; outdoor pool/terrace; room service; Wi-Fi (free).

Soniat House ★★ Inside these unassuming Creole townhouse exteriors lies an oasis of indulgent calm. The staff spoils guests; Frette linens cradle them; the sweet courtyards, candlelit at night, soothe them. The handsome rooms differ in size and furnishings. Most in the main house have high ceilings; all have well-selected artwork; some have balconies (a room with both helps justify the rates). Bathrooms are small, though some have Jacuzzi tubs. It's more about ambience than amenities here, as the experience is unobsequiously elegant, romantic, and adult.

1133 Chartres St. www.soniathouse.com. © **800/544-8808** or 504/522-0570. 31 units. $295–$375 queen or king room, $400–$795 and up suites. Optional continental breakfast $12.50. Valet parking $39. No children 10 and under. **Amenities:** Concierge; honor bar; complimentary access to nearby New Orleans Athletic Club; Wi-Fi (free).

Moderate

Homewood Suites ★★ The hulking exterior of this 2017 newbie doesn't even offer a nod to its historic locale, but like many good things, the enticements are on the inside. This one also happens to be well-situated on the edge of the French Quarter, along the Rampart streetcar line (an older Homewood Suites is in the Warehouse District, p. 72). Like its Homewood brethren, the one- and two-bedroom suites have a functioning kitchen and a parlor area (with sofa bed) separate from the bedroom, and rates include an ample full breakfast buffet daily plus light cocktails and food Monday to Thursday evenings. This one squeezes in a slender pool, putting green, and even a BBQ grill between its two elongated buildings, and hips up the lobby with a sleek fireplace, wood board games and a pool table. Room decor is freshly contemporary if simple; the few balcony rooms don't offer much worth paying more for. A third-floor room facing Rampart Street is the best bet for a wee bit of rooftop and downtown views, but those facing the courtyard may be quieter if the pool is not party central.

317 N. Rampart St. http://homewoodsuites3.hilton.com/en/hotels/louisiana/homewood-suites-by-hilton-new-orleans-french-quarter-MSYFRHW/index.html. © **504/930-4494.** 207 units. $123–$123 double. Rates include full breakfast buffet daily and basic dinner Mon–Thurs. Valet parking $38 or lots nearby. **Amenities:** In-room kitchens; convenience/snack shop; concierge; business center; coin laundry; fitness room; putting green; outdoor pool; BBQ grills; pool table; Wi-Fi (free).

Grenoble House ★★   This midrange property, which opened in 2013 after a lengthy post-Katrina closure, does a few things very well. The 17 suites have full kitchens (for cereal eaters and leftover snackers, the dining-out savings add up). A heated pool, spa, and spacious courtyards link three 19th-century buildings. Decor is comfy traditional; room sizes and configurations vary (some work well for families or small groups). There's a basic continental breakfast and occasional events at an outdoor bar and BBQ area (available for rent). Street noise can be an issue for front-facing rooms; third-floor rooms are less expensive for a reason: no elevators. Staff is friendly and helpful, though. The property uses a key hold system (guests "check" keys at front desk when leaving).

323 Dauphine St. www.grenoblehouse.com. ℂ **504/522-1331.** 17 units. $129–$399 suite (advance payment required). Rates include continental breakfast. Parking garage 1 block away, $30. **Amenities:** Pool; spa; Wi-Fi (free).

Hotel Provincial ★★   This family-run hotel has a healthy dose of character, from the flickering gas lamps and jumbly layout to the rumored ghosts (it's a former Civil War hospital). The quiet, high-ceilinged rooms were renovated in 2017; those facing the street still get a bit of noise but nothing serious). The better ones have non-working fireplaces or huge windows; the best—on the upper floors, accessible only by stairs—reward climbers with peek-a-boo river views. We're also fond of those that open onto the small courtyard and fountain; another courtyard is mostly pool. Rooms were spruced in 2017, when a nod to modernity was added to the mix of antiques, reproductions, and hotel traditional; rooms also have a sweetly sequestered bar. The lobby's **Ice Bar** feels like your own private space.

1024 Chartres St. www.hotelprovincial.com. ℂ **800/535-7922** or 504/581-4995. 92 units. $109–$319 double; $229–$369 suite. Valet parking $30. **Amenities:** Bar; 2 pools; restaurant; mini-fridge; Wi-Fi (free).

Le Richelieu Hotel ★   Located in the quiet, residential end of the French Quarter, this former row house (and macaroni factory) has clean, basic rooms and, usually, fair prices. The public spaces feel sorta like Daddy-cave additions to a suburban home: a small wood-paneled bar, a glassed-in, poolside cafe, and a dunking pool. It's definitely dated but somehow oddly cozy and welcoming, especially to Beatles fans who can sleep where Sir Paul McCartney and family did while in town recording Venus and Mars.

1234 Chartres St. www.lerichelieuhotel.com. ℂ **800/535-9653** or 504/529-2492. 88 units. $110–$225 double; $195–$550 suite. Extra person, including children $15. Self-parking $30. **Amenities:** Restaurant (breakfast and lunch only); bar; concierge; in-room fridge, unheated saltwater pool; room service; Wi-Fi (free).

New Orleans Courtyard Hotel ★   This boutique inn on the Tremé side of Rampart Street offers French Quarter proximity at reasonable rates and pleasantly authentic ambience. They've worked hard to raise their standards over the past few years, and it shows, including upgrading the hotel-generic room furnishings (though there's still work to do—starting with bathroom

French Quarter & Faubourg Tremé

SPARE ROOMS: THE airbnb EFFECT

At press time, the New Orleans City Council had passed a 9-month moratorium on issuing new licenses for short-term rentals in most residential districts. The ban was initiated at the same time the City Planning Commission is close to completing a study on the effects of short-term rentals and whether more regulations are needed.

The moratorium addresses ongoing concerns about the effect these short-term rentals have on affordable housing for locals. New Orleans is awash in these listings: **Airbnb, Homeaway, Vrbo,** and their ilk (the moratorium does not affect those already licensed, nor those operating outside existing regulations). Many offer wonderful spaces and access to neighborhoods out of the fray. New Orleans' economy is indelibly tied to the tourism industry, and its workforce—the servers, cooks, bartenders, and performers whose talents and hospitality you are presumably coming to enjoy—relies on reasonably priced, available housing stock. Even in the most urban environments, there is a delicate balance between commercial and residential; an expectation of stability, peace, and neighborliness. And crucially, in New Orleans the precious evolution of culture and transfer of traditions occurs within long-established communities. All are considerations when it comes to choosing your lodging.

updates). Two multi-hued, low-ceilinged buildings are joined by a courtyard and goodly expanse of pool (which the breakfast room overlooks, and a sister property—the **French Quarter Suites**—shares). We're partial to the carriage-house rooms, with wood floors, exposed brick, and shutters—though a nearby laundry station means much staff scurrying about. Interior rooms fare best; those facing Rampart suffer from traffic and streetcar noise. Deep discounts and self-serve breakfast waffles add guest appeal.

1101 N. Rampart St. www.nocourtyard.com. © **504/522-7333.** 21 units. $129–$219 double. Rates include continental breakfast. On-site parking $25–$35. **Amenities:** Wi-Fi (free).

Place d'Armes Hotel ★ If you're planning to spend a lot of time sightseeing, this is a good choice for French Quarter lodging, especially given the relatively decent rates (which include basic continental breakfast). You're a hop-skip from Jackson Square and Café du Monde, and it's hard to have a care when you're lounging around an amoeba-shaped pool shaded by palm trees. If, however, your vacation fantasies include much lolling about in plush rooms, or you live for light-filled mornings, this may not be for you. Several buildings are knit together by brick hallways and awfully pretty, awfully vieux courtyards. Rooms and bathrooms, while perfectly serviceable, are showing their age. Some rooms are dark or windowless, even, but a few splendid ones have terraces with a Jackson Square corner view.

625 St. Ann St. www.placedarmes.com. © **800/626-5917** or 504/524-4531. 84 units. $93–$154 double; $359–$479 suite. Rates include continental breakfast. Valet parking $30. **Amenities:** Pool; Wi-Fi (free).

Hotel St. Marie ★ We've always been fond of **Vacherie** (p. 94), the restaurant in the St. Marie. After a recent renovation, the rest of the property has caught up. Given its Bourbon Street proximity and choice of on- or off-street rooms, it's a good mid-level option with a very good French Quarter location, and room rates can be downright bargains during low season. There's nothing to knock your socks off here, but the staff has a friendly, helpful vibe, and we especially like that 80% of the rooms have balconies overlooking the street or the modest pool. Get it while it's fresh.

827 Toulouse St. www.hotelstmarie.com. ✆ **888/626-4812.** 103 units. $149–$179 double, $249–$289. Valet parking $34. **Amenities:** Restaurant, bar; concierge; pool; Wi-Fi (free).

Inexpensive

Chateau Hotel ★ Location, location, location is the draw here, along with a friendly staff and prices that can dip below $100 during non-festival weeks. Set in a restored 18th-century mansion, this is definitely not a chain hotel experience. That being said, some of the fussy decor is tired and unremarkable and amenities scant, but the leafy courtyard and pool are lovely, and there's that central location. If you aren't spending a lot of time in the room, this budget sleep delivers. Upgrades are promised in the coming year, so stay tuned.

1001 Chartres St. www.chateauneworleans.com. ✆ **504/524-9636.** 49 units. $109–$359. Rates include continental breakfast. Children 11 and under free. Valet parking $38.51. **Amenities:** Pool; Wi-Fi (free).

MARIGNY & BYWATER

A few inns and a slew of B&Bs (many newly minted) dot this gentrified-meets-working-class area. Artists' workshops, galleries, dive bars and a fresh crop of good restaurants are scattered throughout.

Best for: Artists and art appreciators; bohemians and alternative scenesters; B&B fans; people seeking a less-bustling, neighborhood experience; who prefer staying among the like-minded; LGBTQ; music lovers and street partiers who want to fall out of bed and onto Frenchmen Street.

Drawbacks: Some parts are walking distance to the French Quarter; others are too far from the action or from public transportation, warranting a car or bike. Dicey, rundown shotgun homes commingle with cool renovations.

Expensive

Claiborne Mansion ★★ Secreted a block from the boisterous hordes of Frenchmen Street, this stately edifice hides unexpected elegance and serenity. What appears to be a private home is a bed-and-breakfast with two drop-dead stunning suites and a fabulous swimming pool that might tempt you away from the nearby clubs. Those suites, done up in whites and creams, take full advantage of the home's original architecture: soaring ceilings, crown moldings, fireplaces (nonworking), and huge windows. Upstairs rooms in the main house are pretty in a lesser way; the carriage-house rooms are just ordinary. Continental breakfast is in a communal indoor/outdoor kitchen in the expansive backyard, where kitties lounge in the sun and orange trees provide fresh juice, when in season. Hospitality is more sufficient than solicitous, but architecture buffs will enjoy the owner's insights.

2111 Dauphine St. www.clairbornemansion.com. ℂ **504/301-1027.** 7 units. $125–$170 single, $225–$300 suite. Rates include continental breakfast. Limited on-site parking and street parking. **Amenities:** Saltwater pool; Wi-Fi (free).

Royal Frenchmen ★★ If your plans include extensive Frenchmen Street nightclubbing (p. 196), this is a good option. The freshly renovated historic building (previously a Boys & Girls Club) is a soothing, somewhat more sophisticated respite from the street scene, and your bed is within stumbling distance of all the action. The building facing Frenchmen houses 13 rooms with double queen or king bedrooms; those upstairs have French doors leading to small balconies where you can check out the street scene (and vice-versa). The indistinct suites are in a quieter back building. Betwixt them is a pleasant brick courtyard with soothing fountain and occasional live music. Guest-room character comes from original or reproduced architectural touches like fireplaces (nonworking), crown moldings, and window shutters, which complement the simple antique reproduction furnishings and small but nicely updated bathrooms. The handsome, white-marble-laden lobby features dramatic paintings by surrealist artist Vladimir Kush. Complimentary continental breakfast (fresh fruit, yogurt, bagels) is a nice plus, as is free gated on-site parking. The calm, cozy **bar** serves unexpectedly good small plates (the food and beverage team is mostly Commander's Palace alum; service throughout is casual and friendly). Soundproofing is decent, but expect some street noise. For many visitors, that's a plus—but if you're not among that number, march on.

700 Frenchmen St. www.royalfrenchmenhotel.com. ℂ **504/619-9660.** 16 units including 3 suites. $219–$309 double queen, $299–$399 suite. Rates include continental breakfast and gated parking. **Amenities:** Bar; concierge; Wi-Fi (free).

Moderate

Auld Sweet Olive Bed & Breakfast ★★ Sweet is the operative word for this newly spiffed butter-yellow Creole cottage, from the laziness-inducing wicker porch chairs to the yummy-delish breakfast muffins to the four clean, airy rooms (and one separate kitchenette suite) custom-painted with pretty botanical patterns. But it's genuine and unfussy, just like hospitable owner Nancy Gunn. She's free with the what-to-do tips (it's near the St. Claude Ave. clubs), but hides her Emmy Award (she's a former reality-TV and documentary producer) on kitchen shelves of pretty reclaimed wood.

2460 N. Rampart St. www.sweetolive.com. ℂ **877/470-5323** or 504/947-4332. 5 units. $145–$300 double and suite. Rates include buffet breakfast. Street parking. **Amenities:** Wi-Fi (free).

B&W Courtyards Bed & Breakfast ★★   The simple exterior masks a serene courtyard, a soothing hot tub, and a six-room B&B—4 blocks and a world away from the Frenchmen crowd. They've had some mix-and-match fun here, blending tropical West Indies hues with French antiques and Oriental touches, and each clever room is unique (sometimes even strange—you enter one through the bathroom; saloon-style swinging doors lead from the bathroom to the bedroom); all have been recently updated. The hosts are music lovers who freely share insider club tips and occasionally jam with guests; they also serve a killer hot breakfast (that tasso cheddar frittata is memorable, oh baby).

2425 Chartres St. www.bandwcourtyards.com. ℂ **800/585-5731** or 504/322-0474. 5 units. $145–$195 double. Rates include full breakfast. Street parking. **Amenities:** Hot tub; Wi-Fi (free).

Maison de Macarty ★★★   Tucked away in the Bywater neighborhood is a Victorian treasure with one of the better backyards we've seen, with a big mineral-water pool, a fire pit, and a **cabana bar** that exerts a strong gravitational pull (it also pulls in a lot of weddings, so it's not always available). Six rooms are in the high-ceilinged main house, and two are in separate private cottages; all are smartly decorated (not overly so) with old and new pieces, plus soothing aromatherapy machines and those Himalayan lamp things. Room sizes vary, as do bathrooms (some are shower-only style; others have a deep Jacuzzi tub). The Storyville room works well with its loft space but is not for the claustrophobic; the others are amply sized, and some open over the courtyard for added airiness. Add plush bedding, optional breakfast (additional cost), and the pet-friendly, inherently neighborly ambience, and you're nearly a local. You'll definitely want a car or bike.

3820 Burgundy St. www.maisonmacarty.com. ℂ **504/267-1564.** 8 units. $149–$225. Limited street parking. **Amenities:** Pool; Wi-Fi (free).

Royal Street Inn & R Bar ★   The fact that the name of this all-suite guesthouse includes the name of the attached bar is not incidental. You're welcomed with complimentary drink tokens, and you should count on participating in the bar action (here or elsewhere) late into the night—lest you become its victim. As long as you're aware that this is part of the experience here (music, billiards, cigarette smoke, and all), it's all good—including the actual rooms. All have just undergone a redo, and the result is a clever mix of platform bedding, Pottery Barn–ish leather seating, mood lighting, pops of color with the existing wood-and-brick vibe—comfortable and worn-in but hip, like your favorite torn jeans. It's the free-spirited, decidedly Marigny attitude at play—which also describes the service and the clientele—but it's also Quarter- and Frenchmen-close; location and atmosphere help you feel a bit like a local (free crawfish boil on Fridays during crawfish season; on Mondays, dudes can get a $10 shot and a haircut).

1431 Royal St. www.royalstreetinn.com. ℂ **504/948-7499.** 5 units. $169–$499. Rates include bar beverage. Limited street parking. **Amenities:** Bar; Wi-Fi (free).

Inexpensive

Olde Town Inn ★ This is the hotel version of a neighborhood dive bar: friendly if slightly tired. But the price is right, location works, and it's just fine when you just need something basic. Especially for those on a budget, who want to explore the Marigny and Bywater or hang out on Frenchmen Street. Some rooms have remnants of charm, like arched doorways or (nonworking) fireplaces, but expect basic pressboard reproduction furnishings. Rates includes continental breakfast (yes, with waffles!), served in a sweet, covered outdoor patio. Two long row houses, joined by a narrow brick courtyard, are a bit ramshackle, but staff works hard to keep things tidy, usually succeeding. Three small shotgun houses facing Marigny Street serve as kitchenette suites with a dorm-style group room. The property, and these in particular, are popular with bachelor parties.

1001 Marigny St. www.oldetowninn.com. © **800/209-9408.** 30 units. $79–$169 double; $189–$229 suite. Rates include continental breakfast. Street parking, or limited availability in secured, private lot $15/day. **Amenities:** Mini-fridge; Wi-Fi (free).

MID-CITY/ESPLANADE

This thriving area encompasses diverse socioeconomies and architectural styles amid quiet neighborhood streets and busy commercial corridors. It includes a number of B&Bs along sometimes grand, sometimes shabby Esplanade Avenue.

Best for: Repeat visitors seeking to experience the city more like a resident; those who prefer B&Bs; Jazz Fest and Voodoo Experience goers; bike riders.

Drawbacks: You'll rely on a car, bikes, taxis, or public transportation. It's a large area with some altogether lovely sections; other neighborhoods are more ramshackle.

Expensive

Ashton's Bed & Breakfast ★★★ Ashtons stops just short of lavish, remaining comfortable rather than over-the-top. We might even call it homey—if home was a genteel, Esplanade Avenue antebellum mansion. Once you sink into your comfy bed, you may not want to leave the romantic, pastel-walled, antiques-filled room. But you will, for stellar breakfasts like eggs *cochon de lait*. The main-house rooms are plenty spacious; ceilings are ridiculously high, sheets silky. Room #4 has a half-tester bed and an extravagant rain shower; #7 has a clawfoot whirlpool tub. It's all light and bright, from the wide front gallery to the oak-shaded backyard, and the on-site hosts are most congenial. Excellence is in the details, and the owners have carefully attended to them.

2023 Esplanade Ave. www.ashtonsbb.com. © **800/725-4131** or 504/942-7048. 8 units. $178–$228 double. Rates include full breakfast, beverages. **Amenities:** Secure free parking on-site; Wi-Fi (free).

1896 O'Malley House ★★★   A quiet, nondescript Mid-City neighborhood unexpectedly houses this splendid B&B, antiqued but not frilly, steps from the Canal Street streetcar line. Fine art, stunning woodwork, and a gorgeous fireplace add architectural flair. Tasty breakfast is in the formal dining room, or you can take your homemade muffin to the pleasant but unexceptional outdoor space. The largest rooms are on the second floor, where the impressive decor ends at the bathroom door (though most have Jacuzzi tubs, so we'll deal). The smaller, garret-like rooms on the third floor make clever use of their odd shapes and bleached wood. Ghost hunters should request the haunted room. Host Larry and the family golden retrievers add a pleasantly personal touch.

120 S. Pierce St. www.1896omalleyhouse.com. ✆ **866/226-1896** or 504/488-5896. 8 units. $155–$230. Rates include breakfast, snacks, beverages. Limited free off-street parking. **Amenities:** In-room iPad Concierges; Wi-Fi (free).

Moderate

Antebellum Guest House ★★★   Grandiosity, check. Antiques everywhere. High ceilings. Elaborate breakfast. Check, check, check, all here. The real difference is in the experience, and the hosts. You could spend your entire visit chatting with them about New Orleans, art, travel, history, and whatever far-flung topics arise. They're interesting and interested, which describes much of New Orleans' population, but now you're at home with them (home being an 1830s Esplanade Avenue glamour gal, the former "party home" to a wealthy plantation family, now tarted up to the nines). Quibblers (Instagram posters of scuffed baseboard shots—who probably shouldn't come to a 300-year-old city) will find things to complain about. The anachronistic, 1970s bathrooms are ho-hum, for starters. But there are loaner bikes to get you to the nearby French Quarter or City Park. And when you step into the dreamy, moss-hung backyard, with its hot tub and secret garden, magic begins.

1333 Esplanade Ave. www.antebellumguesthouse.com. ✆ **504/943-1900.** 3 units. $165–$185 double, $260–$365 suite. Rates include full breakfast. Street parking. **Amenities:** Hot tub; bicycles; mini-fridge; Wi-Fi (free).

The Drifter ★★★   The pool-centric Drifter is on a whole other hipness plane. It's just barely removed from its previous life as a boxy midcentury-modern, no-tell motel on an as-yet untrammeled stretch of Tulane Avenue (5–15 Lyft min. to the Warehouse or Marigny). Yet it's eons beyond that blah existence. Beds have Casper mattresses and Frette linens, but the 22 smallish, cement-walled rooms have no TVs and deliberately few amenities (save a mini-fridge, a couple of swank magazines, and a Tivoli radio/speaker)... because life here revolves around the ample bar and spacious, clothing-optional pool area, where parties large and small happen year-round (in winter they spark up the fire pits and set the water heater at 95; occasionally a custom catwalk spans the pool; on Sat there's poolside yoga). The understated high design engages without engulfing, from the lobby's wall-size crawling ivy sculpture and '60s furniture to the so-new-yet-looks-so-old floor tiles and outdoor mirror balls. Naturally there's a good coffee bar and decent snacks. Let the fun begin.

3522 Tulane Ave. www.thedrifterhotel.com. ℂ **504/605-4644.** 22 units, some with bunk beds. $150–$240 double queen or king; $210–$320 queen bunk (four queen beds). Free or street parking. Not appropriate for kids. **Amenities:** Coffee bar; juice, snack and cocktail bar; pool; Wi-Fi (free).

Hotel Storyville ★ Great location (especially for Jazz Fest–goers), friendly host, clean and unfussy rooms with kitchenettes: all good. The exterior looks fittingly New Orleanian, with tall columns and wide double galleries, and its mint-green color hints at the hotel's beachy vibe (aqua, and laidback). Rooms vary in size and configuration, from a tiny single to a multi-bedroom. The gorgeous back courtyard is event-ready, which may or may not work to your benefit (if a crawfish boil is on, you're probably invited; if a wedding is on—which is often—there's a party in your yard). Other amenities are scant, so don't expect to be doted on, but the on-site innkeeper is accessible and the price is surely right.

1261 Esplanade Ave. www.hotelstoryville.net. ℂ **504/948-4800.** 7 suites, 1 studio. $89–$299 single and double. Secured off-street parking $5, or limited free off-street parking. **Amenities:** Wi-Fi (free).

Inexpensive

India House Hostel ★ Foreign travelers and students (passport or student ID required) looking for budget lodging and an instant party, welcome home. The four buildings house private rooms (some with their own bathrooms), standard bunk-bed dorms, and a usable kitchen that also serves good, cheap meals. A pool, deck stage, and outdoor bar make for a ready-made social scene and frequent events. It's close to buses and the Canal Street streetcar, and tour companies pick up here regularly. It's funky but not filthy, friendly, and backpacker-ready. Book directly for the best rates.

124 S. Lopez St. www.indiahousehostel.com. ℂ **504/821-1904.** 168 beds. $22–$99. Some off-street parking; street parking. **Amenities:** Kitchen use; pool; Wi-Fi (free).

CENTRAL BUSINESS DISTRICT

The "CBD" abuts the French Quarter along Canal Street and extends west to include the Warehouse District, with loft-conversion hotels, a thriving club scene, and the arts district. As the city's commerce center, modernity and history mix—as do tourists and businesspeople. Some of the city's finest restaurants and hotels are here, as are some good deals (especially on weekends and off-season). Most of it is still walking distance to the French Quarter action.

Best for: Hipsters; foodies; conventioneers; Superdome attendees; museumgoers; the budget-minded; families (lots of suite and chain hotels are here).

Drawbacks: It's not New York, but this is a city center, with people working and view-obstructing office buildings (and nonstop construction—ask what's nearby when making reservations). Parking is pricey; do without a car or save a few bucks and minutes by using a nearby private lot rather than the valet.

Expensive

Ace Hotel ★★   If a hotel could have a soul patch, the Ace would. Every hipster-bait amenity is attended to. Situated in a converted Art Deco building, this outpost of the Portland-based chain sports photo booths; in-room turntables and vintage vinyl; room snacks of ramen and Bulleit bourbon. Not that there's anything wrong with all this—it all works. The chocolate-and-charcoal rooms look great, with their nominal, angular furnishings and custom painted armoires, but they aren't built for deep comfort. No worry, cuz you be chillin with the <30 crowd in the action-packed lobby bar, excellent **Josephine Estelle** restaurant (p. 114); stellar rooftop pool and bar **Alto; Three Keys** club; and terrif **Seaworthy** oyster bar. The **Stumptown Coffee** shop and **Freda** boutique further augment the hipness. Bring the swag and you'll fit right in.

600 Carondolet St. www.acehotel.com/neworleans. ✆ **504/900-1180.** 235 units. $169–$259 classic room; $369–$969 suite. Pets under 25 pounds $25 per night. Valet parking $39. **Amenities:** 2 restaurants; 3 bars; coffee cafe; music/performance venue; gym; outdoor pool; room service; Wi-Fi (free).

Catahoula Hotel ★★   Hiding in plain sight on a CBD side street, this stylish 2016 boutique hotel is cool but not cold, and feels practically private. The scale is modest throughout: Rooms sport comfy Casper mattresses and historic architectural features, but few amenities (offering hooks instead of closets). Showers that open to the bedroom (and vanities in the bedroom) mean roommates better be very close. The best rooms—those with chic seating areas and small patios facing Union St.—won't reach their greatness potential until the construction project across the street is complete (do inquire). But the public spaces are why you stay here: the so-on-trend **Piscobar** and pop-up kitchen offerings and in-the-works Peruvian café; clandestine, twinkle-lit courtyard with the soaring mural of local burlesque star Trixie Minx; and hip rooftop terrace and bar with occasional DJs, screenings, and bands. Don't overpay.

914 Union St. www.catahoulahotel.com. ✆ **504/603-2442.** 35 units. $125–$399 king; $389–$449 suite. Rates include complimentary morning pastries. Pay parking lots nearby. **Amenities:** Café; bar; coffee bar; rooftop bar/terrace; Wi-Fi (free).

Loews New Orleans Hotel ★★★   We're fans of the crisply contemporary Loews, with its judicious sprinkles of New Orleans flavor and the consistently genteel, professional service. The bright, expansive freshly spiffed rooms come with local photography, understated furnishings, and sophisticated finishes in a muted palette. Many rooms have fab river views that are worth the upgrade (others face surrounding buildings). Even the smallest are on the large size, though the handsome wood and granite bathrooms—which still have tubs—are just average). All get access to the steamy indoor pool and well-equipped fitness room, not to mention the persistently fine **Café Adelaide** (part of the Commander's Palace family) and the excellent **Swizzle Stick Bar.**

300 Poydras St. www.loewshotels.com/neworleans. ✆ **866/473-8970** or 504/595-3300. 285 units. $239–$439 room; $459–$1,800 and up suite. Valet parking $42. Pets allowed

($100 nonrefundable fee, plus $25/day). **Amenities:** Restaurant; bar; concierge; exercise room; indoor pool; room service; spa; Wi-Fi (free).

NOPSI Hotel ★★   Ninety years after it first opened, this 1927 building got a massive renovation that brought smiles to many local faces, who recalled paying utility bills, buying bus passes, or ogling newfangled appliances here in years past (NOPSI stands for New Orleans Public Service Inc.). We like it too, not least for the grandiose lobby boasting soaring, 20-foot vaulted ceilings and the stunning recasted moldings. The central CBD location is also a big plus, and **Above the Grid** rooftop pool and bar boast impressive Superdome views. Given all that grandeur, the well-appointed rooms are surprisingly staid in style, what with their yacht-y navy, white, and tan scheme, but they're comfortable and crisp, spacious and smart. Best of all might be the bathrooms, which clearly denote NOPSI as a woman-owned property: they're big, with double sinks, an enormous shower, and a separate lighted vanity tucked just outside the oft-steamy space. Plenty of mirrors and storage space also feature into the well-thought-out spaces. All-around pro service is the capper.

317 Baronne St. www.nopsihotel.com. *②* **844/439-1463.** 217 units, including 81 suites. $189–$269 standard room, $259–$339 deluxe king suite. Valet parking $45. **Amenities:** Restaurant; 2 bars; concierge; fitness room; gift shop; pool; 24-hr. room service; spa; Wi-Fi (free).

Q&C ★★   Reborn in 2015 after a $10-million renovation (and sold to Marriott in 2016), Q&C is one of the better of the new crop of millennial-targeting hotels. It's got the requisite distressed leather sofas in the "living room"–style lobby; industrial lighting and hardware bits; scratchy blues tunes playing in the hallways; and communal tables where you can plug in and collectively stare at screens. But there's also a vintage shuffleboard table, a terrific selection of art and music coffee-table books for perusing in stylized nooks, and wink-wink cameo silhouettes of Fats Domino and Duke Ellington. Also, while many of the millennialist properties have slashed food and drink options down to the grab-and-go variety, Q&C has a darn good lobby restaurant and bar. The property shares two buildings split by a narrow street. Rooms are small but stylish in muted grays, browns, whites, and brick; subway-tiled, single-sink bathrooms have metal barn doors and half-glass shower doors. In Building A, the third-floor rooms have huge windows; otherwise try for one with a view (floors 8–12); in Building B, snag #14 or #23. Rooms down low can face other buildings or suffer from street noise. Service-wise, it's not the Ritz, but staff is cute, friendly, and generally on top of things.

344 Camp St. www.qandc.com. *②* **504/587-9700.** 196 units. $100–$409 double. Valet parking $38. Pets allowed (fees apply). **Amenities:** Restaurant; bar; fitness room; Wi-Fi (free).

Renaissance Arts Hotel ★★   A film-crew favorite for its loft-conversion style; proximity to the Howlin' Wolf (p. 199) and other Warehouse area attractions; spacious rooms; and terrific modern art. Nothing's to die for, but everything is clean-lined and well-done—and the staff is particularly efficient. The large rooftop pool adds a lot, with spectacular views and a jumping social scene. Streetside rooms have large, original windows; the interior overlooks the '70s-era atrium and courtyard or neighboring buildings.

700 Tchoupitoulas St. www.renaissanceartshotel.com. ✆ **504/613-2330**. 217 units. $120–$329 double; $329–$529 suites. Valet parking $43. **Amenities:** Restaurant; bar; concierge; sundries shop; fitness center; newspaper delivery on request; rooftop pool; room service; Wi-Fi (free in public spaces; $13/day in-room; waived for Marriott members).

The Roosevelt ★★ This grandiose Waldorf property is regal throughout, but the movie-star-glamorous, block-long lobby is positively magnificent, and the history and pedigree equally impressive. Sizes and views in the well-appointed, traditional rooms vary: Luxury suites are more than ample, but the smallest rooms are simply too small for what you're probably paying, even if the upholstery is striped silks and/or deeply tufted. Some have tubs (even clawfoots!); others on the upper floors overlook the city or the fourth-floor pool. All have luscious beds. But guest rooms really take a back seat to the exceptional lobby and other common areas: the sumptuous **Waldorf Astoria Spa, Domenica** restaurant (p. 113), **Sazerac Bar** (p. 208), and the historic **Blue Room** club. Service sometimes feels stretched. Check for occasional good package deals and seasonal rates. Holiday season here is dreamlike.

123 Baronne St. www.therooseveltneworleans.com. ✆ **800/925-3673** or 504/648-1200. 504 units, including 125 suites. $243–$599 double, $329–$999 suite. Valet parking $46. Pets less than 25 lbs. allowed ($175 fee). **Amenities:** 2 restaurants; coffee shop; bar; spa; concierge; fitness room; gift shop; Jacuzzi; pool; room service; Wi-Fi (free in lobby and cafe; $15/day in room; free for Hilton Honors members).

Windsor Court ★★★ There's a kind of hush at this ultra-fine hotel, for decades the center of New Orleans high society. Everything is serene and mannerly, from the proper high tea and mind-blowing hallway galleries of original 17th- to 19th-century art, to the restaurant—the highest-end **Grill Room.** The spacious accommodations are traditional if not particularly distinctive in silvery blue, gold, and creamy ivory. Suites are large-windowed, light-filled, and enormous. Those with balconies and river views are exceptional (though some "view" rooms are only partial views); a ritzy club level adds 24/7 concierge service. It has indisputably the city's best hotel spa. The outstanding rooftop pool is one of several superb places to enjoy a smart beverage along with the chichi **Polo Club** (p. 207).

300 Gravier St. www.windsorcourthotel.com. ✆ **888/596-0955** or 504/523-6000. 316 units. $205–$525 double, $395–$695 suite, $575–$935 club level. Children 17 and under free in parent's room. Pets allowed ($150 fee). Valet parking $45. **Amenities:** 2 restaurants; coffee bar; 2 lounges; poolside bar; concierge; fitness center; pool; room service; spa; Wi-Fi (free).

Moderate

Cambria & Suites ★★ The Cambria, Choice Hotels' upscale imprint, reels you in with a good location and selfie-inducing design. Although new in late 2017, its worn brick and exposed piping help the boxy seven-story building fit into the artsy, historic Warehouse District. Even before you see your room, you'll surely post from the oversize wing chairs under the blue neon "THE BIG EASY" sign. Art glorifies local and pop culture (famed New Orleanian Ellen Degeneres is painted in Renaissance wear). Look closely and you'll notice that the black walled hallways are actually dark plum; in the rooms, skulls are woven into the damask wallpaper pattern, and upholstery is metallic or faux gator. Design is paramount, but the subway-tiled bathrooms are well-sized, and rooms are perfectly practical, with plenty of outlets, a Roomio device streaming, bougie chaise longues, functional wheeled nightstands, and thick mattresses. Warehouse nods come from the rooms' floor-to-cement-ceiling windows; some look directly onto neighboring buildings, but the best have a bridge view. The main entrance around back off Commerce Street lends a private-entry feel (drivers take note: it's unsafe to pull over at the actual address on Tchoupitoulas Street; a pedestrian "back" door there connects to the main lobby via a gallery). A restaurant, bar, and grab-and-go shop offer convenience in a neighborhood flush with activity.

632 Tchoupitoulas St. www.cambrianeworleans.com. ℂ 504/524-7770. 152 units including 9 suites. $139–$489 double, $339–$789 suite. Valet parking $43. **Amenities:** Restaurant; bar; grab-and-go market, fitness room; Wi-Fi (free).

Drury Inn & Suites ★★
The looming, generic exterior hides a better-than-expected interior and a ton of amenities. Most of the spacious rooms, in monochromes with pops of local art, have high ceilings; avoid the darker ones on the lower floors and shorter ones on floors 4 and 5. Suites, though not luxurious, are downright huge. A free hot breakfast buffet and generous evening "kick-back" drinks and snacks aren't fancy but add big value. Staff is invariably friendly, and the serviceable fitness room looks onto the good-size pool and whirlpool spa. All that, a good location, and reasonable rates make this one of the best deals in town.

820 Poydras St. www.druryhotels.com. ℂ 800/378-7946 or 504/529-7800. 214 units. $149–$289 regular room, $209–$379 suite. Rates include full breakfast plus weekday evening snacks. Valet parking $30. **Amenities:** Fitness room; heated courtyard pool and spa; Wi-Fi (free).

Fairfield Inn & Suites Downtown ★★
The recent $10-million redo of this 103-suite hotel makes it a stunner of a budget property, with great French Quarter proximity. The historic hotel, built in 1910 as the Interstate Electric Company, shows off details like 13-foot ceilings in the guest rooms, exposed original brick interior walls and support beams. Like most other Fairfields, the Marriott brand delivers great value including hot breakfast and in-room microwave and mini-fridge; unlike most others, this one has a bar, **346 BLU,** and jazz-themed lobby decor. Distinctions like these elevate it beyond the brand's traditional standards.

346 Baronne St. www.marriott.com. ℂ 504/309-0800. 103 units. $149–$229. Valet parking $34. **Amenities:** Free breakfast, fitness center, Wi-Fi (free).

Homewood Suites ★★
This was already one of our top choices, given all its inclusive fringe bennies. Now, after a recent top-to-bottom renovation,

it's pretty dazzling in a Hilton-brand, cookie-cutter sort of way. Speaking of cookies, they're among the freebies here. Add a full hot breakfast buffet; the perfunctory but perfectly good free "social" dinner (think lasagna or fried chicken, salad bar, and wine or beer!); indoor pool—and the savings really add up. Plus, the XL all-suite rooms have a living room, microwave, and fridge, so if you'd rather spend on sights than tastes and don't need luxury, decamping here will save you tons on dining out (and on transportation, given the convenient location). The fresh decor is simple but well turned-out, and the exterior has plenty of historical appeal so you don't feel completely "chained" in. When rates are at midrange or lower, it's a super value, especially for families and extended stays.

901 Poydras St. www.homewoodsuitesneworleans.com. © **504/581-5599.** 166 units. $169–$279 one-bedroom suite. Rates include full breakfast buffet daily and basic dinner Mon–Thurs. Valet parking $35. **Amenities:** Snack shop; concierge; business center; coin laundry; fitness room; indoor pool and whirlpool; Wi-Fi (free).

Jung Hotel ★★★ This 1907 building was once the largest hotel in the city at 1,200 rooms, hosting many dignitaries and landing on the National Register of Historic Places. After a massive renovation, it's down to a mere 207 (the upper floors are apartments). It's still quite grandiose and coolly elegant (somewhere a marble pit yearns for its missing quarry). Unsurprisingly given its girth, the rooms and bathrooms are plenty large and comfortable, styled in tan, pale teal, and woodgrain. A few more outlets would help, but all is forgiven when you're chillaxing in the spiffy recliner chairs (exec suites add a separate kitchen and dining area and in-room washer/dryer). The property's original, multi-building footprint has made for some oddball configurations, including loooong, *Shining*-like hallways (those skinny faux doorways are the originals), a spacious pool and urban-view deck on the 6th floor, and a too-small lobby bar. That's resolved with a corridor of chic, semi-private seating areas—perfect schmoozing spots—and river-themed abstract artwork throughout, including in the coffee bar and restaurant (which is still getting its footing). The Jung is a few blocks from the French Quarter and Central Business District, yet easy walking distance. So if it's not full with meeting and event visitors, it's well worth checking to see if good rates are available to fill the ample space.

1500 Canal St. www.junghotel.com. © **504/522-5864.** 207 units. $169–$299 double, $249–$379 suite. Valet parking $36. **Amenities:** Restaurant; bar; coffee cafe; fitness room; rooftop pool; Wi-Fi (free) and bottled water.

The Old No. 77 Hotel & Chandlery ★★ Set in an 1854 warehouse formerly called the Old No. 77—a name borrowed from the former warehouse's I.D. number—this Warehouse Arts District hotel dishes history with original hardwood floors, exposed brick walls and interesting ghost signs uncovered during the hotel's renovation. Several rooms are windowless and priced accordingly, but in general the sleep space is comfortable and oozes local charm. This 167-room hotel is all about local art and products, from New Orleans makers including New Orleans Center for the Creative Arts and

Where Y'art Gallery for exhibits and artist-curated loft suites. The good hotel shop has local gifts from the likes of Dirty Coast, Defend New Orleans, and Mad Darling. Chef Nina Compton's superb **Compère Lapin** restaurant (p. 109) might be the hotel's best feature.

535 Tchoupitoulas St. www.old77hotel.com. © **504/527-5271.** 167 units. $97–$313 double, $450–$550 suites. Pets allowed ($45 fee). Valet parking $40. **Amenities:** Coffee shop; restaurant/bar; Wi-Fi (free).

Troubadour Hotel ★★ As tempted as you'll be to ooh and aah over the eye-popping art and sleek, contemporary design in the Troubadour lobby, first you need to take the elevator to the 17th floor and prepare to be gobsmacked. New Orleans unfurls in every direction from the spectacular 360-degree views at the **Monkey Board** rooftop bar, which has date night written all over it. Other reasons to check in to the 184-room boutique hotel, which opened in late 2016, are the crisp, comfy guest rooms (each has a cocktail station complete with go-cups, a retro Igloo mini fridge, and iPads for room-service orders) with lots of handy bathroom storage space. The location is within strolling distance of the French Quarter, the Superdome, and the lively dining and entertainment scene in the Warehouse District.

1111 Gravier St. https://thetroubadour.com. © **888/858-6652** or 504/518-5800. 184 units. $189–$279 double, $289–$849 suite. Pets allowed (no fees). Valet parking $39. **Amenities:** Restaurant/bar (Jayne Bistro & Bar); rooftop bar; fitness center; room service; Wi-Fi (free).

Inexpensive

Nada. Some of the above moderate to higher-priced CBD hotels run specials, especially over summer; and the many chains here might work if convention business is slow that week. But there are no year-round inexpensive options in this area that we'd guide you toward, dear reader. Just being honest.

UPTOWN/GARDEN DISTRICT

The residential Garden District offers iconic Old South charm, complete with moss-laden greenery and palatial, columned homes. Not all of Uptown is as grandiose as the name might suggest—there are many more modest, no less charming properties—but the best sections are both spacious and gracious.

Best for: Repeat visitors; romantics; history buffs; claustrophobes; garden lovers; style-seeking shoppers (for nearby Magazine St.).

Drawbacks: Allow extra time and expense to get around—you're not in the thick of the action or near the city's top attractions. You'll likely be close to public transportation, but may prefer a car or bike.

Expensive

Henry Howard Hotel ★★★ A top-to-bottom 2016 renovation turned this stunning, 18-room, 1867 townhome with classic columns and soaring ceilings into a drop-dead gorgeous, super-stylish choice, where crisp,

Uptown Hotels

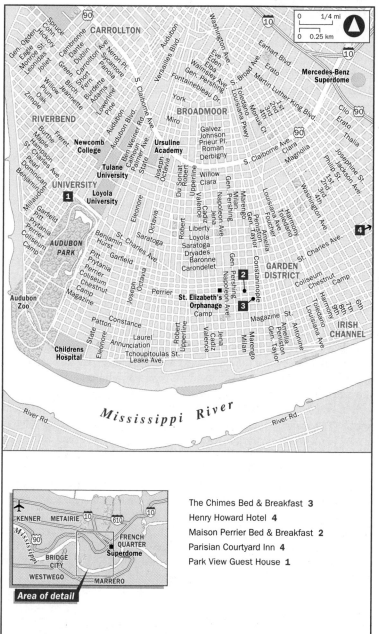

The Chimes Bed & Breakfast **3**
Henry Howard Hotel **4**
Maison Perrier Bed & Breakfast **2**
Parisian Courtyard Inn **4**
Park View Guest House **1**

white-black-blue decor and sleek, custom touches meet classy antiques. Second-line instruments as artwork and (limited) amenities like a small, butler-style bar in the polished parlor keep it friendly; the wide front gallery, complete with dawdle-ready wicker rockers, keeps it welcoming. Second-floor rooms with private balcony spaces feel positively Southern-belle chic. The Lower Garden District locale is a bit off the beaten path but convenient to the streetcar line.

2041 Prytania St. www.henryhowardhotel.com. (*C*) **504/313-1577.** 18 units. $219–$349 double. Street parking. **Amenities:** Concierge; parlor bar; Wi-Fi (free).

Maison Perrier Bed & Breakfast ★★★　The impressive exterior of this former house of ill repute is frillier than inside, though there is still plenty to impress here. Antiques abound, and a smattering of country touches help create genuine, warm comfort. The beds are deep and piled with soft, girly linens; and room configurations are amenable to couples, families, and friends (two- or four-legged). Nearly all the well-appointed bathrooms have whirl-pool tubs—some big enough for two. A full breakfast with Southern special-ties like puffed pancakes; an honor bar; helpful hosts; ample supply of homemade sweets; and weekend wine and cheese parties round out the very pleasing experience here. Check the website for excellent seasonal deals.

4117 Perrier St. www.maisonperrier.com. (*C*) **888/610-1807** or 504/897-1807. 9 units. $149–$340 double. Rates include tax, breakfast, snacks. Limited free on-site parking or street parking. **Amenities:** Concierge; Wi-Fi (free).

Ponchartrain Hotel ★★★　The 2016 reopening of the Pontchartrain rekindled some heavy trips down memory lane around here. The 1920s apart-ment building was reborn in the '40s as a high-end hotel, hosting presidents, movie stars, and Tennessee Williams (whose portrait adorns guest rooms now) and throwing storied parties for the likes of Sinatra, the Doors, and many a well-heeled local. The latest post-slump redo, a $10-million job, is splendid. Guest-room decor maintains a throwback feel with traditional furnishings, crystal chandeliers, and luxe fabrics (leather, velvet); patterns and accessories evoke tropical colonialism by way of Morocco. Modern needs are well met with the expected comforts and conveniences and spaciousness (even more so in the impressive suites). The cheery St. Charles Avenue location, outside more touristed areas and a pleasant walk from some stunning manses, is part of the experience. But the common areas really reel us in, from the foyer forward: the sweet **Silver Whistle** café; gentlemanly **Bayou Bar;** and the swank **Living Room** lounge outside **Jack Rose** restaurant, where a wall of campy floral still-lifes surround an enormous, glossy Ashley Longshore (p. 215) painting of Lil' Wayne chowing a slice of the hotel's legendary Mile High Pie. And then there's **Hot Tin** on floor #11. Arguably the city's best rooftop bar, the converted penthouse is styled after a 1940s writer's salon, if said author had stunning 270-degree views. If only these walls could talk.

2031 St. Charles Ave. http://thepontchartrainhotel.com. (*C*) **800/708-6652.** 120 units. $159–$549 double, $399–$799 suite. Valet parking $30. **Amenities:** Restaurant/lounge; bar; cafe; rooftop bar; concierge; Wi-Fi (free).

Moderate

The Chimes Bed & Breakfast ★★★   This gem has no grand airs, just pure charm and contentment in a true neighborhood setting. Rooms vary in size, but all are a tasteful, unfussy, unpretentious mix of antiques, modernity, creature comforts, and thoughtful amenities. Linens are particularly pretty, and a gallery wall displays striking black-and-white photographs of local musicians—the work of one of the many repeat guests. The hosts bring fresh baked breakfast pastries (even tastier in the pretty courtyard) and 25+ years of hospitality experience (they built the Chimes themselves). It shows in the details.

1146 Constantinople St. www.chimesneworleans.com. ℂ **504/899-2621** or 504/453-2183. 5 units. $138–$250 double. Rates include breakfast. Street parking available. **Amenities:** Wi-Fi (free).

Parisian Courtyard Inn ★★   Hospitality and location are the keywords here, though the accommodations in this converted 1846 mansion are by no means slouchy. The Lower Garden District locale is far enough from the name-brand action to merit slightly lower rates, but close enough to access it all by foot or nearby streetcar. The affable hosts will ably direct you and ply you with afternoon brownies, and perhaps some musician friends will entertain you in the soignée parlor where elaborate ceiling details and porcelain chandeliers are among the many fab light fixtures. Rooms have plenty of carved antiques; sizes vary from liberal to slight (we like the second-floor balcony suites; the third and fourth floors have angled ceilings). But if you're one of those vacationers who seek the best in rest(rooms), these teensy tubless ones won't cut it. The outdoor courtyards are sweetly pleasant, and a smattering of antiques come with interesting stories. Just ask…perhaps over the hot breakfast buffet.

1726 Prytania St. www.theparisiancourtyardinn.com. ℂ **504/581-4540.** 8 units. $167–$235 double. Rates include breakfast, snacks. Street parking. **Amenities:** Wi-Fi (free).

Park View Guest House ★★   For Tulane and Loyola visitors and others staying far uptown, this late-1800s boardinghouse with St. Charles Avenue frontage (easy streetcar access) is a splendid choice. The wide porch is stellar for sitting for a spell out front. The park in view is verdant Audubon Park, which adds serenity and spaciousness to the large breakfast room and park-facing guest rooms, all with updated bathrooms (with deep tubs). Antique-laden decor is Victoriana-meets-reproduction; smaller and non-view rooms can feel cramped. The Wi-Fi signal is stretched and may not reach rooms in the back. The ample buffet breakfast also ranks high. Daily cookies and evening sherry add delightfulness; warm, helpful staff multiplies it.

7004 St. Charles Ave. www.parkviewguesthouse.com. ℂ **888/533-0746** or 504/861-7564. 21 units. $169–$359 double. Rates include continental breakfast, afternoon wine, and snacks. Street parking available. **Amenities:** Wi-Fi (free).

Inexpensive

Auberge NOLA Hostel ★ This mellow, clean youth hostel has a helpful staff, a decent shared kitchen, and standard-issue metal bunk beds in mixed and single-gender dorms. It's not party-central like some hostels in town—just friendly. The big selling point is location: It's a few blocks off the St. Charles Streetcar line, and a few blocks the other direction into the heart of the CBD. Another plus: on-site bikes for rent (but not enough of them), a small courtyard, and a bit of old NOLA character in the converted home. A small apartment has a private kitchen and bath and two double-bunk beds.

1628 Carondelet St. www.aubergenola.com. ℂ **504/524-5980.** 34 beds. $20–$68 bed. Rates include breakfast and linens. Street parking. **Amenities:** Shared kitchen; concierge; courtyard and TV room; lockers; rental bicycles; Wi-Fi (free).

The Quisby ★★★ The newer youth hostels are, as they say, lit. Unlike the derelict dives of yore, some are super sleek and even—yes—clean. The Quisby is one of the best. Opened in 2017 after gutting a long-shuttered historic building, the Quisby and its techno lobby area—sleek bar, sculpted industrial lighting, and graphical mural—sets the poppin' social scene. There, $2 PBR rules at happy hour and Friday night pop-ups are—as they also say—legion (tamales and DJ, for example). The beds offer the best evidence that the Quisby is something special: no rickety, Ikea-style pole kits, these; they're handsome, sturdy, XL beech bunks built by a noted local wood craftsman, with memory-foam mattresses. Each has an adjacent booklight, charging outlet, accessory cubby, and oversize storage locker. Most of the 26 coed or female-only en-suite rooms have four beds (two bunks); a few have two or six beds. Perhaps the Quisby's single best feature is its streetcar-adjacent St. Charles Avenue location (to snag a window-laden room overlooking the avenue during Mardi Gras, book 8–12 months ahead). All ages welcome.

1225 St. Charles Ave. www.thequisby.com. ℂ **504/208-4881.** 120 beds. $30–$40 bed, $60–$100 during events. Rates include free continental breakfast. Street parking. **Amenities:** Bar with snacks; on-site laundry room; Wi-Fi (free).

St. Charles Guest House ★ The three 1890s buildings are humble, funky, old, slightly crumbling, and not for everyone. But if you're a non-partying budget traveler and don't demand modern amenities, you'll appreciate the rare combination of value, location, pool, and even the offbeat charm (if the owner is around, chat him up for some great tales of yore). Some rooms are downright spartan (no A/C), while others are larger and even furnished with antiques; upkeep is inconsistent. Keep expectations in check (generally, and specifically regarding the continental breakfast), and don't overpay for accommodations during big events—that will only leave you bitter.

1748 Prytania St. www.stcharlesguesthouse.com. ℂ **504/523-6556.** 25 units; 22 with private bathroom. $55–$105 double. No credit cards; PayPal accepted. No in-room phones. Parking available on street. **Amenities:** Outdoor pool, Wi-Fi (free).

WHERE TO DINE

T he late New Orleans restaurant matriarch Miss Ella Brennan once said that whereas in other places, one eats to live, "In New Orleans, we live to eat." It seems that as soon as you step foot in this city, your appetite for just about everything somehow increases: adventure, romance, joy...and food food food.

Here, we don't call a friend and ask, "How are you?" Instead, it's either the colloquial "Where y'at?" or, more often, "What're you eatin'?" Here, cuisine is community, cuisine is culture, cuisine is practically church (literally and figuratively—except for the fact that Church is church). Food forms the crucial threads of the city's multicolored fabric: It weaves through the people, the music, the history, the parties, the traditions. A style of gumbo can define a neighborhood. A roux technique can unite (or divide) generations of families.

New Orleans has always been recognized by food lovers, but with the advent of the foodie movement, the restaurant scene has positively erupted, and the city is undeniably a foodie destination. At last count New Orleans had more than 1,400 restaurants, so there's goodness in every direction and on every level: in centuries-old grande-dame restaurants and the corner po' boy shops; in a gas station with shockingly good steam-table food; and in the sleek bistro of a brash, upstart culinary-school grad fusing Grandma's recipes with unpronounceable techniques and ingredients. And that's not even counting the many bars and nightclubs serving seriously stellar snacks. Or the much-anticipated restaurants that are *about* to open as we're turning in this book, including **Longway Tavern,** the **Pythian, Thalia,** and an unnamed spot from Justin Devillier of La Petite Grocery. Culinary training grounds like **Café Reconcile** (1631 Oretha Castle Haley Blvd.; www.cafereconcile. org; ✆ **504/568-1157**) and **Liberty's Kitchen** (300 N. Broad St. and 1615 Poydras St; www.libertyskitchen.org; ✆ **504/822-4011**) serve sturdy meals while preparing young men and women for careers in food service. And fourth-generation chefs work backstreet dives whose menus and ingredients haven't varied since, well, forever.

You are going to want to eat a lot here. And you are going to want to eat here, a lot. And then you are going to talk about it. You'll probably adopt the local custom of talking about dinner while you're at lunch (and lunch while you're breakfasting). The food here is utterly, unashamedly regional, which isn't to say that (in some cases) it's not also utterly of the moment, sophisticated, and/or redolent of other influences as well. But it's ingredient- and chef-driven, which makes it uniquely New Orleanian: It will never be Copenhagen or Bilbao, or New York for that matter, nor does it want (or need) to.

In many restaurants, certainly in the more traditional ones, dishes are based largely on variations of Creole recipes. Others, the innovators, take Creole as a cue and go wildly afield. Creole food was originally based on recipes brought by the French settlers, the herbs and filé (ground sassafras leaves) used by the Native Americans, and saffron and peppers introduced by the Spanish. From the West Indies came new vegetables, spices, and sugarcane, and when slave boats arrived, an African influence was added. Today, the Italian influence runs deep, and even Vietnamese has found its way onto the plate, the gift of a newer wave of immigrants. And while nearly all restaurateurs source fresh ingredients from local purveyors, the ban on butter never took hold here (thankfully). Flavor comes first.

So indulge and enjoy. It's what you do here. Try some of everything. We're particularly big on lunching, since many of the best restaurants have terrific prix-fixe lunch deals that include dishes that'd cost twice as much during dinner. Then start planning the next trip, so you can do it again.

Please keep in mind that all prices, hours, and menu items in the following listings are subject to change according to season, availability, or whim. You should call in advance to ensure the accuracy of anything of import to you.

Make sure to check out our "**Best of**" recommendations in chapter 1.

OF BEIGNETS, BOUDIN & DIRTY RICE

Many of the foods in New Orleans are unique to the region and consequently may be unfamiliar. This list should help you navigate local menus:

Andouille (ahn-doo-*we*)   A spicy Cajun sausage made with pork.

bananas Foster   Bananas sautéed in liqueur, brown sugar, cinnamon, and butter, drenched in rum, set ablaze, served over vanilla ice cream.

barbequed shrimp   Not actually grilled or BBQ-sauced, but a butter-soaked, garlicky, pepper-shot peel-and-eat Gulf specialty.

beignet (bin-*yay*)   A big, puffy, deep-fried, hole-free doughnut, liberally sprinkled with powdered sugar—the more sugar, the better.

boudin (boo-*dan*)   Cajun liver-and-rice sausage of varying spice levels.

café brûlot (cah-*fay* brew-*low*)   Coffee, spices, and liqueurs, served flaming.

crawfish   A tiny, lobsterlike creature common locally and eaten in every conceivable way, including boiled whole with spices and peeled by hand.

debris   The rich, juicy bits of meat that fall off during roasting and carving.

dressed   A "dressed" po' boy comes with lettuce, tomato, mayonnaise, and sometimes pickles.

étouffée (ay-too-*fay*)   A Cajun stew (usually containing crawfish or shrimp) served with rice.

filé (*fee*-lay)   Ground sassafras leaves, frequently used to thicken gumbo.

gumbo   A thick, spicy soup of poultry, seafood, and/or sausage, with okra in a roux base, served with rice. Gumbo z'herbes, a Good Friday tradition, eschews meat for greens.

holy trinity   Onions, bell peppers, and celery: the base of much Creole and Cajun cooking.

Hurricane   A local drink of rum and passion-fruit punch.

jambalaya (jum-ba-*lie*-ya)   A simmer of yellow rice, sausage, seafood, poultry, vegetables, and spices.

lagniappe (lan-*yap*)   A little something extra: a bonus freebie.

mirliton (*mur*-li-tone)   A pear-shaped squash also called chayote.

muffuletta (moo-foo-*let*-ta or moo-fuh-*lot*-ta)   A mountainous sandwich made with Italian deli meats, cheese, and olive salad, piled onto a specially made seeded round bread.

oysters Rockefeller   Oysters on the half shell in a creamy spinach sauce, so called because Rockefeller was the only name rich enough to match the taste.

po' boy, po-boy, poor boy   A sandwich on long French bread, similar to submarines and hoagies. Often filled with fried seafood or roast beef, or famously with French fries and gravy, they can include most anything. The story goes that they were originally a free sustenance offered to striking transit workers, those "poor boys." After decades of apostrophe and hyphen use, some purists are returning to the full "poor boy" name. They're delish in any spelling.

pralines (*praw*-leens)   A sweet confection of brown sugar and pecans.

rémoulade   A spicy sauce, usually over shrimp, made of mayonnaise, boiled egg yolks, horseradish, Creole mustard, and lemon juice.

roux   A mixture of flour and fat that's slowly cooked over low heat, used to thicken stews, soups, and sauces.

Sazerac   The official cocktail of New Orleans, consisting of rye whiskey (or sometimes cognac), sugar, and bitters.

shrimp Creole   Shrimp in a tomato sauce seasoned with what's known around town as the "holy trinity:" onions, bell peppers, and celery.

THE FRENCH QUARTER

Expensive

Antoine's ★★ CLASSIC CREOLE   We're sentimental about Antoine's, it being one of the first fine-dining restaurants in the New World. It's been owned and operated by the same family (and serving generations of patrons' families) for more than 175 amazing years. It's as classic as New Orleans dining gets, but truth be told, the food and presentation can be uneven. Still, the experience is well worth it. The best strategy: Go for conviviality, classics, and

Fair Grounds Racetrack (Jazz Fest)

FAUBOURG ST. JOHN

MID-CITY

TREMÉ DISTRICT

Louis Armstrong Park

St Louis Cemetery

Mercedes-Benz Superdome

Lafayette Square

Angelo Brocato Ice Cream & Confectionery **4**	Gabrielle **19**
Addiction Coffeehouse **21**	Gene's Po'Boys **47**
Adolfo's **45**	Herbsaint **29**
Annunciation **33**	The Joint **59**
Arabella Casa di Pasta **49**	Josephine Estelle **27**
Auction House Market **30**	Junction **53**
Bacchanal **60**	Kebab **50**
Bevi Seafood **4**	Kukhnya **48**
Biscuits & Buns on Banks **2**	La Boca **41**
Blue Oak BBQ **11**	Liberty's Kitchen **17**
Buffa's **44**	Lil' Dizzy's **35**
Bywater American Bistro **52**	Liuzza's **6**
Bywater Bakery **58**	Liuzza's by the Track **14**
Borgne **25**	Lola's **12**
Café Degas **13**	Mandina's **5**
Café Du Monde **8**	Marcello's **29**
Café Sbisa **43**	McHardy's Chicken **18**
Cajun Seafood **34**	Melba's **46**
Cochon **42**	Merchant **24**
Cochon Butcher **42**	Meril **28**
Compère Lapin **39**	Mother's **37**
Country Club **55**	Nor-Joe Importing **1**
Dat Dog **22, 45**	Paloma Café **56**
Domenica **23**	Pandora's SnoBalls **9**
Dooky Chase **20**	Paradigm Gardens **31**
Drago's **38**	Parkway Bakery and Tavern **15**
Elizabeth's **57**	Peche **30**
Emeril's **40**	Praline Connection **45**
Frady's **56**	Ralph's on the Park **7**
French Truck Coffee **32**	

Red's Chinese **54**
Restaurant August **36**
Revelator Coffee **39**
Ruby Slipper Cafe **16**
Sac-a-Lait **33**
St. Roch Market **51**
13 Monaghan **45**
Toups Meatery **10**
Willa Jean **26**
Willie Mae's Scotch House **19**
Ye Olde College Inn **3**

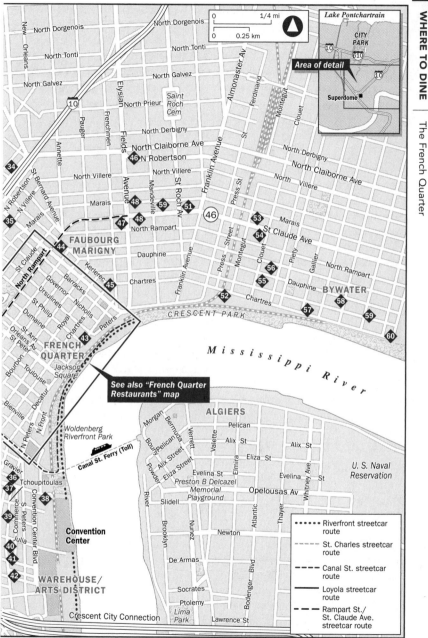

See also "French Quarter Restaurants" map

Riverfront streetcar route

St. Charles streetcar route

Canal St. streetcar route

Loyola streetcar route

Rampart St./ St. Claude Ave. streetcar route

drama. Request Johnny or Sterling as your server. Befriend neighboring guests. Order the spinach-soaked baked oysters Rockefeller (invented here); buttery, crab-topped trout Pontchartrain; and a side or two of the hollowed soufflé potato puffs. Finish with a *café brûlot* (see "Anythin' Flamin'," p. 118) and the frivolous, football-size baked Alaska. Get the daily featured 25¢ cocktails. Then tour some of the 15 (!) memorabilia-packed rooms, peek at the astounding wine alley, and catch some good local music in the **Hermes Bar.** The seasonal three-course weekday lunch at $20.17 (it goes up a penny a year) is worth every penny. Make dinner reservations well in advance during peak periods.

713 St. Louis St. www.antoines.com. ⓒ **504/581-4422.** No shorts, sandals, or T-shirts; collared shirts for gentlemen (jackets welcome, not required). Main courses $27–$48. Mon–Sat 11:30am–2pm and 5:30pm–9pm; Sun 11am–2pm.

Arnaud's ★★★ CLASSIC CREOLE Arnaud's isn't the best-known of the old New Orleans restaurants, but it tops them in quality, and far exceeds them in the cocktail arena. Arnaud's, which celebrated its centennial in 2018, is classically atmospheric with white tile floors and dark wood accents, and the recipes are classics as well. Thus, it's not wildly innovative, but the quality and attention to detail are there. Have the signature shrimp Arnaud appetizer (topped with a spicy rémoulade sauce) and the spicy pompano Duarte or the definitive *filet au poivre*. We also love the quail Elzey—petite, elegant fowl stuffed with foie gras mousse, wrapped with bacon, and ensconced in a truffle-wine sauce—and no one should leave without ordering some puffy soufflé potatoes and bananas Foster, flamed tableside (see the "Anythin' Flamin'" counsel, p. 118), although our resident crème brûlée expert rates theirs very high. Allow time to visit the impressive Mardi Gras museum upstairs. A more casual **jazz bistro room** features nighttime entertainment (a $4 cover goes to the band)—all of which makes Arnaud's a good fine-dining introduction for well-behaved children. Make dinner reservations well in advance during peak periods.

813 Bienville St. www.arnaudsrestaurant.com. ⓒ **866/230-8895** or 504/523-5433. Reservations suggested. Business casual. Main courses $27–$42. Dinner nightly 6–10pm; Sun jazz brunch 10am–2:30pm.

Bayona ★★ CONTEMPORARY SOUTHERN/INTERNATIONAL After celebrating 25 years, we'll forgive chef/owner Susan Spicer if her modern classic restaurant has slipped a notch. The food, cocktails, and wine list are still thoughtful and inspired, if no longer at the tippy-top of the heap. The ambience inside and out is positively lovely, although service can be annoyingly spotty. Begin with the signature cream of garlic soup; and select among extremes of sweetbreads with lemon caper butter (another signature), any rabbit preparation, or whatever vegetarian dish is on—ever-changing preparations of the latter are consistently superb. At lunch, the famed smoked duck with cashew butter and pepper jelly is still a clever flavor bomb. Desserts

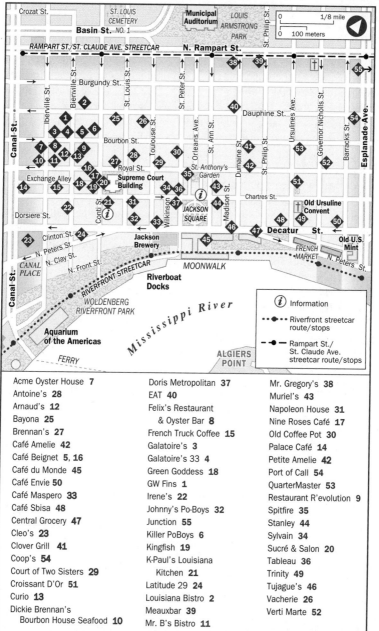

Acme Oyster House **7**

Antoine's **28**

Arnaud's **12**

Bayona **25**

Brennan's **27**

Café Amelie **42**

Café Beignet **5, 16**

Café du Monde **45**

Café Envie **50**

Café Maspero **33**

Café Sbisa **48**

Central Grocery **47**

Cleo's **23**

Clover Grill **41**

Coop's **54**

Court of Two Sisters **29**

Croissant D'Or **51**

Curio **13**

Dickie Brennan's
   Bourbon House Seafood **10**

Doris Metropolitan **37**

EAT **40**

Felix's Restaurant
   & Oyster Bar **8**

French Truck Coffee **15**

Galatoire's **3**

Galatoire's 33 **4**

Green Goddess **18**

GW Fins **1**

Irene's **22**

Johnny's Po-Boys **32**

Junction **55**

Killer PoBoys **6**

Kingfish **19**

K-Paul's Louisiana
   Kitchen **21**

Latitude 29 **24**

Louisiana Bistro **2**

Meauxbar **39**

Mr. B's Bistro **11**

Mr. Gregory's **38**

Muriel's **43**

Napoleon House **31**

Nine Roses Café **17**

Old Coffee Pot **30**

Palace Café **14**

Petite Amelie **42**

Port of Call **54**

QuarterMaster **53**

Restaurant R'evolution **9**

Spitfire **35**

Stanley **44**

Sylvain **34**

Sucré & Salon **20**

Tableau **36**

Trinity **49**

Tujague's **46**

Vacherie **26**

Verti Marte **52**

center on seasonal fruits, like the divine mango cheesecake flan with pistachio crust and blackberries. Reservations required for dinner; book early.

430 Dauphine St. www.bayona.com. ℂ **504/525-4455.** Main courses $15–$17 lunch, $28–$34 dinner. Wed–Sat 11:30am–1:45pm; Mon–Thurs 6–9:30pm; Fri–Sat 5:30–9:45pm.

Brennan's ★★★ MODERN CREOLE   After a fall to lesser heights, brief closure, ownership change, and all-in $20-million-plus renovation, Brennan's is back in all its pink glory and then some. The look and feel of the elegant dining room and charming courtyard and the attentive service all scream old New Orleans, but there's nothing tired on the plate: The terrific new chef twists Creole classics into updated plates of newfound awesome. Still service-driven, it's polished and exciting (breakfast at Brennan's is an automatic celebration). First course: cocktails, as in a rum-spiked milk punch or a Ramos Fizz. Chef does well with breakfast meats, and the egg preparations are pretty perfect, so we choose his house-smoked duck ham or crispy veal cheek grillades. You need a side of the BBQ lobster, slow-roasted in the shell with mild Creole spice. At dinner, the crispy, Sazerac lacquered roast duck is phenomenal; beef Stanley with mushrooms, caramelized banana, and a truffle-infused sauce stands out. The signature turtle soup is well sherried, and we're promised that the turtles living on the premises won't ever…well, you know. Bananas Foster, born here in 1951 and prepared tableside, make for a flaming fun finale. Come back Friday for the 5pm Champagne sabering ceremony. Deal alert: The two-course breakfast/lunch menu is a steal for $28.

417 Royal St. www.brennansneworleans.com. ℂ **504/525-9711.** Main courses $16–$28 breakfast, $21–$45 dinner. Mon–Fri 9am–2pm; Sat–Sun 8am–2pm; dinner nightly 6–10pm. Dress code.

Café Sbisa ★★★ CREOLE   This atmospheric stunner sashays with original wood, intimate balcony and patio dining, and a staircase that harks back to a golden age. As of 2016, Chef Alfred Singleton, who worked his way up from busboy to chef until Katrina devastated the restaurant, is now back in the kitchen—and a partner. His outstanding French-Creole cuisine includes blue crab cakes and an amazing turtle soup laced with sherry, served under the watchful eyes of a bawdy George Dureau mural (which somehow survived the mold that bloomed after the flood). During Sunday brunch, live jazz fills the restaurant, providing a wonderful ambience in which to enjoy Creole classics like crawfish and andouille omelette, cheese grits, and smoked-salmon Benedict. Reserve a table on the balcony for alfresco dining.

1011 Decatur St. www.cafesbisanola.com. ℂ **504/522-5565.** Main courses $12–$26 brunch, $20–$32 dinner. Wed–Sun 5:30–10pm; Sun 10:30am–2:30pm.

Court of Two Sisters ★ CLASSIC CREOLE   No doubt about it, this is one of the prettiest places around, thanks to the huge, wisteria-shaded courtyard and the 200-year-old building, and you should soak up that ambience by enjoying a smart cocktail or two. Then you should head elsewhere to eat.

Sadly, the food is nothing special. The daily jazz brunch buffet is nonetheless popular, and we do get the attraction: There are plenty of items available, it's well-priced, and you get all that jazz and atmosphere; so fill up and enjoy the company. Make brunch reservations well in advance.

613 Royal St. www.courtoftwosisters.com. ✆ **504/522-7261.** Dinner main courses $25–37; brunch buffet $30 adults, $13 children. Daily 9am–3pm for jazz brunch buffet and 5:30–10pm dinner.

Curio ★★ BISTRO, CONTEMPORARY CREOLE

New in 2018, Curio is a reboot of a space that was most recently a Chase bank. You'd never know it from the classically pretty decor and enticing wraparound patio upstairs—on a nice day, a hard spot to leave. Creole cuisine also gets a reboot here: It's an accent to American bistro cuisine rather than the main event. So local oysters show up in a chopped Cobb salad and a BL(O)T, but you can also get a very good 'ole American burger. Appetizers that shine include shrimp *boulettes* (breaded and fried golf-ball-size balls with buttermilk-chive dipping sauce) and a generous plate of delicate tuna and scallop carpaccio. Short ribs are sweetly glazed with cane syrup and accompanied by cheesy grits, while grilled salmon with lemon-shallot vinaigrette is a delightful antidote to heavier fare. Allow room for the luscious café au lait crème brulee with mini donuts.

301 Royal St. www.curionola.com. ✆ **504/717-4198.** Main courses $13–$26 lunch, $23–$34 dinner. Sun–Thurs 11am–11pm; Fri–Sat 11am–midnight; Sat–Sun brunch 9am–3pm.

Dickie Brennan's Bourbon House Seafood ★★ SEAFOOD

Although it looks a bit sprawling and formulaic from the street, this modern version of a classic New Orleans fish house has much to recommend it. Hang out at the super-fresh raw bar, or order the head-turning *fruits du mer* platter. A simple grilled redfish is perfect (top it with fresh lump crabmeat for $14 more, a worthy addition). In a city of good BBQ shrimp dishes (shrimp sautéed in a buttery, garlicky, spicy sauce—bread-sopping heaven), we love their bourbon-finished version. Leave room for a frozen bourbon milk punch, a dreamy booze-shake. (Naturally they're committed to, and knowledgeable about, all things bourbon.) Great happy hour with $1 oysters, $5 small plates, $3 Abita Amber, plus a good shucker show. Parking is guaranteed to be available and can be purchased in advance online.

144 Bourbon St. www.bourbonhouse.com. ✆ **504/522-0111.** Main courses $12–$22 breakfast, $14–$28 lunch, $24–$36 dinner. Daily 6:30–closing; Sun brunch 10am–3pm.

Doris Metropolitan ★★ STEAK

Upscale Doris audaciously displays its dry aging beef in the front window like an Amsterdam madam. Besides the distinctive, slightly pungent flavor of dry-aged steaks (theirs are sourced from raised-to-specification cattle), the Israeli-based restaurant brings some Middle Eastern touches to its menu, like a delectable charred eggplant appetizer with glossy tahini. Servers are warm and knowledgeable to the allowable extent (the "classified cut" is described by flavor and texture, but the actual cut is not betrayed; we'll spill: it's a luscious rib-eye cap). The room's indisputably handsome presentation—beginning with the artsy olive oil—is downright beautiful. Locals have embraced the hopping bar with its beguiling wines and open-kitchen view, and a luxe, chill vibe permeates the moneyed air in the comfortable dining rooms. The juicy pan-glazed chicken that knocked us over wouldn't be our logical first choice; the silken tuna tartare is superb. But ultimately, it's about the beef. After a couple of initial missteps, in due time we found the carnivorous knowledge we sought in the Butcher's Cut, its crunch of char displaying a perfectly marbled, ultra-flavorful, and densely sensuous mouthful.

620 Chartres St. www.dorismetropolitan.com. © **504/267-3500.** Main courses $32–$82. Daily 5:30–10:30pm; Fri–Sun noon–2:30pm.

Galatoire's ★★ CLASSIC CREOLE/FRENCH Considered New Orleans' consummate old-line Creole French restaurant, Galatoire's is a time-honored, fine-dining classic beloved by generations—perhaps because their families are beloved by Galatoire's. Or perhaps because Tennessee Williams supped here, as did his characters Stella and Blanche in *A Streetcar Named Desire.* It oozes tradition: Ceiling fans whir, bentwood chairs strain, mirrored walls reflect the civilized frivolity. But the jovial obsequiousness that the tuxedoed waiters lavish upon their regulars isn't always bestowed upon *moi et toi.* Things are a tad more somber in the (lesser—but perfectly fine) upstairs dining room. Either way, the drinking commences upon arrival, and doesn't (and shouldn't) let up for a few hours.

No one comes here for great gastronomy, but Galatoire's does know fish (it's had 110 years of practice, after all). Go with a classic shrimp rémoulade, crab maison, or the eggplant fingers. Ask the waiter which fish is best today, get it a la meunière and topped with crabmeat; or order the soft-shell crab if available and some creamed spinach. We're not fond of the heavy sauces they ladle on the fine fish, but don't scoff at asparagus with spot-on hollandaise. The puffy soufflé potatoes are legally required. Skip the meh desserts; order a glass of port instead. Reservations accepted for upstairs only; reserve well in advance. Worth mentioning: Galatoire's regulars have known for years that these seafood specialists grill a mean steak. That's the specialty at **Galatoire's 33,** the offshoot next door (which also corners the Galatoire's bar scene).

209 Bourbon St. www.galatoires.com. © **504/525-2021.** Jackets required after 5pm and all day Sun. Main courses $19.75–$44. Tues–Sat 11:30am–10pm; Sun noon–10pm; Fri lunch: Recommend lining up 45–60 min. before opening. **Galatoire's 33:** 215 Bourbon St. www.galatoires33barandsteak.com. © **504/335-3932.** Main courses $29–$70. Sun–Thurs 5–10pm; Fri–Sat 5–11pm; lunch Fri 11:30am–3pm.

GW Fins ★★★ SEAFOOD This modern seafood shrine is one of the city's best restaurants, period. It is polished from the top down, in service and seafood sourcing, with a shipment of fresh fish arriving straight from the Gulf and beyond at 4pm daily. Stylish preparations include the signature "scalibut" (thin-sliced scallop "scales" atop grilled halibut) on lobster risotto, worthy of its fame. A diverting starter of watermelon and pork belly, or the lobster

YOU GOT cajun IN MY CREOLE!

The difference between Cajun and Creole cuisine lies chiefly in distance between city and countryside. Cajun cooking came from the Acadians who settled in the swamps and bayous of rural Louisiana and adapted the recipes of their French heritage to their new location. Their cuisine is like their music: robust and full of flavor (and despite the reputation, not necessarily spicy). They used available ingredients like sausage, seafood, poultry, and rice in single-pot stews that fed large families and farms. Creole dishes, on the other hand, were developed by French and Spanish city dwellers and feature fancier sauces and ingredients. Today, the two cuisines have a happy marriage, often blurring the distinctions and inviting other influences. Our advice? Disregard the classifications, try it all, and decide what *you* prefer.

dumplings with a light brush of fennel, are both to be savored. The wine list is thoughtfully complementary, with a good range of midpriced bottles and an extensive array of finer pours by the glass. Order the pretzel-crusted salty-malty ice cream pie, even if you only have room for a bite. The large, tiered dining room is handsome and high-ceilinged yet conversation-conducive. We particularly love those high-backed gangsta booths along the back wall.

808 Bienville St. www.gwfins.com. © **504/581-3467.** Collared shirts for men; better jeans; no shorts or flip-flops. Main courses $21–$46. Sun–Thurs 5–10pm; Fri–Sat 5–10:30pm (summer from 5:30pm).

Irene's Cuisine ★★★ ITALIAN   If you detect the scent of simmering garlic from blocks away and aren't lured to its source, Irene's may not interest you. No worry—that leaves more of the French Provincial and Creole-Italian cooking for the rest of us. Irene (herself a Quarter institution) and her friendly crew create delectable house-made pastas and sauces, but the *secondi* are the real standouts. Locals come on Thursdays for the ginormous osso buco flavor bomb, and someone at the table needs to order Duck St. Phillip (with raspberry-pancetta demi-glace) so that everyone can taste it and wish they had ordered it. The seemingly simple *pollo rosemarino*—marinated, par-cooked, re-marinated, and roasted—is nearly perfect. The multiple smallish, warmly-lit rooms (designed to resemble those of the beloved original location) engender a genial time, and chat between the closely-set tables is common. Would that the desserts were a little bit better, but the cheesecake will do.

529 Bienville St. © **504/529-8811.** Main courses $18–$38. Mon–Sat 5:30–10pm. Closed major holidays and week of Labor Day.

Kingfish ★★ CONTEMPORARY SOUTHERN   Craft-cocktail guru Chris McMillan came out of retirement to open Kingfish. The ample bar space, surrounded by the elongated, brick and tin-paneled dining room, has the edge over the kitchen—the drinks are stellar, it's open to the street, and it's a good hang while taking in the easygoing Southern fare, hearty stuff with smarts. We like the boudin tamale and the BBQ shrimp with waffles. Although the signature "King" pompano, seared and served on a salt brick, didn't live up to expectations, we do like the creative impulses behind it. Kingfish succeeds with seasonal salads and their little surprises: fresh plums in one, couscous with Creole tomatoes in another.

337 Chartres St. www.kingfishneworleans.com. © **504/598-5005.** Main courses $20–$39. Sun–Thurs 11am–10pm; Sun 11am–11pm.

K-Paul's Louisiana Kitchen ★★ CAJUN/CREOLE   Paul Prudhomme started the Cajun cooking craze in the 1980s and is responsible for introducing the term "blackened" to our culinary vocabulary. Prudhomme's sauce-and-spice empire still thrives, and the restaurant remains a standard-bearer for American regional food—but it's difficult to justify the high prices at dinner. We're partial to the blackened beef tenders with debris from the rotating menu, and now that the classic blackened drum is served (albeit on a po' boy) during the "deli lunch," that's how we roll: with counter service, paper plates, and entrees about $25 less than dinner. Reserve in advance for dinner. The restaurant requests no cellphones while dining, but that's hard to police.

416 Chartres St. www.kpauls.com. © **504/596-2530.** Business casual; no tank tops for gents. Main courses $13–$15 lunch, $33–$38 dinner. Thurs–Sat 11am–2pm; Mon–Sat 5:30–10pm.

Louisiana Bistro ★★ CONTEMPORARY CREOLE   You've seen the movie. On a ramble through Paris, you stumble into *une petite cafe,* just 11 tables, with a nutty chef at the helm. You can hear him shouting at someone from behind the kitchen doors; waiters roll their eyes conspiratorially and shrug. Then Chef Mars appears at your side, flashing a charming smile, saying "Trust me, you'll like it." So you do, and you do. The a la carte menu here is just a concession to the three-, four-, and five-course "Feed Me" tasting menus, made to order based on market availability and Chef Mars' whim. Call it Louisiana *omakase.* You might get dreamy crawfish beignets in brown *beurre,* or maybe a cast-iron-bronzed Louisiana swordfish with a shocking drizzle of jalapeño hollandaise. It's good. It's fun. It's good fun. Skip dessert, not wine.

337 Dauphine. www.louisianabistro.net. © **504/525-3335.** Entrees $19–$42; "Feed Me" tasting menu: 3 courses $50, 4 courses $60, 5 courses $70. Wed–Sun 6–10pm.

Meauxbar ★★★ BISTRO   We thought this decidedly French locals' favorite was a perfect pearl before it changed hands in 2014. But the new chef-owners topped that high bar. Meauxbar is no flash—and no flaws. That doesn't mean it's boring. It's just that everything is done right. Service in the crisp espresso and white room is smart but unhurried, friendly but unforced. The spot-on wine selection includes half-bottles and carafes. Small and large plates feature French-based standards with an accent on now. Quality local ingredients shine through the exacting flavor profiles, as in the meaty speckled trout heaped with toasted almonds; the delicate *moules* tickled with fennel and topped with model-thin *frites;* the bone-deep richness of braised beef and onions on feloniously large, Gruyère-topped brioche slices. For a fine *finis,* just say *oui* to Grandma's Coming for Mardi Gras, a bourbon milk-punch cheese-cake with root beer caramel. A wonderful addition to the Friday lunch scene.

942 N. Rampart St. ℂ **504/569-9979.** www.meauxbar.com. Reservations suggested. Main courses $16–$43. Sun–Thurs 4–10pm; Fri 10:30am–2pm; Fri–Sat 4pm–midnight; Sat–Sun 10:30am–2pm.

Mr. B's Bistro ★★ CONTEMPORARY CREOLE   The "B is for Butter."

BBQ shrimp is the claim to fame here, and that's what you should get. Other dishes tempt as well (the gleaming ginger-glazed pork chop is terrific, for example), but the plump, peppery house special is the standout and indeed the distinguishing feature here. The hunt-club motif draws a businessman's lunch crowd for the strong drinks and attentive service, and the roving-band jazz brunch is a hit with all ages.

201 Royal St. www.mrbsbistro.com. ℂ **504/523-2078.** Business casual; no shorts or tank tops. Main courses $17–$32 lunch, $26–$39 dinner; jazz brunch entrees $22–$33. Mon–Sat 11:30am–2pm; bar menu 2–5:30pm; dinner 5:30–9pm; Sun jazz brunch 10:30am–2pm.

Muriel's ★ CONTEMPORARY CREOLE   The dreaded "fine." That's

how we feel about perennially popular Muriel's. We want to fall in love with, or at least *in* their romantic, red-walled dining rooms, and pose on the elegant balconies overlooking Jackson Square. We want to *ooh* over the crawfish and goat-cheese crêpes, like others seem to do. But except for the admittedly fab atmosphere, there's just nothing especially inspired or inspiring here, on the plate or working the floor. That said, there's no denying that the table d'hôte menus are good value. So we opt for the safety of the pan-roasted half-chicken or the generous double-cut pork chop. Visit the ghost's table, have your palm read in Jackson Square, and the night is still, well, fine. Muriel's is popular with groups, so reserve in advance during peak periods.

801 Chartres St. (at St. Ann). www.muriels.com. ℂ **504/568-1885.** Main courses $14–$25 lunch, or 2 courses $19; dinner $19–$39, or 3 courses $43; brunch entrees $17–$25. Mon–Sat 11:30am–2:30pm; Mon–Fri 5:30–10pm; Fri–Sat 5:30–10:30pm; Sun jazz brunch 10:30am–2pm.

Palace Café ★★ CONTEMPORARY CREOLE   A good standby for low-

key, non-intimidating Creole dining, this historic, two-story restaurant (for-merly the famed Werlein's music store) has sidewalk seating for people-watching and a craft cocktail bar upstairs. It comes with the stamp of New Orleans authenticity that Brennan-family ownership conveys, and the crabmeat cheese-cake appetizer makes people pound the table. The Andouille-crusted fish is a winner, and the pleasantly familiar rotisserie chicken with truffle-mashed potatoes is done well. They invented white-chocolate bread pudding, so go there (we like coming just for dessert at the streetside tables). Also the "$5 after 5pm" happy-hour small plates, and the summertime "Temperature Lunch": two courses priced (in cents) at 10 times the prior day's high temperature.

605 Canal St. www.palacecafe.com. ℂ **504/523-1661.** Main courses $14–$28 lunch, $21–$36 dinner, $15–$32 brunch. Mon–Fri 8–11am, 11:30am–2:30pm, 5:30–'til closing; Sat–Sun brunch 10:30am–2:30pm.

Restaurant R'evolution ★★ MODERN LOUISIANA This extravagant spot, helmed by food-world icons (John Folse and Rick Tramonto) keys the cuisine to New Orleans' globe-hopping cultural influences. Go big at this big-idea, big-ticket spot in a fanciful but refined setting, with unpretentious service and beautiful plating. It's Event Dining, so save up your paycheck and make it truly memorable. Tour the rooms (better yet, book one, like the stunning Storyville Parlor, or come for the festive jazz brunch). Indulge in something marvelous from the wine list, so enormous that only an iPad can contain it, and augment your order with sides, sauces, and toppings. Lead with the rich "Death by Gumbo" and gently crisped crab beignets, each with a different rémoulade dollop. A terrine of lustrous duck-liver mousse and rugged country pâté terrines are the best bang. Shrimp and grits get a chili-and-ginger Asian kick; the voluminous veal chop bursts with flavor. A jewelry box of tiny cookies is a darling lagniappe, but get "beignets with coffee" anyway. Service can be a bit casual for a restaurant of this caliber and cost, but we'll take that over snooty.

777 Bienville St. (in the Royal Sonesta Hotel). www.revolutionnola.com. © **504/553-2277.** Main courses $17–$36 lunch, $25–$68 dinner, $24–$36 brunch. Reserve well in advance for dinner. Daily 5:30–10pm; Fri 11:30am–2:30; Sun 10:30am–2pm.

Tableau ★★ CLASSIC CREOLE Tableau's pristine white space, soaring staircase, and high-arched entries are impressive…but that balcony view overlooking Jackson Square is peerless. Relish an afternoon there with a well-balanced classic cocktail, slices of the addictive tart bread, and a "Grand Royal" quartet of seafood starters—including sublime bacon-wrapped, rosemary-skewered oysters. In cooler climes, opt for a hearty red and the heartier, hopped-up onion soup. The airy main dining room looks onto the gleaming open kitchen and brick courtyard. Things we like there: servings in full or demi portions, aiding those who want less *or* more; the juicy dark and white portions of chicken Tableau in a rich béarnaise sauce; time-honored poached-egg dishes on the dinner menu (and at the rollicking brass-band brunch); the logo-branded crème brûlée, served in a shallow, wide bowl (as at other Brennan's restaurants), to maximize the crispy-crust-to-silken-custard ratio. Service could use a little smoothing out, but the overall experience is classic New Orleans, turned up enough to honor gastronomy in 1880 as well as today.

675 St. Peter St. www.tableaufrenchquarter.com. © **504/934-3463.** Main courses $12–$26 lunch, $21–$34 dinner, $8–$26 brunch. Mon–Thurs 11am–10pm; Fri–Sat 10am–11pm; Sat–Sun 10am–2:30pm brunch, 2:30–10pm lunch & dinner.

Trinity ★★ CONTEMPORARY CREOLE/CONTEMPORARY SOUTHERN This stylish newish arrival sports more marble per square foot than a quarry, but the food, which stops just short of fussy, is easy to like. The duck-fat hush puppies are addictive; other starters are a bit pricey, but the luscious ricotta gnudi with wine-soaked mushrooms are worth the cost. A simple sliced Wagyu strip steak stands out, as does the beautifully textured pork shank, first cooked sous vide, then seared, dotted with green lentils and served over melted apples. The slender space and sleek gray booths don't quash the liveliness, thanks to sociable service and a genial cocktail scene (including well-crafted low-alcohol options). In fact, a seat at either bar—oysters and cocktails in front, open kitchen in back—adds to the experience. So does the Fat Elvis peanut butter/banana/bacon sundae—but it's over the top, even for us. We loved the tender rhubarb cheesecake.

1117 Decatur St. www.trinityrestaurantneworleans.com. © **504/325-5789.** Main courses $26–40; brunch $12–$24. Sun–Thurs 6–10pm; Fri–Sat 6–11pm; Fri–Sun 11am–3pm.

Tujague's ★ CLASSIC CREOLE Spared the wrecking ball in 2013 (it almost succumbed to a T-shirt-shop takeover), this 1856 landmark is now more precious than ever. The threat of closure also kick-started some needed changes to the old-line menu and decor (style-wise, you'd never know; but trust us, it's eons spiffier). They still make a perfect Sazerac, and the anti-nouvelle, fork-tender brisket still rules the traditional six-course prix-fixe menu; also worthy are the soft-shell crab meunière (when in season) and the off-menu baked garlic chicken Bonne Femme. It's solid if not earth-shattering, authentic Creole cooking, from the sinus-clearing shrimp rémoulade appetizer to the last bite of bread pudding. Do visit their famous **bar** (p. 206) before or after dinner.

823 Decatur St. www.tujaguesrestaurant.com. © **504/525-8676.** Main courses $14–$26 brunch, $14–$18 lunch, $25–$42 dinner; add $28 to entree price for 5-course dinner. Mon–Fri 11am–2:30pm; Sat–Sun 10am–2:30pm; daily 5–10pm.

Moderate

Café Amelie ★★ CONTEMPORARY SOUTHERN/CASUAL FARE The pretty-as-a-chocolate-box, greenery-laden brick courtyard is Amelie's calling card; and it's the place where Beyoncé & Jay-Z dined quite publicly days after the scandalous Solange elevator, uhm, incident. Expect cafe standards with something for everyone. Crab cakes, goat cheese and beet salad, local fave cochon de lait pork sandwich, and grilled catfish with a kick stand out. The relaxing spot calls loudly for a lemonade or mint julep and slice of lemon doberge cake. (Fair warning: Call ahead, it's frequently closed for weddings.) Reserve in advance for Sunday brunch. We quite like offshoot **Petite Amelie** ★, a few doors down, for quick and tasty prepared takeaway meals, soups, salads, cheeses, pastries, and such via counter service.

912 Royal St. www.cafeamelie.com. © **504/412-8965.** Main courses $24–$28 lunch, $24–$29 dinner, brunch $12–$26. Wed–Sun 11am–3pm and 5–10pm (Fri–Sat till 10pm); Sun brunch 11am–3pm. Closed occasionally for special events; call to check. **Petite Amelie:** 900 Royal St. Wed–Sun 8am–8pm.

EAT New Orleans ★★ CONTEMPORARY CREOLE/CASUAL
FARE This charming bilevel corner spot in a tucked-away French Quarter section attracts plenty of locals. The chatty, efficient servers will make you feel like one of them. Trust them when they suggest the hearty, down-to-earth chicken and dumplings or the surf-and-turf stuffed red pepper. At brunch, eggs Dumaine are just what the hangover ordered. We're also fond of their

sister restaurant, **Vacherie,** in the Hotel Ste. Marie (827 Toulouse St.). *Note:* Proximity to a nearby school means no liquor license, but they will gladly serve whatever you bring from nearby **Matassa's** (1001 Dauphine St.).

900 Dumaine St. www.eatnola.com. ℭ **504/522-7222.** Main courses $10–$19 lunch, $18–$27 dinner, $12–$19 brunch. Tues–Fri 11am–2pm; Tues–Sat 5:30–10pm; brunch Sat–Sun 9am–2pm.

Green Goddess ★★ INTERNATIONAL   The raffish Green Goddess may not be the trendier-than-thou phenomenon and critics' darling that it once was, but that's just because other restaurants have caught up to its ground-breaking gastronomic globetrotting. Seated at alleyway tables, you'll find cocktails and food inspired by Spanish, Indian, Hawaiian, and Middle Eastern cuisines (for starters). The imaginative, vegan- and vegetarian-friendly cuisine is good to very good—ditto for the offbeat atmosphere and fair prices (service, never stellar, hasn't changed). Top choices include the shrimp-and-pork-belly *banh mi;* a watermelon and burrata cheese salad; and Father Pat's grilled cheese, made with Guinness and pear butter. Pair with something from the thoughtful, interesting wine list. For dessert, the bacon sundae is always an indulgence, as is the sultan's nest, a sort of baklava reconstructed as a sundae—in fact, if you just come for dessert and the still-superb cocktails, you'll be in good stead. Reservations not accepted.

307 Exchange Place. www.greengoddessrestaurant.com. ℭ **504/301-3347.** Main courses $10–$15 lunch, $14–$22 dinner. Wed–Sun 11am–9pm.

Latitude 29 ★★ INTERNATIONAL/POLYNESIAN   When rumors first arose that Jeff "Beachbum" Berry was moving to New Orleans and opening up a bar/restaurant, the buzz in the tiki community (yes, there is one) was deafening. After all, Berry literally wrote the book on tiki. That the cocktails deliver was never in doubt, but Lat 29 succeeds because it's all the tiki you could hope for and less: There's bamboo, wood, and thatch decor, but it's understated; the fun, made-for-sharing rum bombs in bowls and giant clam-shells are nuanced and ingredient-driven. The ratcheted-up Polynesian fare is less cloy, more Cantonese-meets-Creole-meets-craft than the midcentury version. But do expect elaborate garni, cute umbrellas, and kitschy custom stir sticks. And don't skip the riblets or the light veggie poke with the oddly excellent pistachio froth.

321 N. Peters St. in the Bienville House hotel. www.latitude29nola.com. ℭ **504/609-3811.** Main courses $14–$23. Sun–Thurs 3–11pm; Fri–Sat 1pm–midnight.

Port of Call ★★ HAMBURGERS   For a decade or two before the great national gourmet burger tsunami overtook New Orleans, Port of Call was putting out a product that drew hordes. That hasn't changed. This is not a burger for teeny-patty people. It's a dripping, half-pound monster, served with a massive loaded baked potato. You're probably going to wait a good while for it (the fruity signature Monsoon cocktail helps pass the time), and you'll barely be able to see it inside the dark den of a dining room. (a good thing since the restaurant has needed a redo for years). They have steaks, but they're

BACK-ROOM bites

Long before there were pop-up restaurants, there were back-room deli counters in unassuming corner stores. It's how a lot of French Quarter residents still eat, because it's fast, cheap, diverse, available 'round-the-clock, and often surprisingly good. Take it out or have it delivered, and be sure to ask for utensils. True locals eat while leaning against a wall or seated on someone's front stoop.

- **Frady's** ★ (This one's in the Bywater at 3231 Dauphine St.; ⓒ **504/949-9688**; Mon–Fri 9am–6pm, Sat 9am–3pm). Best choice: Hot sausage or oyster po' boy.

- **QuarterMaster** ★ (1110 Bourbon St.; ⓒ **504/529-1416**; 24/7). Best choice: Basic po' boys, especially the French-fry po' boy, and greasy burgers.

- **Verti Marte** ★★ (1201 Royal St.; ⓒ **504/525-4757**; 24/7). Best choice: anything in the deli case or from the mother lode of a menu, especially the day's specials, like Grandma's Boardinghouse Meat Loaf or catfish Bienville. Also salads, specialty sandwiches, and loads of veggies.

irrelevant. Sometimes you just need a good burger, and even with the serious contenders around town now (if the line is hideous, hightail it to **Company Burger** on O'Keefe or on Freret St.), Port of Call's still holds up. No reservations.

838 Esplanade Ave. www.portofcallnola.com. ⓒ **504/523-0120.** Cheeseburger $12, rib-eye $23. Sun–Thurs 11am–midnight; Fri–Sat 11am–1am.

Sylvain ★★★ BISTRO The tradition-bound French Quarter is surprisingly devoid of coolness, save for a few spots including gastropub Sylvain, with its side-alley entrance, resident ghost, Civil-War-meets-Soho vibe, and literary heritage (it was the home of a tall, feisty Storyville madam who was the inspiration for Faulkner's "Miss Reba," in both *Sanctuary* and *The Reivers*). Fortunately, it's delicious, friendly, and unexpectedly unpretentious, even when packed and loud. The lush chicken liver crostini and the "Buffalo"-style sweetbreads are worthy starters. Try the absurdly tender beef cheeks; signature "Chick Sylvain" fried chicken sandwich; or a brightly delightful shaved-apple and Brussels sprout salad. Since the menu doesn't skew light, share the chocolate pot du crème. On a nice evening, the discreet back-alley tables have their own cool vibe (a quieter one).

625 Chartres St. www.sylvainnola.com. ⓒ **504/265-8123.** Main courses $14–$29 dinner, $13–$23 brunch. Mon–Thurs 5:30–11pm; Fri–Sun 10:30am–2:30pm and 5:30pm–midnight; Sun 10:30am–2:30pm and 5:30–10pm.

Inexpensive

Acme Oyster House ★★★ SEAFOOD/CASUAL FARE Is it worth the wait, you ask, eyeing the block-long lineup? They're Gulf oysters, people, and this is the oldest oyster bar in the French Quarter. In other words, yes (unless you're famished—then just go across the street to **Felix's;** see below).

WHOLE LOTTA muffuletta GOIN' ON

Muffulettas are sandwiches of (pardon the expression) heroic proportions, enormous concoctions of round seeded Italian bread, Italian cold cuts, cheeses, and olive salad. One person cannot (or should not) eat a whole one—at least not in one sitting. A half makes a good meal; a quarter is a filling snack. They may not sound like much on paper, but once you try one, you'll be hooked. Vegetarians swear they're delicious done meatless.

Several places in town claim to have invented the muffuletta and also claim to make the best one. You decide: Comparison-shopping can be a rewarding pastime.

The lunchtime line can be daunting but moves fast (and it's part of the aura) at world-famous **Central Grocery** ★★★, 923 Decatur St. (𝄫 **504/523-1620**). There are a few seats at the back of this crowded, garlic-scented Italian grocery, or you can order to go. Best of all, they ship, so you can satisfy your craving or throw an envy-inducing party.

Eat it across the street on the banks of the Mississippi for an inexpensive, romantic meal ($22 for a whole, with tax). The impersonal staff at Central Grocery starts making and wrapping their sandwiches early in the day, so they're ready for the rush. Don't worry about freshness; it actually helps when the olive flavors soak through the layers. It's open daily 9am to 5pm.

Are the hot muffulettas at **Napoleon House** ★★ (p. 204) better or blasphemy? It's a different taste sensation, and a heated debate. Feeling experimental? Drive to **Nor-Joe's Importing Co.** ★★, 505 Friscoe, in Metairie (𝄫 **504/833-9240**), where the ginormous, outstanding muffulettas, constructed with iconoclastic ingredients like prosciutto and mortadella, have their own cult following. Then there's **Cochon Butcher** ★★★ (p. 113), whose house-cured meats form the basis of what may actually be our favorite 'letta. Okay it is. There, we said it.

The oysters are tastiest when you're standing at the bar, talking tourist trash with the shucker, piling up shells to be tallied later, knocking back some oyster shooters (chilled vodka, cocktail sauce, erster, gullet). But if you sit at a checked-cloth-covered table, you can also order a dozen or two of the garlicky charbroiled oysters, which may change your life. Or po' boys served in red plastic baskets, and Creole standbys (jambalaya, gumbo, red beans and sausage), good enough for those who do not slurp oysters. It's boisterous and there's much waiter scurrying, so things do move fast once you're inside. No reservations.

724 Iberville St. www.acmeoyster.com. 𝄫 **504/522-5973.** Oysters $15.50/dozen raw, $20 charbroiled; po' boys & platters $10–$24. Sun–Thurs 10:30am–10pm; Fri–Sat 10:30am–11pm.

Café Beignet ★ CAFE/BAKERY   Some swear the beignets here are better than those at Café du Monde, and we can attest that they're usually fresh out of the deep fryer, but we're true to the CdM for just the right chewiness and puffiness. Still, you won't find insane lines here, and you will find waffles, brioche French toast, gumbo, and simple sandwiches and salads. Both locations have nice patios; there's even live jazz Thursday through Sunday afternoons and evenings at the Bourbon Street location, a respite from the street's insanity.

334B Royal St. www.cafebeignet.com. ⟲ **504/524-5530.** Most items under $10. Daily 7am–10pm. Also at 311 Bourbon St. (⟲ **504/525-2611;** daily 8am–midnight) and Jax Brewery, 600 Decatur St. (⟲ **504/581-6554;** daily 8am–10pm).

Café Maspero ★ CAFE/SEAFOOD/CASUAL FARE   Why is it always so crowded here? We'll give you five good reasons: the big menu, decent food, inexpensive prices, large portions, plus you can watch the Decatur action go by. It may not merit an Instagram post, but it's an easy stop for a burger, club sandwich, onion soup, or muffuletta (regular or veggie).

601 Decatur St. www.cafemaspero.com. ⟲ **504/523-6250.** Main courses $8.50–$10. No separate checks. Sun–Thurs 11am–10pm; Fri–Sat 11am–11pm;

Clover Grill ★ DINER   The burger here is just a frozen patty thrown on the grill, but it's cooked under a hubcap (the better to seal in the juices), available at 4am, and served by a sassy queen in a "Clever Girl" T-shirt, making it so very worthwhile. Basic egg breakfasts and standard diner fare are also available. Bonus points for: excellent '80s jukebox, Formica counter, red vinyl stools you can spin around on, pie. But mostly for aforementioned sass, which they have in spades here, 24/7.

900 Bourbon St. www.clovergrill.com. ⟲ **504/598-1010.** All items under $10. Daily 24 hr.

Coop's ★ CREOLE/CASUAL FARE   This divey, former locals-only hangout has long since been discovered by tourists, which may mean an unjustifiably long wait: It's good, but not OMG! awesome. Except for the well-known rabbit-and-sausage jambalaya, and the fried chicken, both of which really are pretty awesome. Decent food, friendly prices, late hours, and a menu that covers all the bases make this a good fallback if the line isn't crazy prohibitive. No kids; it's 21 and older only.

1109 Decatur St. www.coopsplace.net. ⟲ **504/525-9053.** Main courses $10–$20. Daily 11am–close (at least 10pm, later on weekends). 21 and older only.

Felix's Restaurant & Oyster Bar ★★ SEAFOOD/CREOLE   Seventy-year-old Felix, Acme's friendly rival across the street, has two rooms: the original, a down-home, nuthin'-fancy oyster bar/diner (entrance on Iberville), and a new, spiffier spot around the corner (entrance on Bourbon St.). In both locales the dozens come out fresh and bitterly chilled, needing nothing more than a spritz of lemon. You can also have them in stews, soups, pastas, or omelets, broiled, fried, or baked. And if it's crawfish season, order up a spicy pile. It's not nearly as much of a scene as Acme (a big plus), and the shuckers have fast hands and quick wit—even, nay especially—Mr. Paul, in his mid-80s and going strong. *Tip:* If there's a line at the Iberville entrance, check the Bourbon Street entrance. They seat separately.

739 Iberville St. and 208 Bourbon St. www.felixs.com. ⟲ **504/522-4440.** Oysters $15/ dozen raw; po' boys $9–$17; main courses $12–$21. Sun–Thurs 11am–10pm; Fri–Sat 11am–11pm.

Johnny's Po-Boys ★ CASUAL FARE   Johnny's is the standard-bearer for po' boys in the French Quarter—in fact, it's the only proper po' boy joint in the area. They'll put almost anything on that crunchy, fluffy Leidenheimer bread, but they're best known for their roast beef po' boy. We have a soft spot for the fried pork chop version, just 'cause it's hard to find one elsewhere. The line moves fast; don't be discouraged. Little-known insider fact about the family-owned fave: It's also a good, cheap, quick breakfast spot. Other little-known fact: They deliver to French Quarter hotels.

511 St. Louis St. ✆ **504/524-8129.** Most items $8–$16; specials may be more. No credit cards. Daily 8am–3pm (to 4:30pm Fri–Sun).

Mr. Gregory's ★★ CAFE/BAKERY/CASUAL FARE   *Bienvenue!* This welcome addition to the upper Quarter brings much-needed coffee, breakfast, and lunch options to this area, all done with a French accent. Pastries are baked on-site, including the elusive proper croissant and decadent *pain perdu* muffins, so gooey with crème Anglaise that they must be et with knife and fork. Soups, salads, quiches, and *croque* sandwiches (with Gruyére! and house-cured tuna!) round out the lunch menu—and now they even host seasonal crawfish boils on their balcony overlooking Armstrong Park. Year-round, there's simple goodness and brewed-to-order French-press coffee for $2.50. *Mais oui.*

806 N. Rampart St. www.mistergregorys.com. ✆ **504/407-3780.** Everything under $13. Thurs–Mon 9am–9pm; Tues–Wed 9am–2pm.

Nine Roses Cafe ★★★ VIETNAMESE   Outside the Crescent City, it's not widely known that New Orleans has a huge Vietnamese population. The delicate, refreshing flavors of Vietnamese food can be a welcome counterpoint to traditional Creole fare. The original location of this family-run legend has been destination dining for decades; now it has an outpost smack in the middle of the French Quarter, and it's very, very good. A fresh shrimp spring roll or pork bun is quick, reasonable, and delicious; at $9, the grilled chicken vermicelli bowl is a tasty bargain. In cool weather (or after an indulgent night), the steaming, deeply flavored beef pho hits it just right. Wine and beer only.

620 Conti St. www.nineroses restaurant.com. ✆ **504/324-9450.** Everything under $15. Sun–Thurs 10:30am–9:30pm; Fri–Sat 10:30am–10pm.

The Old Coffee Pot ★ CASUAL FARE   Known for being one of the few places that serve calas, sweetened fried rice cakes that date to the mid-1800s. The egg dishes are okay, but it's the calas you want. The menu overall is unremarkable, but the high-ceilinged room, fading murals, and outdoor courtyard will immerse you in the French Quarter aura (it dates to 1894). The service is full of "hons" and "dahlins," though no one's moving too fast.

714 St. Peter St. www.theoldcoffeepot.com. ✆ **504/524-3500.** Breakfast $9–$14; dinner $16–$25. Mon, Thurs, Sun 8am–9pm; Tues–Wed 8am–2pm; Fri–Sat 8am–10pm.

Stanley ★★ CONTEMPORARY CREOLE/CASUAL FARE   It's cute and convenient (right on the corner of Jackson Square) and serves well-prepared "regular" food that kids and grown-ups like (pancakes, good burgers, and an old-fashioned soda fountain serving homemade ice cream). So naturally it's popular as all get-out; try to go during off-peak hours. The takeout shop next door has coffee, ice cream, and ready-made sandwiches to go, which is awfully convenient. But if you choose the sit-down restaurant, the cornmeal-crusted oyster po' boy is a good way to go. For breakfast (served all day), those oysters come Benedict style, with poached eggs and hollandaise. Yum.

547 St. Ann St. (corner of Jackson Sq. and St. Ann). www.stanleyrestaurant.com. © **504/587-0093.** Everything under $20. Daily 7am–7pm.

THE FAUBOURG MARIGNY & BYWATER

For restaurants in this section, see "New Orleans Restaurants" map on p. 82.

Moderate

Bacchanal ★★★ INTERNATIONAL   It's a ramshackle old building and a big backyard. It's a wine store. It's a bar. It's a jazz club. And now, it's an actual restaurant. Whatever it is, it epitomizes New Orleans, and it's one of our favorite spots anywhere. The unusual, European-leaning wine selection and funky, twinkle-lit outdoor garden with the corner jazz combo attracts locals kicking back in plastic chairs, steampunk wine snobs in deep discussion, maybe a smattering of out-of-towners enlightening to the "real" New Orleans…all tantalized by the romantic ambience and Spanish-inspired small plates. You order at a window and grab your own utensils, and a starter of grilled corn with Cotija cheese, crema, and spices (or bacon-wrapped dates with chorizo, or smoked trout crostini with crisp apples) shows up. An attic converted to a dining room means it's accessible even on rainy days, but ahh, that garden. It won't be the best meal you have in New Orleans (its ★★), but it's frequently tasty, never boring, and ultra-atmospheric. It all seems thrown together, but it melds into something much greater than the sum of its parts (thus the ★★★).

600 Poland Ave. www.bacchanalwine.com. © **504/948-9111.** Tapas and small plates $6–$16. Daily 11am–midnight (Sun–Thurs kitchen closes at 11pm).

Bywater American Bistro ★★★ INTERNATIONAL/CONTEMPORARY SOUTHERN   About a week after opening BABs, as Nina Compton's second New Orleans restaurant is known, she snagged the James Beard award for Best Chef: South for **Compère Lapin** (p. 109), her flagship locale. No pressure. And still she persists . . . and rises to meet her own high bar. This more casual spot is no less inventive, featuring flavor profiles—and techniques and ingredients from NOLA and the Caribbean by way of Europe—that spark the palate in ways both newfound and comforting. A crispy fried brick of hearty hog's head boudin sausage balances the rustic side, while tender, sweet duck breast satisfies for sophistication. Flavor-packed crab fat

There's talent in the clubs *and* the kitchens of St. Claude Avenue, where a burgeoning homegrown, farm-to-hipster restaurant scene is incubating some crushing creativity at bargain prices. **St. Roch Market ★★★**, a controversial if stunning food hall showcasing 12 varied vendors, anchors the avenue's many options (2381 St. Claude Ave.; www.strochmarket.com; ✆ **504/609-3813;** Sun–Thurs 7am–10pm; Fri–Sat 7am–11pm). These are some of our other faves:

o **Arabella Casa di Pasta ★★** Order mixy-matchy style from tasty house-made pastas and sauces, plus add-ins like veggies, shrimp, and sausage. Consulting Italian Grandma Nettie says check YES box next to the meatballs; ditto the filled-to-order cannoli (2258 St. Claude Ave.; www.arabellanola.com; ✆ **504/267-6108;** Mon–Thurs noon–10pm, Fri–Sat noon–11pm).

o **Junction ★★** High-quality burgers (beef sourced from a small-production, local cattle farm) on soft, sweet brioche buns baked by Dong Phuong (p. 126). Straight up or with specialty toppings plus one of 40 tap craft beers (3021 St. Claude Ave.; www.junctionnola.com; ✆ **504/272-0205;** daily 11am–2am). Also a pop-up in **Molly's at the Market** (p. 204).

o **Kebab ★★** Very good doner kebabs, falafel, and gyro sandwiches. Immorally good Belgian-style fries. Sauces made and bread baked in-house. Vintage pinball machines. 'Nuff said? (2315 St. Claude Ave.; www.kebabnola.com; ✆ **504/383-4327;** Sun–Mon & Wed–Thurs 11am–11pm; Fri–Sat 11am–midnight).

o **Kukhnya ★★** Well-conceived Slavic soul food in the back of a punk bar for the low-wage crowd. Pierogi. Beet burger. Grilled asparagus. Yup. More on p. 102 (2227 St. Claude Ave. inside Siberia; www.siberianola.com/page/kukhnya; ✆ **504/265-8855;** daily 4pm–2am).

o **Red's ★★** Between the cooks and the clientele, there's plenty of fodder for a game of "I Spy," St. Claude Ave. style ("I spy with my eye a tattoo of a _____"), while waiting for soul-warming ginger scallion noodles, or nearly famous Kung Pao pastrami and honey-lacquered General's chicken. (3048 St. Claude Ave. (no sign, just a square red light); www.redschinese.com; ✆ **504/304-6030;** daily noon–11pm).

rice and the anything-but-innocuous roasted cabbage round out a fine meal. That said, the biggest hit is the simple spaghetti pomodoro: It's perfection. Desserts didn't wow (we'll give it time) but the bar program is solid, and a seat there is a fun hang.

2900 Chartres St. www.bywateramericanbistro.com. ✆ **504/605-3827.** Main courses $20–$26. Wed–Sun 5–10pm; Sun brunch 10am–2pm.

The Country Club ★★★ MODERN CREOLE The Country Club, located in a stunning plantation house in Bywater, celebrated 4 decades in 2017 with a slew of great changes. New executive chef Chris Barbato, formerly of Commander's Palace, has reinvigorated the locally inspired menu, with its nod to Italian-French and Creole-Southern heritages, with dishes from barbecue shrimp and grits to an 18-ounce chateaubriand, jumbo sea scallops, and Louisiana speckled trout. Long known for its free-wheeling backyard pool scene, the Country Club has been spruced up inside and out with eye-popping murals and a lush redo of the outside space, including an outdoor kitchen for poolside nibbles (guests pay a day rate for pool access). Drag brunch on Saturdays is a hoot, as gaggles of lively bachelorette parties digging into truffled mac 'n' cheese or debris and eggs can attest (it books up months in advance).

634 Louisa St. www.thecountryclubneworleans.com. ⓒ **504/945-0742.** Main courses $9–$21 brunch/lunch, $8–$24 dinner. Sun–Thurs 10am–9pm; Fri–Sat 10am–10pm; brunch Sat–Sun 10am–3pm.

Elizabeth's ★ CREOLE They were driving the bacon truck long before the bandwagon hooked on, and Elizabeth's is rightly famous for its brown-sugar-coated praline bacon. If the quality's dropped a bit since that heyday and service leans toward perfunctory, this is still a solid choice, especially for breakfast or brunch, for the bacon and more. Like the rarely-seen fried chicken livers with pepper jelly, or bleu cheese oyster appetizer. The bananas Foster *pain perdu* is a perennial winner. The dinner menu is stacked with solid Southern staples: stuffed catfish, crab cakes (thumbs up), an impressive and well-priced ($25) smoked rib eye. Dessert? More praline bacon, please.

601 Gallier St. www.elizabethsrestaurantnola.com. ⓒ **504/944-9272.** Breakfast and lunch everything under $15; dinner $15–$26 (specials higher). Mon–Sun 8am–2:30pm; Mon–Sat 6–10pm.

The Joint ★★★ BARBECUE When you think of barbecue, you might conjure up Memphis, St. Louis, Texas, the Carolinas…now think Bywater (unless you're in Mid-City, then think **Blue Oak** ★★★, 99 N. Carrollton Ave.; www.blueoakbbq.com; ⓒ **504/822-2583**). When that smoked-meat hankering hits, the Joint stands up to the best of them. Its location in an old corner store is less joint-like and more modern roadhouse, with picnic tables inside and out. The luscious babybacks and lean, smoldering brisket are sublime; for something truly local, try the Cajun sausage. Save room for the peanut butter pie.

701 Mazant St. www.alwayssmokin.com. ⓒ **504/949-3232.** Main courses $8–$28. Mon–Sat 11:30am–10pm.

Paloma Cafe ★★ LATIN/CARRIBEAN We just want to put Paloma in our pocket and carry it around with us. This darling, affordable neighborhood restaurant charmed us with mussels steamed in beer broth dotted with house-made chorizo, a simple plate of perfect shrimp in garlic butter, and juicy pork skewers with chimichurri. It chilled us with understated lighting and under-powered music (as in, just right). The goodnight kiss that sealed the deal: fluffy, crunchy, cinnamon-dusted, just-made warm churros with chocolate chili dipping sauce and a perfect, satiny flan accompanied by a Revelator coffee café au lait. Breakfast and cocktails are also on point.

800 Louisa St. www.palomanola.com. ⓒ **504/304-3062.** Main courses $10–$13 lunch, $12–$16 dinner. Mon–Tues 8am–6pm; Wed–Sat 8am–11pm; Sun 9am–4pm.

Praline Connection ★ CREOLE/SOUL FOOD The servers in their cute bowler hats and skinny ties are undeniably adorable, but the food and service aren't as adorable as they used to be. The fried chicken is still dependably juicy, though, and our top choice, with some fried pickles. The rest of the menu is only okay, too much something (sweet, in the yams), not enough of something else (flavor, in the greens). But we've had good luck with the nightly specials, and it's conveniently located on Frenchmen Street.

542 Frenchmen St. www.pralineconnection.com. ✆ **504/943-3934.** Main courses $13–$24. Mon–Sat 11am–10pm; Sun 11am–9pm.

Inexpensive

Bywater Bakery ★★★ CASUAL FARE The only bad thing about Bywater Bakery is that it closes too early. This casual Bywater breakfast-lunch cafe is a multi-threat, with delicious pastries, scrumptious savories, really cool local art (usually), and local talents tinkling the ivories on the old upright in the center of the room (often, especially on weekends). We're fond of the thick-crusted hand pies with rotating fillings, from fresh fruit to a gumbo-like stew; the ya-ka-mein (a locally beloved noodle soup specialty, chock-a-block full of hangover-curing ingredients); and the breakfast-in-a-go-cup options. The dazzling cakes lure us with their good looks and keep us with their good taste.

3624 Dauphine St. www.bywaterbakery.com. ✆ **504/336-3336.** Everything under $10. Daily 7am–3pm.

Gene's Po' Boys ★ CASUAL FARE Just outside the tourist zone is a serious po' boy for people who are serious about po' boys: Gene's homemade hot sausage patty with American cheese. (And we do mean hot—the building is Pepto-pink for a reason.) No chips, no dessert, no atmosphere, comes with a soda, open 24 hours. That's all she wrote and all you need to know.

1040 Elysian Fields Ave. ✆ **504/943-3861.** Everything under $10. Cash only. Daily 24 hr.

Kukhnya ★★ INTERNATIONAL Some of the best cheap eats do in fact operate out of a neon-lit window at the back of a dicey, punk-meets-metal nightclub whose Wi-Fi password is "Satan." Once we got past the bouncer (just explain you're there for the food), we fell hard for this place, starting with the pucker-inducing pickled veggies and a simple $2.50 side of crisp, grilled asparagus. The heartier mushroom-and-spinach blini was a bit greasy, but we made return visits for the locally made kielbasa po' boy with spicy cabbage and searingly hot mustard, and the beet-and-lentil burger topped with goat cheese. You can take your order or hang in the club if you like what you're hearing; in that case, pay the cover and order something from the decent beer list. This "Slavic soul food" isn't like anything from the old country; it's just satisfying, adventurous, affordable bar eats like you probably haven't seen before.

2227 St. Claude Ave. (inside Siberia nightclub). www.siberianola.com. ✆ **504/265-8855.** Everything under $11, cash only. Daily 4pm–midnight; Sat–Sun 10am–4pm.

Closed occasionally due to club capacity. Consider calling ahead; phone orders accepted.

McHardy's Chicken and Fixin' ★★★ SOUL FOOD   Popeye's will do when we're far from New Orleans, but if we're in town, it's gotta be family-owned McHardy's for take-out fried chicken. It's moist, tender, slightly crispy-skinned, perfectly seasoned, and cheap. Stellar. We never have a party without it, and often *make* a party *just* to have it. The other "fixins" are okay—the mustardy, nearly mashed homemade potato salad is a standout—but the bird is the word here. *Tip:* Cheap, hot to-go breakfasts, too; cooked fresh from $2 up.

1458 N. Broad St. www.facebook.com/pages/McHardys-Chicken-Fixin/176427879083461. © **504/949-0000.** 5-piece box $6; 100-piece (!) $96.60. Mon–Fri 6:30–9am; Mon–Thurs 11am–6:30pm; Fri–Sat 11am–7:30pm; Sun 11am–3pm. Takeout only.

MID-CITY/TREMÉ/BAYOU ST. JOHN

For restaurants in this section, see "New Orleans Restaurants" map on p. 82.

Expensive

Gabrielle ★★★ CONTEMPORARY CAJUN   We're so glad that this charming neighborhood gem is back, 12 years after its watery demise. And that the revered, signature roast duck is back on the menu in all its dusky sweetness. The warm French blue exterior in the midst of Orleans Avenue in the Tremé is a welcoming beacon to the creative Cajun and Creole riffs within (i.e., why have garlic butter frites when you can have *guava* garlic butter frites with hanger steak?). Regulars table-hop between bowls of smoked quail gumbo, a concoction that reaches to the delicious depths of dark roux. The BBQ shrimp-sweet potato pie appetizer positively works; braised rabbit comes delicately topped with rose-petal syrup, grapes, and caramelized onion. And then, all the desserts. We mean it. We can't pick.

2441 Orleans Ave. www.gabriellerestaurant.com. © **504/603-2344.** Main courses $16–$30. Tues–Thurs 5:30–10pm; Fri–Sat 5:30–11pm.

Ralph's on the Park ★★★ CONTEMPORARY CREOLE   Huge picture windows look out on Spanish moss–draped oaks in City Park. **Joe Krown**'s stylish stride piano seeps from the lounge and across the cream-upholstered dining room. You're sipping a French 75, eagerly anticipating the turtle soup and brown-butter sweetbread starters, gazing upon the setting sun, glistening rain, or your sweetheart's baby blues. Whatevs—it's dreamy here. The fare takes a fresh global approach with a pinch of Creole. A polished version of ya-ka-mein, the local ramen-like hangover cure, is soothing surprise. Roast cobia comes topped with a light hollandaise, faintly redolent of the crawfish fat used deep in the recipe. Shrimp and grits gets a curry and yogurt twist. Desserts are crowd-pleasing: Just say chocolate crème brûlée. The whole experience epitomizes Southern elegance—a vacation within a vacation, it's easily reachable by cab or the City Park streetcar, and there are usually multi-course specials. Allow time to hear Mr. Krown at happy hour or brunch.

900 City Park Ave. www.ralphsonthepark.com. © **504/488-1000.** Main courses $18–$21 lunch, $25–$37 dinner, $17–$23 brunch. Mon–Sun 5:30–9pm; Fri–Sat 5:30–9:30pm; Tues–Fri 11:30am–2pm; Sun 10:30am–2pm.

Moderate

Café Degas ★★★ BISTRO/FRENCH   Every neighborhood in every city should have a charming, casual French bistro that serves a perfect salad Niçoise and has a tree growing in the middle of the indoor/outdoor dining room. But only Faubourg St. John can claim it. Café Degas is darling, perfectly suited to a romantic dinner or a gals' lunch. Favorites like escargot, hanger steak, and rack of lamb are straightforward, flavorful, and generous; a delicate roast quail starter was tempting to double as an entree. It's a popular spot, particularly for brunch and the $18 two-course prix-fixe weekday lunch, so reserve ahead. Check the website for coupons. Reserve ahead during peak periods.

3127 Esplanade Ave. www.cafedegas.com. © **504/945-5635.** Main courses $12–$18 lunch/brunch, $14–$31 dinner. Wed–Sat 11am–3pm and 5:30–10pm; Sun 10:30am–3pm and 5:30–9:30pm.

Dooky Chase ★★ SOUL FOOD/CREOLE   First, the important Dooky trivia: Ray Charles (among other musicians) hung out here after shows and wrote "Early in the Morning" about it. Leah Chase, chef, hostess, and the late Dooky's wife (aka the "Queen of Creole Cuisine"), has won just about every culinary award in existence (and was the model for Tiana in Disney's delightful *The Princess and the Frog*). In the '60s, Dooky Chase was an important meeting place for civil rights leaders. Now well into her 90s, Leah remains a vibrant, revered, and important civic figure. After Hurricane Katrina, the couple lived in a FEMA trailer across the street for 2 years while they rebuilt the restaurant. Oh, and presidents Obama and Bush I both dined at Dooky's (not together). It's not quite what it was in the glory days, but us lesser folk can partake of the weekday lunch buffet of Creole standards in the handsome art-filled dining room. A better choice: Friday dinner, when the neighbor-saturated atmospher sizzles like the crisp fried chicken—a serious contender for the city's best. Come for the hallowed history; stay for the fried chicken.

2301 Orleans Ave. www.dookychaserestaurant.com. © **504/821-0600.** Lunch buffet $18; dinner main courses $20–$25. Tues–Fri 11am–3pm; Fri 5–9pm. Dinner service Thurs–Sat are in the works, so check website.

Liuzza's ★★ CREOLE/ITALIAN   Actual Liuzza's moment: Crusty waitress hands customer a menu ("Here you go, Bay-bee"), then abruptly closes it. "Bay-bee," she instructs, gesticulating with intent, "Numba One, or Numba Two—but *definitely* Numba One." Naturally, the Number One special was ordered (a seafood lasagna, dripping with a white cream sauce) and promptly devoured, in all its enormity. If you've been wondering what Creole Italian is all about, come here. This is a true, humble neighborhood institution, and we're pretty sure it gets the same regulars that were here before it took on 8 feet of Katrina waters. So when the waitress talks, you betta listen. There's nothing subtle about the hearty, saucy comfort food and po' boys; it's solid and rib-sticking. Do get a massive frosted mug of Abita Amber and the famous deep-fried dill pickles. "You people will batter and deep-fry anything that isn't nailed down!" exclaims yet another astonished visitor. Good times. (And credit cards are now accepted.)

3636 Bienville St. www.liuzzas.com. © **504/482-9120.** Main courses $12–$22. Sun–Mon 11am–4pm; Tues–Sat 11am–10pm.

Lola's ★★ INTERNATIONAL/SPANISH   For something very European yet very local—and completely different—try the Spanish fare at teeny Lola's in the Bayou St. John neighborhood. Start with garlic soup (one of several good vegetarian options; another is refreshing gazpacho). Then get a sizzling platter of paella—we prefer the mussel-loaded combination. If there's a wait, relax with a carafe of red or white sangria; if there isn't, relax with a carafe of red or white sangria. Once you're seated, service is prompt, though cooked-to-order paellas take about 30 minutes. Close with the silky homemade flan. A very good day can be had by ending up here after spending time in City Park or at the New Orleans Museum of Art (p. 151).

3312 Esplanade Ave. www.lolasneworleans.com. © **504/488-6946.** Main courses $16–$32; paellas $18–$54. Sun–Thurs 5:30–9:30pm; Fri–Sat 5:30–10pm.

Mandina's ★★ CREOLE/ITALIAN   Dis is da ultimate N'Awlins neighbahood restaurant, owned by the same family since the late 1800s—and largely unchanged—as it should be. Nothing innovative here, just heart, soul, and comfort food the way Maw Maw made it (including canned veggies—skip 'em), served by someone who looks like her. If the daily specials aren't to your liking, get some butter-soaked garlic bread to share, and the right and true seafood gumbo or turtle soup au sherry. Then go for the sweet Italian sausage and spaghetti combo, or the brown-buttery trout meunière. The cocktails are strong here; so is the A/C. Bring a sweater.

3800 Canal St. www.mandinasrestaurant.com. © **504/482-9179.** Main courses $13–$28. Mon–Thurs 11am–9:30pm; Fri–Sat 11am–10pm; Sun noon–9pm.

Marjie's Grill ★★ CONTEMPORARY SOUTHERN/INTERNATIONAL Oddball menu, off-cuts of meats and poultry, weird location, weirder flavor mash-ups. No worry, it mostly works. Adventurous Marjie's fuses Thai, Cambodian, and Filipino ingredients with NOLA standards and, in many cases, smokes them over coal or wood. It's not all rabbit livers and lamb belly (just some of it), but the novel results do include chili-spiked pig knuckles glazed with cane syrup, or spicy raw seafood salad with a hit of lime and mint. Cool it down with smashed cucumbers and sticky Thai-style BBQ ribs. A side of roast sweet potatoes is necessary. Service and space are mismatched-dish-style casual; weather permitting, the outdoor wood deck is the sweet spot here.

320 South Broad St. www.marjiesgrill.com. © **504/603-2234.** Entrees $12–$30. Mon–Fri 11am–2:30, 4–10pm; Sat 4–10pm.

Toups' Meatery ★★ CONTEMPORARY CAJUN   Just another neigh-borhood spot with killer food, mostly of the porky variety. Chef Toups speaks our oinky language. As you are being seated, order some crunchy porkalicious cracklins to munch on while you're deciding what to eat. As the name implies, one should order the charcuterie plate here. Another should get the cheese plate, just to even things out. We're actually more a fan of lunch here than dinner, but we'll happily eat the short ribs if they're on the oft-changing menu. And despite this pork- and red-meat-centric advice, the mussels, the sky-high chicken sandwich, and a rich confit of chicken thighs are all worthy. Abso-lutely get whatever variety of multilayered Debbie Does Doberge cake is available. At **Toups South,** the second location in the Southern Food & Bever-age Museum, the menu has a slightly less meaty bent and is more expansive of Southern cooking.

845 N. Carrollton Ave. www.toupsmeatery.com. ✆ **504/252-4999.** Main courses $11–$18 lunch, $22–$29 dinner (large plates). Tues–Sat 11am–2:30pm and 5–10pm; Fri–Sat 5–11pm. **Toups South:** 1504 Oretha Castle Haley Blvd. www.toupssouth.com. ✆ **504/304-2147.** Mon–Fri 11am–10pm; Fri–Sat 11am–11pm; Sun 10am–3pm.

Ye Olde College Inn ★★★ CREOLE/CASUAL FARE   This high-ceilinged 1930s hangout has been smartly renovated with an inviting bar, murals, and store signs reminiscent of ye olde New Orleans. The cuisine is more refined than that implies, particularly in the inventive daily specials, and they take farm-to-table seriously (their own farm, complete with chick-ens, is across the street). A succulent, perfectly grilled lamb loin comes topped with sun-dried tomatoes and shiitake mushrooms in a red-wine reduc-tion. Throwback options are crafted with a deft touch, like the platter-size breaded veal cutlet, a steal at $16, including spinach and mashed potatoes. The familiar bleu-cheese-and-pecan salad is elevated by aromatic roast duck. For sheer decadence, the award-winning oyster, Havarti cheese, and bacon po' boy is hard to top, but if that's your goal, order the fried bread pudding po' boy. A tower of onion rings for the table is legally mandated. Ask your server for the deets about the discounted admission to Rock 'n' Bowl, right next door (same owners).

3000 S. Carrollton Ave. www.collegeinn1933.com. ✆ **504/866-3683.** Main courses $14–$35. Tues–Sat 4–11pm.

Inexpensive

Bevi Seafood ★★★ SEAFOOD/CASUAL FARE   Bevi is a smidge more proper and pricey than a divey corner seafood shack, but make no mistake, they know how to berl (boil) and fry up a downright fine batch of shrimp, oysters, crab, or crawfish. The seafood is fresh, seasonal, and local—and the spice is right, even in the tangy slaw. Carnivores have excellent options too. Consider making the Messi Swine po' boy (pork belly, cochon, ham, and—for good measure—bacon fat mayo) your last meal. Even unintentionally. It's counter service with just a few tables, but don't get fried stuff to go: a concise fryer-plate-mouth interval is essential. ***Bonus:*** It's a few doors from **Angelo Brocato's** (p. 130), thus amortizing the Mid-City Lyft ride.

236 N Carrollton Ave. www.beviseafoodco.com. ℂ **504/488-7503.** Everything under $20. Tues–Sat 11am–8pm; Sun–Mon 11am–4pm.

Biscuits & Buns on Banks ★ CAFE/CASUAL FARE   Indulge yourself here with the fluffy eponymous biscuits, with honey or Steen's cane syrup, or laden with immoral Andouille-chorizo gravy. Or try the crispy waffle sandwiched with brie cheese and blueberry compote. Crisp, Andouille-pecan-crusted shrimp, in a taco with tangy avocado mango salsa, nicely sauced and balanced with mirliton slaw? Yes, please.

4337 Banks St. www.biscuitsandbunsonbanks.com. ℂ **504/273-4600.** Breakfast and lunch main courses $9–$14. Daily 8am–3pm.

Lil' Dizzy's ★★ CREOLE/SOUL FOOD   This Tremé mainstay is another quintessential family-owned neighborhood restaurant. It's lively with locals at the mostly average breakfast (the homemade hot sausages are slightly above that, and the catfish and eggs are a winner) and for the lunch buffet. If you're a light eater, it might be a bit high-priced as well, so come hungry and dig into the terrific fried chicken, okay gumbo, and red beans—and a few other soul-food standards (also come early; they do run out). Better yet, order a la carte: the aforementioned chicken or our favorite, the standout trout Baquet: a delicate fish filet topped with garlic-butter sauce and lump crabmeat.

1500 Esplanade Ave. www.lildizzyscafe.com. ℂ **504/569-8997.** Lunch buffet $16 ($7 kids 8 and under), a la carte lunch items under $15, Sun brunch buffet $18. Mon–Sat 7am–2pm; Sun 8am–2pm.

Liuzza's by the Track ★★★ CREOLE/CASUAL FARE   When friends fly in for a visit, we stop here on the way home to get them in the gumbo groove. Liuzza's by the Track has one of the best in town. The BBQ-shrimp po' boy is their signature, overstuffed with peppery, butter-soaked shrimp, but we're partial to the garlic oyster sammie. When we're feeling feisty, we switch to the drippy garlic-stuffed roast beef, with a pinch of horseradish in the mayo (we'll often get the cup of gumbo and half po' boy deal, which excludes that BBQ shrimp). Specials can be pretty special, so check the board. The veggie-deprived should opt for the Portobello salad, and everyone here should strike up a conversation with whoever's nearby. It's that sort of place. Avoid prime weekday lunch hours if you can.

1518 N. Lopez St. www.liuzzasnola.com. ℂ **504/218-7888.** Everything under $20. Mon–Sat 11am–7pm.

Parkway Bakery and Tavern ★★★ CASUAL FARE   It's hard to believe that this corner shop began life as a bakery more than 100 years ago. Or that it was shuttered for years in between then and now. Or that it was essentially under water after Katrina. Now, after getting love from umpteen magazines and travel- and food-channel shows (plus a visit from the Obamas), people literally come by the busload. Try to sit inside or on the original deck;

either has more charm than the massive outside picnic area, thrown up to accommodate the popularity surge. But don't be put off—what matters is that the po' boys still hold up terrifically. Claims to fame are the fried shrimp and juicy roast beef—our favorite in the city, even if (maybe because) it's among the sloppiest. We're fond of the Reuben or lighter caprese, too. The home-made potato salad is killer, and the banana pudding is old-skool lip-smacking. Round it all out with a bottled Barq's and a stroll along nearby Bayou St. John. Oysters are on the menu Monday and Wednesday only and are available with bacon! (Just say yes.) The line can be daunting but moves pretty fast (more so with a beer in hand, so hit up the bar), or try for off-peak hours.

538 Hagan Ave. www.parkwaypoorboys.com. ℭ **504/482-3047.** Everything under $18. Wed–Mon 11am–10pm; closed Tues.

Willie Mae's Scotch House ★★ SOUL FOOD   Since the 1970s, this humble chicken shack in a not-great part of the Tremé neighborhood was known mainly to locals, the budding foodie community, and a few enterprising tourists. In 2005, octogenarian Willie Mae and her secret-recipe fried chicken were designated "American classics" by the James Beard Foundation, and the world came knocking. Weeks later, her home and restaurant were 8 feet under water. The remarkable, volunteer-driven recovery began quickly, with hands-on support from local restaurateurs—a testament to New Orleans' supportive food community. Nowadays, with the matriarch's family helming the fryers, the chicken is still beautifully spiced and crisped—on a good day. Which is much more common than a bad (dry or oversalted) day, but we've had them. For safety, order the fried pork chops, and always get the creamy butterbeans (which don't get *near* the attention the chicken does, but should). Plan to wait in line—for service (maybe), then for the fried-to-order bird. Or trade the character of the original Tremé location for the efficiency of the newer Uptown location.

2401 St. Ann St. www.williemaesnola.com. ℭ **504/822-9503.** Mon–Sat 10am–5pm. Uptown: 7457 St. Charles Ave. ℭ **504/417-5424.** Mon–Thurs 11am–8pm; Fri–Sat 11am–9pm. Everything under $15.

CENTRAL BUSINESS DISTRICT & WAREHOUSE DISTRICT

For restaurants in this section, see "New Orleans Restaurants" map on p. 82.

Expensive

Annunciation ★★ CONTEMPORARY CREOLE   Annunciation mines the classic bentwood-chair, white-tablecloth decor and "good time was had by all" tone we love so well in New Orleans, as well as some time-honored reci-pes and attentive service. The fried oysters with spinach and brie, and buttery, crispy chicken Bonne Femme au jus, two signature dishes, both belong on the table. A salad of abundant crab and a creamy herb dressing is delicious; and the tender veal with crawfish and Andouille cornbread dressing is a little bit Southern, a little bit city, and a lot of flavor. A stunning soft-shell-crab special was enough for two, but too good to share. Despite the cool brick, jet-black stained floors, and angular black-and-white abstract artwork, there's a warmth to the room that sets the mood on genial, owing largely to Richard Williams, the ever-gracious, perpetually bow-tied maître d'. If form follows, good moods mean wine and dessert. The wine list is a bit more interesting, but a simple tawny Port and the budino will lengthen a lovely night of lingering.

1016 Annunciation St. www.annunciationrestaurant.com. ⓒ **504/568-0245.** Main courses $24–$32. Mon–Thurs and Sun 5:30–10pm; Fri–Sat 5:30–11pm.

Borgne ★★ SEAFOOD   We like Borgne's easygoing vibe and the well-versed servers who show up when we want them to and don't when we don't. We like most of the items we've tried here, with their interesting Spanish accents. We love that they serve a $10-plate lunch every day, especially Tuesday's ropa vieja. We like the cool-looking, shell-crusted columns, the loooong bar and the friendly service there. In fact, we quite like dining in the bar, strung with televisions and still sometimes quieter than the expansive dining room. The better to discuss how good the soothing oyster spaghetti is, or ask our friend if she's going to eat that last bacon-jalapeño duck popper. Whatever's on special is a good bet here. Skip the signature Hummingbird cake and stick with the chocolate hazelnut puddin'.

601 Loyola Ave., in the Hyatt Regency. www.borgnerestaurant.com. ⓒ **504/613-3860.** Main courses $10–$30 lunch, $22–$34 dinner; plate lunch $10. Sun–Thurs 11am–10pm; Fri–Sat 11am–11pm.

Compère Lapin ★★★ CONTEMPORARY SOUTHERN/INTERNA-TIONAL   *Top Chef* alumni and St. Lucia native Nina Compton's tasty culinary tricks blend Caribbean, French, Italian, and Creole influences into James Beard award–winning dishes that are just exotic enough: deeply flavored, wonderfully textured curried goat with sweet plantain gnocchi; perfectly jerked crisped local drum with lush caramelized sunchokes; island-inflected hot fried chicken. At the commodious bar, munch on seasoned corn and pig's ears with spiked aioli (c'mon, try 'em) while sipping shimmery, beautifully balanced drinks. Stellar lighting, blue highlights, and the dotted bunny logo help update the lively room's warehouse-y bones (huge windows, weathered wood and brick), though it but suffers on the noise front thanks to those hard surfaces and its shared space with the Old No. 77 Hotel lobby.

535 Tchoupitoulas St., in Old No. 77 Hotel. www.comperelapin.com. ⓒ **504/599-2119.** Main courses $16–27 lunch, $26–$34 dinner. Mon–Fri 11:30am–2:30pm; nightly 5:30–10pm; Sat–Sun 10:30am–2pm.

Emeril's ★★★ CREOLE/MODERN LOUISIANA   He heads an empire and pioneered New Orleans' modern restaurant scene, but Emeril's flagship restaurant has never flagged. It's still high quality (and high priced), interesting, exciting dining with dishes that build meaningfully on tradition. The wine list is intelligent and broad; service is helpful and professional but unstuffy; and noise is well-managed in the buoyant room. The plate shows clear commitment to first-rate, locally sourced ingredients: A salad of local tomatoes and melon is dotted with tiny, crispy duck hearts and a wisp of herb in the vinaigrette. Grilled pork chops, done perfectly despite their girth, are artfully glazed with tamarind and tomatillo molé sauces. Meyer lemon crème elevates brandied lobster bucatini. Order chocolate soufflé with your entrée but get banana cream pie too. *Tips:* The open-kitchen bar seating is perfect for single diners; the $23 three-course lunch is a great deal. Reserve well in advance.

800 Tchoupitoulas St. www.emerils.com. 𝒞 **504/528-9393.** Main courses $12–$29 lunch, $25–$50 dinner; degustation by advance arrangement; 3-course lunch $35. Mon–Fri 11:30am–2pm; daily 6–10pm.

Herbsaint ★★★ BISTRO Donald Link may not be a Food Channel staple like Emeril, but he's right up there in terms of modern New Orleans restaurant royalty. His sweet, window-lined bistro, rooted in French, Italian, and Creole traditions and helmed by Rebecca Wilcomb, who earned the James Beard Best Chef: South award for 2017, is one of New Orleans' best restaurants. It's usually packed and always lacks elbow room, but it's uphill from there. Herbsaint dishes some of the city's best gumbos, including a meatless, herb-based gumbo z'herbes version we crave. The winning signature starter of homemade spaghetti with a creamy, guanciale-spiked sauce is topped with a batter-fried poached egg (yes, you can—and should—double it as an entree); a watermelon gazpacho with lump crab is a simple little cup of summer. For heartier fare, a slow-cooked lamb neck is astoundingly sized, equally tender, and rich with flavor, and arrives on a well-paired bed of saffron fideo. Desserts here are terrific—try whatever they put in a tart shell. A bistro menu served from 1:30 to 5:30pm features light entrees from both the lunch and dinner menus. Reserve well in advance.

701 St. Charles Ave. www.herbsaint.com. 𝒞 **504/524-4114.** Main courses $16–$34. Mon–Fri 11:30am–10pm; Sat 5:30–10pm.

La Boca ★★★ STEAK One might not think of New Orleans as a steak town, but it's yet another tradition that runs deep here—this is the city that gave us Ruth's Chris, after all. You choose your cut and your knife at this Argentinean steakhouse, and you should get the transcendent 3-day fries regardless of what else you order. But for the best-flavored beefiness, we suggest the *entraña fina* skirt steak (which can also be had skin-on, interesting but unnecessary) or the *centro de entraña* hanger steak. Temperatures are proper; the trio of chimichurri sauces add zip. Servers know their meats and are helpful about the (accordingly Argentinian) wines, but aren't particularly sociable. We miss the secretive, cavern-like ambience of its original location, but the commodious, loft-like new room does make it easier to get a table.

870 Tchoupitoulas St. www.labocasteaks.com. 𝒞 **504/525-8205.** Appetizers $9–$22, steaks $16–$54. Mon–Wed 5:30–10pm; Thurs–Sat 5:30pm–midnight.

Marcello's ★★ ITALIAN Marcello's bills itself as a "wine bar and bistro," and indeed the back dining room doubles as a well-stocked, decently priced wine shop to peruse between courses. Fun idea, but in truth we prefer the smaller, more traditional, white-tile-floored front dining room. There's nothing edgy about the recognizable Sicilian-focused menu—it's just inviting and well executed. Dressings and sauces pop, each distinctive flavor showing spryly on the palate and not overwhelming the just-chewy housemade pastas. Traditional parmigiana with eggplant (available as an appetizer or entree, or with chicken or veal), so often plagued with a heavy hand, lets the fresh tomato sauce and aubergine shine. Comforting, herbalicious cioppino bursts with local seafood, while lamb ragu over silken pappardelle satisfies the craving for something robust. Our accommodating server extolled the tiramisu; it proved to be a fluffy, superb example of the familiar standard.

715 St. Charles Ave. www.marcelloscafe.com. ℰ **504/581-6333.** Main courses $14–$19 lunch, $19–$37 dinner. Mon–Fri 11:30am–10pm; Sat–Sun 5–10pm.

Meril ★★ CONTEMPORARY AMERICAN Meril is Emeril Lagasse's newest concept, breezy and casual in style, lower in price point, and small plates focused. The bustling space opens onto a large horseshoe-shaped bar, next to an expansive dining room with floor-to-ceiling windows. The bar's creative cocktail program centers on local ingredients and fresh herbs. Dishes feature inventive takes on some of Lagasse's favorite foods, influenced in part by the docu-series "Eat the World with Emeril Lagasse." Look for Mexican-inspired tamales made with boudin topped with a roasted tomatillo sauce; Korean short ribs cooked on a Japanese robata-style grill, served with kimchi cucumbers; and linguine and clams made with guanciale and blistered tomatoes.

424 Girod St. www.emerilsrestaurants.com/meril. ℰ **504/526-3745.** Snacks and small plates $5–$12, main courses $10–$16. Sun–Thurs 11:30am–10pm; Fri–Sat 11:30am–11pm.

Peche ★★★ SEAFOOD There's nary a dud on the menu of wood-fired seafood at this uber-popular, mega-award winner (Best New Restaurant, Best Chef Ryan Prewitt, blah blah). The raucous room works best for plate-sharing parties, not dates or deep convos. You can skip the shrimp toast and Betty Crockery tuna, but not the beer-battered fish sticks (really); hearty crawfish gratinée; or onion dip with pepper jelly and freshly fried chips. The whole grilled fish (our last one was a buttery, fire-crusted redfish with salsa verde one night) is fab. The raw bar is equally fine and fun. Make full use of the terrific craft beer, cocktail, and European wine menus. For your dessert, the salted caramel cake, of course. Reserve well in advance.

800 Magazine St. www.pecherestaurant.com. ℰ **504/522-1744.** Snacks and small plates $9–$13, grilled entrees $14–$27, whole grilled fish $45–$69. Mon–Thurs 11am–10pm; Fri–Sat 11am–11pm.

Restaurant August ★★★ CONTEMPORARY SOUTHERN/FRENCH If you live under a rock (aka, don't watch TV food shows or read the news), you may not know Chef John Besh, the one-time shooting star of TV food shows and now fallen star of the New Orleans restaurant scene. August, the fine-dining flagship restaurant of the culinary empire Besh started and has since left, is helmed by Todd Pulsinelli and an attentive front-of-house staff and remains a marvel of Frenchified Creole and Cajun creativity. There is the rare mishit here, when a boundary-pushing dish goes one ingredient beyond the limit, or an ordinary dish reaching for extraordinary doesn't get there (an overcomplicated pappardelle Bolognese on one occasion). But on the whole your experience will be decorous, cultured, stunningly plated, expensive—and memorable.

These are masters of foie gras. It's unfailingly off the charts, done "Three Ways" or in any incarnation. As well, salads are invariably perfectly composed standouts. Softly lush gnocchi done with sweet blue crab and slabs of earthy truffles melt on the palate. The signature breaded trout Pontchartrain, in its envelope of paper-thin white bread (!), with shrimp, crab, and local mushrooms, is a fine plate of Gulf goodness. Slowly roasted lamb spiked with Andouille produces an orchestra of earthy, rich flavor. A Wagyu hangar steak is about as perfect in temperature, texture, and taste as could be wished for. At the other extreme, the vegetarian tasting menu, including buttermilk-laced spring pea soup and squash blossoms stuffed with a smoked eggplant puree, enticed an entrenched carnivore to gustatory ecstasy.

The sweets are urbane yet playful. The deconstructed banana pudding has a following; we're more taken with a summery pineapple soufflé. Service is utterly professional and unhurried. Tables are well-spaced in the sedate main dining room, where chandeliers glint off the tall windows; the warm, wood-paneled wine room with the clever overhead cellar is slightly less formal. If the prices are off-putting (don't expect serving sizes to justify them), the Friday prix-fixe lunch, three courses at $28, makes August indisputably doable. Alternately, if the degustation is doable for you, do it.

301 Tchoupitoulas St. www.restaurantaugust.com. ℃ **504/299-9777.** Reservations recommended. 3-course lunch $28; dinner main courses $34–$49; 3-hr. degustation menu $97 per person ($152 with wine). Daily 5–10pm; Fri 11am–2pm.

Sac-a-lait ★★★ CONTEMPORARY SOUTHERN   Rustic doesn't mean unpolished at tradition-flipping Sac-a-lait, named for the official state freshwater fish of Louisiana. The hunting/fishing-camp-driven fare includes thin filets of venison backstrap fried to a high crunch and painted with a creamy peppery sauce; house specialty Lost Fish (ours a speckled trout) is *"perdu"* style: dredged through an egg and cream froth, pan-fried to create a crisp crust, and served on a bed of creamy crawfish étouffée in a double-win. If your party is game, a whole, 3-pound richly roasted pheasant comes ready for sharing and carving (you can do it or they will). It's a festive presentation. As long as you're sharing, spring for a flask of barrel-aged Sazeracs. The owners hand-built much of the decor in the large converted mill, using reclaimed materials from a shuttered broom factory across the street. Expect plenty of old pine, whitewashed brick, subtle river murals, and those clamor-causing high ceilings (and ask about the Angola gray chairs).

1051 Annunciation St. www.sac-a-lait restaurant.com. ℃ **504/324-3658.** Main courses $22–$45. Tues–Sat 5:30–10pm; Fri–Sun 11am–2pm.

Moderate

Auction House Market ★★ FOOD HALL   This super-chic new food hall is ideal for solos, groups, the multi-palated and the indecisive. Ten vendor options ranging from Indian to oysters to empanadas to avocado toast surround a sleek (and seemingly always busy) marble bar. Sushi, sandwiches, and coffee are also available; all are enjoyed by a lively mix of locals, conventioneers, business lunchers, and moms with strollers. Our faves: Happy Jaxx sandwiches and salads, Elysian Seafood for shrimp cocktail and oysters, dosas from Tava, and the Empanolas (handmade empanadas with fillings like gumbo and crawfish étouffée). Definitely use the bathroom here. When you go, you'll know.

801 Magazine St. www.auctionhousemarket.com. © **504/586-8305.** Items $4–$18. Sun–Thurs 7am–10pm; Fri–Sat 7am–11pm.

Cochon ★★★ CONTEMPORARY CAJUN   Chef/owners Donald Link and Steve Stryjewski pay homage to all things swine at this inspired and authentic Cajun restaurant with a serious moonshine list. It's good, sometimes very good, and one of the few games in town for Cajun food—the rustic country cousin to big-city Creole cooking (see p. 115). Cochon's version is, of course, amped up several notches: This is Cajun via Donald Link and Steve Stryjewski, after all. All visits to Cajun country should kick off with some cracklins and a good local beer, like the Parish Canebrake. Follow with the boudin balls—crunchy outside, savory and porky inside—with a side of creamy, burnished mac 'n' cheese. For a hog break, the briny bite of wood-fired oysters bathed in chili garlic butter or the chicken livers with pepper jelly are astoundingly good. The fork-tender pork cheeks are disappointing only in terms of serving size (so get two orders), and the skillet-baked rabbit and dumplings is a soul-warming dish that, if you skip everything else, should not be missed. Oops, same goes for the mac 'n' cheese, which is life changing. The ambrosia cake is a potluck-perfect finish—a creamy, fruity, happy ending. Reserve well in advance.

930 Tchoupitoulas St. www.cochonrestaurant.com. © **504/588-2123.** Reservations strongly recommended. Small plates $8–$14; main courses $19–$32. Sun–Thurs 11am–10pm; Fri–Sat 11am–11pm.

Domenica ★★ ITALIAN   Bittersweet chocolate walls, soaring ceilings, great art, glossy surfaces, small bar, large crowd. Which all sets the scene for perfectly bubble-edged Neapolitan pizzas, arguably the best salumi in the city, and a kitchen that knows its way around a vegetable. We rarely make it to the *secondi* here because it's so easy, and such a pleasure, to load up on antipasti, *primi*, and a pizza or two. Buttery sautéed chanterelle mushrooms are flavored with marrow and cut through with parsley—decadently rich. A whole, deeply roasted cauliflower makes an impressive presentation and a delicious addition to the table. Fresh tagliatelle is sauced with rabbit and porcini mushrooms, hearty and divine, and we'd never leave home if Mom could make a *stracci* with oxtail and fried chicken livers. End with the satiny chocolate hazelnut budino. Domenica's superb happy hour, with half-price pizzas from 2 to 5pm,

7 days a week, helps explain why it's often cacophonous. The bar pours well-priced boutique Italian wines and popular homemade cellos. Okay, service is inconsistent, ranging from prompt and knowledgeable to perfunctory. And still it's worth it. Reserve in advance. Also consider the casual uptown outpost, **Pizza Domenica** ★★ (www.pizzadomenica.com; ℰ **504/301-4978**).

123 Baronne St., in the Roosevelt Hotel. www.domenicarestaurant.com. ℰ **504/648-6020.** Reservations recommended. Pizza $13–$18; antipasti $14–$24; main courses $24–$30. Daily 11am–11pm.

Drago's ★★ SEAFOOD   The booming Hilton lobby isn't too conducive to an atmospheric experience. Fortunately, that's irrelevant, because you're here for one thing and one thing only (okay, two): Drago's buttery, garlicky, Parmesan-y, charbroiled oysters—your new paramour, the one you can't get enough of. Other places do them, but none so well. They're like a home-renovation project: However many you think you want to order, double it. The bargain-priced Maine lobsters are also worth your while, but not much else matters. Sports-minded folks can sit at the bar, order oysters, and watch what's on—there are worse ways to take in a game (though it has no beers on tap—wassup with that?). Be mindful that the sprawling dining room can fill up, and they don't take reservations, so a wait is possible.

2 Poydras St., in the Hilton Riverside. www.dragosrestaurant.com. ℰ **504/584-3911.** Also 3232 N. Arnoult Rd., Metairie. ℰ **504/888-9254.** Raw oysters $13/dozen, charbroiled $20; dinner appetizers $12–$18, main courses $20–$29, Maine lobster $27–$52. Daily 11am–10pm.

Josephine Estelle ★★ ITALIAN   Located in the über-hip Ace Hotel, the restaurant is not at all too cool for regular people. In fact, it's surprisingly sprawling, high-ceilinged, and bright in a somewhat uncool way (although those dark-green velvet booths are v. cool). The Ace bar is really where the hipness happens (with some spillover), but at Josephine Estelle it's about the food. Highlights include any of the crudo starters—the snapper melts in the mouth. Also get the generous order of meatballs, and then do your best to work your way through the pasta selection—the entrees pale in comparison. Standouts include the delicate agnolotti with creamy sweetbreads and rustic wild mushrooms, and the very tasty, very traditional mafalde "with maw maw's gravy," which means red gravy, aka marinara sauce. You could also make a meal of the very good veggie sides. Cocktails are just fine. Do save room for the delectable peanut butter budino.

1600 Carondelet St. www.josephineestelle.com. ℰ **504/930-3070.** Entrees $14–$35. Mon–Fri 7am–11pm; Sat 8am–11pm; Sat–Sun 8am–10pm.

Maypop ★★★ INTERNATIONAL   Possibly our all-around favorite new-ish spot in the city; hands-down our favorite spot for Asian Italian Indian Southern-American cuisine (sometimes all in one dish). The inventive, flavor-packed cooking surprises rather than stuns, satisfying both the serious foodie and the food-shy (especially at the more affordable lunch). Don't skip the standard-sounding bibb lettuce salad. You'll do well with the hot fried chicken vindaloo or hand-pulled pasta. Servings aren't huge, thus everyone should get their own slice of Maypop pie. It's all beautifully plated, in keeping with the room's high style. Make sure to check out the lenticular mural from both sides.

611 O'Keefe Ave. www.maypoprestaurant.com. © **504/518-6345.** Main courses $15–$18 lunch, $17–$34 dinner. Sun–Thurs 11am–10pm; Sat–Sun 11am–11pm.

Inexpensive

Cochon Butcher ★★★ CONTEMPORARY CAJUN/CASUAL FARE This could easily be a three-word review: Just. Eat. Everything. As the name belies, they butcher and cure on-site, turning house-smoked meaty goodness into small plates and world-rocking sandwiches. The boudin sausage is the best east of Lafayette; the muffuletta may surpass Central Grocery's; pork belly with cucumber and mint is wondrous. Get the vinegary Brussels sprouts, some potato chips, and dreamy mac 'n' cheese or rue your bad decision. Dessert, like everything else, must be had; order the swoonful caramel doberge cake if it's available Casual, high-top tables open to the street via garage-style doors, and good local beers are offered at the full bar. Bonus points for the mad "Star Wars" diorama/table.

930 Tchoupitoulas St. www.cochonbutcher.com. © **504/588-7675.** Sandwiches $8–$12, charcuterie plate $14, sides and small plates $3–$6. Mon–Thurs 10am–10pm; Fri–Sat 10am–11pm; Sun 10am–4pm.

Mother's ★ CREOLE/SOUL FOOD/CASUAL FARE Legendary Mother's gets the "touristy" rap, but hey, Paris is touristy. And if it's good enough for Beyoncé and Jay-Z (who selfied from here), it's…actually that has no bearing on anything. Its worth is in proportion to line length: If there are more than four parties ahead of you, go elsewhere. If you can waltz right in, the combo platter makes a decent introduction to Creole cuisine. Best bet is any poor boy with Mother's signature baked ham, like the top-selling Ferdi (ham, roast beef debris), or with turkey and cheese, our preference (or with biscuits at breakfast). Guffaw at the bread pudding's retro inclusion of canned fruit cocktail, but it's freakishly good. Follow the line rules lest you get some hostess lip: 1) no table-saving; 2) get steam-table items; 3) order and receive drinks; 4) pay; 5) then and only then find a table—don't send a scout to save one; 6) a server delivers the rest of the food.

401 Poydras St. www.mothersrestaurant.net. © **504/523-9656.** Menu items $6–$27. Mon–Sun 7am–10pm.

Willa Jean ★★★ BAKERY/CASUAL FARE When John Besh's longtime pastry chef Kelly Fields opened her own casual restaurant, we went, 'natch. And then we went back. Then we tried to lease a table, because we saw no reason to leave. Every Southern-accented food and beverage need is not just covered, but done exceedingly well and with just enough flair—including the cocktails and the coffee (Intelligentsia). We know you like specifics, but seriously, anything containing flour is awesome. So pick whatever bread or pastry item appeals to you. Then get a loaf of the cornbread. Yes, you heard right: a loaf. You can thank us later. Biscuits with crab and hollandaise or classic sausage gravy rock your breakfast. For lunch, get the fried chicken on a housemade Hawaiian roll with jalapeño slaw, or the griddled meat loaf with tomato jam. Or the grilled fig and goat cheese sandwich. Lunch gets crazy busy so a reservation is not unwise. Dinner entrees are less interesting, or maybe we're just full after eating breakfast and lunch here.

611 O'Keefe Ave. www.willajean.com. ℂ **504/822-9503.** Breakfast/lunch everything under $19; dinner main courses $18–$22. Sun–Thurs 7am–9pm; Fri–Sat 7am–10pm.

UPTOWN/THE GARDEN DISTRICT/CENTRAL CITY

Expensive

Avo ★★★ ITALIAN   Bet someone $5 that you'll witness a marriage proposal tonight. Then book a table on the ultra-romantic, candle-lit patio at Avo. Even if you don't witness The Big Moment, you're a winner when you dine at this uptown beauty, considering chef-owner Nick Lama's impressive and indisputable qualifications: deep Sicilian roots; experience in some of the city's best kitchens; his family's decades-long immersion in New Orleans' food scene. When his talents met this tantalizing locale, lightning—and love—struck. We fell for the perfectly charred, tender octopus, and a just al dente pasta with crabmeat, Calabrian chili, and a creamy herb sauce. The delicious meatballs and lasagna don't stray far from tradition; both are simultaneously hearty and delicate; pistachio-crusted halibut is divine. Everything is seasoned. Just. So. Skip the cocktail standards and go straight to the winning, almost all-Italian wine list. Service is prompt and perfunctory. If only the desserts were must-do's (you're too full anyway). We're excited to try the just-launched brunch.

5908 Magazine St. www.restaurantavo.com. ℂ **504/509-6550.** Reservations recommended. Main courses $26–$36. Mon–Sat 5–10pm.

Brigtsen's ★★★ CONTEMPORARY CAJUN/CREOLE   Brigtsen's was one of the early modern Creole revolutionaries, and one of the first to convert a beautiful, 19th-century house into an upscale neighborhood restaurant way back in 1986. This perennial favorite still maintains a warm, romantic intimacy, with the hostess circulating amiably though the sweet little memorabilia- and mural-decorated rooms. The service and cuisine—which shows homey, Cajun-country roots—have been polished to consistent excellence. The "Shell Beach Diet," the famously grand seafood platter, changes seasonally but includes five to six sauced, baked, or otherwise unfried seafood items—an impressive extravagance for sharing or for a hungry, indecisive diner. Chef Brigtsen has a special touch with game and rabbit. His panéed sesame-crusted version in a tangy Creole mustard sauce, as well as his crispy, moist roast duck, are known far and wide; his pecan pie with its perfect, copious crust is also justifiably revered. A modest wine list satisfies but could be

Uptown Restaurants

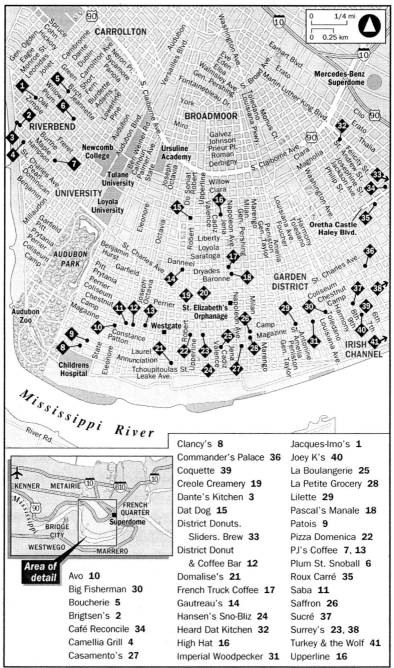

Avo **10**
Big Fisherman **30**
Boucherie **5**
Brigtsen's **2**
Café Reconcile **34**
Camellia Grill **4**
Casamento's **27**

Clancy's **8**
Commander's Palace **36**
Coquette **39**
Creole Creamery **19**
Dante's Kitchen **3**
Dat Dog **15**
District Donuts.
   Sliders. Brew **33**
District Donut
   & Coffee Bar **12**
Domalise's **21**
French Truck Coffee **17**
Gautreau's **14**
Hansen's Sno-Bliz **24**
Heard Dat Kitchen **32**
High Hat **16**
Imperial Woodpecker **31**

Jacques-Imo's **1**
Joey K's **40**
La Boulangerie **25**
La Petite Grocery **28**
Lilette **29**
Pascal's Manale **18**
Patois **9**
Pizza Domenica **22**
PJ's Coffee **7, 13**
Plum St. Snoball **6**
Roux Carré **35**
Saba **11**
Saffron **26**
Sucré **37**
Surrey's **23, 38**
Turkey & the Wolf **41**
Upperline **16**

Once upon a time, while waiting for Casamento's to open and just moments from an oyster loaf, three youngish tourist gals struck up a chat (as happens nearly automatically in New Orleans) with three Uptown ladies-of-a-certain-age ahead of them. They were St. Charles–born and –bred, dined at Casamento's weekly, and offered us NOLA newbies some well-tested tips. The one that still sticks sounds best when read with a high-pitched, breathy lilt: "You simply *must* go to any of the fine old French restaurants, and when you do, why you just order anythin' flamin'." Meaning, go to Antoine's, Arnaud's, Commander's Palace, or Galatoire's, and get bananas Foster, baked Alaska, *café brûlot*, or anything prepared tableside and involving conflagration. Naturally we bought the ladies a round, and to this day we're still living by the "anythin' flamin'" creed: Indulge a bit, relish fun, and while one needn't embrace drama in all aspects of life, when it comes to dessert, *bring it on.*

expanded. Reserve well in advance during peak periods, and expect a comfortable, relaxed, thoroughly adult evening.

723 Dante St. www.brigtsens.com. ℰ **504/861-7610.** Reservations highly recommended. Main courses $21–$34. Tues–Sat 5:30–10pm.

Clancy's ★★★ CONTEMPORARY CREOLE

Clancy's epitomizes the New Orleans tradition of fine neighborhood dining, where white tablecloths meet good ole boys. Thing is, everyone's a good ole boy here—it's been that way for 70 years. It's got the look: tuxedoes on the waiters, linen on the laps, beadboard on the walls. It's got the attitude: It's fun, fine dining, aspirational for some, a weekly ritual for others. It's got a menu full of new Creole classics, superbly done: flash-fried oysters topped with brie; creamy, succulent shrimp and grits; a colossal smoked duck leg that stands on its own with the simplest of sides. When softshell crab is in season, it's de rigueur on every menu in town, but Clancy's is smoked—and it's a wonder. We've had great success with veal here, lighter than usual, with luscious Béarnaise and crabmeat. If we were going all in, we'd order several of the pricey starters—the mussels with Andouille in tomato broth and crawfish vol au vent, to name two. Alas, the ample wine list is short on lower-end options. But once you give in to the kind of splendid evening to be had here, you may choose to give in to all that, too, and commune over conversation and cognac. Make reservations.

6100 Annunciation St. www.clancysneworleans.com. ℰ **504/895-1111.** Main courses $17–$20 lunch, $27–$40 dinner. Mon–Sat 5:30–10:30pm; Thurs–Fri 11:30am–2pm.

Commander's Palace ★★★ CONTEMPORARY CREOLE

The Commander's Palace miracle: If there is a sliding scale of formality, they have an uncanny ability to serve up just the amount your mood requires (and a room to match it). An elegant "event" evening? Got it. Rollicking (civilized) good time? Jaded foodie who wants a wow? They're on it. Marriage proposal in the offing? Just tell them when to serve the ring. They understand that service reigns supreme, and in the ultimate New Orleanian experience—stately needn't be stuffy, formal can still be fun, and sometimes innovation is the best way to honor tradition—they immerse you in it. They're also leaders in mentoring and fostering the city's culinary scene: A who's who of New Orleans restaurant owners, chefs, and front-of-house managers resembles a Commander's family tree. Yet regardless of how many "best of" lists and awards Commander's racks up, they never rest on their laurels.

The continually changing menu reflects 2013 James Beard award–winning "Best Chef" Tory McPhail's commitment to local ingredients and fervent imagination, on best display in the seven-course "Chef's Playground." The a la carte menu mixes its classics—spicy-sweet shrimp and tasso henican (the gateway drug of Commander's Palace dishes); consistently perfect pecan-crusted Gulf fish—with seasonal newbies, like a sublime boudin-stuffed quail with a pepper jelly and sugarcane reduction. The gumbo can be a tad salty; opt for the robust turtle soup instead. For enders, the famed bread pudding soufflé is a puff of gladness with whiskey sauce. The wine list is one of the finest in this or any city, with a good selection offered by the glass in half or full pours. Everyone should dine at Commander's, and everyone can. Its unintimidating finery—plus multicourse lunch and happy-hour deals start under $18 (less than some po' boys, not to mention 25¢ martinis!); $39 at dinner. So worth it. Reserve well in advance.

1403 Washington Ave. www.commanderspalace.com. ⓒ **504/899-8221.** No shorts or T-shirts; jackets preferred for men at dinner. Main courses $28–$45; chef's tasting menu $95 add $56 for wine pairing; 3-course dinner $39–$42. Mon–Fri lunch only 25¢ martinis. Mon–Fri 11:30am–1:30pm; brunch Sat 11am–1pm and Sun 10am–1:30pm; daily 6–10pm (June–Aug from 6:30pm).

Coquette ★★★ BISTRO It's hard to believe that Coquette will turn just 10 this year. It feels like it's occupied this tin-ceilinged, chandeliered, bistro-chic space forever. We mean this in the best way—it's smart and polished, and altogether comfortable in its skin, even if that skin changes daily. We're sure that somewhere in an attic Chef/Owner Michael Stoltzfus has a menu that's aging—because his well of culinary creativity seems to keep Coquette eternally fresh. That, plus dedication to ingredient perfectionism, and top talent heading the bar and pastry programs, lands Coquette firmly in the upper echelon of New Orleans's restaurants and makes it one of our perennial favorites. For it to get any better, they'd have to add another one of the city's best chefs. Wait, that's Kristin Essig, and you'll want to dine here while she is in the house.

Whatever we suggest will be long gone by the time you dine (and what you should really do if possible is spring for the five-course blind tasting menu; on some Tuesdays it's discounted to a ridiculous $45—the single best deal in town). Tuna crudo interspersed with compressed cantaloupe and garnished with herb-dusted popcorn had us chuckling with delight. Chicken-fried sweetbreads on a blueberry puree are a miracle in the mouth; baby eggplant paired with ricotta gnocchi over a chilled peach-tomato sauce wasn't a beautiful sight, but was altogether divine on the palate. If any version of cheesecake is on the menu, make that your choice, unless you're a chocolate lover. Then get the pudding and the delicate strawberry vacherin (for balance). If all this sounds a bit daunting, the $30 three-course lunch menu is more than a po'boy, but a great deal for the quality.

2800 Magazine St. www.coquettenola.com. © **504/265-0421.** Reservations highly recommended. 3-course lunch $30, lunch entrees $11–$18, 5-course blind tasting $70 (wine pairing $35), dinner entrees $18–$34. Fri 11:30am–2:30pm; dinner nightly 5:30–10pm; Sat–Sun brunch 10:30am–2pm.

Gautreau's ★★ CONTEMPORARY SOUTHERN Tucked away in a residential Uptown neighborhood, with no signage to speak of, is a reclusive spot that pretty much every major food magazine has managed to find. It's been lavished with praise, and garnered umpteen awards, and appeared on *Top Chef Masters.* There's a finery to the food that hews close to that of classic French treatments, but steps forward by virtue of modernity, ingredient perfection, and artisanal everything. A dewy foie-gras torchon adds a reduction of stone fruit and huckleberries, with bits of macadamia for crunch. A bright starter marries jicama and watercress with roast pineapple. Moist, seared yellowfin snapper is uncluttered by a snappy salsa verde and richly roasted fennel. The grownup wine list matches the low-ceilinged room, with its trompe l'oeil linen walls and warm lighting. Service is flawless. Reserve in advance.

1728 Soniat St. www.gautreausrestaurant.com. © **504/899-7397.** Appetizers $16–$22; main courses $25–$45. Mon–Sat 6–10pm.

Jacques-Imo's ★★ CREOLE/SOUL FOOD Speaking of food trucks, the gator-painted pickup in front of Jacques-Imo's actually has a table set up in its bed, where some lucky couple can dine (they'll have way more space than in the crowded dining room). This funky, colorful spot with the long line (longer in proportion to who's playing next door at the **Maple Leaf;** p. 200) is hugely popular for all that jacked-up fun, not to mention the giant portions and Creole soul-food stylings. Fortunately, the drinks are well made, and as soon as you're seated you'll be appeased with righteous cornbread muffins. The signature shrimp and alligator-sausage "cheesecake" (more like a quiche) has fans and detractors (we're on board); the diamond-hard crunchy fried chicken and less-complicated Creole specialties fare best: Blackened redfish with a crab-chili hollandaise is a winner, and the lightly batter-fried softshell-crab "Godzilla" worked. The food may ride a bit on the coattails of the rowdy party atmosphere, and you'll feel that you've earned it after the wait.

8324 Oak St. www.jacques-imos.com. © **504/861-0886.** Reservations for 5 or more required; smaller parties are first-come, first-served. Main courses $20–$33. Mon–Thurs 5–10pm; Fri–Sat 5–10:30pm.

La Petite Grocery ★★★ BISTRO Among the many bistros along Magazine Street, this way-Uptown standard-bearer is more traditionally French than some in terms of decor and wine selections. Ambience-wise, there's a comfortably welcoming groove here. Food is a distinctive mélange of Creole creativity, local ingredients, keen, classic technique, and the adroit palate of chef/owner/*Top Chef* contestant Justin Devillier. We believe deeply in the steak tartare (which comes and goes from the menu), and require the blue crab beignets as well as the ricotta dumplings with lobster and fresh peas. The chefs are also soup geniuses here, making preliminary courses a tough choice. For entrees, the smoky shrimp and grits with roasted mushrooms is one of the better treatments we've tried; and the beef tenderloin gets a deep, satisfying sear from the pan roasting. They also deliver a perfect cheeseburger with perfect fries. Save space for dessert, where superstar pastry chef Bronwen Wyatt crushes it. Her floral addition to a simple local strawberry shortcake changed our view of that dessert forever; she exalts a silky cheesecake with cardamom and candied kumquats. The bar can get pretty lively—good or not-so-much depending on your goals for the evening (we start there, munching on sides of fried green beans). The usually on-point service might suffer a tad during peak periods.

4238 Magazine St. www.lapetitegrocery.com. © **504/891-3377.** Main courses $16–$48 lunch and dinner. Tues–Sat 11:30am–2:30pm; Sun 10:30am–2:30pm; Sun–Thurs 5:30–9:30pm; Fri–Sat 5:30–10:30pm.

Lilette ★★★ BISTRO   Lilette's pedigreed chef-owner brings to bear his training in some of New Orleans' finest kitchens and at Michelin-starred restaurants in France, resulting in an artistic, serious approach. The NOLA classic space—high-ceilinged, columned, tiles—is made East Village–ready with tobacco-toned walls. Lunch is thick with business people and ladies who lunch; dinner (which gets dear) sees a staid mixed crowd of tourists, neighbors, and young hipsters, all here for the chef's tasteful, clean lines. Start with the truffled Parmigiano toast with wild mushrooms, marrow, and veal glace (you may end with it, too; it's divine) or the chunky crab claws doused in slightly sweet passion fruit butter, rich yet restrained (if you stop now, you've done well). A roast chicken breast with Brussels sprouts and balsamic-glazed onions is flawless simplicity; gnocchi with intensely unctuous beef cheeks and chanterelles is immorally rich. Desserts are worth the indulgence, notably the curious signature of goat-cheese crème fraîche rounds, paired with vanilla-poached pears sprinkled with pistachios and lavender honey. If you're a wine enthusiast trying to decide between the Uptown bistros, opt for Lilette.

3637 Magazine St. www.liletterestaurant.com. © **504/895-1636.** Main courses $19–$24 lunch, $26–$60 dinner. Tues–Sat 11:30am–2pm; Mon–Thurs 5:30–9:30pm; Fri–Sat 5:30–10:30pm.

Paradigm Gardens ★★★ CONTEMPORARY SOUTHERN   We're including this even though it's seasonal, because we hope you're here when it's open. Working at a portable kitchen surrounding a rustic outdoor oven in the midst of this verdant urban garden (complete with goats—and goat yoga for that matter)—guest chefs prepare a multi-course dinner while local musicians do their thang. Communal picnic tables engender a social scene, aided by wine and spirits (included in the prix fixe, although those in the know BYO supplements). Other nights feature wood-oven cooked pizzas or à la carte items. It's all lovely and funky and friendly and as farm-to-table as it gets.

1131 S. Rampart St. www.paradigmgardensnola.com. ℂ **504/344-9474**. March–May; check websites for dates. $10 entrance fee for à la carte nights. $80 multi-course concert dinners.

Patois ★★★ BISTRO/CONTEMPORARY CREOLE   Can we just cut to the chase and say that this is a near-perfect bistro? The tucked-away restaurant is chic but inviting; the locally sourced ingredients are bright with freshness; service is practiced; and the menu is French meets modern Southern bistro. We sampled an octopus carpaccio made lively with a pepper-and-chorizo citrus vinaigrette, and loved a simple lamb ribs appetizer—just right with a dollop of marinated eggplant and Creole tomato jam. The grilled hanger steak, in a rich red-wine bone-marrow reduction, is deeply flavored, and local dessert favorites are tweaked in amusing, inviting ways—king-cake bread pudding with Creole cream-cheese ice cream (though the pretzel-crust peanut-butter cup gives it a run). All are sweet and worthy. Reserve well in advance during peak periods.

6078 Laurel St. www.patoisnola.com. ℂ **504/895-9441.** Main courses $22–$30 dinner, $12–$21 lunch. Wed–Thurs 5:30–10pm; Fri 11:30am–2pm and 5:30–10:30pm; Sat 5:30–10:30pm; Sun 10:30am–2pm.

Saffron ★★★ INDIAN   Who comes to New Orleans and eats Indian food? Smart people who appreciate stellar, unpretentious service and elevated, sophisticated, delicately seasoned food in a comfortable, elegantly contemporary setting. Share a few sathi, small bowls served with crisp roti flatbread for dipping or spooning: an excellent daal (lentil stew) or saag paneer. And/or the chargrilled oysters, a NOLA staple done here with curry leaf. Standout entrees include the goat masala, subtle and unctuous, and a spice-crusted gulf fish—another perfect melding of the two cuisines. Cocktails mirror the menu, with crafty hints of tamarind or cardamom; beer and wine are thoughtfully paired. If you think Indian desserts are an immaterial afterthought, the ethereal "Curry is My Jam" ginger cake will change your mind.

4128 Magazine St. www.saffronnola.com. ℂ **504/323-2626.** Main courses $18–$32. Tues–Thurs 5–9:30pm; Fri–Sat 5–10:30pm; Sun 11am–2pm.

Upperline ★★★ CONTEMPORARY CREOLE   Genial owner/host JoAnn Clevenger has maintained the hospitable vibe that has been a touchstone at this charming residential spot for a quarter-century—no wonder she was named Outstanding Restaurateur by the James Beard Foundation in 2016. We love the "Taste of New Orleans" dinner: seven traditional local specialties on small plates ($48), crafted here with far more care than most other "samplers" around town. Standout appetizers include fried green tomatoes with shrimp rémoulade sauce (an oft-copied dish that was invented here) and a gumbo as rich as Bill Gates (and many shades darker). For entrees, the moist roast duck with a spry ginger-peach sauce is crispy perfection on a plate (though the plating could be sharpened); a mellow, sautéed drum comes with a shock of spicy shrimp. If you're in town in the summer, the all-garlic menu is great fun. Don't leave without succumbing to the warm honey-pecan bread pudding, touring the art-filled restaurant, and thanking JoAnn (though she'll probably get to you first to do the same). Take the streetcar—it's an easy walk and the combo makes for a stellar evening. Reserve in advance during peak periods.

1413 Upperline St. www.upperline.com. ℰ **504/891-9822.** Reservations suggested. Main courses $22–$34; 3-course prix-fixe menu $40. Wed–Sun 5:30–9:30pm.

Moderate

Boucherie ★★★ CONTEMPORARY SOUTHERN When Boucherie opened, we wrestled with the selfish, tell-or-don't-tell moral dilemma. We told, as did everyone, and last year it moved to a larger location. Spiffed up the menu a wee bit too—the better to detach from its former locale's new life as **Bourrée,** which is crushing it as an amped-up wing, barbecue, and daiquiri shack. The food retains its original sense of playfulness (and prices remain solidly affordable for what chef/owner (and *Chopped* alum) Nathaniel Zimet calls "fine dining for the people." The menu is limited, but most everything has Cajun-inflected, meaty goodness (and dashes of global influences). At dinner, the deeply savory brisket is piled with crispy, Parmesan-sprinkled fries (too good to share; get an extra side); at lunchtime you can rock a po'boy loaf, topped with fresh horseradish sauce, or the sweet pulled-pork cake piled with tangy, acidic purple slaw or slivers of pickled pear. We wouldn't ignore the blackened shrimp and grit cake, either. Super-sweet Krispy Kreme bread pudding is no longer the hilarious curiosity it once was; choose the Thai chili chocolate pie instead (or don't choose—get both).

1506 S. Carrollton Ave. www.boucherie-nola.com. ℰ **504/862-5514.** Dinner small plates $7–$15, large plates $18–$26. Tues–Sat 11am–3pm; Mon–Sat 5:30–9:30pm; Sun 10:30am–2:30pm. **Bourrée:** 1510 S. Carrolton Ave. (www.bourreenola.com; ℰ **504/510-4040;** wings $7–$9; Sun–Thurs 11am–10pm, Fri–Sat 11am–11pm).

Dante's Kitchen ★★ BISTRO/CONTEMPORARY CREOLE Locals give this low-profile spot steady love, understandably given the shrewd use of seasonal and local products, cheerful *This Old House* interior, and obliging staff. The lively New Orleans cuisine comes with little surprises, alternately simple and refined. At dinner, hope that the herb-suffused redfish "on the half shell" is on the menu, or go for crispy confit pork steak with braised greens and an apple compote—just like Mom never made. Despite these pork-focused suggestions, most everything they do with veggies is wondrous; you could make a meal of just them (a pea soup with crab butter and bacon counts). Brunch is a strong alternative. We like their reworked Benedict, in which tender rosemary-crusted pork replaces Canadian bacon, honey sweetens the hollandaise, and a caramelized biscuit supports it all. It's a ways from the FQ, but just 2 blocks off the St. Charles streetcar line where it makes the big turn onto Carrollton Avenue (Hampson stop). Reserve in advance during peak periods (reservations not accepted for brunch).

736 Dante St. www.danteskitchen.com. ℰ **504/861-3121.** Main courses $10–$17 brunch, $23–$27 dinner. Wed–Mon 6–till late, Sat–Sun brunch 10:30am–2pm.

IN-THE-KNOW treasure TROVES: OC HALEY & FRERET

Like a proper Southern belle, lesser-known foodie zones beckon with a "come hither" wink. The up-and-coming **Oretha Castle Haley Blvd.** scene is anchored by the **Southern Food & Beverage Museum** (p. 153), where **Toup's South** dishes Southern porcine goodness (1504 Oretha Castle Haley Blvd.; http://toupssouth.com). At nearby **Roux Carré,** brightly painted, upcycled shipping containers house several good, inexpensive food vendors (2000 OC Haley Blvd.; www.rouxcarre.com). In the expansive **Dryades Public Market,** food stalls, a fresh pasta maker, and oyster and cocktail bars hide under soaring ceilings in a converted school (1307 OC Haley Blvd.; www.dryadespublicmarket. com). Over on **Freret Street,** the food scene is up and came: **Ancora's** excellent wood-fired pizza (4508 Freret St.; www.ancorapizza.com), Wayfare's artisan sandwiches (4510 Freret St.; www.wayfarenola.com), and our beloved **High Hat** (p. 124) get the block party started. **Cuzco** Peruvian (4714 Freret St.; www.facebook.com/Grupo5rest), **Good Bird** rotisserie chicken (5031 Freret St.; www.goodbirdnola.com), and **Piccola Gelateria** (4525 Freret St.; www.piccolagelateria.com) are worthy recent adds to the scene. **Company Burger** (p. 95) and **Dat Dog** (p. 127) started here, and famed **Cure** (p. 207), arguably the city's foremost craft drinking and small-plate locale, started it all.

High Hat ★★★ CONTEMPORARY SOUTHERN   If you make it here (by cab or car), you'll reap the fringe benefit of checking out Freret Street, a booming restaurant street and one of the best post-Katrina success stories. This casual neighborhood spot had nothing to go on but an idea and original tile floors, and what a go they've made of it. It's become one of our no-fail, go-to spots for unfussy lunches and dinners made with obvious care. We come for the always interesting drinks. We come for the graceful oyster fennel soup, and the upgraded Southern comfort foods, like a mound of fork-tender, slow-roast pork with sublime braised greens and addictive mac 'n' cheese. But mostly we come for the plateful of fried awesome that is their catfish: crispy, light, piled high, and accompanied by tangy slaw and housemade tartar sauce (everything here save the Delta tamales is chef-made on-site, even the condiments). Then we get whatever oven-fresh pie is available, and the insane Grills with—a grilled donut topped with melting ice cream—because it would be equally insane to skip it.

4500 Freret St. www.highhatcafe.com. © **504/754-1336.** Everything $20 and under. Daily 11am–9pm.

Pascal's Manale ★★★ ITALIAN/STEAK/SEAFOOD   We adore the old-school neon, and the where-everybody-knows-your-name feel at this century-old neighborhood joint. But more than anything we love the barbecued shrimp—the bowl of colossal, buttery crustaceans that made Manale (mu-*nah*-lee). Make sure you get them (schedule a long workout tomorrow), some turtle soup, and—trust us—classic spaghetti and meatballs, but start the meal at the oyster bar. The bivalves might be frigid (in contrast to their effect, some might say), but if Thomas "Uptown T" is shucking, his repartee is hot. Ask him anything, and your party is officially started. When it's crowded it can be boisterous—Pascal's is the kind of place where neighboring tables spontaneously converse, but unlike at a cozy bistro, it's a welcome intrusion (people eat with their hands and wear bibs, fer Pete's sake).

838 Napoleon Ave. www.pascalsmanale.com. ℂ **504/895-4877.** Main courses $21–$39. Mon–Fri 11:30am–9pm; Sat 5–10pm.

Saba ★★★ ISRAELI/INTERNATIONAL   Soon after Alon Shaya left the eponymous, mega-award-winning restaurant he helped originate (we'll spare you the breakup details), Chef Shaya roared back by opening Saba, just blocks away. The menu and amped-up Israeli recipes resemble those at Shaya: the fresh, modern Middle Eastern flavorings are intact, with a bit more localism woven through. That's evident in the blue crab topping the velvety hummus, and the rich duck broth in the matzo ball soup. The Middle Eastern herbs and spices are as subtle as the textures are supple, and the menu encourages a table full of shared plates—tiny, small, medium, and major. Start with some pretty plates of salatim, like the *ikra* (lox shmear on steroids) or *lutenitsa,* oven-fired peppers, tomatoes, and eggplant pureed and seasoned to pure perfection. At three for $15, order as many plates as your table can fit. That way they'll keep bringing the glorious, steam-puffed pita bread, piping-fresh from the wood oven. The whole harissa-roasted chicken is moist and perfect, and the astute wine list is wisely stocked with a contingent of beautifully complementary rosés. Close with the divine labneh cheesecake, grit notwithstanding, and the carob-fudge cake with black sesame gelato, carob notwithstanding.

5757 Magazine St. https://eatwithsaba.com. ℂ **504/324-7770.** Salatim & small plates $5–$18; family-style dinner main courses $45–$60. Wed–Thurs 11am–10pm; Fri 11am–11pm; Sat 10am–11pm; Sun 10am–10pm.

Inexpensive

Big Fisherman ★★ SEAFOOD   This. Is. The. Stuff. If you really want a true local experience, that means eating a sack of boiled seafood—crawfish, shrimp, crab, whatever's in season. Order shellfish by the pound, and potatoes, half-cobs of corn, heads of boiled garlic, maybe some sausage by the piece. Grab a beer or sweet tea to soothe the spice, plenty of paper towels, and a fistful of newspapers by the door. That's to dump your hot seafood onto, and rip into 'em all primal-like, often done on a patio table in a park, or sitting atop a levee watching the river run (there's no seating here). No reason it can't be done in a hotel room (as long as you're okay with some lingering eau de shellfish). Contrary to logic, go at peak times, even if there's a line. Boiled seafood is best when it's straight out of the pot. They ship or pack for travel, too, so you can have a home boil.

If you're on other ends of town, **Cajun Seafood** ★★ (www.cajunseafood nola.com; 1479 N. Claiborne St.; ℂ **504/948-6000;** daily 10:30am–8:30pm;

You can snag plenty of good eats in the city's nearby suburbs and parishes. These local favorites are well worth the 10- to 30-minute drive.

o **Blue Crab** ★★ For a city that lies between two bodies of water, there's scant waterfront dining. Here's your opportunity. It's seafood, 'natch. Boats tie up. Partying happens (7900 Lakeshore Dr., Metairie; www.thebluecrabnola. com; © 504/284-2898; $12–$24; Tues–Sun 11am–9pm, Fri–Sat 11am–10pm, Sat–Sun 7:30am–11am).

o **Dong Phuong** ★★★ Thanks to its huge Vietnamese population, New Orleans has excellent *banh mi*, *pho*, and other specialties. Head east for the best, as a 2018 James Beard award corroborated (14207 Chef Menteur Hwy., N.O. East; © 504/254-0214; $3–$10; Mon and Wed–Sun 8am–4pm; bakery till 6pm).

o **Middendorf's** ★★★ Classic on-the-water joint that fries up the crispiest, freshest catfish imaginable (30160 Hwy. 51 South, Akers; © 985/386-6666; $12–$23; Wed–Sun 10:30am–9pm).

o **Mosca's** ★★★ Generations of New Orleanians make the drive, wait the wait for killer old-school Italian, and categorically deny allegations that it's an old mob hangout (4137 U.S. Hwy. 90 West, Avondale; www.moscasrestaurant. com; © 504/436-8950; $12–$40; no credit cards; Tues–Sat 5:30–9:30pm).

o **R&O's** ★★ Thoroughly unpretentious old-school neighborhood joint serving po' boys, fried seafood, Italian essentials (216 Hammond Hwy., Metairie; http://r-opizza. com; © 504/831-1248; $9–$23; Mon–Fri 11am–3pm, Wed–Thurs 5–9pm, Fri 5–10pm, Sat 11am–10pm, Sun 11am–9pm).

o **Sal's Seafood** ★★★ Many locals cite the fresh, meaty, spiced-just-right boiled crawfish at this hole-in-the-wall as the best around (1512 Barataria Blvd., Marerro; © 504/341-8112; boiled seafood $3–$9/lb. [market price]; Tues–Sat 9:30am–9:30pm, Sun 9am–noon).

also at 2730 S. Broad St., © **504/821-4722;** daily 10:30am–9pm) provides a similar experience and quality, with table seating and prepared foods, too.

3301 Magazine St. www.bigfishermanseafood.com. © **504/897-9907.** Boiled seafood $3–$12/lb. (market price). Mon–Fri 11am–6pm; Sat 10am–6pm; Sun 10am–5pm.

Camellia Grill ★★ DINER/CASUAL FARE Even though it's only been a part of the city's food culture since 1946, the white-columned Camellia Grill seems to have always been here. We go for luncheonette-style counter service with white linens, Southern hospitality, witty banter dished out by white-jacketed servers, and a classic grill-top burger. The omelets manage to be simultaneously hefty and fluffy and come in the standard varieties (if it's been a rough night, we go with chili cheese; that would be American cheese—the square stuff). Late-night hours make both locations popular after-club spots, but any time is good for the chocolate pecan pie (heated on the grill and a la mode, please). Good prices, true character.

Uptown: 626 S. Carrollton Ave. ☎ **504/309-2679.** All items under $12. Sun–Thurs 8am–midnight; Fri–Sat 8am–2am.

Casamento's ★★★ SEAFOOD   Probably the best "erster" joint in the city, Casamento's takes its oysters so seriously that it simply closes down when they're not in peak season (well, Gulf oysters are always in season nowadays, but everyone needs a vacation). The subway-tiled restaurant has been family-owned since 1919. The oysters are scrubbed clean and well selected; the shucker is a hoot (if you dare him, he'll shoot a bivalve into your mouth from across the room). You should absolutely take the plunge and order the oyster loaf: a whole loaf of bread fried in butter, filled with oysters (or shrimp), and fried again to seal it. Seriously.

4330 Magazine St. www.casamentosrestaurant.com. ☎ **504/895-9761.** Dozen raw oysters $15, main courses $9–$24, market price on some items. No credit cards. Thurs–Sat 11am–2pm and 5:30–9pm, Sun 5–9pm. Closed May 26–Sept 14 and major holidays.

Dat Dog ★ CASUAL FARE   This darling of the gourmet hot-dog boom ought to satisfy any dog-related craving, what with 16 types of franks and sausages (including vegan options) and umpteen toppings. Success depends on your personal selections, and as dog traditionalists we prefer the brats and imported German wieners over the gator, turducken, or crawfish dogs. Still, we admit the duck version with blackberry sauce was darn good, and the fluffy buns held up well. There are burger and chicken-breast sammies too. The bright blue buildings at all three locales make for an easy, fun hang with a brew and your crew (the gallery overlooking Frenchmen St. is a stellar view) and an inexpensive dinner (though it's still a $7–$9 hot dog).

5030 Freret St. www.datdog.com. ☎ **504/899-6883.** All items under $10. Cash only; ATM on-site. Mon–Sat 11am–10pm; Sun 11am–9pm. Also at 3336 Magazine St. ☎ **504/324-2226.** Mon–Thurs 11am–10pm; Fri–Sat 11am–11pm; Sun 11am–9pm. And one more at 601 Frenchmen St. ☎ **504/309-3362.** Sun–Wed 11am–midnight; Thurs 11am–1am; Fri–Sat 11am–3am.

District Donuts. Sliders. Brew ★★ LIGHT FARE/BAKERY   The idea sounds like it emerged from a 4am brainstorm after a very long frat party. At the genius frat. The sliders come in cheeseburger, fried chicken, and tofu every day and three other rotating varieties. Pork belly and oyster show up frequently (which is to your benefit). They're invariably carefully topped with housemade dressings, slaws, or a balancing bit of greenery—like a spicy avo-cado goat-cheese schmear on soft-shell crab. Donuts follow a similar pattern: You can always get a good ol' glazed, chocolate, or cinnamon sugar, and then the donut heavens open. Fresh-fruit-jelly-filled (pomegranate, muscadine, whatever's at the farmer's market), Nutella-drenched, tart lemon ginger, maple bacon Sriracha…Ri.Diculous. Surprisingly, their "Brew" has nothing to do with beer—pardon our misguided frat presumption. It's coffee, pulled from taps, including a super-smooth nitrogen cold-brewed version. Go at off-peak times to avoid lines. The Uptown outpost, **District Hand Pie & Coffee Bar,** offers savories and sweetness tucked into a dainty, buttery half-moon crusty.

2209 Magazine St. http://districtdonuts.com. ℂ **504/570-6945.** Everything under $6. Daily 7am–9pm. **District Hand Pie & Coffee Bar:** 5637 Magazine St. (ℂ **504/313-1316;** daily 7am–4pm).

Domilise Po' Boys ★★ LIGHT FARE   Under "Neighborhood Joint," reference materials list a picture of Domilise's (or could). At the century-old, cluttered, lowdown poor-boy shop tucked away Uptown, your hands-down order is the wet-dry, battered-and-fried-to-order shrimp, piled onto puffy poor-boy loaves by friendly fry-counter ladies. Peak lunchtime can move slowly along (take a number), and tables are scant.

5240 Annunciation St. www.domilisespoboys.com. ℂ **504/899-9126.** $9–$18. Mon–Fri 10am–6:30pm; Sat 10:30am–7pm.

Heard Dat Kitchen ★★ SOUL FOOD   The restaurant seats four people—but the napkins are linen. The neighborhood looks sketchy—but the neighbors are friendly. It makes no matter—the food is worth the trip for those interested in "The Real New Orleans" (you're well out of the tourist zones, into an area where the city's 24% poverty rate is evident). You'll also see some beautiful old homes, a sparkling new community center, and plates presented with the pride of ownership that Jeff Heard imbues in all his soulful, home-cooked dishes. His "Superdome," a dome of mashed potatoes atop a crispy catfish filet, topped with wafer-thin onion rings and surrounded by crab and crawfish creamed corn, is pretty much all you need to eat this week—and so worth it. But get the stuffed bell pepper if it's available.

2520 Felicity St. www.facebook.com/Heard-Dat-Kitchen-671484922957250. ℂ **504/510-4248.** Mon–Sat 11am–7pm.

Joey K's ★ CREOLE/SEAFOOD/DINER   This corner hangout gets locals and a few visitors, who know that the trout Tchoupitoulas—a rocking pan-fried trout topped with grilled veggies and shrimp—is worth a stop if you're out for a shop. Service is beyond friendly, and the menu is a solid mix of local dishes. The daily blackboard specials such as brisket, lamb shank, and white beans with pork chops are tasty, and somehow we often end up around this stretch of Magazine when hunger strikes.

3001 Magazine St. www.joeyksrestaurant.com. ℂ **504/891-0997.** Main courses $10–$21. Mon–Sat 11am–9pm.

Surrey's ★★★ CASUAL FARE   No embellishment needed: just a straightforward, unfancy breakfast and lunch cafe with a straightforward menu and fresh-juice bar, and where most everything is homemade and really good. Corned-beef Andouille hash is outstanding; deeply house-smoked turkey uplifts a no-fuss turkey-avocado sandwich. OMG award goes to the felonious sugar- and rum-drenched French toast stuffed with bananas Foster. The

A snoball's CHANCE

Shaved-ice clone, let us assure you: It's no such thing. These mouthwatering concoctions are made with custom machines that shave the ice so fine that skiers envy the powder. And the flavors—including exotic ones such as wedding cake (almond, mostly), nectar (think cream soda, only much better), and orchid cream vanilla (bright purple that must be seen to be believed)—are absolutely delectable (the better proprietors make their own flavored syrups). Order them with condensed or evaporated milk if you prefer your refreshing drinks on the more decadently creamy side, or go further— some shops have started spiking them with booze. Or double the decadence with a **hot rod**—a snoball stuffed with ice cream. At any time on a hot day, lines can be out the door, and like so many other local specialties, loyalties are fierce. You should stop in at any snoball stand you see, but the following are worth seeking out. Hours vary, so call ahead; most open midday till 7 or 8pm, and many close for winter. Go with a sweet tooth and get plenty of napkins.

The snoballs at **Hansen's Sno-Bliz** ★★★ (4801 Tchoupitoulas St.; www.

snobliz.com; ✆ **504/891-9788**) are a revered city tradition, still served with a smile by third-generation owner Ashley Hansen, who officially took over after her grandparents died in the months following Katrina (and won the 2014 James Beard "American Classic" award). Those grandparents invented the shaved-ice machine in use here and elsewhere, and concocted their own proprietary syrups. Snoballs come in a souvenir cup. Try the bubble-gum-flavored Sno-bliz. **Plum St. Snoballs ★★★** (1300 Burdette St.; www.plumstreetsnoball.com; ✆ **504/866-7996**) has been cooling New Orleanians for more than 70 years, serving favorites in Chinese food containers. Fans of **Pandora's ★★★** (901 S. Carrollton Ave.; ✆ **504/289-0765**) say its ice is the softest anywhere, and the flavor list is so long it's taking over the neighborhood. You'll have to fight the hordes of school kids in line, even, it often seems, during school hours. **Imperial Woodpecker** has the edge on exotic and contemporary flavors, like black sesame, cardamom, and cereal cream (3511 Magazine St.; www.iwsnoballs.com; ✆ **251/366-7777**).

creamy crab melt isn't far behind. No wonder there's always a line of locals at both locations (no reservations).

Lower Magazine: 1418 Magazine St. ✆ **504/524-3827.** Uptown: 4807 Magazine St. ✆ **504/895-5757.** www.surreysnola.com. Daily 8am–3pm. Menu items $7–$13.

Turkey & the Wolf ★★★ CASUAL FARE Prestigious *Bon Appetit* magazine named this Irish Channel hideaway best new restaurant in the country in 2017. *In the country*, people. *For a sandwich shop*. With counter service. Go…taste…understand. The goodness stems from comfort, creativity, a dollop of hilarity, a side of wackiness, and talent. Thick-cut, fried custom-made bologna, kettle chips, and gooey American cheese are stuffed between fat white bread slabs. Even slow-stewed, heat-spiked collard greens make their way into a sandwich, oozing with cheese and Russian dressing. Deviled eggs are topped with chicken-skin *chicarrones* and housemade hot sauce. Then, for those who have (or make) room, homemade vanilla soft serve comes with rainbow sprinkles (okay) or tahini and date molasses (whoa). I mean, you gotta laugh. And you gotta eat. *Bonus:* drinks are equally creative and carefully wrought. *Double-bonus:* adorbs vintage salt & pepper shakers.

739 Jackson Ave. www.turkeyandthewolf.com. ⓒ **504/218-7428**. Sandwiches & casual fare $4–$13. Mon, Wed–Sat 11am–5pm; Sun 11am–3pm.

COFFEE, BAKERIES & DESSERTS

For other sweet treats, see the section on "**Candies, Pralines & Pastries**" in chapter 9, p. 219.

Angelo Brocato Ice Cream & Confectionery ★★★ ICE CREAM/
DESSERT   Though this sweet, genuine ice cream parlor celebrated its 100th birthday under 5 feet of water, it's long since come back—and ostensibly not a thing has changed. The Brocato family (who have run this since 1905) make rich Italian ice cream and ices, cookies, and pastries amid a wonderful throwback atmosphere (anchored by a portrait of Angelo himself, and a stunning, copper and brass espresso machine). Italian flavors like *stracciatella* (chocolate chip) and panna cotta are capital-P Perfect; hard-to-find specialties like spumoni and casatta are spot-on; and the fresh lemon ice is legendary (don't try to decide between that and seasonal fresh fruit ices, blood orange or passion fruit; just get both). After that we get a freshly filled cannoli. Heck yeah, we do. And a slice of the ricotta torta. We tell them it's for a party.

214 N. Carrollton Ave. www.angelobrocatoicecream.com. ⓒ **504/486-1465.** Everything under $10. Tues–Thurs 10am–10pm; Fri–Sat 10am–10:30pm; Sun 10am–9pm; closed Mon.

Café du Monde ★★★ COFFEE/DESSERT   Excuse us while we wax
rhapsodic. Since 1862, iconic Café du Monde has been selling café au lait and beignets (and nothing but) on the edge of Jackson Square. A New Orleans landmark, it's a must-stop for fried goodness and people-watching, 24 hours a day. A beignet (ben-*yay*) is a square French doughnut–type object, steaming-hot and covered in powdered sugar. You might be tempted to shake off some of the sugar. Don't. Trust us. Spoon more on, even (just beware not to inhale as you ingest); at three to an order for under $2.50, they're a hell of a deal. Wash them down with chicory café au lait (good with extra powdered sugar) or really good hot chocolate. Feeling guilty? The fresh orange juice is excellent, too, and presumably has vitamins. *Tip:* Don't wait for a clean table. Just sit—if it's dirty, the surly servers will eventually clear them. *Tip #2:* The takeout line is around the back. But if the line is long, you're better off just waiting for a table. That line moves much faster. *Tip #3:* Or just go to the location in the Outlet Collection at Riverwalk (p. 213).

French Quarter: 800 Decatur St., ⓒ **504/525-4544.** Daily 24 hr. Mon–Thurs 6am–11pm; Fri–Sat 6am–1am. **Outlet Collection:** 500 Port of New Orleans. ⓒ **504/218-7993**. Mon–Sat 8am–9pm, Sun 8am–7pm. All closed Christmas Eve & Day. www.cafedu monde.com. 3 beignets for $2.42. Cash only.

bean FREAKS

Single-source, third-wave, cold-pressed, pour-over-only people might be satisfied at one of these spots. Might. All except purist Spitfire offer some variation on pastries and light savory fare. See also: **Sucré** (p. 132), **District Donuts** (p. 127), **Willa Jean** (p. 115).

- **Addiction** ★★ (Tremé): 1009-1015 N. Claiborne Ave. (http://addictioncoffee.house; ℂ **504-475-9948;** Mon–Sun 7am–7pm).

- **French Truck** ★★★: www.frenchtruckcoffee.com. **French Quarter:** 217 Chartres St. (ℂ **504/605-2899;** Mon–Fri 7am–6pm, Sat–Sun 8am–6pm. **Lower Garden District:** 1200 Magazine St. (ℂ **504/298-1115;** Mon–Fri 7am–6pm, Sat–Sun 8am–6pm). **Uptown:** 4536 Dryades St. (ℂ **504/702-1900;** Mon–Fri 6:30am–6pm; Sat–Sun 7:30am–6pm).

- **Merchant** ★★★ (CBD): 800 Common St. (www.merchantneworleans.com; ℂ **504/571-9580;** Mon–Fri 7am–5:30pm, Sat–Sun 7am–3pm).

- **Revelator** ★★★ (CBD): 637 Tchoupitoulas St. (www.revelatorcoffee.com; daily 7am–6pm).

- **Spitfire** ★★ (French Quarter): 627 St. Peter St. (ℂ **504/384-0655;** daily 8am–8pm).

- **Solo Espresso** ★★★ (Bywater): 1301 Poland Ave. (www.soloespressobar.com; ℂ **504/408-1377;** Mon–Sat 7am–3pm, Sun 8am–1pm).

- **Stumptown** ★★ (CBD): 610 Carondelet St. (www.stumptowncoffee.com/locations/new-orleans; ℂ **855/711-3385;** daily 7am–7pm).

Café EnVie ★ COFFEE/BAKERY/CASUAL FARE   This handsome coffeehouse has locations on both ends of Decatur in the French Quarter. Expect a nice selection of drinks, pastries, bagels, panini—and a full breakfast stuffed into a go-cup. Good for a shot of espresso while waiting for the clubs on Frenchmen to get cranking.

308 Decatur St. (ℂ **504/598-5374**) and 1241 Decatur St. (ℂ **504/524-3689**). www.cafeenvie.com. Everything under $10. Sun–Thurs 7am–midnight; Fri–Sat 7am–1am.

Creole Creamery ★★★ ICE CREAM/DESSERT   Shakes and malts and scoops, oh my! Thick, luscious, truly fabulous ice cream and sorbets with a rotating list of standard and exotic flavors, from lavender-honey and absinthe to red velvet cake and tiramisu. Fortunately they offer a sampler of four or six mini-scoops. Refreshing, maybe even mandatory in summer, and open late enough for a scoop on the way to or from an Uptown club or bar.

4924 Prytania St. (look for the old McKenzie's sign). www.creolecreamery.com. ℂ **504/894-8680.** Everything under $10 except 8-scoop "Eating Challenge" and whole cakes. No credit cards. Sun–Thurs noon–10pm; Fri–Sat noon–11pm.

Croissant D'Or ★★ COFFEE/BAKERY   A quiet and calm place with the same snacks you might find in a cosmopolitan coffeehouse, and you can almost always find an open table inside or in the pretty courtyard. Are the pastries and croissants made of gold? The prices feel like it sometimes, but they are credibly, crustily French. Quiches and light sandwiches as well.

617 Ursulines St. www.croissantdornola.com. © **504/524-4663.** Sandwiches and pastries under $8. Wed–Mon 6am–3pm.

La Boulangerie ★★ BAKERY/CASUAL FARE Crusty baguettes and oven-warm loaves of many varieties; fresh fruit tarts and Danish; house-smoked salmon on house-baked bagels; sandwiches with cured meats from Cochon Butcher (p. 113); and homemade ice cream (on waffle cones baked here)…this French bakery is a neighborhood staple, with good reason. Don't let anyone tell you how good it was under the former owner—just enjoy how good it is now, especially as they add even more lunch options.

4600 Magazine St. (Uptown). https://laboulangerienola.com. © **504/269-3777.** Breads, pastries, sandwiches $3–$11. Mon–Sat 6am–6pm; Sun 7am–4pm.

Morning Call ★★ COFFEE/DESSERT/LIGHT FARE The original French Quarter Morning Call and Café du Monde were beignet rivals back in the 1870s. They still are: at press time, the two were in court battling over this space, a 1913 Spanish Mission-Revival style building in the midst of Mid-City's glorious, oak-filled City Park. You're here for café au lait and beignets, 3 for 2 bucks and change, usually fresh from the fryer and delivered by non-chalant servers. You self-sprinkle powdered sugar atop them to your liking (pro tip: just remove the shaker bottle's lid and have at it). They also have a few Creole standbys, jambalaya and red beans and such, which are awfully handy at 4am or if you're famished from a longer-than-expected museum visit.

3325 Severn Ave., in the Casino Building, City Park (east of the Sculpture Garden). © **504/885-4068.** $2–$10. Cash only. Daily 24 hr. Closed Christmas.

P.J.'s Coffee & Tea Company ★★ COFFEE This local institution has many locations and offers a great variety of teas, coffees, and espressos and roasts its own coffee beans. The iced coffee is made with a 12-hour cold-water process. The granita "slushee" is great on hot, muggy Louisiana days.

5432 Magazine St. www.pjscoffee.com. © **504/355-2202.** Drinks and pastries $1–$6. Daily 6am–9pm (sometimes later on Sat and Sun). About 30 other locations, including Tulane University (© **504/865-5705**); 644 Camp St. (© **504/529-3658**); and 7264 Maple St. (© **504/861-5335**).

Sucré and **Salon** ★★★ DESSERT/CASUAL FARE See the listing for these fabulous confectioners under "Candies, Pralines & Pastries," on p. 219.

3025 Magazine St. www.shopsucre.com. © **504/520-8311.** Sun–Thurs 9am–10pm; Fri–Sat 9am–11pm. 622 Conti St.: © **504-267-7098.** Shop: Sun–Thurs 9am–10pm; Fri–Sat 9am–11pm Salon: Thurs, 10am–9pm; Sun 10am–9pm; Fri–Sat 10am–10pm. All desserts under $10, except full cakes.

EXPLORING NEW ORLEANS

We've made no secret of our favorite New Orleans activities: walking, eating, people-watching, listening to music, dancing, and eating again. But between those activities, there's much to see, do, and experience. New Orleans is a vibrant, visual, utterly authentic city with a rich history and gobs of culture worthy of your time.

While the French Quarter is certainly a seductive place, going to New Orleans and never leaving the Quarter is like visiting Times Square and believing you've seen New York. Stroll the lush Garden District, marvel at the live oaks in City Park, ride the streetcar on St. Charles Avenue and gape at the gorgeous homes, or go visit some gators on a swamp tour. Take a walk along Bayou St. John, tour the remarkable Tremé neighborhood, or ride a bike through the Bywater. We'll guide you to some of the city's amazing museums, diverse neighborhoods, and prettiest parks, with suggestions for action-lovers and armchair adventurers, history buffs, and party animals.

THE FRENCH QUARTER

Those who have been to Disneyland might be forgiven if they experience some déjà vu upon first seeing the French Quarter. The same might be said for those who have visited Paris. It's more worn than Disneyland, of course, and more compact than Paris, on which it was based. But despite the fact that Walt actually did replicate a French Quarter street in Disneyland's New Orleans Square, there ain't nothing like the real thing, baby—and there's certainly no other square mile in the U.S. that resembles the French Quarter. This one turned 300 years old in 2018 and is one of the most visually interesting neighborhoods in America. The endless eyefuls of florid architecture, the copious cultural oddities, and the stories that seem to emanate from the very streets make it easy to look beyond the ubiquitous souvenir shops and bars. We certainly make the occasional foray to Bourbon Street in all its tacky, outlandish glory, and believe it should be experienced (at least once). But the operative word is "occasional," and the key to this city is getting out and fully exploring it.

New Orleans Attractions

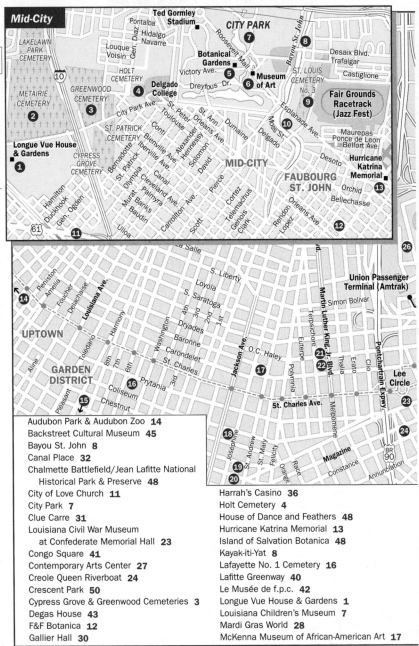

Mid-City

LAKELAWN PARK CEMETERY

Pontalba
Hidalgo
Navarre
Gen. Diaz
Louque
Voisin

Ted Gormley Stadium

CITY PARK ⑦

⑧

Roosevelt Mall

Bayou St. John

Desaix Blvd.
Trafalgar

Castiglione

HOLT CEMETERY

Botanical Gardens ⑤
Victory Ave.

Museum of Art ⑥

ST. LOUIS CEMETERY No. 3

METAIRIE CEMETERY ②

GREENWOOD CEMETERY ③

⑩ Delgado College ④
Dreyfous Dr.

⑨

Fair Grounds Racetrack (Jazz Fest)

City Park Ave.
St. Peter
Orleans Ave.
St. Ann
Dumaine
Esplanade Ave.
Moss St.
Delgado

Maurepas
Ponce de Leon
Belfort Ave.

Longue Vue House & Gardens ①

ST. PATRICK CEMETERY

CYPRESS GROVE CEMETERY

Bernadotte
St. Patrick
Iberville Ave.
Olympia
Cleveland Ave.
Murat
Palmyra
Banks
Baudin

Toulouse
Conti
Bienville Ave.
Iberville Ave.
Canal
Alexander
Hennessy
Solomon
David

Desoto
MID-CITY

FAUBOURG ST. JOHN

Hurricane Katrina Memorial ⑬

Orchid
Bellechasse

Hamilton
Duckhook
Gen. Ogden

Ulloa

Carrollton Ave.
Scott
Pierce
Cortez
Telemachus
Genois
Clark

Orleans Ave.
Rendon
Lopez

⑫

61

⑪

La Salle

⑳

Penston
Amelia
Foucher
Delachaise

Louisiana Ave.

Harmony

S. Liberty
Loyola
S. Saratoga
4th
3rd
2nd
1st

Martin Luther King Jr. Blvd.

Simon Bolivar

Union Passenger Terminal (Amtrak)

⑭

UPTOWN

Aline
Toledano
8th
7th
6th

Washington
Dryades
Baronne
Carondelet
St. Charles

Jackson Ave.

O.C. Haley

Terpsichore
Euterpe
Polymnia

Pontchartrain Expwy.

Clio
Erato
Thalia

Lee Circle

GARDEN DISTRICT

Pleasant
Coliseum
Chestnut

⑯
Prytania
3rd

⑰

St. Charles Ave.

㉑
㉒

Melpomene

㉓

⑮

⑱
Josephine
St. Andrew
St. Mary
Felicity

Magazine
Race
Orange
Constance

BR 90
㉔

Annunciation

⑲
⑳

㉖

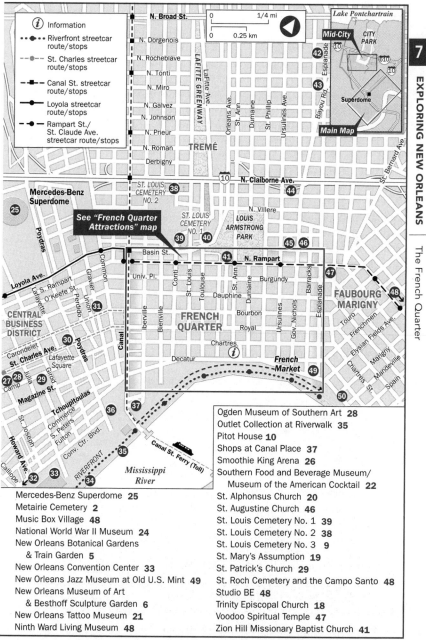

Ogden Museum of Southern Art **28**
Outlet Collection at Riverwalk **35**
Pitot House **10**
Shops at Canal Place **37**
Smoothie King Arena **26**
Southern Food and Beverage Museum/
   Museum of the American Cocktail **22**
St. Alphonsus Church **20**
St. Augustine Church **46**
St. Louis Cemetery No. 1 **39**
St. Louis Cemetery No. 2 **38**
St. Louis Cemetery No. 3 **9**
St. Mary's Assumption **19**
St. Patrick's Church **29**
St. Roch Cemetery and the Campo Santo **48**
Studio BE **48**
Trinity Episcopal Church **18**
Voodoo Spiritual Temple **47**
Zion Hill Missionary Baptist Church **41**

Mercedes-Benz Superdome **25**
Metairie Cemetery **2**
Music Box Village **48**
National World War II Museum **24**
New Orleans Botanical Gardens
   & Train Garden **5**
New Orleans Convention Center **33**
New Orleans Jazz Museum at Old U.S. Mint **49**
New Orleans Museum of Art
   & Besthoff Sculpture Garden **6**
New Orleans Tattoo Museum **21**
Ninth Ward Living Museum **48**

A French engineer named Adrien de Pauger designed the Quarter in 1718. Today it's a great anomaly in America, where many other cities have torn down or gutted their historic centers. Thanks to a strict local preservation policy, the area looks much as it always has and is still the heart of town.

Jackson Square bustles with musicians, artists, fortune-tellers, jugglers, and those peculiar "living statue" performance artists entertaining for change (we try to always carry some $1 bills, so we're prepared to throw something in the hat of those who catch our eye or ear). Pay attention to that seemingly ad-hoc jazz band that plays right in front of the Cabildo—these talented musicians might be in jeans now but may very well be in tie and tux later, playing high-end clubs. **Royal Street,** our favorite street for strolling, is home to stellar street musicians, numerous antiques shops, and galleries, with other interesting stores on **Chartres** and **Decatur streets** and the cross streets between.

The closer you get to **Esplanade Avenue** and toward **Rampart Street,** the more residential the Quarter becomes (in the business sections, the ground floors are commercial and the stories above are often apartments). Peep in through any open gate; surprises await in the form of graceful brick- and flagstone-lined courtyards filled with foliage and bubbling fountains. At the same time, be mindful that throughout the Quarter, you are walking by people's homes. Please be courteous, quiet, and clean, folks.

The Vieux Carré Commission is ever vigilant about balancing contemporary economic interests in the Quarter with historical preservation. There are few chain stores or restaurants, and no traffic lights in the whole interior of the French Quarter (they're relegated to fringe streets); streetlights are the old gaslight style. Large city buses are banned, and during part of each day Royal and Bourbon streets are pedestrian malls. No vehicles are *ever* allowed around Jackson Square. The Quarter streets are laid out in an almost perfect rectangular grid, so they're easily navigable. It's also well-traveled and thus relatively safe. Again, as you get toward the fringes and as night falls, you should exercise caution; stay in the more bustling parts and try not to walk alone.

The French Quarter **walking tour** in chapter 10 will give you the best overview of the historic structures in the area and its history. Many other attractions that aren't in the walking tour are listed in this chapter (and mapped on p. 137), so make sure to cross-reference as you go along.

As mentioned elsewhere, driving in the French Quarter isn't ideal. But if you must, and you're planning a full day of sightseeing in the Quarter, check out our parking tips on p. 266.

Major Attractions

Audubon Aquarium of the Americas ★★★
Penguin evacuees made a star-studded post-Katrina return via a chartered FedEx flight here, waddling home down a (FedEx) purple carpet as news cameras rolled. Then, rescued sea turtles were rehabilitated here after the Gulf oil spill. These instances point up just how topical and relevant this world-class aquarium is, besides being full of cool fishies. Its focus on the Mississippi and Gulf of

French Quarter Attractions

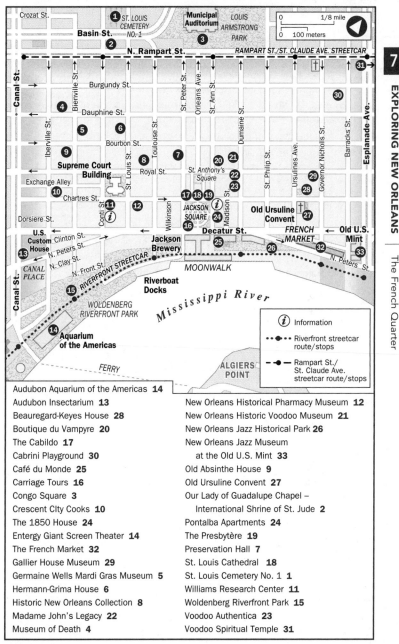

Audubon Aquarium of the Americas **14**
Audubon Insectarium **13**
Beauregard-Keyes House **28**
Boutique du Vampyre **20**
The Cabildo **17**
Cabrini Playground **30**
Café du Monde **25**
Carriage Tours **16**
Congo Square **3**
Crescent City Cooks **10**
The 1850 House **24**
Entergy Giant Screen Theater **14**
The French Market **32**
Gallier House Museum **29**
Germaine Wells Mardi Gras Museum **5**
Hermann-Grima House **6**
Historic New Orleans Collection **8**
Madame John's Legacy **22**
Museum of Death **4**

New Orleans Historical Pharmacy Museum **12**
New Orleans Historic Voodoo Museum **21**
New Orleans Jazz Historical Park **26**
New Orleans Jazz Museum
   at the Old U.S. Mint **33**
Old Absinthe House **9**
Old Ursuline Convent **27**
Our Lady of Guadalupe Chapel –
   International Shrine of St. Jude **2**
Pontalba Apartments **24**
The Presbytère **19**
Preservation Hall **7**
St. Louis Cathedral **18**
St. Louis Cemetery No. 1 **1**
Williams Research Center **11**
Woldenberg Riverfront Park **15**
Voodoo Authentica **23**
Voodoo Spiritual Temple **31**

Mexico is highly entertaining and painlessly educational for kids and grown-ups. There's plenty of interactivity, like the "Geaux Fish!" exhibit that follows fish from the waters to the plate. We love the huge interior rain forest complete with birds and piranhas, and being able to peer below the surface of a swamp. Not to be missed are a fine exhibit on frogs, a rare albino gator, and a manta-ray touch tank. The outdoor splash fountain is irresistible on a warm day. Right on the edge of the Quarter, it's a handy refuge from the heat or rain and part of a complex of Audubon attractions, including the Imax-style **Entergy Giant Screen Theater** next door; the **Insectarium** (see below) a block away; and the **Audubon Zoo** (p. 159) uptown. *Tip:* If you plan to visit more than one, the combination admission package saves up to $30 per person.

1 Canal St., at the river. www.auduboninstitute.org. © **800/774-7394** or 504/861-2537. Aquarium $25 adults, $19 seniors and children 2–12. Entergy Theater $7 adults, $6 seniors and children. Four-attraction combo ticket: $45 adults, $38 seniors, and 35 children 2–12. Aquarium and Entergy Theater daily 10am–5pm. Labor Day–Feb 28 closed Mon. Call for theater showtimes. Closed Mardi Gras, Thanksgiving, and Christmas.

Audubon Insectarium ★★
This fascinating museum is dedicated to all things bug and arachnid, specifically 900,000 species of critters that creep, crawl, and flutter. Located in the old U.S. Customs House, it's the largest free-standing museum in the world dedicated to its multi-legged, winged subjects.

The journey through creepy-crawlies begins in the Prehistoric hallway with 30-inch insect replicas. A gallery that simulates the experience of being underground exposes the tiny world living in our soil. Get up close and personal with the touchable bugs in **Boudreaux's Bait Shop; Bug Appetit Cafe** even serves a few creepy-crawler-based snacks. Finally, the Asian-inspired butterfly gallery, full of fluttering beauty, is a peaceful departure from the hustle outside.

423 Canal St. www.auduboninstitute.org. © **800/774-7394** or 504/861-2537. Admission $23 adults, $20 seniors, and $18 children 2–12. Daily 10am–5pm; Labor Day–Feb 28 closed Mon. Last entry 4pm. Closed Mardi Gras, Thanksgiving, and Christmas.

The French Market ★★
Legend has it that the site of the French Market was originally used by Native Americans as a bartering market. It grew into an official market in 1812. From around 1840 to 1870, it was part of Gallatin Street, a rough area full of bars, drunken sailors, and criminals. Today it's a mixed bag, and not nearly as colorful as its past, but a fun amble. The food-stuffs, from produce and seafood to more tourist-oriented items like hot sauces and Cajun spice mixes, are pricier than at local supermarkets—but here they'll pack it for air travel or ship it home. Snacks like gator on a stick will amuse the kids, while the oyster bar and food vendors will satisfy the grown-ups (**Meals from the Heart** is a standout). Try to come on Wednesday or Saturday when a **farmer's market** and entertainment (music, cooking demos) liven things up and harken back to what it was once like here. The famed **flea**

market section is kind of junky, but sprinkled among the T-shirts, caps, and cheap sunglasses are a few original art vendors (original art here is tax-free). It's convenient for souvenir shopping and New Orleans–related trinkets, especially inexpensive silver jewelry and all manner of fleur-de-lis. If you've outshopped your luggage, you can pick up a duffle bag or small suitcase. There are all-important clean public bathrooms here.

1235 N. Peters St.; starts across from Jackson Square; continues to Barrracks St. www. frenchmarket.org. ✆ **504/522-2621.** Daily 10am–6pm (tends to start shutting down about an hour before closing). Farmer's market: Wed noon–5pm and Sat 10am–2pm.

St. Louis Cathedral ★ The St. Louis Cathedral prides itself on being the oldest continuously active cathedral in the United States. It's not the prettiest, though—the outside is all right, but the rather staid interior wouldn't give even a minor European church a run for its money. Still, history and spirituality seep from within, so it's worth a look—if you're lucky, you may catch a choir practice. Volunteer docents, available most weekdays, are full of fun facts about the windows and murals and how the building nearly collapsed once from water-table sinkage. Note the sloping floor: Clever architectural design somehow keeps the building upright even as it continues to sink. Outside, a statue and plaque mark the visit by Pope John Paul II in 1987.

The cathedral formed the center of the original settlement, and remains the French Quarter's central landmark. This is the third building to stand on this spot. A hurricane destroyed the first in 1722. On Good Friday 1788, its bells were kept silent for religious reasons (or wind, some say) rather than ringing out the alarm for a fire—which eventually burned down the cathedral and 850 other buildings. It was rebuilt in 1794 and remodeled and enlarged between 1845 and 1851. The structure's bricks were taken from the original town cemetery and covered with stucco to protect the mortar from dampness. That issue arose again during Katrina, which caused a leaky roof to ruin the $1-million organ (it's been rebuilt and returned). Outside in back, two magnificent, ancient live oaks fell, narrowly missing a statue of Jesus. His thumbs were amputated, however, and Archbishop Hughes, in his first post-Katrina sermon in the cathedral, vowed not to replace them until all of New Orleans is healed. The dramatically lit statue makes a resplendent, if somewhat eerie, nighttime silhouette. Well, we think so; others call it "Touchdown Jesus"—do make a point to walk by at night to see why.

615 Pere Antoine Alley. www.stlouiscathedral.org. ✆ **504/525-9585.** Free admission. Self-guided-tour brochure available ($1 donation); formal tours by advance reservation. Open 8:30am–4pm daily; Mass Mon–Fri at 12:05pm; Sun at 9am and 11am.

Historic Buildings

Beauregard-Keyes House ★ This "raised cottage," with its Doric columns and handsome twin staircases, was built as a residence by a wealthy New Orleans auctioneer, Joseph LeCarpentier, in 1826. Confederate General P. G. T. Beauregard (of the recently deposed monument, p. 148) lived here between 1865 and 1867. From 1944 until 1970 it was the residence of Frances

Parkinson Keyes (pronounced *Kize*), who wrote many novels about the region. Her most famous, *Dinner at Antoine's,* was written here, as was *Madame Castel's Lodger,* concerning General Beauregard's stay in this house. Mrs. Keyes left her home to a foundation. The house, gardens, and her collections of dolls and porcelain veilleuse teapots are open to the public.

7 1113 Chartres St., at Ursuline St. www.bkhouse.org. © **504/523-7257.** Admission $10 adults; $9 seniors, students, and AAA members; $4 children 6–12; free for active military and children 5 and under. Mon–Sat 10am–3pm. Tours on the hour. Closed holidays.

The 1850 House ★★

James Gallier, Sr., and his son designed the historic Pontalba Buildings for the Baroness Micaela Almonester de Pontalba, who had them built in 1849 in an effort to combat the deterioration of the older part of the city (see box on p. 143). The rows of townhouses on either side of Jackson Square were the largest private buildings in the country at the time. Legend has it that the baroness, miffed that her friend Andrew Jackson wouldn't tip his hat to her, had his statue erected in the square, where to this day he continues to doff his chapeau toward her top-floor apartment. It's probably not true, but we never stand in the way of a good story.

This **Louisiana State Museum** presents a demonstration of life in 1850, when the buildings opened for residential use. The self-guided tour uses a fact-filled sheet explaining the history of the interior. Period furnishings vividly illustrate the difference between the upstairs portion of the house, where the upper-middle-class family lived in comfort (and the children, largely confined to a nursery, were raised by servants), and the downstairs, where the staff toiled in considerable drudgery to make their bosses comfortable. It's a surprisingly enjoyable look at life in the good, or not so good, old days.

Lower Pontalba Bldg., 523 St. Ann St., Jackson Sq. www.louisianastatemuseum.org. © **800/568-6968** or 504/524-9118. Admission $3 adults; $2 students, seniors, and active military; free for children 12 and under. Tues–Sun 10am–4:30pm (free museum tour if you take the **Friends of the Cabildo** French Quarter walking tour, p. 227, which starts here). Closed Mon and all state holidays.

Old Absinthe House ★

The Old Absinthe House was built in 1806 and now houses a bar and restaurant. The drink for which the building and bar were named was once outlawed in this country (certain chemical additives, not the actual wormwood used to flavor the drink, caused blindness and madness). Now you can legally sip the infamous libation in the bar and feel at one with the famous types who came before you, listed on a plaque outside: William Thackeray, Oscar Wilde, Sarah Bernhardt, Walt Whitman, Andrew Jackson—and the Lafitte brothers, who plotted their desperate defense of New Orleans here in the War of 1812.

The house was a speakeasy during Prohibition, and when federal officers closed it in 1924, the interior was mysteriously stripped of its antique fixtures—including the long marble-topped bar and the old water dripper that was used to infuse water into the absinthe. Just as mysteriously, they reappeared in another bar down the street, and then once again returned to one of the restaurants on this site. The bar is now covered with business cards (and drunks), so don't come looking to recapture some kind of old-timey classy atmosphere. But it's still a genuinely fun, historic hangout.

240 Bourbon St., btw. Iberville and Bienville sts. www.ruebourbon.com/oldabsinthe house. ✆ **504/523-3181.** Free admission. Daily 9am–3am.

Old Ursuline Convent ★★ Forget tales of America being founded by brawny, brave, tough guys in buckskin and beards. The real pioneers—at least, in Louisiana—were well-educated Frenchwomen clad in 40 pounds of black wool robes. That's right; you don't know tough until you know the Ursuline nuns, and this city would have been a very different place without them.

The Sisters of Ursula came to the mudhole that was New Orleans in 1727 after a journey that nearly saw them lost at sea or succumbing to pirates or disease. Here, they provided the first decent medical care (saving countless lives) and later founded the first local school and orphanage for girls. They also helped raise girls shipped over from France as marriage material for local men, teaching them everything from languages to homemaking of the most exacting sort (laying the foundation of many local families).

The convent dates from 1752 (the sisters themselves moved uptown in 1824, where they remain to this day), and it is the oldest building in the Mississippi River Valley and the only surviving building from the French colonial period in the United States. It also houses Catholic archives dating back to 1718.

The **self-guided tour** of the convent shows rooms typical of the era, as well as religious and artistic icons (the top floor, where a ghost supposedly lives, is off-limits, unfortunately). It includes access to St. Mary's Church, original site of the Ursuline convent and a former archbishop's residence. The whole convent can be viewed in an hour or less.

1100 Chartres St., at Ursuline St. www.oldursulineconventmuseum.com. ✆ **504/529-3040.** Admission $8 general admission, $7 seniors, $6 students. Mon–Fri 10am–4pm; Sat 9am–3pm (last admission 15 minutes before close).

Our Lady of Guadalupe Chapel—International Shrine of St. Jude ★ This "funeral chapel" was erected in 1826 conveniently near St. Louis Cemetery No. 1, specifically for funeral services, so as not to spread disease through the Quarter. We like it for three reasons: the catacomb-like devotional chapel with plaques thanking the Virgin Mary for favors granted; the gift shop full of religious medals including a number of obscure saints; and the statue of St. Expedite. The saint got his name, according to legend, when his crate arrived with no identification other than the word EXPEDITE stamped on the outside. Now he's the "saint" you pray to when you want things in a hurry (we are not making this up).

411 N. Rampart St. at Conti St. www.judeshrine.com. ✆ **504/525-1551.** Gift shop Mon–Sat 9am–5pm; Sun 7am–6pm. Masses Mon–Sat starting at 7am, Sun from 7:30am.

Museums

In addition to the destinations listed here, you might be interested in the **Germaine Wells Mardi Gras Museum** at 813 Bienville St., on the second floor of **Arnaud's** restaurant (p. 84; www.arnaudsrestaurant.com/about/mardi-gras-museum; ✆ **504/523-5433**). It has a collection of Mardi Gras costumes and ball gowns dating from 1910 through 1960. Admission is free, and the museum is open daily during restaurant hours.

The Cabildo ★★ One of two fine museums flanking St. Louis Cathedral in the heart of the French Quarter, the Cabildo houses the premier collection of New Orleans and Louisiana historical artifacts. It starts with the earliest explorers and covers slavery, post–Civil War reconstruction, and statehood. It is well qualified to do so: The Cabildo is the site of the signing of the Louisiana Purchase transfer (this 1795 building was the seat of government at the time; at other times it served as a courthouse and a prison). The detailed history is covered from a multicultural perspective and touches on topics like antebellum music, mourning and burial customs (a big deal during the yellow fever epidemics), immigration and assimilation, and the role of the Southern woman. Portraits of historical figures and incidents are hung throughout, and the **Napoleon Room** (opening May 2016) houses the crown jewel: Napoleon's death mask. The item and its story (it almost ended up in a trash dump) are quite fascinating. It's a dense but terrific museum.

701 Chartres St. www.louisianastatemuseum.org ✆ **800/568-6968** or 504/568-6968. Admission $12 adults; $10 students, seniors, and military; free for children 6 and under. Discounts for visiting multiple Louisiana State museums. Tues–Sun 10am–4:30pm; closed Mon and state holidays.

Gallier House Museum ★★ James Gallier, Jr. (it's pronounced *Gaul-ee-er*, by the way—he was Irish, not French), and his father were the leading architects in New Orleans in the mid-1800s. They designed the French Opera House, Municipality Hall (now Gallier Hall), and the Pontalba Buildings. This was Junior's personal home. It's meticulously restored, with the fancy furnishings appearing much as they would have when the family resided there (some claim Gallier's ghost still does). The home displays some of his innovations—such as early indoor plumbing—and a decided lack thereof in the slave quarters. It's made even more gorgeous for holiday season, with period decor; check the website for other special programs. ***Fun fact for Anne Rice fans:*** This house was her model for Louis and Lestat's New Orleans residence in *Interview with the Vampire.* Discounted combination tickets with the Hermann-Grima House are available.

1118 and 1132 Royal St., btw. Gov. Nicholls and Ursuline sts. www.hgghh.org. ✆ **504/525-5661.** Admission $15 adults; $12 seniors, students, children. Guided tours Mon, Tues, Thurs, Fri at 10 & 11am, 12, 1, and 2pm; Sat noon, 1, 2, and 3pm. Fewer tours in summer; call to confirm. Usually closed 1–2 weeks in Aug and during Mardi Gras.

lady bountiful: **BARONESS DE PONTALBA**

New Orleans owes a great debt to Baroness Micaela Almonester de Pontalba and her family. Without them, Jackson Square might still be a soggy mess. Her father, Don Almonester, used his money and influence to have St. Louis Cathedral, Cabildo, and Presbytère built. The baroness was responsible for the two long brick apartment buildings that flank Jackson Square and for the renovation that turned the center of the Quarter into what it is today.

Born in 1795 into the most influential family in New Orleans, the baroness married her cousin, who subsequently stole her inheritance. When she wanted a separation, at a time when such things were unheard of, her father-in-law shot her several times and then shot himself. She survived, though some of her fingers did not (nor did he). In subsequent portraits, she would hide the wounded hand in her dress. In the end, she got her money back—she used it for those French Quarter improvements—and also ended up caring for her slightly mad husband for the rest of his life. She died in Paris in 1874; her home there is now the American ambassador's residence. The book *Intimate Enemies,* by Christina Vella (Louisiana State University Press, 1997), details this remarkable woman's life.

Hermann-Grima House ★★ This symmetrical Federal-style building (perhaps the first in the Quarter) is very different from its French-style neighbors. The house, which stretches from St. Louis Street to Conti Street, passed through two different families before becoming a boardinghouse in the 1920s. It has been meticulously restored and researched, and a tour of the house is one of the city's more historically accurate offerings. The knowledgeable docents make this a satisfactory stop at any time, but keep an eye out for the occasional special tours. At Halloween the house is draped in typical 1800s mourning cloth, as docents explain mourning customs. On most Thursdays from October through May, cooking demonstrations take place in the authentic 1830s kitchen, using methods of the era. The house also contains one of the Quarter's last surviving stables, complete with stalls. Discounted combination tickets with the Gallier House are available.

820 St. Louis St. www.hgghh.org. © **504/525-5661.** Admission $15.45 adults; $12.36 seniors, students, and children 8–18; free children 7 and under. Guided tours Mon, Tues, Thurs, Fri at 10 & 11am, 12, 1, and 2pm; Sat noon, 1, 2, and 3pm. Fewer tours in summer; call to confirm. Usually closed 1–2 weeks in Aug.

Historic New Orleans Collection—Museum/Research Center ★★ This complex of historic buildings in the middle of the French Quarter is secreted away with little fanfare. But it's a true treasure and an excellent look at what once was. The main galleries at the recently expanded Royal Street campus are chock full of wonderful artworks, maps, and historic documents. There are docent tours of the galleries, the multiple buildings in this compound (one a rare survivor of the great fire of 1794), and the elegant former residence of General and Mrs. Williams. It's all of great relevance to anyone interested in architecture or local history—each building has a centuries-old tale to tell. Around the corner, the **Williams Research Center,** 410 Chartres St. (© **504/598-7171**), is a grandly restored, Beaux-Arts-style building also belonging to the complex. It serves as a research center for academics and the public. If you're curious about anything regarding New Orleans or Louisiana history, the answer is probably here.

533 Royal St., btw. St. Louis and Toulouse sts. www.thnoc.org. © **504/523-4662.** Free admission; guided tours $5. Tues–Sat 9:30am–4:30pm; Sun 10:30am–4:30pm. Tours Tues–Sat 10am, 11am, 2pm, and 3pm; Sun 11am, 2pm, and 3pm. Closed major holidays and Mardi Gras.

Madame John's Legacy ★ This is the second-oldest building (well, parts of it) in the Mississippi Valley, after the Ursuline Convent, and a rare example of Creole architecture that miraculously survived the 1794 fire. Built around 1788 on the foundations of an earlier home that was destroyed in the fire of *that* year, the house has had a number of owners and renters (including the son of Governor Claiborne), none of them named John—or even Madame! It acquired its moniker courtesy of author George Washington Cable, who used the house as a setting for his short story *'Tite Poulette.* The protagonist was a quadroon, Madame John, named after the lover who willed this house to her. It's of interest mostly for its unusual exterior architecture, but the occasional art exhibit makes a peek inside worth the (free) price.

632 Dumaine St. www.louisianastatemuseum.org. © **800/568-6968** or 504/568-6968. Free admission. Tues–Sun 10am–4:30pm. Closed Mon and state holidays.

Museum of Death ★ If you find vampire tours positively banal and need more death in your death, here's all the gore you could ask for. It's graphic, no-holds-barred gruesome, for the thick-skinned only (there are rocking chairs in the lobby for companions who opt out; those going through the collection are advised to "sit on one of the coffins if you feel faint"). It's an outpost of a similar museum in Hollywood, one man's lurid collection of crime, accident, and autopsy photos (gunshot victims, dismemberments); serial killers' correspondence, diaries, and doodles (John Wayne Gacy's clown drawings; love letters to Jeffrey Dahmer); videos of a cannibal discussing his act; and much more. Perhaps the most thought-provoking item is the rare Thanotron, Dr. Kervorkian's suicide machine. Not judging, just…sitting on a coffin. Pick up a serial-killer "tarot card" T-shirt on the way out.

227 Dauphine St. www.museumofdeath.net/nola. © **504/593-3968.** $15. Daily 10am–6pm.

New Orleans Historical Pharmacy Museum ★★ Leeches. LEEEEECHES. Yeah, they're here. So are many other icky things, and fascinating potions, and instruments-of-torture-looking artifacts (antique surgical devices, in actuality). The first licensed pharmacist in the United States, Louis J. Dufilho, Jr., opened an apothecary shop in this Creole-style townhouse in 1823. This bizarre and beguiling museum opened in 1950 and displays old apothecary bottles, Voodoo potions, opium products of every ilk, suppository molds, and all variant of snake oil—in exquisite wood and glass cases. Also interesting are old makeup and perfume paraphernalia, which were brewed up by pharmacists back in the day. You'll never appreciate a modern doctor's appointment more. Go for the insightful, sometimes shocking guided tour.

514 Chartres St., at St. Louis St. www.pharmacymuseum.org. ℭ **504/565-8027.** Admission $5 adults, $4 students and seniors, children 5 and under free. Tues–Sat 10am–4pm. Guided tours Tues–Fri 1pm. Closes early for private events some Sat; call ahead.

New Orleans Historic Voodoo Museum ★
This small museum is packed with dusty displays of Voodoo objects from around the world and right here in New Orleans, including some that allegedly belonged to the legendary Voodoo queen, Marie Laveau. While serious practitioners might scoff at the tourist orientation of this place, it offers a good introduction to the truth behind the myths of this much-maligned practice. You'll get the most out of your visit if you engage with whoever is manning the front desk, someone usually involved in Voodoo, and invariably happy to discuss it with those with a sincere interest. They can even arrange a reading or custom gris-gris bag for you or hook you up with herbs or Voodoo dolls. Why not? (Don't confuse this place with the Marie Laveau House of Voodoo on Bourbon Street.)

724 Dumaine St., at Bourbon St. www.voodoomuseum.com. ℭ **504/680-0128.** Admission $7 adults; $5.50 students, seniors, military; $4.50 high-school students; $3.50 children 11 and under; mention website offer for discount. Daily 10am–6pm.

The Presbytère ★★★
The Presbytère, which flanks St. Louis Cathedral to the right, was originally built to house the clergy serving in the cathedral. That never came to pass, and the clergy's loss is our gain. It's now a museum with two excellent permanent exhibits. Upstairs, the Mardi Gras exhibit walks visitors through the holiday's history—which is so much more (and so much more interesting) than cwazy kids doing cwazy kid stuff. It shows ornate Mardi Gras Indian costumes and antique Mardi Gras Queen jewels, and there's even a replica float so you can toss mock beads at mock crowds. (To see the real thing, visit Blaine Kern's **Mardi Gras World;** p. 150.) On the first floor, the multimedia exhibit "Living with Hurricanes: Katrina and Beyond" is an in-depth look at the human drama of hurricanes. First-person audio, video, and interactive displays create an educational but wholly accessible experience, and an emotionally evocative one at that (but with enough optimism, humor, and science to keep it from being too downcast). One man's "IN CASE OF EMERGENCY" memo hangs on a wall: his jeans, scrawled with his name, blood type, and next of kin. A reproduction of a small attic with a rough hole chopped through its ceiling—and the very axe one woman used to commit a similar act—accompany her voiceover describing the incident. It's powerful stuff.

751 Chartres St., Jackson Sq. www.louisianastatemuseum.org. ℭ **800/568-6968** or 504/568-6968. Admission $6 adults; $5 seniors and students; free for children 12 and under. Discounts if visiting multiple Louisiana State museums. Tues–Sun 10am–4:30pm. Closed Mon and state holidays.

Woldenberg Riverfront Park ★★   This 20-acre park along the river serves as promenade and public art gallery, with numerous works by popular local and internationally known artists amid green lawns and hundreds of trees. Seek out the kinetic Holocaust memorial sculpture by noted Israeli sculptor Yaacov Agam, and make a slow circle around it to get the full impact of its changing perspectives, which use a rainbow to unexpected symbolic effect. At the upriver end, you're rewarded with a splash fountain for a soggy cool-down. An excellent incentive to get kids to take a scenic walk.

It connects to the nearby **Moonwalk** ★★★, a paved pedestrian thorough-fare along the river, a wonderful walk on a pretty New Orleans day but really a must-do for any weather other than pouring rain. Newly renovated steps allow you to get right down to Old Muddy—on foggy nights, you feel as if you are floating above the water. There are many benches from which to view the city's busy port—perhaps while enjoying sugar-dusted beignets to a street musician's song, or watching the moon rise over the river. To your right is the Greater New Orleans Bridge and the World Trade Center of New Orleans skyscraper as well as the Toulouse Street wharf, the departure point for excursion steamboats. All of the French Quarter's riverfront walkways and greenways will soon be renovated and connected in a contiguous path, meeting up with **Crescent Park** where the Quarter borders the Faubourg Marigny.

Along the Mississippi from the Moonwalk at the old Governor Nicholls St. wharf to the Aquarium of the Americas at Canal St. ℂ **504/861-2537.** Daily dawn–dusk.

OUTSIDE THE FRENCH QUARTER

Visiting Uptown, the Garden District & Bayou St. John

If you can see just one thing outside the French Quarter, make it the Garden District. These two neighborhoods are the first places that come to mind when one hears the words "New Orleans." The Garden District has no significant historic buildings or important museums—it's simply beautiful—enough for authors as diverse as Truman Capote and Anne Rice to become enchanted by its spell. Gorgeous homes stand quietly amid lush foliage, elegant but ever so slightly (or more) decayed. You can see why this is the setting for so many novels; it's hard to imagine that anything real actually happens here.

But it does. Like the Quarter, this is a residential neighborhood, so please be courteous as you wander about. To see the sights, you need only mosey around and admire the exteriors and gardens of beautiful houses. We've mapped out a comprehensive **walking tour** (p. 227) to help guide you to the Garden District's treasures and explain a little of its history. Naturally it starts with a ride on the St. Charles streetcar. You might also check out the listings starting on p. 214 to find the best shops, galleries, and bookstores on **Magazine Street,** the eclectic shopping strip that bounds the Garden District.

Meanwhile, a little background: Across Canal Street from the Quarter, "American" New Orleans begins. After the Louisiana Purchase of 1803, an essentially French-Creole city came under the auspices of a government determined to develop it as an American city. Tensions between Creole society and the encroaching American newcomers began to increase. Some historians lay this tension at the feet of Creole snobbery; others blame the naive and uncultured Americans. In any case, Creole society succeeded in maintaining a relatively distinct social world, deflecting American settlement upriver of Canal Street (Uptown). The Americans in turn came to outpace the population with sheer numbers of immigrants. Newcomers bought up land in what had been the old Gravier Plantation (now the Uptown area) and began to build a parallel city. Very soon, Americans came to dominate the local business scene, centered along Canal Street. In 1833, the American enclave now known as the Garden District was incorporated as Lafayette City, and—thanks in large part to the New Orleans–Carrollton Railroad, which ran the route of today's St. Charles Avenue streetcar—the Americans kept right on expanding until they reached the tiny "resort town" of Carrollton, a few miles away. It wasn't until 1852 that the various sections came together officially as a united New Orleans.

Bayou St. John, Esplanade & Lake Pontchartrain ★★★ Bayou St. John is one of the key reasons New Orleans exists. This body of water originally extended from the outskirts of New Orleans to Lake Pontchartrain. Jean-Baptiste Le Moyne, Sieur de Bienville, was commissioned to establish a settlement in Louisiana that would both make money and protect French holdings in the New World from British expansion. Bienville chose the spot where New Orleans now sits because he recognized the strategic importance of the Bayou St. John's "back-door" access to Lake Pontchartrain, and ultimately to the Gulf of Mexico. Boats could enter the lake from the Gulf, then follow the Bayou to its end. From there, they were within easy portage distance of the mouth of the Mississippi River. Native Americans had used this route for years.

The early path from the city to the bayou is today's Bayou Road, an extension of Governor Nicholls Street in the French Quarter. Modern-day Gentilly Boulevard, which crosses the bayou, was another Native American trail—it led around the lake and on to settlements as far as Florida.

As New Orleans grew and prospered, the bayou became a suburb as planters moved outward along its shores. In the early 1800s, a canal was dug to connect the waterway with the city, reaching a basin at the edge of Congo Square (which begat today's Basin Street). The Bayou became a popular recreation area, lined with fine restaurants and dance halls (and meeting places for Voodoo practitioners, who held secret ceremonies along its shores). Gradually, New Orleans reached beyond the French Quarter and enveloped the whole area—overtaking farmland, plantation homes, and resorts.

The canal was filled in long ago, and the bayou is a meek re-creation of itself (though reopening nearby floodgates, allowing more natural ebb and flow from Lake Pontchartrain, should bring its ecosystem closer to its thriving original state). It is no longer navigable (even if it were, bridges were built too low to permit the passage of watercraft other than kayaks), but residents still prize their waterfront sites, and kayaks, rowboats and paddleboards make use of the bayou's smooth surface. This is one of the prettiest areas of New Orleans—full of the old houses tourists love to marvel at without the hustle, bustle, and confusion of more high-profile locations. A stroll along the banks and through the nearby neighborhoods is one of our favorite things to do on a nice afternoon.

GETTING THERE   The simplest way to reach St. John's Bayou from the French Quarter is to drive or ride straight up Esplanade Avenue about 20 blocks (or grab the bus that says ESPLANADE at any of the bus stops along the avenue). Right before you reach the Bayou, you'll pass **St. Louis Cemetery No. 3** (just past Leda St.). It's the final resting place of many prominent New Orleanians, among them Father Adrien Rouquette, who lived and worked among the Choctaw; Storyville photographer E. J. Bellocq; and Thomy Lafon, the black philanthropist who bought the old Orleans Ballroom as an orphanage for African-American children and put an end to its infamous "quadroon balls" (p. 230). Walking just past the cemetery, turn left onto Moss Street, which runs along the banks of St. John's Bayou. To see an example of an 18th-century West Indies–style plantation house, jog left at Moss Street and stop at the **Pitot House,** 1440 Moss St. (p. 158).

Esplanade leads into **City Park** (p. 160) at Wisner Boulevard—you'll see an equestrian statue in the center of the traffic circle just outside City Park's grand entrance—that block of marble is where a sculpture of Gen. P.G.T. Beauregard stood until its recent removal, one of four monuments to the Confederacy that were de-perched. Turn left on Wisner for about 3 miles as it hugs the border of City Park. It'll jog right into Beauregard Street; then turn right on Cloverleaf and look for water—and Lakeshore Drive. Turn left. You've reached Lake Pontchartrain, which you've probably figured out. Meander along Lakeshore Drive for a couple of miles until you reach a marina (the road will curve and become West End Blvd.). It's hard to believe that this area (called **Lakeshore**), home to commercial fishing since the late 1800s, was totally devastated by the 17th Street Canal breech. The storm piled boats atop each other, smashed buildings into rubble, and destroyed a lighthouse. Now, there's a thriving restaurant hub and shopping along Harrison Avenue, and the nearby **Lakeview** residential neighborhood boasts some of the highest property values around. That canal is just ahead of you, as is the fishing-oriented **Bucktown** neighborhood. But this is probably a good spot to turn back—or hit up **Deanie's** (www.deanies.com) for old-school seafood just like a local.

Lake Pontchartrain, technically an estuary connected to the Gulf of Mexico, is some 40 miles long and 25 miles wide, and is bisected by the 24-mile **Greater New Orleans Causeway,** the world's longest over-water bridge.

Museums & Galleries

Backstreet Cultural Museum ★★★ This small cultural gem in the heart of the Faubourg Tremé is dedicated to certain wholly unique New Orleans cultural traditions, mostly of the African-American community. The social aid and pleasure clubs, the second-line parades, brass bands, Mardi Gras Indians, and jazz funerals are all well documented and recollected here. We guarantee that the Mardi Gras Indians' ornate beaded costumes are like nothing you've ever seen, and best appreciated up close. But the suits are just an entree into the intriguing traditions. Founder Sylvester Francis is often in the house (this scrupulous collection is largely his own). He's a fount of knowledge and a true New Orleanian, so spend a few minutes with him if you can, and say thanks.

1116 Henriette Delille St. www.backstreetmuseum.org. ✆ **504/657-6700** or 504/606-4809. Admission $10. Tues–Sat 10am–4pm.

Contemporary Arts Center ★★ The CAC's three stories of airy galleries anchor the city's thriving arts district. The center shows influential work by regional, national, and international artists in various mediums, and often presents theater, performance art, dance, or music concerts. It's worth a walk-by to check out whatever provocative, large-scale installation is showing in the street-level windows—and often worth checking out in deeper detail.

900 Camp St. www.cacno.org. ✆ **504/528-3805.** Gallery admission $10 adults; $8 seniors and college students; free for K–12 students. Performances may be additional. Wed–Mon 11am–5pm.

Le Musee de fpc ★ Louisiana's history of slavery is well-known. In this elegant 1859 Greek Revival house, the lesser-known chronicle of the **free people of color (fpc)** is told through a one-of-a-kind personal collection of artworks and documents. These educated, sophisticated, and industrious men and women of French, African, and Caribbean origin populated New Orleans since the early 1700s, and their cultural and commercial impact on the city was massive. Exhibited works range from gallant formal portraits of finely attired men and women to copies of the Dred Scott decision and Civil War–era activist newspapers. The **McKenna Museum of African American Art,** a sister museum in Central City, also houses a terrific collection (www.themckennamuseum.com; ✆ **504/323-5074;** by appt. only).

2336 Esplanade Ave. www.lemuseedefpc.com. ✆ **504/323-5074.** Admission $15; $12 students. Tours on the hour Tues–Fri 1–4pm; Sat 10am–2pm; Sun 1–4pm. Call ahead; museum sometimes closes for private events.

Louisiana's Civil War Museum at Confederate Memorial Hall ★★ Here is the Confederate flag, that hot-button epicenter of controversy, displayed with no glamour or judgment: It's a history museum, after all, and a good one if you're interested in the Civil War. Or architecture: The unusual, circa-1891 pressed-brick Romanesque building is a stunner inside and out. Among thousands of relics (the second-largest collection in the U.S.) are weapons, uniforms, portraits, and the personal effects of Jefferson Davis and Robert E. Lee. Of note: an elegant piano, saved from a fine Mississippi home pre-razing, that was carried into a trench mid-battle (for safekeeping!), where it was protected—and played—as cannonballs flew. Also: a great seal of the (short-lived) Confederate States of America, circa 1862; and an Alabama Legion battle flag with 83 painstakingly mended bullet holes.

929 Camp St., at St. Joseph's. www.confederatemuseum.com. ⓒ **504/523-4522.** Admission $10 adults; $5 children 7–14; free for children 6 and under. Tues–Sat 10am–4pm.

Mardi Gras World ★★   The Kerns are the first family of float-making, and this is their headquarters. The Kerns design and build some 75% of the floats used by the Mardi Gras krewes during Carnival Season, so you'll see floats from previous years and those in the works for the next season. Sketches, sculptures (and sculptors at work), engineers' drawings, and king cake and coffee are all included on the tour—plus you can try on some of the elaborate, sparkling costumes that float riders wear. It's pretty nifty to see the handiwork up close, and if you can't come for Mardi Gras, at least you can get a taste here—and a better understanding of what goes into it.

1380 Port of New Orleans Place. www.mardigrasworld.com. ⓒ **504/361-7821.** Admission $22 adults, $17 students and seniors (65 and over), $14 children 2–11. Daily 9:30am–5:30pm. Last tour at 4:30pm. Closed Mardi Gras, Easter, Thanksgiving, Christmas.

National World War II Museum ★★★   This must-see, world-class facility boasts a collection of artifacts that is beyond abundant. The exhibits also include stellar videos and advanced digital techniques, but still manage to emphasize the personal side of war, highlighted by audio and video of civilians and soldiers recounting their first-hand experiences. Descriptions don't do justice to the incredibly moving, interactive experiences.

Founded by the late historian and best-selling author Stephen Ambrose with support from Tom Hanks (Ambrose wrote *Band of Brothers* and consulted on war film *Saving Private Ryan*, both of which starred Hanks), the museum now spans 6 acres and multiple buildings. Visitors are given the dog tag of a soldier whose story unfolds when the tag is scanned at stations along the route. In the **Road to Berlin** and **Road to Tokyo** exhibits, atmospheric, floor-to-ceiling decor re-creates battle locations—right down to the temperature and scent. In the U.S. Freedom Pavilion, seven original warplanes hang from a 10-story ceiling. From the ground up, it's an imposing sight; from eye level, it's an almost intimate perspective. Other exhibits of note are the "What Would You Do?" kiosks, which pose thoughtful moral and technical questions; a short, shocking film about the atomic bomb (not for kids)—appropriately silent except for a few excerpts of classical music; a copy of Eisenhower's backup speech apologizing to the nation in the event that D-Day failed; and the amazing story of the B-17 known as **"My Gal Sal"**—its desolate downing, the daring rescue, and its comeback decades later.

BB Stage Door Canteen lightens the mood with live, 1940s-era USO-style shows. It's good, clean swinging fun for a dinner or brunch show ($39–$65 with modest discounts for kids under 12; $30 show only). (**The American Sector,** the museum's restaurant, is pretty good.) Showing in the **Solomon Victory Theater,** *Beyond All Boundaries* is a short film with "4-D" multisensory effects—shaking seats, flashing lights, falling snow—which may be moderately successful at interesting kids in war history ($6). Time is better spent on **"Final Mission: USS Tang,"** which enlists visitors into "silent service" inside a realistic mock submarine as it undergoes its harrowing final sea battle ($6—this one's worth it). Perhaps most affecting are the intimate stories told through the artifacts and personal items of former soldiers and their loved ones. Take every opportunity to hear these first-person audio stories at the listening stations.

War veterans and civilians who were involved in the war effort often volunteer at the museum. Say thanks, and talk with them. We met Jim Weller, who told us how he lied about his age to enlist; he showed us his photo at the Battle of the Bulge, and said of the woman and baby next to us: "that's why I won the war—for the babies." That's about the best possible museum experience one can have. You could spend days here, but allow at least 3 hours.

945 Magazine St.. www.nationalww2museum.org. ℂ **504/528-1944.** Museum admission $27 adults; $23.50 seniors; $17.50 K–12 students and military with ID. Free for WWII veterans and children 4 and under. Second-day pass $6. Other discounts apply for combination tickets. Daily 9am–5pm. Closed holidays.

New Orleans Jazz Museum at the Old U.S. Mint ★★

Dedicated to an original American art form, this still-evolving museum steps from Frenchmen Street features stellar collectibles like Louis Armstrong's first cornet, Sidney Bechet's soprano saxophone and Edward "Kid" Ory's trombone. The rotating exhibits come from an archive of irreplaceable treasures ranging from costumes, photos, manuscripts, and historic recordings to rare film footage. Best of all, the gorgeous third-floor performance space has **free 2pm concerts** every open day (and evening shows often). The building, the only mint that was both a U.S. *and* a Confederate mint, and also has exhibits of interest to numismatists (O-minted coins, struck right here!) and regular, curious folk. *Fun fact:* Ghost hunters believe William Mumford, who met the noose here in 1862, still hangs around.

400 Esplanade Ave. www.louisianastatemuseum.org and www.musicatthemint.org. ℂ **800/568-6968** or 504/427-2190. Admission $6 adults; $5 students, seniors, and military; free for children 6 and under. Discounts for visiting multiple Louisiana State museums. Tues–Sun 10am–4:30pm. Closed Mon and state holidays.

New Orleans Museum of Art ★★★

The crown jewel of City Park, and of New Orleans art, NOMA houses a 40,000-piece collection of 16th-through 20th-century European paintings, drawings, sculptures, and prints; early American art; Asian art; pre-Columbian and Native American ethnographic art; a gallery entirely devoted to Fabergé; and one of the largest decorative glass collections in the country. Not everything is on display, of course, and this very manageable museum does not need to take hours to visit.

Curation here has been impressive of late, with unfailingly interesting exhibits. From the front, the original 1911 neoclassical building is an imposing sight among the greenery of City Park. The contemporary rear portion is all angles and curves, steel and glass; and the handsome interior galleries are well lit and organized. It all works to the visitor's advantage. (Well, Lichtenstein's *Five Brushstrokes* sculpture, prominently installed at the front entrance in late 2013, met with comparisons to streaky bacon. But what's art without controversy?)

Next door is the superb **Besthoff Sculpture Garden ★★★,** which spotlights 60 modern sculptures amid 5 serene, landscaped acres winding around reflecting lagoons (11 acres by the time you read this). Artists' works by George Segal, Henry Moore, Elisabeth Frink, Gaston Lachaise, and a version of Robert Indiana's famous pop-art *LOVE* sculpture are here. It's a cultural highlight, and admission is free. We like to grab a **Parkway Bakery** po' boy (p. 107) on the way there and picnic amid the artwork. Alternately, **Ralph Brennan's Cafe NOMA** inside the museum has light lunch fare and wine during museum hours; and **Morning Call** (p. 132) is just a short walk away.

1 Collins Diboll Circle, at City Park and Esplanade. www.noma.org. ℭ **504/658-4100.** Museum admission $12 adult; $10 seniors (65 and over) and students; $8 children 7–17; free for kids 6 and under and local students. Tues–Thurs 10am–6pm; Fri 10am–9pm; Sat 10am–5pm; Sun 11am–5pm. Closed most major holidays. Sculpture Garden free admission; Mon–Fri 10am–6pm; Sat–Sun 10am–5pm.

The New Orleans Tattoo Museum ★

This off-the-beaten-path oddity houses a working tattoo studio, a 2,000-square-foot room museum, and Don "Doc" Lucas, historian, curator, collector, author, storyteller, artist, and the museum's most interesting exhibit. Doc's work graces the skin of Aaron Neville and Anne Rice, among thousands of others. To be sure, it's for those with a specialized interest in the tattoo arts, but most anyone will succumb to Doc's knowledge of technique and enthusiastic recounting of life among the classic ink giants. The walls are plastered with old-time flash and photos; pigments and tattoo machines through the ages are nicely displayed in glass cases.

1915 Martin Luther King Jr. Blvd, Central City. www.nolatattoomuseum.com. ℭ **504/218-5319.** Free admission (donations accepted). Tues–Sat 1pm–7pm.

Ninth Ward Living Museum ★★

Situated in a former home in a residential section of the 9th ward, the scant few rooms of this modest museum hold a world of insight. The moving oral histories, exhibits, and videos (and often, the people here) tell the story of this area—not just of the levee failure and its devastation, but of the centuries leading up to it—and why all are so deeply intertwined. It's illuminating, thought-provoking, and as relevant now as ever. If you are interested in this area and its people, this museum is a must.

1235 Deslonde St. http://l9livingmuseum.org. ℭ **504/220-3652.** Free admission; leave a generous donation. Tues–Sun noon–5pm.

The Ogden Museum of Southern Art ★★★

If NOMA is the crown jewel, this is the crown. It's the premier collection of Southern art in the United States. The artists' works are impressive, and the graphics are informative and even clever. We particularly like the permanent exhibit of self-taught and outsider art, including some from the local area. Though the building itself is quite dazzling, anchored around a sky-high atrium, one can't help wondering if that soaring space could be put to better use if it were hung with even more fine Southern art (we do appreciate the Poydras St. sculptures that the Ogden installed in 2013). If you're able, come on a Thursday for music in the atrium during Ogden After Hours. It might be old Delta blues, the New Orleans Philharmonic, 1930s country, or straight-up jazz, but on the list of special New Orleans treats, these evenings are near the top. We're also keen on the well-curated gift shop, which has consistently covetable souvenirs with a local spin.

925 Camp St. www.ogdenmuseum.org. ℂ **504/539-9600.** Admission $13.50 adults; $11 seniors, students and military; $7.25 children 5–17. Wed–Mon 10am–5pm; Thurs 10am–8pm (6–8pm live music).

Sculpture for New Orleans ★ Not a museum you can visit, per se, but if you're curious about the eye-popping outdoor sculptures along Poydras St., this is the organization responsible. Born in the wake of Hurricane Katrina to brighten a blighted landscape and spotlight the city's visual artists, it's since placed 75 artworks in public places, including the moving "Eleven" on Elysian Fields at Dauphine, artist Jason Kimes' tribute to the 11 men who died when BP's Deepwater Horizon oil rig exploded in the Gulf in 2010.

www.sculptureforneworleans.org. ℂ **361/441-6527.**

Southern Food & Beverage Museum & Museum of the American Cocktail ★ The South's first food-and-beverage museum reopened in this mid-renaissance, off the tourist-beat part of town. The large room features clusters of alimental artifacts from each Southern state. It's a jumbled but informative assemblage, showcasing farms, tables, and everything in between, and illustrating how different ethnic groups, geography, and time have contributed to the regional cuisines of the American South. A Creole cooking class with tastes in the gorgeous demo kitchen runs $45 (including museum admission). Interesting events and rotating exhibits—always its forte—detail obscure but fascinating food topics from absinthe drips to Appalachian soups.

The **Museum of the American Cocktail** (MoTAC), a stumble through 200 years of cocktail history and New Orleans' vital role in same, is also here. Founder Dale "King Cocktail" Degroff and curator Ted "Dr. Cocktail" Haigh's mind-blowing collection offers an original and lively glimpse into the history of everyone's favorite poison. The booze-obsessed will lose it over the extensive historical artifacts here, including defunct product packaging, glassware, and Prohibition-era photos. (We love the bottles of commercially sold gin, rye, and bourbon flavoring used to spike homemade rotgut to make it palatable.)

1504 Oretha Castle Haley Blvd. www.southernfood.org and www.museumoftheamerican cocktail.org. ℂ **504/569-0405.** Admission to both museums: $10.50 adults; $5.25 seniors, active military, and students with ID; children under 12 free with adult. Wed–Mon 11am–5:30pm.

Studio BE ★★★ The power of artist, activist, and educator Brandan "BMike" Odums' astounding work is evident on first glimpse of the murals covering this 35,000-square-foot gallery/museum/warehouse/shop. But the large-format spray-painted and sculptural works inside, of iconic figures important to civil rights, are reflective, instructive, inspiring, and jaw-dropping.

2941 Royal St. www.facebook.com/exhibitbe. ℂ **504/330-6231.** $10 admission, waived for students and educators. Wed–Sat 2–8pm.

Historic New Orleans Churches

Church and religion are not likely to be the first things that jump to mind in a city known for its debauchery. But New Orleans remains a very pious, mostly Catholic city—don't forget that Mardi Gras is a pre-Lenten celebration. Religion of one form or another directed much of the city's early history and molded its culture in countless ways. (For a detailed review of the **St. Louis Cathedral,** see p. 139 earlier in this chapter.)

St. Alphonsus Church ★ The interior of St. Alphonsus is probably the most stunning of any church in the city, right up there with some of the lusher Italian splendors. The Irish built St. Alphonsus Church in 1855 because they refused to worship at St. Mary's (see below) with their German-speaking neighbors. The gallery, columns, and sharply curving staircases lead to spooky, atmospheric balconies where the paint and plaster are peeling off in chunks.

The church no longer holds Mass. Ironically, when St. Mary's was restored, St. Alphonsus closed, and the congregation moved there. Hopes for similar restoration here are high, but it's no small undertaking. Katrina caused half a million dollars in damage, and the downriver bell tower was blown dramatically across the street. Meanwhile, it's used for events. You can visit the still fabulous-looking museum interior; free tours (donations gratefully accepted and much in need) are conducted on an informal schedule (Tues, Thurs, and Sat 10am–2pm or by advance arrangement; calling ahead is recommended).

2025 Constance St., at St. Andrew St. www.stalphonsusno.com. ℂ **504/524-8116** (for additional info call Friends of St. Alphonsus at ℂ **504/482-0008**).

St. Augustine Church ★★ One of the great cultural landmarks of New Orleans' black history, St. Augustine has been a center of community life in the troubled but striving Tremé neighborhood since the mid-1800s. This church was founded by free people of color, who also purchased pews to be used exclusively by slaves (to the frustrating dismay of their white masters). This was a first in the history of slavery in the U.S., and resulted in one of the most integrated churches in the country. In the modern era, under the direction of its visionary and charismatic then-pastor, Father Jerome LeDoux, St. Augustine integrated traditional African and New Orleans elements into its services. Homer Plessy, Sidney Bechet, and Big Chief Tootie Montana all called this their home church. In late 2005 the archdiocese decided to close St.

REAL GOSPEL, NO brunch

You could do the slick "Gospel Brunch" at the House of Blues, or you could experience the real thing in a real place of worship. Don't expect fancy robes or masses of choir members, just rooms full of spirit and a seriously joyful noise. Try **Zion Hill Missionary Baptist Church,** 1126 N. Robertson St. (𝐶 **504/525-0507**). It's humble, right, and true (and Pastor Joshua's preaching can get pretty fiery). You may well be the only non-parishioner there, but the modest congregation is welcoming; show some mutual respect when the collection plate comes 'round. Sunday services are at 10:30am to noonish; communion service on the first Sunday of the month runs longer.

At the other end of the spectacle spectrum, Bishop (and Internet star) Lester Love incorporates his smooth soul vocals into his powerful sermons, adding an R&B backing band and singers at his mini-mega, full-gospel **City of Love Church** (8601 Palmetto St. in the Gert Town neighborhood; www.thecityoflove.com; 𝐶 **504/895-5410;** Sun 7:30 & 10am). Inspiration is practically preordained. Or take in the jazzy Sunday 10am Catholic mass at historic **St. Augustine's** (see above). Home church for many a famous local musician, the service incorporates New Orleans–tinged music. And if you must have that brunch, get to nearby **Lil Dizzy's** afterward, p. 107.

Augustine because of diminished membership, but a major public outcry bought a reprieve, and it's going strong again. Services here are remarkable, especially when the jazzy 10am **Sunday Mass** features a soul-stirring guest performer like James Andrews or John Boutté. Frequent art exhibits celebrating the neighborhood and the deeply moving **Tomb of the Unknown Slave** (outside on the right side) make this worth a stop anytime (but call ahead to make sure it's open). Don't forget to leave a donation to help keep St. Aug going.

1210 Governor Nicholls St. www.staugustinecatholicchurch-neworleans.org. 𝐶 **504/525-5934.** Mass: Sun 10am; choir rehearsal: Tues 6pm. Call to arrange a tour.

St. Mary's Assumption ★ Built in 1860 by German Catholics, this is an even more baroque and grand church than its Irish neighbor across the street (St. Alphonsus Church, above), complete with dozens of life-size saints' statues. The two churches make an interesting contrast to one another. Also inside the church is the national shrine to the hero of the 1867 yellow-fever epidemic, Blessed Father Francis Xavier Seelos, who was beatified (one step away from sainthood) in 2000. See his original coffin, some of his personal belongings, a display containing recently discovered locks of his hair, and the centerpiece of the shrine, a reliquary containing his bodily remains. Should Father Seelos become a saint, expect this shrine to be a big deal and place of pilgrimage.

2030 Constance St., at Josephine St. www.stalphonsusno.com. 𝐶 **504/522-6748.** Mass: Mon–Sat 8am, Sat 4pm, Sun 10:30am.

St. Patrick's Church ★★ The original St. Patrick's was a tiny wooden building founded to serve the spiritual needs of Irish Catholics—a far cry from this elaborate structure. Begun in 1838, it was built around the old one, which was then dismantled. The distinguished architect James Gallier, Sr., designed much of the interior including the altar. It opened in 1840, proudly proclaiming itself as the "American" Catholics' answer to the St. Louis Cathedral in the French Quarter (where, according to the Americans, God spoke only in French).

724 Camp St., at Girod St. www.oldstpatricks.org. ℂ **504/525-4413.** Mass: Mon–Fri 11:30am, noon; Sat 4pm, 5:30pm; Sun 8am, 9:30am (Latin), 11am, 5:30pm. Adoration: Mon–Fri 11am–1pm, Sun 3–5pm.

St. Roch and the Campo Santo ★★

A local priest prayed to Saint Roch, patron saint of plague victims, to keep his flock safe during an epidemic in 1867. When everyone came through all right, the priest made good on his promise to build Saint Roch a chapel. The Gothic result is fine enough, but what is better yet is the small room just off the altar, where successful supplicants to Saint Roch leave gifts, usually in the form of plaster anatomical parts or medical supplies to represent what the saint healed for them. The resulting collection of bizarre artifacts (everything from eyeballs to false limbs) is either deeply moving or among the greatest creepy spontaneous folk-art installations you've ever seen. The chapel, located on the cemetery grounds, isn't always open despite the posted hours, so hope for the best. This area isn't great, so be aware.

1725 St. Roch Ave., at N. Derbigny St. ℂ **504-482-5065.** Mon–Fri 8:30am–4pm except during inclement weather.

Trinity Episcopal Church ★

This is a very pretty church, outside and in. Outside, the Gothic Revival construction dates to 1853; inside, elaborate carved wood panels show off a 5,000-pipe organ. But the big attraction here is that it gets regular play. Weekly pipe organ concerts by the Church's retired music director, **Albinas Prizgintas,** often accompanied by local singers and musicians, feature traditional repertoire by names you know, like Bach, Pachelbel, Led Zeppelin, and Michael Jackson. Tuesday the organ accompanies a meditative, candle-lit labyrinth walk. On the list of eclectic things to do in New Orleans on a Tuesday or Sunday evening, this is up there.

1329 Jackson Ave. www.trinitynola.com. ℂ **504/522-0276.** Church open Mon–Fri 7:30–4:30pm; Sun mass with organ 10:30; Sun concert, usually with organ, 5pm. Tues traditional labyrinth walk 6pm.

A Few More Interesting New Orleans Buildings

Degas House ★ Legendary French Impressionist Edgar Degas had a tender spot in his heart for New Orleans. His mother and grandmother were born here, and he spent several months in 1872 and 1873 visiting his brother at this house. The trip resulted in a number of paintings, and this is the only residence or studio associated with Degas anywhere in the world that is open to the public. One of the artist's paintings showed the garden of a neighboring house. His brother liked that view, too; he later ran off with the wife of the judge who lived there. The brother's wife and children then took back her

floating ACROSS THE RIVER TO ALGIERS POINT

Algiers, annexed by New Orleans in 1870, is about a quarter-mile across the Mississippi River from the city. Generally ignored because of its location, it became a sort of God's country after the hurricane because it did not flood at all; many services, such as mail delivery, were restored quite quickly. It still has the feel of an undisturbed turn-of-the-20th-century suburb, and strolling around here is a delightfully low-key way to spend an hour or two (daytime only). It is easily accessible via the Algiers ferry that runs from the foot of Canal Street. This unfancy ferry is one of New Orleans' best-kept secrets—it's a great way to get out onto the river and see the skyline (and at 30 min. it's perfectly timed for kids' attention spans). See schedule and fares on p. 269.

maiden name, Musson. The Musson home, as it is formally known, was erected in 1854. It has since been sliced in two, redone in an Italianate manner, and restored as a B&B. It's open to the public daily for tours (you can also combine the tour with a Creole breakfast or painting party here).

2306 Esplanade Ave., north of the Quarter, before N. Broad Ave. www.degashouse. com. ✆ **504/821-5009.** Guided tours $29/person; senior, student, military discounts available. Tour plus breakfast and mimosas $50. Breakfast 9am; tours daily 10:30am and 1:45pm. Reservations required.

Gallier Hall ★ This impressive Greek Revival building was the inspiration of James Gallier, Sr. Now an events hall, it was erected between 1845 and 1853, served as City Hall for over a century, and has been the site of many key events in the city's history—especially during the Reconstruction and Huey Long eras. Several important figures in Louisiana history lay in state in Gallier Hall, including Jefferson Davis and General Beauregard. Of late, local music legends Ernie K-Doe and Earl King were so honored. Five thousand mourners paid respects to K-Doe, who was laid out in a white costume with a silver crown and scepter. A $10-million exterior renovation was completed in 2017, followed by an interior spiff.

545 St. Charles Ave. www.nola.gov/gallier-hall. ✆ **504/658-3627.** Not usually open to the public.

The Mercedes-Benz Superdome ★ Completed in 1975, the Superdome is a landmark civic structure that took on a new worldwide image when it was used as shelter during Katrina. Intended as an evacuation locale of last resort, the Superdome quickly turned into hell on earth when tens of thousands of refugees ended up here in a scene of suffering and despair. People were trapped without sufficient food, water, medical care, or, it seemed, hope.

Just months later, the New Orleans Saints reopened the Superdome in 2006 to much hoopla for their first home game (and a halftime show featuring U2), and went on to the playoffs. Three years later they won their first Super Bowl ever (in Miami), to rejoicing far beyond the city boundaries. Atop the team's gleaming success and the Dome's $118-million renovation, the entire building was then "reskinned" in glittery gold tone, a shining beacon of what can arise from the darkest Katrina days. What arose 2 years later was a lucrative naming-rights deal with Mercedes-Benz and the 2014 Super Bowl—capping a huge symbolic comeback. Do join the locals in a chant of "WHO DAT?!"

The stats: It's the largest fixed-dome structure in the world (680 ft. in diameter, covering 13 acres), a 27-story windowless building with a seating capacity of 76,000. Inside, there are no view-obstructing posts. Besides sports events, this flying-saucer-like building hosts conventions, balls, and concerts, as does its sister **Smoothie King Center** next door. **Champions Square,** its adjoining outdoor plaza, has become pre- and post-game central and home to many a festival and special event.

1500 block of Poydras St., at LaSalle St. www.mbsuperdome.com. © **504/587-3663.**

Pitot House ★★   Set along pretty Bayou St. John, the Pitot House is a typical West Indies–style plantation home, restored and furnished with early-19th-century Louisiana and American antiques. Dating from 1799, it originally stood where the nearby modern Catholic school now stands. In 1810 it became the home of James Pitot, the first mayor of incorporated New Orleans (he served from 1804–05). Tours, given by knowledgeable docents or architecture students, are surprisingly interesting and informative.

1440 Moss St., near Esplanade Ave. www.pitothouse.org. © **504/482-0312.** Admission $10 adults, $7 seniors and students, free children 6 and under. Wed–Sat 10am–3pm (last tour at 2:15pm).

PARKS, GARDENS & A ZOO

New Orleans' verdant vegetation and expansive tree canopy is one of its many charms, with greenery bursting from small condo courtyards, lavish mansion landscaping, abundantly overflowing terrace pots—and wonderful public parks and gardens. Glorious live oaks are a city hallmark, spreading across streets and over roofs everywhere (an amazing 320 million trees were lost to Hurricane Katrina, including many old oaks; thankfully, plenty survived). The city's parks and gardens can be an inviting respite from pounding the sightseeing pavement.

Audubon Park ★★   Across from Loyola and Tulane universities, Audubon Park and the adjacent Audubon Zoo (see below) sprawl over 340 acres, extending all the way from St. Charles Avenue to the Mississippi River. This tract once belonged to city founder Jean-Baptiste Le Moyne and later was part of the Etienne de Boré plantation, where sugar was first granulated in 1794. Although John James Audubon, the country's best-known ornithologist, lived only briefly in New Orleans (at what is now the **Audubon Cottages** hotel; p. 54), the city has honored him by naming the park, zoo, and even a golf course after him.

The huge trees with black bark are live oaks; some go back to plantation days, and more than 200 were planted to replace the many that did not survive Hurricane Katrina. Other than the trees, it's not the most visually arresting park in the world—it's just pretty and a nice, wide-open place to be. Visitors can enjoy a shaded picnic among statuary, fountains, and gazebos, feed ducks in a lagoon, and pretend they're Thoreau. Or they can look with envy at the lovely old houses whose backyards abut the park. The most utilized feature is the 1¾-mile paved, traffic-free walking, running, skating, and biking road that loops around the lagoon and golf course (which a lovely café overlooks). Along the track are 18 exercise stations. There are tennis courts, baseball diamonds, and horseback-riding facilities, and Audubon Zoo is toward the back of the park across Magazine Street. Behind the zoo, the pavilion and popular green space on the riverbank, called Riverview but nicknamed the **Fly,** has pleasant views of Frisbee players and the Mississippi.

6500 Magazine St., btw. Broadway and Exposition Blvd. www.auduboninstitute.org. © **504/861-2537.** Daily 5am–10pm.

Audubon Zoo ★★★   This is a place of justifiable civic pride that delights even non–zoo fans—small enough to be manageable, but big enough to cover all the important zoo bases including elephant and orangutan exhibits with some bonuses, like the amazing white tiger and Malayan sun bears. Some 15,000 animals (including rare and endangered species) live in natural habitats of subtropical plants, waterfalls, lagoons, and a Louisiana swamp replica complete with rare white gators. There are some great hot-day diversions for kids, including a wading pond for the little ones, and the **Cool Zoo** splash park with the **Gator Run** lazy river for inner-tube floating. So bring swimsuits and towels if the weather warrants (open seasonally, check website). There are misters and shady oaks for humans of all ages, but hot is hot: For maximum animal action, plan your visit to avoid midday, when the animals are sleeping off the heat. We like taking the St. Charles Avenue streetcar to Audubon Park, where a free shuttle from the park to the zoo departs every 20 to 30 minutes.

6500 Magazine St. www.auduboninstitute.org. © **504/861-2537.** Admission $23 adults, $20 seniors, $18 children 2–12. Add-ons: Cool Zoo $12; Aquarium/IMAX/Zoo combo tickets and shuttle bus tickets available (see Aquarium listing for details, p. 136). March to Labor Day Mon–Fri 10am–5pm, Sat–Sun 10am–6pm; after Labor Day Zoo is closed 1 hour earlier and all day Mon. Closed Mardi Gras Day, 1st Fri in May, Thanksgiving, and Christmas.

Chalmette Battlefield/Jean Lafitte National Historical Park & Preserve ★★   These are the grounds where the bloody **Battle of New Orleans** was won on January 8, 1815. Ironically, it should never have been fought: A treaty signed 2 weeks before in Ghent, Belgium, had ended the War of 1812. But word had not yet reached Congress, the commander of the British forces, or Andrew Jackson, who stood with American forces to defend New Orleans and the mouth of the Mississippi River. The battle did, however, succeed in uniting Americans and Creoles, and in making Jackson a hero in this city.

Markers on the battlefield allow you to follow the course of the battle (or you can just watch the film in the visitor center). Inside the park is a national cemetery, established in 1864. It holds only two American veterans from the Battle of New Orleans and some 14,000 Union soldiers who fell in the Civil War. For a terrific view of the Mississippi River, climb the levee in back of the Beauregard House.

8606 W. St. Bernard Hwy. www.nps.gov/jela. © **504/281-0510.** Free admission. Daily 9am–4pm. Visitor center closed Sun–Mon. Park closed Mardi Gras and federal holidays (open Veterans and Memorial days).

City Park ★★★   Once part of the Louis Allard plantation and named one of America's "Coolest Parks," City Park has seen it all—including that favorite pastime among 18th-century New Orleans gentry: dueling. At the entrance, note the empty marble platform, where a statue of General P. G. T. Beauregard (whose order to fire on Fort Sumter kicked off the Civil War) was one of four Confederate monuments that were recently removed. The 1,300 beautifully landscaped acres provide a charming spot for a jog, bird-watching, or just gazing at the moss-dripping live oaks (the largest collection in the world!). It's also a treasure trove of culture and activity, with botanical gardens, a conservatory, picnic areas, lagoons for boating and fishing, **pedal boats** (p. 183), and bike paths and **rentals** (p. 268). But wait, there's more: a brand-spanking-new golf course and tennis center, a New Orleans–themed **miniature golf** course (p. 183), a bandstand with summertime concerts, two stadiums, playing fields, and a miniature train you can ride in. That's just a start. **Carousel Gardens** is a kids' amusement area with rides; **Children's Storyland,** inside the Carousel Gardens, has fairy-tale figures for kids to scamper on and over and an antique carousel (see "Especially for Kids," later in this chapter). At Christmastime, the mighty oaks are strung with light displays—quite a magical sight—and during Halloween the park hosts the massive **Voodoo Experience** music festival.

You'll also find the **New Orleans Museum of Art** (p. 151) at Collins Diboll Circle, on Lelong Avenue, in a building that is itself a work of art. Next to it is the wonderful **Besthoff Sculpture Garden** (p. 152). Tucked away inside the **Botanical Gardens** is one of the oddest and most charming attractions in this odd and charming city, the **Train Garden.** Imagine a massive train set, the kind every 9-year-old kid (or kid at heart) would kill for. Now imagine that it's located in Dr. Seuss's basement, if Dr. Seuss was obsessed with both New Orleans and organic materials. Along 1,300 feet of track are exacting, $\frac{1}{22}$-scale replicas of 1890s streetcars and ornately detailed, bizarrely beautiful representations of actual New Orleans neighborhoods and landmarks—all made from plant matter! In a town of weird and wonderful attractions, this is one more. The Botanical and Train Gardens are open for viewing year-round from 10am to 4pm daily; trains operate Saturdays and Sundays only (weather permitting).

1 Palm Dr. www.neworleanscitypark.com. © **504/482-4888.** Park open daily sunrise–sunset. Free admission to park. Admission to Botanical Gardens and $8 adults, $4 kids

5–12, 4 and under free. Train Garden: $6 adults; $3 kids 5–12, 4 and under free. For hours and rates of other attractions, see separate listings. Admissions and hours may vary seasonally, so check website or call.

Crescent Park ★★   This newish, river-hugging green space paralleling the Marigny and Bywater neighborhoods is ideal for a picnic, run, or walk, or just to get a different, thoroughly modern perspective on New Orleans. That starts as you cross the enormous, rust-colored steel arc, aka the Piety Street Bridge (aka the Rusty Rainbow), to reach the park. Or access it via the less dramatic, wheelchair-accessible Mandeville Crossing closer to the French Quarter. From the freshly planted and paved paths, the French Quarter is a mysterious, distant vision; from the expansive waterfront stage set amid decayed wharves, the area's industrial legacy nips at the heels. Watch for concerts and other events at this substantial, welcome space.

Enter from bridges at N. Peters St. at Marigny St. (ADA accessible and closest to the French Quarter; diagonally across from the U.S. Mint); Piety St. and Chartres St. (stairs only—lots of 'em); Mazant St. at Chartres St. (ADA accessible). Free admission. Daily 6am–7:30pm (may close earlier during winter).

Lafitte Greenway ★★   This 2.6-mile walking trail and bikeway is a former railway and post-Katrina success story that now connects neighbors and neighborhoods: It starts just above the French Quarter and traverses the Tremé, Bayou St. John, and Mid-City. If you're renting a bike (p. 268), the greenway will facilitate your explorations with nary a pothole in sight. (Bonus: It passes almost right by **Parkway Bakery,** p. 107 and other enterprising, adjacent eat- and drinkeries.) It's well lit, but use caution after dark. Check the website for events along the greenway, as well as info about planned walking tours that explain the very important history of this area and the storm-water management techniques it incorporates.

Trailhead begins at Basin and St. Louis sts. just outside the French Quarter (near St. Louis Cemetery #1); look for signage. Other access points intersect its route. www. lafittegreenway.org. ✆ **504/462-0645.** Open 24/7.

Longue Vue House & Gardens ★★   Longue Vue mansion is a little pocket of the unexpected. Just 20 minutes from the city center, near the more interesting end of suburban Metairie, is a unique expression of Greek Revival architecture set on an 8-acre estate, constructed from 1939 to 1942 and listed on the National Register of Historic Places. It's like stumbling across a British country-house estate, and while it was never a plantation, it may just satisfy your Tara-esque cravings if you can't get out to River Road (p. 174)—and it's a nice place to ramble on a pretty day.

The mansion was designed to foster a close rapport between indoors and outdoors, with vistas of formal terraces and pastoral woods. The charming gardens were partly inspired by the Generalife, the former summerhouse of the sultans in Granada, Spain; look also for fountains and a colonnaded loggia. Unlike some attractions for garden enthusiasts, kids can actually have fun here in the delightful **Discovery Garden,** with clever and amusing exhibits where kids can play (and maybe even learn).

7 Bamboo Rd., near Metairie. www.longuevue.com. ☏ **504/488-5488.** Admission $12 adults; $10 seniors; $8 students; $5 children 3–10. Free for AAA members and active military. Mon–Sat 10am–5pm; Sun 1–5pm. Tours on the hour till 4pm. Closed most major holidays.

NEW ORLEANS CEMETERIES

Along with Spanish moss and lacy cast iron balconies, the cities of the dead are part of the indelible landscape of New Orleans. Recognized the world over for their elaborate and beautiful aboveground tombs, their ghostly and inscrutable presence enthralls visitors. There are 45 cemeteries in New Orleans—31 are considered historic, and 5 are officially listed in the National Register of Historic Places. Iconic tourist attractions as much as Jackson Square or Bourbon Street, the cemeteries have a fascinating backstory—one that has become twisted over time by mythology. But the truth is so fascinating that it needs little embellishment.

Sometimes called "Cities of the Dead" for their resemblance to urban centers, the cemeteries have, of course, been a part of New Orleans nearly since its founding. For the earliest settlers, dying wasn't that big of a deal; everyone was doing it, and the dead were buried in common graves or along the riverbanks (except the hoitiest of the toity, who were buried at St. Louis Cathedral). But when the river rose or a major rain caused minor flooding, that didn't work out too well. Old Uncle Etienne had an unpleasant habit of bobbing back to the surface, doubtless no longer looking his best. This practice gave rise to some good stories (though experts debate their veracity) of coffins floating downriver, bodies weighted down with rocks, and holes drilled in caskets to let the water through and prevent them from popping up from the ground like deathly balloons.

Add to that cholera and yellow-fever epidemics, which helped increase the number of bodies and also the possibility of infection. Given that the cemetery of the time was *inside* the Vieux Carré, it's all pretty disgusting to think about.

Around the late 1780s, death was getting to be a bigger deal. Well, death was getting to be more *prevalent,* what with fires and yellow-fever epidemics and such; *honoring* death and the dead was indeed getting to be a bigger, more ceremonial deal. When new cemeteries became necessary, they were plotted on the outskirts of town where illness and odor were less likely to be troublesome. The first, St. Peter, was begun in 1725 by the Catholic Diocese, and rests where a Superdome parking lot now sits. Bodies were buried in the soil there. When St. Peter was full, the famed St. Louis No. 1 came about, in 1789, on what is now Rampart Street. The first major city of the dead, with fancy tombs and a parklike setting, provided a more fitting tribute to departed loved ones. When it filled up, others soon followed, improving on the haphazard layout of St. Louis No. 1 to form designated "streets" in a grid pattern.

Following Old-World Style

It's true that the high water table and muddy soil here influenced the popularity of the above-ground "condo crypt" look—the dead are placed in vaults that look like miniature buildings. But they are actually customary in France and Spain (and elsewhere), so it was just another tradition that the colonists brought with them to New Orleans. Some say St. Louis No. 1 was inspired by the famous Père Lachaise cemetery in Paris. Perhaps it's just because they are such an impressive, prestigious sight.

The above-ground vaults are also often adorned with stunning works of sculptural art, decorations that represent the family name, occupation, or religion (which was invariably Catholic; the first Jewish cemetery was not founded until 1828). Some tombs were not owned by families, but by a group, like the firefighters, police, or a benevolent society. These were decorated thusly: witness the enormous elk visible from the corner of Canal Street and City Park Avenue. These were helpful for families who could not afford a family tomb. The cemeteries may also have fancy ironwork in the gates and fences—and on the whole are well worth a visit.

Hi Honey, I'm Home

So . . . all that tomb for one dead guy? Not so much. The tombs indeed host multiple bodies. The methodology is actually fairly clever. Inside the tomb are long chambers, one above the other, separated by shelves. When a casket goes in, it rests on the top shelf, and the vault is re-sealed with simple brick and mortar. Heat and humidity act like a slow form of cremation. After a year and a day (by custom and rule—to accommodate the traditional year-long mourning period), another family member may be buried here. Whatever's left of the first one is moved to the bottom level, and the casket bits are removed. In some tombs, that shelf has a gap toward the back, and the remnants just get pushed back, where they fall through the gap to the vault below. Everyone eventually lies jumbled together to continue their quest for a dusty family reunion. And so room is made for a new casket, and the exterior is closed up once again. The result is sometimes dozens of names, going back generations, on a single spot. It's an efficient, space-saving system that gives new meaning to the phrase "all in the family." If a family loses two people within the year, one of them rests in a temporary holding vault until that year-and-a-day period has passed.

Upkeep Issues

By law, families must maintain their tombs. Traditionally, All Saints' Day (Nov 1) is when families gather to honor their dead, and in the days leading up to it you will still see people busily tidying up and washing down the sun-bleached, whitewashed brick buildings. Some are treated with lime, leaving a yellow or green tint. Flowers, candles, photos, and memorabilia are left on and around the tombs of loved ones. To this day, if you go to a cemetery on November 1 (which we recommend), you may see a tender graveside party atmosphere.

Safety First

You may be warned against going to the cemeteries alone and urged to go with a scheduled tour group (see "Organized Tours," later in this chapter). Visitors were once prime pickings for muggers, due to the cemeteries' locations and layout (vault-sized crypts that can obscure bad guys). Nowadays they are popular with visitors, and we simply don't hear about actual incidents.

Nevertheless, besides offering peace of mind, a good tour is totally worthwhile (and required if visiting St. Louis #1). If you're going to make a day of visiting the cemeteries, think about renting a car and visiting tombs farther away, safely, and at your own pace. If you opt to visit lesser-known cemeteries in rough parts of town, use common sense.

But many graves have fallen into disrepair, when family members are no longer willing, able, or around to do the maintenance. There are laws that allow the city to take over and transfer a neglected tomb, but these are largely unenforced (and there's the creepy factor). Other laws and customs around these centuries-old tombs are murky, and responsibility for the expensive upkeep gets shifted or shunted off. So sadly, many cemeteries today face moderate to severe dishevelment. For years, crypts lay open, exposing their pitiful contents—if they weren't robbed of them—bricks, shattered marble tablets, even bones, lay strewn around. Several of the worst eyesores have been cleaned up; others still remain in deplorable shape.

Some restoration and cleanup efforts have been spearheaded by the nonprofit **Save Our Cemeteries** (www.saveourcemeteries.org; © **504/525-3377**). Consider throwing a few, um, bones their way, or even volunteering. The website accepts online donations. Save Our Cemeteries also offers tours and occasional lectures.

Survivors

A faux Voodoo practice continues in some of the St. Louis cemeteries, where visitors scrawl Xs on the tombs. Please don't do this; not only is it a made-up Voodoo ritual, but it destroys the fragile tombs.

Concerns were high for the fate of the iconic cemeteries during the Katrina disaster days, but "the system worked": The tombs survived unscathed, except for some high-water marks much like those borne by any other flooded structure. Shockingly, some unscrupulous visitors and even a terrible tour guide will still revile the tombs with graffiti or other abuse. Call police if you spot this abhorrent, illegal behavior.

For more information, we highly recommend Robert Florence's *New Orleans Cemeteries: Life in the Cities of the Dead* (Batture Press, 1997). It's full of photos, facts, and human-interest stories for those with a deeper interest in this fascinating aspect of New Orleans culture, and is available at bookstores throughout the city.

Three Cemeteries You Should See with a Tour

All of the organized tour companies listed on page 171 provide cemetery tours. If you haven't pre-planned, there are often tour operators available for hire at the entrances to St. Louis No. 1 and Lafayette No. 1.

Lafayette Cemetery No. 1 ★★★   Right across the street from Commander's Palace restaurant, this is the lush uptown cemetery. Once in horrible condition, it's been mostly restored. Anne Rice's Mayfair witches have their family tomb here. See p. 169.

1400 block of Washington Ave.

St. Louis Cemetery No. 1 ★★★   Actually you can *only* see this one with a tour. It's the oldest extant cemetery (1789) and the most iconic. Here lie Marie Laveau (p. 167), Bernard Marigny, and (eventually) Nicolas Cage, in the pyramid he had inscribed *"Omnia Ab Uno"* (Everything From One). It's also recognizable for the acid-dropping scene from *Easy Rider* shot here.

Basin St. btw. Conti and St. Louis sts.

St. Louis Cemetery No. 2 ★   Established in 1823, it's the city's next-oldest cemetery. Although the neighborhood is much improved, its reputation as a rough one has kept most tours away. Caution is still advised, and **Save Our Cemeteries** (p. 177) does offer tours in combo with St. Louis No. 1. The Emperor of the Universe, R&B legend Ernie K-Doe, was laid to rest here in 2001; his widow, Empress Antoinette, joined him in 2009. Claude Tremé, founder of the historic neighborhood that bears his name (see p. 31), also rests here.

N. Claiborne Ave. btw. Iberville and St. Louis sts.

Some Cemeteries You Can See on Your Own

Most of these cemeteries (such as St. Louis No. 3 and Metairie) have offices that can provide maps or direct you to a grave location. All have sort-of-regular hours—anytime from 9am to 4pm is a safe bet.

Cypress Grove and Greenwood Cemeteries ★★   Located across the street from one another, both were founded in the mid-1800s by the Firemen's Charitable and Benevolent Association. Each has some highly original tombs; keep your eyes open for the ones made entirely of iron. These are an easy streetcar ride up Canal Street from the Quarter. Just take the streetcar called "Cemeteries." Duh.

120 City Park Ave. and 5200 Canal Blvd. By car, take Esplanade north to City Park Ave., turn left. The entrance to Greenwood is on the immediate right; Cypress Grove is across the street. Daily 8:30am–4:30pm.

Holt Cemetery ★★★   This one is for the more intrepid. It's not so easy to reach or find, but it's worth seeking out. Dating to the mid-1800s, this former burial ground for indigents is the rare New Orleans cemetery with nearly all in-ground graves. They are maintained by the families—or not maintained at all, in many cases—which results in its particular, folk-art appeal, with hand-drawn markers and family memorabilia scattered about. It's incredibly picturesque and poignant in its own way.

635 City Park Ave. (turn down tiny Rosedale Ave., across City Park Ave. from the Burger King and next to Delgado College). Mon–Fri 8am–2:30pm; Sat 8am–noon.

Hurricane Katrina Memorial ★   On the former site of Charity Hospital's paupers' field, this ominous but oddly affecting circle of tombs holds the bodies of 85 unclaimed victims of the 2005 levee failures and the names of others who perished. It's an unfussy place that's easily missed, the better for contemplative solitude, perhaps. Surrounded by a storm-shaped series of pathways, the memorial does its duty in giving one substantial pause.

5056 Canal St. Take the Canal St. streetcar to City Park Ave. Mon–Fri 8am–2pm.

Metairie (Lake Lawn) Cemetery ★★   Don't be fooled by the slightly more modern look—some of the most amazing tombs in New Orleans are here. Don't miss the pyramid-and-sphinx Brunswig mausoleum, the "ruined castle" Egan family tomb, and the former resting place of Storyville madam Josie Arlington. Her mortified family had the madam's body moved when her crypt became a tourist attraction (her move may have also resulted from the complaints of blue-blood families, themselves mortified at Josie's proximity). But the tomb remains exactly the same, including the statue of a young woman knocking on the door. Legend has it that the young woman is Josie herself being turned away from her father's house, or a virgin being denied entrance to Josie's brothel—she claimed never to despoil anyone. The reality is that it's just a copy of a statue Josie liked. Other famous residents include Confederate General P. G. T. Beauregard, jazz greats Louis Prima and Al Hirt, and Ruth Fertel of Ruth's Chris Steakhouse (in a marble edifice that oddly resembles one of her famous pieces of beef). You'll have to drive or taxi here, but you can also drive the lanes through the cemetery, a good option for a rainy day.

5100 Pontchartrain Blvd. ℱ **504/486-6331.** Daily 7:30am–5:30pm. By car, take Canal St. to City Park Ave.; turn left until it becomes Metairie Ave., turn right onto Pontchartrain Blvd. (signs for I-10), then make a quick left under highway; stay on Pontchartrain and into entrance.

St. Louis Cemetery No. 3 ★★★   Conveniently located next to the Fair Grounds racetrack (home of Jazz Fest), St. Louis No. 3 was built on top of a former graveyard for lepers. Storyville photographer E. J. Bellocq lies here. It's a scenic cemetery and neighborhood near **Bayou St. John,** accessible via Esplanade Avenue.

3421 Esplanade Ave. ℱ **504/482-5065.** Mon–Sat 9am–3pm; Sun 9am–noon. Holiday closings vary.

VOODOO MYSTIQUE

Voodoo's mystical presence is one of the most common New Orleans motifs—though it is mostly reduced to a tourist gimmick. With kitschy dolls for sale and exaggerated mythology surrounding Voodoo queen Marie Laveau, a very real, culturally important religion with a serious past gets lost amid all that camp.

Voodoo's roots can be traced in part back to the religion of West Africa's **Yoruba** people, which incorporates the worship of several different spiritual forces that include a supreme being, a pantheon of deities, and the spirits of ancestors. When Africans were kidnapped, enslaved, and brought to Brazil, Haiti, and, ultimately, Louisiana, they brought their religion with them.

Later, other African religions met and melded, and when slaves were forced to convert to Catholicism, they found it easy to merge and practice both religions and rituals. Rites involved dancing and singing to intricate drum rhythms. Some participants might even fall into a trancelike state, during which a *loa* (a spirit and/or lower-level deity intermediary between humans and gods) would take possession of them.

Voodoo was banned in Louisiana until the Louisiana Purchase in 1803. The next year, the Haitian slaves overthrew their government, and new immigrants came to New Orleans, bringing along a fresh infusion of Voodoo.

Napoleonic law (which still holds sway in Louisiana) forced slave owners to give their slaves Sundays off and to provide them with a gathering place: **Congo Square** on Rampart Street, part of what is now Louis Armstrong Park. Voodoo practice there, including dancing and drumming rituals, gave slaves a way to have their own community and a certain amount of freedom. These gatherings naturally attracted white onlookers, as did the rituals held (often by free people of color) along **St. John's Bayou.** The local papers of the 1800s are full of lurid accounts of Voodoo "orgies" and of spirits possessing both whites and blacks. The Congo Square gatherings became more like performance pieces rather than religious rituals, and legend has it that nearby madams would come down to the Sunday gatherings and hire some of the performers to entertain at their houses.

During the 1800s, the famous Voodoo priestesses came to some prominence. Mostly free women of color, they were devout religious practitioners, very good businesswomen with a steady clientele of whites who secretly came to them for help in love or money matters. During the 1900s, Voodoo largely went back underground.

It is estimated that today as much as 15% of the population of New Orleans practices Voodoo, though the public perception—casting spells or sticking pins in Voodoo dolls—is largely Hollywood nonsense.

Most of the stores and places in New Orleans that advertise Voodoo are set up strictly for tourism. This is not to say that some facts can't be found there or that you shouldn't buy a mass-produced souvenir. For an introduction to Voodoo, check out the **New Orleans Historic Voodoo Museum** (p. 145) or

Voodoo Authentica (p. 225). For true Voodoo, however, seek out real Voodoo temples or practitioners. You can find them at the temples listed below or by calling **Ava Kay Jones** (http://yorubapriestess.tripod.com; ✆ **504/484-6499),** who creates custom gris-gris bags (packets of meaning-infused herbs, stones, and other such bits), potions, candles, and dolls by appointment only. If you happen into one of these temples and find no one about, come back or wait quietly; they may be conducting a reading in a side room. And be sure to check out Robert Tallant's book *Voodoo in New Orleans* (Pelican Pocket, 1983).

Voodoo Temples

The city has several authentic Voodoo temples and *botanicas* selling everything you might need for potions, spells, and ritual implements for altars. The public is welcome, and employees are happy to educate the honestly inquisitive.

The **Island of Salvation Botanica** in the New Orleans Healing Center, 2372 St. Claude Ave. in the Marigny (http://islandofsalvationbotanica.com); ✆ **504/948-9961**), is run by Voodoo priestess **Sallie Ann Glassman.** The botanica is open Monday to Saturday 10am to 5pm and Sunday 11am to 6pm, but call first to make sure they are not closed for readings (or to schedule a reading).

Priestess Miriam, who practices at the **Voodoo Spiritual Temple,** 1428 N. Rampart St. (www.voodoospiritualtemple.org; ✆ **504/943-9795**), is the real McCoy, a serene spirit and practitioner in the traditions of the West African ancestors. No pins in dolls here, folks, but healings, prayers, blessings, spiritual consultations, and training are available. The temple is just off Esplanade Avenue, easily accessed from the French Quarter or via the Rampart streetcar. Interested, respectful tourists are welcome. Call for an appointment. Primarily a store, **Voodoo Authentica,** 612 Dumaine St. (www.voodooshop.com; ✆ **504/522-2111**), also has working altars and often a practitioner in attendance, reading cards and performing cleansings. It's open Monday to Sunday 11am to 7pm. For related supplies, see p. 225.

Visiting Marie Laveau

Marie Laveau is the most famous New Orleans Voodoo queen. Though she was a real woman, her life has been so mythologized that it is nearly impossible to separate fact from fiction. But who really wants to?

Certainly it's known that she was born a free woman of color in 1794. A hairdresser by trade, Marie became known for her psychic abilities and powerful gris-gris. Her day job allowed her into the best houses, where she heard all the good gossip and could apply it to her other clientele. In one famous story, a young woman about to be forced into a marriage with a much older, wealthy man approached Marie. She wanted to marry her young lover instead. Marie counseled patience. The marriage went forward, and the happy groom died from a heart attack while dancing with his bride at the reception. After a respectable time, the now-wealthy widow was free to marry her lover.

Marie wholeheartedly believed in Voodoo—and business. Her home at what is now 1020 St. Ann Street was purportedly a gift from a grateful client.

A devout Catholic, Marie attended daily Mass and was well known for her charity work. Her death in 1881 was even noted by the *Times-Picayune.*

Her look-alike daughter, Marie II, took over her work, leading some to believe (mistakenly) that Marie I lived a very long time, looking quite well indeed—which only added to her legend. But Marie II allegedly worked more for the darker side than her mother. Her eventual reward, the story goes, was death by poison (delivered by whom is unknown). Today, visitors bring Marie tokens (candles, beads, change) and ask her for favors—she's buried in **St. Louis Cemetery No. 1.** (The misguided or outright disrespectful mar the tomb with X's. Despite what you may hear, this does nothing except dishonor her and damage her resting place. It's a horrifying, illegal fail. Don't do it.)

Anne Rice's New Orleans

Long before Sookie Stackhouse or any Originals, before anyone cared whether you were Team Edward or Team Jacob, there was Lestat—and the originator of the modern vampire era, author Anne Rice. Love her or loathe her, the New Orleans native has been one of her hometown's biggest boosters. After *Interview with the Vampire* exploded in the 1980s, hordes of fans descended on her Garden District home, hanging out for days on end, communing with each other and whatever spirits they could conjure. Rice famously egged on the whole spectacle, inviting fans into her home, throwing elaborate Halloween bashes, even making appearances in a coffin. Alas, those heady days are gone, and Rice lives quietly in California now. But visitors still come here to honor the legendary doyenne of fang fiction, including obsessed Twihards mining the eerie ore.

Rice writes seductive descriptions of her hometown and actual locales that are often quite accurate—minus the undead, of course. You can find signed copies of her books at the **Garden District Book Shop,** 2727 Prytania St. (p. 218). The following landmarks play a role in her books, movies, and inspirations.

ANNE RICE IN THE FRENCH QUARTER

The romance of the French Quarter seems to attract vampires, who found easy pickins in its dark corners in the days before electricity.

St. Louis Cemetery No. 1: A tomb (empty, of course) with Louis the vampire's name is located here in the Vampire Chronicle books, and Louis occasionally sits and broods on it. Rumor has it that Rice owns a tomb here for her eventual use. See p. 165.

700 to 900 Royal St.: Exteriors for the *Interview with the Vampire* movie were filmed here—though set decorators had to labor long to erase all traces of the 20th century, covering the streets in mud. What fun for the present-day residents.

Madame John's Legacy: In the *Interview with the Vampire* movie, caskets are being carried from this house as Brad Pitt's voiceover describes Lestat and the little vampire Claudia's night out: "An infant prodigy with a lust for killing that matched his own. Together, they finished off whole families." Yum. See p. 142.

Hotel Monteleone, 214 Royal St.: This was Aaron Lightner's home in *The Witching Hour.* Also see p. 55.

Rice's characters spent time dining well at **Café du Monde** (800 Decatur St.; p. 130), **Court of Two Sisters** (613 Royal St.; p. 86), and **Galatoire's** (209 Bourbon St.; p. 88).

If all this talk of fables and fangs gets you in the mood, head to **Boutique du Vampyre** (709 St. Ann St.; https://boutique-du-vampyre.myshopify.com; 🕿 **504/561-8267**) in the French Quarter, which claims to be the only vampire shop in the country, "Open to both mortals and vampire since 2003." It offers themed tours, custom fangs, coffin-shaped backpacks, capes, and you know, the usual.

ANNE RICE IN THE GARDEN DISTRICT

Rice's books feature many locales in and around the Garden District where she and her family lived and owned properties.

Pontchartrain Hotel, 2031 St. Charles St.: This upscale, 1927 hotel appears in *The Witching Hour.*

Copeland's Cheesecake Bistro, 2001 St. Charles Ave.: The vampire Lestat disappeared from this world through an image of himself in the window of this building.

Commander's Palace, 1403 Washington Ave.: Rice readers will recognize this restaurant as a favorite of the Mayfair family (p. 118).

Lafayette Cemetery No. 1: A frequent setting in Rice's work, especially as a roaming ground for Lestat and Claudia in *Interview with the Vampire* and as the graveyard for the Mayfairs in *The Witching Hour.* See p. 165.

ORGANIZED TOURS

There are great advantages to taking tours. Though they're touristy by definition, someone else does the planning, and it's an easy way to get to outlying areas. A good tour guide can entertain, enlighten, and even inspire. We lean toward some of the smaller companies, in hopes that they may have fewer people than the allowable 28 per group. We like to hang close to the guide in case we have questions; they'll often continue to share knowledge while on the way to the next point of interest—and we find that these kinds of serendipitous personal interactions are easier to come by when fewer people are being herded along. We also like that, for tours to the swamps and plantation homes, say, you'll be saving the earth a bit by carpooling (well, buspooling). Finally, we like the fact that New Orleans tour guides must be licensed, which involves actual study and testing. So not just anyone can load you on a bus and take you for a (literal or figurative) ride.

Tours almost always run rain-or-shine (no refunds), but in some instances you're allowed to move your reservation to another day. Walking tours and large bus tours provide a designated meeting point; smaller van tours usually provide pickup at your hotel. Before booking, check for deals on tickets—they come up pretty regularly on **Groupon** (www.groupon.com) and **Yelp** (www.yelp.com).

Be aware: It's fairly common practice for hotel concierges and storefront tour offices to **earn commission on the tours they sell or recommend** (ditto restaurants). Some may have honest opinions about the merits of one over another, and those may be perfectly good options, but often they're selling you what they get paid to sell. If you're looking for a tour, do the research yourself and cut out the middleman; no matter how you learned about it, pay the fee directly to the company, not to your concierge or a street-corner booth.

And about those **"Free Tours."** It's not that the tours themselves aren't good, per se; it's that they're not really free (and they're always packed to the gills). They usually come with a heavy-hitting request for tips, and by the time you tip the guide, you're not far from the cost of tours from established providers. We don't love the business model and hiring practices either. But when we found large chunks of our published walking tours lifted wholesale and republished on their website—without attribution—well, draw your own conclusions about the authenticity of their tours. We're supportive of legitimate businesses that legitimately support the city we love so much. But that's just us.

Tour Companies

The following companies offer multiple tours (and will often offer discounts if you commit to more than one). Most of them have walking tours of the **French Quarter;** the **Garden District;** and the **cemeteries,** as well as city van tours and tours to the **plantations** and **swamps** (they provide transportation and tickets to an associated swamp or airboat tour). Other specialty tours are noted, but if you have a particular interest you don't see, contact these companies—customized tours can often be arranged.

Cajun Encounters ★★ This is a large company, but it's also locally owned—a point of pride and also a bit of a hallmark, as they like to hire local guides. It's been around for 20 years, and tours are on a 33-seat bus. The City & Cemetery bus tour takes you through the French Quarter, St. Louis No. 1 Cemetery, Warehouse and Central Business districts, City Park, and Garden District, with walk-around opportunities at several stops. It also offers transportation and ticketing to a wonderfully eerie nighttime swamp tour.

941 Decatur St. www.cajunencounters.com. © **866/928-6877** or 504/834-1770. City + Cemetery Tour $52 adults, $36 children. Day or nighttime swamp tour (with hotel pickup) $56 adult, $36 children. Check website for other costs, schedules, and discount offers.

Chris Rose Tours ★★ Chris Rose saved the city's soul, and it very nearly cost him his life. After Katrina, the now-former *Times-Picayune* columnist's words, quite literally, kept people sane, safe, and connected—when their tenuous ties to their city and their dissolved realities were frayed to the barest existence. In the process, he published a *New York Times* best-selling book, won a Pulitzer Prize, and then fell—plunged—from that high-grace, pressure-cooker pinnacle to a fragile subsistence, after depression, addiction, and the deaths of loved ones (and the near-death of mainstream journalism) took their toll. Now healthier and still brilliant and biting, he may be more qualified to tell the story of New Orleans than just about anybody. In his latest incarnation as a licensed tour guide, he's doing just that. Don't expect a soul-searing exposé, though. Do expect a raucous, booze-spiked, F-bomb-laced bombast, told from an erudite, insider's perspective with pathos, attitude, irony, wit, and song. It's a wild, fun ride.

Check schedule, availability, and locations at www.facebook.com/chris.rose.37017794 or contact chrisrose504@gmail.com. Walking tours (2–3 hr.) of the French Quarter focusing on general history or rock 'n roll history: $25 per person.

Cradle of Jazz History Tours ★★★ John McCusker, a New Orleans native and former staff photographer for the *Times-Picayune,* is a passionate authority on early jazz and the role that New Orleans musicians played shaping this uniquely American art form. He offers a **Jazz History Tour, New Orleans Culture Tour, Pro Photography Tour, and Katrina Eye Witness Tour.** McCusker was there when the levees broke in 2005 and shared the 2006 Pulitzer Prize for Public Service Journalism for coverage of Hurricane Katrina and its immediate aftermath. The four-person (max) tours are offered via van Friday and Saturday at 10am. Larger groups can also be accommodated.

http://cradleofjazztour.com. ☏ **504/487-7666.** $50 per person.

G L-f de Villiers Tours ★★★ Multi-degreed, dishy raconteur Glenn de Villiers is a local native who traces his family lineage directly to a key figure in the founding of New Orleans. The city's history, then, is literally in his DNA. The tall, chapeaued bon vivant is worth following around the French Quarter for his laissez-faire saunter and breezy repartee alone, but his insider perspective can't be replicated through a library of books. Glenn describes the customs and culture like he's lived it (he has), and serves up the facts with urbane wit and a generous dollop of gossip. It works best on his Gay Heritage and Drinks "Twirl" tours, though the French Quarter and Louisiana History tours are all worthy. Some might find this personal take tiresome. Not us. Added pluses: He maxes his groups at 12 participants and donates profits to worthy local causes.

www.glfdevilliers.com. ☏ **225/819-7535.** All about 2 hr. and $30. Check website for schedule and meeting places. Private group tours available.

Gray Line ★★ This well-known, well-established (since 1926!) nationwide company runs coach and walking tours of the city, swamps, and plantations—in pretty much every combination (including tour/cruise combos with sister company **Steamboat Natchez,** p. 179). They offer a few more unusual itineraries, like a nighttime tour that goes across the river for fab views and stops at less-traveled night spots; and one that focuses on New Orleans' unique connection to the waterways surrounding it. As the big kahuna of tour companies, they have large groups, full-size buses, and a slicker, more scripted presentation—but also a slick, glitch-free operation, from the call center to the deep bench of backup tour guides to the heavy tour schedule, so one call can set you up.

Toulouse St. at the Mississippi River. www.graylineneworleans.com. ☏ **800/233-2628.** Walking tours start at $27 adults, $15 children. Bus tours start at $44 adults, $15 children. Check website for other tours, prices, and full schedule.

Historic New Orleans Tours ★★★ This is one of our favorite midsize tour companies, mostly because the guides are consistently good. Quite often they have advanced degrees in history or other related disciplines, and they're free to bring their own perspectives and interests to the tour, thereby keeping things fresh. The company emphasizes authenticity over sensationalism, and they're particular experts in cemeteries, with a serious depth of knowledge. They do walking tours of the French Quarter, Garden District, and cemetery; plus a fun adults-only "Scandalous Cocktail" tour, which strings together a series of fascinating tales around local bars and drinks. The tour delves into historic brothels, organized crime, and even the JFK assassination. The colorful bartenders, when not too busy, also tell their own tales (do pace your drinking, though!). They also offer walking and van tours of the Garden District, and a City + Katrina van tour. Other special-interest tours (available by advance arrangement only) include music, literary, Tremé, and Creole Mourning Customs Tours, the latter a particularly novel and fascinating topic. If you can get on a tour led by Milton, Denise, or Dianne, more's the better.

www.tourneworleans.com. ⓒ **504/947-2120.** Most tours $25 adults; $18 students and seniors; $7 children 6–12; free for children 5 and under. Call or link for times/reservations.

Tours by Isabelle ★ This well-established but smaller tour company schedules tours only when a minimum number of people sign up (if they don't hit the minimum, you may have to switch to a different tour). The upside is you'll get more personalized attention, and van tours are maxed out at 13 people. Isabelle's tours (available in English and French) include: New Orleans city overview; plantations; swamps and airboats; and good combination tours—like a 3½-hour City Overview and Katrina Recovery tour; or the City and Estate tour, which adds Longue Vue House and Gardens (p. 161) to a tour of the French Quarter, St. Louis Cemetery No. 3, Bayou St. John, Lake Pontchartrain, and the Uptown and Downtown neighborhoods—a very extensive overview with a broad reach. Isabelle also offers swamp and plantation tours, but no Garden District or walking tours.

www.toursbyisabelle.com. ⓒ **504/398-0365.** City tour combined with Katrina Recovery or Longue Vue $90; swamp plantation combo tours $210.

Two Chicks Walking Tours ★★ This tour company adds a dollop of sass to their tours, but they're nonetheless informative and entertaining. In the Bordellos and Ladies of the Night tour, perky guide Christine, adorned in a rainbow tutu, knows her stuff and weaves plenty of standard history through this soft-focus lens, bringing it new interest. Each tour stop has some relation to the oldest profession, from the Ursuline Convent to Storyville. It's a bit bawdy but not at all frivolous (even with the soundtrack of hooker-related tunes played between stops—think "Roxanne" and "House of the Rising Sun"). Our group had men and women of all ages and a mature teen with her parents, and all were equally engaged. The guide went well off-script answering questions, which personalized the tour even if causing it to run a bit over the 2 hours.

www.twochickswalkingtours.com. ⓒ **504/975-4386.** Most tours $20–$25; St. Louis #1 Cemetery tour $20. Check website for schedules. Reservations required.

French Quarter Intro Walking Tours

Besides the more extensive city tours listed above, these are some good introductory French Quarter walking tours. Needless to say, you can also start with the free, self-guided walking tour we've developed for you on p. 227.

The nonprofit volunteer group **Friends of the Cabildo ★★** (www.friends ofthecabildo.org; ✆ **504/524-9118**) offers an excellent 2-hour walking tour of the Quarter. Docents are mostly Quarter residents (ask about their own family histories). The tour leaves from in front of the 1850 House Museum Store, at 523 St. Ann St., on Jackson Square. The fee is $20 per adult, $15 students, free for children 12 and under. Tours leave Tuesday through Sunday at 10:30am and 1:30pm, except holidays. Purchase tickets online or on-site. Arrive 15 minutes early.

The **Jean Lafitte National Park and Preserve's Folklife and Visitor Center** is at 419 Decatur St., near Conti Street (www.nps.gov/jela/french-quarter-site.htm; ✆ **504/589-2636**). The super-cool National Park Service rangers here lead an excellent, free **"Riverfront History Stroll."** The walking tour covers about a mile along the riverfront and brings to life the city's history and the ethnic roots of its unique cultural mix. No reservations, and only 25 people are taken in a group. The tour starts at 9:30am Tuesday through Saturday (except for Mardi Gras and Christmas); the office opens at 9am; it's strongly suggested that you get there then to ensure you get a ticket.

Beyond the Quarter

A walking tour of the Garden District is offered by **Historic New Orleans Tours** (see above) daily at 11am and 1:45pm. It's 2 blocks from the St. Charles Streetcar line (Washington stop). Reserve in advance or just show up (cash only for walk-ups; $25 adults, $18 seniors, students, kids 6–12). **Gray Line** (see above) also offers a Garden District walking tour, but theirs transports you via bus from their French Quarter "Lighthouse" depot (Toulouse St. at the Mississippi River), then lets you off in the Garden District where the tour begins ($37 adults, $26 kids; March–Dec).

Tours of Katrina devastation and restoration are included in the general city tours offered by most of the listed tour companies above. If observed through the right lens, seeing the still-recovering areas is bearing witness to history, and it's important. That said, the residents rebuilding here became understandably tired of being viewed through that very lens, so tour companies must now skirt the edges of the worst-hit Lower Ninth Ward rather than entering the neighborhood. Coming here remains a double-edged decision.

Plantation tours of the **River Road plantation homes** are offered by the operators listed under "Tour Companies," above. See p. 171 for more info.

Surprisingly, one of the better and more established **walking tours of the Faubourg Tremé,** focusing on African-American history and the incredible cultural and musical legacy of this historic neighborhood, is offered by **French Quarter Phantoms** (www.frenchquarterphantoms.com; ✆ **504/666-8300**). It leaves from 718 N. Rampart St. daily at 10am. Reservations are required; it's $16 when booked online.

The 2-hour van tours by **Tremé & Mardi Gras Indians Tours** (www. tremeindiantours.com; ☏ **504/975-2434**) cover more ground than feet can, going to lesser-known but no less interesting beacons like the Zulu Social Aid & Pleasure Club headquarters. (Plus they serve food samples—always a bonus.) The guides are from this culture, mostly Tremé locals, so given their immersion in, and personal connection to, the area—they are inevitably knowledgeable and sincere; the focus on the Mardi Gras Indian culture is of particular interest. Three tours depart daily from Congo Square. Reservations are required and it only goes out if at least five people reserve. It's $65 adults; $60 seniors and military; $36 kids ages 4 to 12.

Other Special-Interest Tours

Hop On, Hop Off City Sightseeing Tours ★ (www.citysightseeingnew orleans; ☏ **800/362-1811**). We're not crazy about the sight of the familiar but garish **Big Red Bus** splayed across the city's historic streets (couldn't they at least have designed them to resemble our local streetcars?). But admittedly, these double-deckers offer a good way to get oriented, and see the city at your own pace. Like any multi-site, multi-day package, it's a good deal if you're really going to use it. The buses stop at 15 locations—from the French Market to the World War II Museum in the Central Business District and up to Magazine Street. Enough buses circulate so that you'll be picked up within 30 minutes at any of the stops. Onboard the enclosed bus or open-air roof (bring sunscreen), a guide narrates the sights along the way. It's rote but explanatory and helpful, and includes escorted walking tours of the French Quarter and Garden District. You can purchase tickets online, print them, and show up at any stop; or buy a ticket on the bus or at ticket offices at 700 Decatur St., or 501 Basin St. (the Basin St. Station Visitor Center). Buses run continuously from 9:30am to 5:30pm. It's $49 for unlimited hop on, hop off sightseeing over 3 days ($10 children 3–12).

Clue Carré ★ (830 Union St., www.cluecarre.com; ☏ **504/667-2583**), a New Orleans version of the popular **escape room** craze, is a good rainy-day option for couples or small groups. Participants are "locked" in one of five heavily decorated, locally themed rooms and given clues that they must answer to solve a mystery and thereby "escape." It works best when clue hunters' backgrounds and ages are diverse ($28 per person, 8 and older only).

Swamp Tours

A **swamp tour** can be a hoot, particularly if you get a guide who attracts alligators to your boat (please keep your hands inside the boat—they can look a lot like dinner to a gator). On all the following tours, you're likely to see alligators and waterfowl such as egrets, owls, herons, bald eagles, and ospreys. Or less frequently, spot a feral hog, otter, beaver, frog, turtle, raccoon, deer, or nutria. But even during winter hibernation, a morning spent floating on the bayou is mighty pleasant, and learning about how this unique ecosystem contributes to the local culture and economy is quite interesting. Plus, the swamps are simply eerily beautiful.

Most tour operators listed earlier in this chapter under "Tour Companies" (p. 171) provide swamp tours, but they really just coordinate your transportation, narrate the drive, and deliver you to one of the following knowledgeable swamp-tour folks. You can also drive to one of these tours, or contact them directly to arrange your transportation from the city.

Airboat Adventures ★★★ (www.airboatadventures.com; ✆ **888/467-9267**). This ain't no cozy roadside junket. It's a slick operation with an expansive gift shop (which also houses a rare albino gator) and a fleet of boats. And you're likely to see and hear those other boats as you ply the waters, rather than disappearing into swampy seclusion (as you might at some other swamp tour outfits). What you might get that you won't find elsewhere (and we've been on *many* a swamp tour) are brothers Paul and Lance, airboat captains who swim with—and *on*—the abundant gators. These fearless, local good ol' boys get shockingly up close and personal, enough to hand-feed and belly-rub the toothy reptiles. They're actual gator wrestlers who grew up with the beasts and know what they're doing. We think. Controversial? Yes. Cool? Um, sorry but yes. There's also the speeding, screeching boats (noise-blocking headphones provided) that intersperse showboating donuts with peaceful stops amid the primordial beauty of Lafitte National Preserve, to observe flora, fauna, and human-induced petrochemical clear-cutting. Paul and Lance, people—request them by name! Prices are $95 per person for a six- to eight-passenger boat, or $75 for a 15- to 27-passenger boat; fee includes transportation from New Orleans hotels (about 40 min.); deduct $20 if you arrive on your own. Phone reservations required.

Dr. Wagner's Honey Island Swamp Tours ★★★ (www.honeyisland swamp.com; ✆ **985/641-1769** or 504/242-5877), at 41490 Crawford Landing Rd. in Slidell about 30 miles outside of New Orleans, takes you by boat into the interior of Honey Island Swamp to view wildlife with native professional naturalist guides (captains Charlie and Brian both grew up plying these waters). The guides provide a solid educational experience to go with the purer swamp excitement. Tours last approximately 2 hours. Prices are $23 adults, $15 children 11 and under if you drive to the launch site yourself; or $48 adults and $32 children with hotel pickup in New Orleans.

Pearl River Eco-Tours ★★, 55050 Hwy. 90, Slidell (www.pearlrivereco tours.com; ✆ **866/597-9267** or 985/649-4200), is built on Southern hospitality. Captain Neil has been doing tours of Honey Island Swamp for more than 20 years, and the other captains also know their stuff. The swamp is beautiful, even during the cooler months when the gators are less frisky. In addition to the regular 18- to 26-passenger boats, these guys also offer a small six-passenger skiff ($70 per person, $85 with transportation) and **night tours,** which are supremely cool even if they do slightly freak us out ($100 per person/six-person minimum). **Day tours** are $25 adults, $15 children 4 to 12 if you drive; or $52 adults, $33 children including transportation. Tours are daily at 9:45am and 2:30pm.

It's a little farther out and you'll need to provide your own transportation, but we'd be remiss if we didn't add **Annie Miller's Son's Swamp and Marsh Tours ★★**, 4038 Bayou Black Dr., Houma (www.annie-miller.com; ℂ **985/868-4758**). The utterly authentic Jimmy Miller, son of the legendary Alligator Annie, is carrying on in her down-home tradition. Swamp water runs through his veins and he knows every inch of this bayou. Reservations required; call for schedules. Prices are $20 adults, $10 children 4 to 12, free 3 and under; tours run 2 to 2½ hours.

See p. 180 for a swamp tour done by kayak.

Cemetery, Mystical & Mysterious Tours

Interest in the ghostly, supernatural side of New Orleans has always been part of its appeal. But let's blame author Anne Rice's tales and subsequent stories of sparkly vampires for increasing the interest in tours catering to the vampire set. It has also resulted in some rather humorous infighting as rival tour operators steal each other's guides, shtick, and customers. We enjoy a good nighttime ghost tour of the Quarter as much as anyone, but we also have to admit that what's available is really hit-or-miss in presentation (it depends on who conducts your particular tour) and more miss than hit with regard to facts. Go for the entertainment value, not for the education, and you won't be disappointed. All the tours stop outside locations where horrifying things supposedly (or actually) happened, or inexplicable sights have been observed. Allegedly. Just be aware that this isn't a haunted-house tour (except for one tour, you don't enter any buildings other than a bar for a mid-tour break), and no shocking ghouls jump out from around dark corners. If you do see any spectral action, it'll most likely be after that bar stop.

We can send you with a clear conscience on the **Cemetery and Voodoo Tour** offered by **Historic New Orleans Tours ★★★** (www.tourneworleans. com; ℂ **504/947-2120**). It is consistently fact-based and not sensation-based, though no less entertaining. The trip goes through St. Louis Cemetery No. 1 and Congo Square and visits an active Voodoo temple. It leaves Monday through Saturday at 10am and 1pm (Sun 10am only) from the courtyard at 334-B Royal St. Rates are $25 adults, $15 students and seniors, $7 children 6 to 12, free 5 and under. They also offer a **nighttime haunted tour,** 'cause thrills and chills deserve darkness. The tour departs nightly at 7:30pm from Tujague's, 823 Decatur St.

Save Our Cemeteries ★★★ (www.saveourcemeteries.org; ℂ **504/504-525-3377**) is a nonprofit organization dedicated to cemetery maintenance, education, tomb restoration, and authentic tours. They have several daily tours of St. Louis Cemetery #1 ($20); daily 10:30am tours of Lafayette Cemetery ($15); and occasional tours of the little-seen St. Louis #2 ($20) (kids 12 or under free on all tours; add $1.40 per tour online booking fee; $5 for offline). Advance reservations required.

New Orleans Secret Tours does a Voodoo tour led by James Corbyn, a Voodoo practitioner and paranormal historian. He focuses on the actual religion—in history and today—in relationship to slavery and to the City of New Orleans, in myth and reality. The tour visits Voodoo altars and a temple where guests meet with a practitioner. It's $29; departure dates and times vary. Leaves from Mr. Gregory's, at 806 N. Rampart St. Book at www.nosecret tours.com or call ℂ **504/517-5397.**

As for those **vampire tours** . . . sorry to burst your bubble, friends, but vampires are not real. But if they were, they'd hang out in the French Quarter. Both are mysterious. Both are centuries old. Both are sexy. It makes sense. Personally, we prefer our history with a bit of, well, history—but if tales of bloodsuckery and high drama are what you seek, the current reigning kings are at **French Quarter Phantoms** (www.frenchquarterphantoms.com; ℂ **504/666-8300**). Costumes, fake blood, Dickensian delivery—the whole magilla (but not all the guides do it). Tours cost $16 to $18 when booked online; free for kids 7 and under. They leave from the Voodoo Lounge, 718 N. Rampart St., nightly at 6pm and 8pm. The 1½-hour **New Orleans Vampire** tour given by **Haunted History Tours** ★ (www.hauntedhistorytours.com; ℂ **888/644-6787** or 504/861-2727) is a baby step down on the drama ladder. It departs nightly at 8:30pm from outside St. Louis Cathedral and costs $25 adults, $18 students and seniors, $14 kids ages 6 to 11, free for kids 5 and under. Haunted History also offers cemetery and nighttime French Quarter ghost tours.

Popular with visitors of all stripes, these tours usually go out with large groups. Try to stay near the front, so you can see and hear your guide. Even the ones with the most booming voices have to regulate their delivery out of respect for French Quarter residents.

Food & Beverage Tours & Classes

Visitors can take can take their New Orleans culinary experience one tasty step further with a food and beverage tour or class.

Cooking class instructors, just like tour guides, can make or break the experience. We've had great times with the instructors at **Crescent City Cooks** ★★ (201 Chartres St.; www.crescentcitycooks.com; ℂ **504/529-1600**), whose personal commentary and local knowledge enliven what could be a pretty rote recipe recitation. The recipes themselves are local favorites, and the comfortable "classroom" has excellent sightlines and facilities. It's New Orleans, so naturally there's food and beverages before, during, and after the lesson ($30–$40 per person). If you can pop for it, by all means opt for a hands-on class ($150 per person). If you book first, you choose the menu, and the smaller class sizes and participatory lessons make for a much livelier, memorable time. Great for families and small groups.

Destination Kitchen Food Tours ★★ (www.destination-kitchen.com; ℂ **855/353-6634**) delivers Julie Barreda Bruyn's sprightly and cosmopolitan approach to epicurious Big Easy. Bruyn, a natural storyteller and event planner who also offers food tours in Italy, France, and Spain, showcases culinary offerings on Oak Street and Freret Street uptown, along St. Charles Avenue in the Garden District, the lakefront, and tours of the French Quarter with or without a cooking experience. Commentary is offered in English, French, or Spanish, the three languages that New Orleans has spoken for centuries. Tours range from $65 to $129 and are small and intimate. Some include transportation. Tours of Cajun country and weekend getaways and girlfriend experiences also offered.

Drink and Learn ★★★ (www.drinkandlearn.com; ⓒ **504/578-8280**) is Elizabeth Pearce's aptly named company. The noted cocktail impresario and author of *Drink Dat New Orleans* punctuates her walking tour with stops at cocktail-orientated sites, where participants partake of prepoured smart beverages. Pearce's lively delivery, depth of knowledge, and visual aids transport guests through centuries of New Orleans' storied cocktail history. The Cocktail Tour meets most nights (but not all) at 6 or 6:30pm at Vacherie Restaurant (p. 94), 827 Toulouse St., and costs $50 per person (21 and over only). Reservations required. Book in advance; the small groups fill up fast.

NOLA Brewing Brewery Tour ★★ isn't a walking tour but an actual tour through the largest local craft brewery in New Orleans. The 35-minute, brewmaster-led look behind the scenes is wildly popular (read: crowded) for the free samples but also because it's interesting and informative. And because kickass **McClure's BBQ** is on-site, and goes down well with the taproom's brews. For more on local breweries, see p. 208. Tours are offered Friday 2 to 3pm and Saturday and Sunday 2 to 4pm, and the taproom is open daily 11am to 11pm (3001 Tchoupitoulas St.; www.nolabrewing.com; ⓒ **504/896-9996**).

Also see the **Confederacy of Cruisers Culinary Bike Tour,** below.

Boat & Kayak Tours

C'mon, you know you want to. It's a paddle wheeler on the Mississippi, fer the love of Mark Twain. A river cruise is cheesy, refreshing fun, and gives everyone an excuse to bust out their best "Proud Mary."

The steamboat *Natchez* (www.steamboatnatchez.com; ⓒ **800/233-2628** or 504/569-1401), a marvelous three-deck steam-powered stern-wheeler, re-creates the 19th-century version that held the record for fastest steamship till the *Robert E. Lee* famously whipped it in 1870—although the current boat has never lost a race! Now it takes leisurely jazz cruises from 7 to 9pm nightly with the most excellent Dukes of Dixieland providing the tunes. There's narration for a little history and a steam-engine room for gearheads (tickets $48 adults, $24 kids 6–12, free for kids 2–5; with dinner: $83, $38, and $18, respectively). The daily 11:30am or 2:30pm lunch (Sun brunch) cruises are $34, $13 kids 6 to 12, free kids 2 to 5; with lunch or brunch $51, $28, and $18, respectively. *Natchez* is docked at Toulouse Street behind Jax Brewery; its new sister steamboat, the *City of New Orleans,* should be launched by the time you read this.

On the smaller *Creole Queen* (www.creolequeen.com; ⓒ **800/445-4109** or 504/529-4567), Don Vappie, a favorite local banjo player, leads the band during the 7:30pm jazz cruise ($48 adults, $24 kids 6–12, free for 5 and under; with buffet dinner: $79, $16 and $12, respectively). Other logical options include the 2½-hour Historical River Cruise, which stops downriver at Chalmette Battlefield, site of the Battle of New Orleans ($34 adults, $14 kids 6–12, free for 5 and under; add $19 for buffet lunch). There is a snack bar if you opt out of the meal. It's docked at the end of Poydras Street, next to the Outlets at Riverwalk. The Queen is also setting sail a new sister ship in late 2018, the 3,000-passenger, jazz-themed *Louis Armstrong*.

Both ships have outside decks and inside lounges with A/C or heat as needed, and cocktail bars of course. Times vary seasonally, so call ahead. Arrive at least a half-hour early to board. *Tip 1:* Check the online coupon sites for discounts. *Tip 2:* There's better food on land. Just sayin'.

Kayak-iti-Yat ★★★ (www.kayakitiyat.com; ℂ **985-778-5034** or 512-964-9499) explains city lore from the unique perspective of a kayak along Bayou St. John. When the weather's right, it's a sublime way to explore some historic neighborhoods. Tours range from 2 to 4 hours, with increasing intensity of upper-body workouts (the better to justify last night's indulgent dinner). It's not difficult even for the inexperienced, and highly recommended. Tours run daily; times vary, and advance reservations are required. Costs range from $45 to $110. Call for reservations, times, and meeting-place directions. All equipment is provided, but there's no bathroom stop, so plan ahead.

If you're adventuresome and can commit the better part of a day, **Lost Lands Tours** ★★ (www.lostlandstours.org; ℂ **504/858-7575**) takes kayakers to Lake Maurepas, 40 minutes outside of New Orleans, on a 3- to 4-hour paddle through the elegant, mysterious swamps. The focus is on the environmental issues surrounding these vital, rapidly disappearing wetlands. It's beautiful and illuminating. Limited transportation is available; tours are $95 and require a minimum of four to go out, weather permitting.

Bicycle & Other Wheeled Tours

A bike tour is a terrific way to explore some lesser-seen parts of this flat city up close and in depth. Our suggested tours go at an outright leisurely pace, so you needn't be a serious rider, but bike familiarity and a healthy dose of pluck will help you handle the hazards of potholes and traffic (including stretches along some busy avenues). Do opt-in to the optional helmet; bring sunscreen, a hat, rain poncho, and water (though most tours provide a small starter bottle) as conditions dictate. While a restroom stop is included, you'd be wise to take care of that before departure, too. For regular old bike rentals, see p. 268.

Confederacy of Cruisers (www.confederacyofcruisers.com; ℂ **504/400-5468**) offers a bike tour with an itinerary that hits parts of the Marigny, Bywater, 7th Ward, and Tremé on comfortable, well-maintained single-gear cruisers with baskets. The eight-person-maximum, guide-led group pulls over about every 10 minutes at such diverse stops as the New Orleans Center for Creative Arts (NOCCA), St. Roch Cemetery, the Mother-in-Law Lounge, and St. Augustine Church, where guides offer up well-informed cultural and architectural insights. The 3-hour tours are $49 and depart twice daily. The half-day **culinary bike tour** takes different itineraries, but all go to killer, off-the-beaten-track eateries favored by locals. The "tastes" are copious, and guide Cassady's laidback delivery belies a serious depth of food knowledge (and history and architecture), which he imparts between bites. It's $89 all-inclusive, and worth it. Reservations are a must. Depart from Washington Square Park at Elysian Fields Avenue and Royal Street, on the outskirts of the French Quarter.

Freewheelin' Bike Tours (www.neworleansbiketour.com; ✆ **504/522-4368**) has a similar itinerary, with stops for snoballs (during the season) and at St. Louis No. 3 Cemetery, where one of the guides' great-grandparents are buried. It goes out at 10am and 2pm every day. The **Uptown tour** through the Garden District and the Irish Channel goes along St. Charles Avenue for a bit and through the Warehouse District. This one departs daily at 9:30am and 1:30pm; both are $50 and leave from 325 Burgundy St. in the French Quarter. Check the website for their occasional quickie, low-priced tours (1–2 hours), usually offered in off-season or at off times. We like their sturdy, American-made cruisers, which have been custom-constructed for these streets, and that tours max out at 10 passengers.

It's All About the Music (www.nolasocialride.org) is a three-way win: You 1) ride around the city; 2) hang with locals; and 3) hear music at a bunch of clubs. A cool dude leads this casual, free ride every Tuesday night just for fun. He's also a WWOZ DJ, so he's fully dialed in to the local music scene. You need your own bike (see p. 268 for rentals) with a light and a lock. Meet Tuesday 6:30pm at Congo Square (inside Armstrong Park at Rampart St. and Orleans Ave.).

As for other wheeled ways to tour the city, consider the **City Segway,** 214 Decatur St. (http://neworleans.citysegwaytours.com; ✆ **504/619-4162**). There's something disconcerting about seeing these oddball, two-wheeled stand-up vehicles rolling thru the hallowed, centuries-old French Quarter streets. But the thing is, they're kind of a blast. It gets better after the "How to avoid brain trauma" introductory video (the in-store training ends when everyone feels comfortable). Still, when you follow the guide onto those potholed streets, it can be intimidating. Till it turns fun. Which happens quickly. The 3-hour ($75) tour beats the 2-hour ($65) one—you get more stops (mostly to French Quarter and Tremé greatest-hits landmarks), more history, and more leg stretches, which you need. And yes, you get a few minutes in an open space to let those horses loose and see what they can really do (about 10 mph). Multiple departure times daily include evenings; call or check website for schedule and to book.

Corny it may be, but an old **horse-drawn carriage tour** of the Quarter or beyond has a romantic allure. The "horses" are actually mules (they handle the city heat and humidity better), often bedecked with ribbons, flowers, and even hats. Drivers seem to be in a fierce competition to win the "most entertaining" award. They share history and rote anecdotes of dubious authenticity; they'll also customize itineraries on request. Carriages wait on Decatur Street in front of Jackson Square from 8:30am to midnight (except in heavy rain). Private carriages are $200 per 1 hour for up to four people; there are ghost-themed 1-hour group carriage tours for $40 or you can hop into one of the waiting carriages (you may be sharing with other tourists) for $20 per person per ½ hour. Contact www.neworleanscarriages.com or © **504/943-8820** for custom tours and hotel pickups.

ESPECIALLY FOR KIDS

If you plan to give the kids a lifelong complex for confining you to your hotel room when you *know* all that clubbing and fooding is going on outside, then perhaps New Orleans is better done *sans enfants*. But the truth is, despite its reputation as a playground for grown-ups, the Big Easy is a terrific family destination, with oodles of conventional and unconventional only-in-New-Orleans activities to entertain them (and you). **Mardi Gras** (p. 42) and **Jazz Fest** (p. 50) are both doable and enjoyable with kids, as are many of the organized tours (p. 171). *Tip:* Those above spooking age love to tour the cemeteries (no touching!) and haunted places, but long walking tours of historic homes and landmarks may be best left to the grown-ups.

The **French Quarter** in and of itself is cool for kids 6 and over. You can while away a pleasant morning on a Quarter walkabout, seeing the architecture and peeking into shops, checking out the street performers, with a rest stop for powder-sugary beignets at **Café du Monde** (p. 130). If you have kids of museum-going age, the Mardi Gras exhibit at the **Presbytère** (p. 145) or the Hurricane exhibit at the **Cabildo** (p. 142) will hold their attention for a while. You can probably talk them into a riverfront walk along scenic Woldenberg Park, because it ends at a great splash fountain in front of Audubon Aquarium.

Even self-conscious tweens fall for a **horse-and-buggy ride** (see "Bicycle & Other Wheeled Tours," above) around the Quarter (it's text-friendly, after all), and it works for all ages when it's hot and nap time is closing in—it might even rock the little ones to sleep. The **Canal Street Ferry** (p. 269) crosses the Mississippi River and ends just pre-boredom (and makes a great intro to reading *Huckleberry Finn* together). Add a clackety-clacking **streetcar ride** (p. 266), and you've hit the trifecta of ever-fascinating transportation options.

If it's just a matter of needing to run, jump, swing, and blow off some energy, head for **Cabrini Playground** (www.cabriniplayground.com) in the residential, northeast corner of the French Quarter at Barracks and Dauphine streets.

A number of the city's top attractions are obviously family-friendly, including the **Audubon Aquarium of the Americas** (p. 136). Only the most squeamish should skip the **Insectarium** (p. 138), because it's swell.

Outside the Quarter, the highly regarded **Audubon Zoo** (p. 159), complete with a seasonal splash park for the pool-deprived, is both lovely and a great diversion. For more animal action, a **swamp tour** (p. 175) is a sure-fire winner. While you're not guaranteed to see gators, it's a pretty good bet, and even so, hey, you're on a boat in a swamp. Many also offer speedier **airboats** for young adrenaline junkies.

And then there is the wonder that is **City Park.** We've already mentioned some of the all-ages features there (see p. 160, and pay particular attention to the **Train Garden**); every December, thousands of holiday lights turn the City Park landscape into fairy-tale scenery for the **Celebration in the Oaks** (p. 28).

Here are a few more of the city's offerings for kids and parents to love.

Amusement Park and Children's Storyland ★★ The under-8 set will be delighted with this playground (rated one of the 10 best in the country by *Child* magazine), where well-known children's stories and rhymes inspired the charming decor. It offers plenty of characters to slide down and climb on and generally get juvenile ya-yas out.

Kids and adults will enjoy the carousel, Ferris wheels, bumper cars, miniature train, Tilt-a-Whirl, lady-bug-shaped roller coaster, and other rides at the **Carousel Gardens,** also in City Park. Delighting local families since 1906, the carousel (or "da flying horses," as real locals call it) is one of only 100 all-wood merry-go-rounds in the country, and the only one in the state.

City Park at Victory Ave. www.neworleanscitypark.com/in-the-park/carousel-gardens. © **504/483-9403.** Admission to Carousel Gardens, Botanical Gardens, and Storyland $4; rides $4 each, unlimited rides $18. Amusement park mid-Mar through mid-Nov Fri–Sun 11am–6pm; extended weekend hours June 3–Aug 3. Storyland Tues–Fri 10am–5pm; Sat–Sun 10am–6pm. Hours vary by season, so call ahead to be safe.

Big Lake Boating and Biking ★★ Big Lake in City Park is a pretty spot for a boat ride, and the kids can scour the shoreline for turtles. There are **pedal boats** for rent from **Wheel Fun,** which also rents **bicycles, tandems,** and **surreys** for use inside City Park. All that pedaling action can be a workout, which means you can justify a visit to nearby **Angelo Brocato's** ice cream parlor afterward (p. 130). Life jackets (provided) required. Check website and www.groupon.com for discounts.

Wheel Fun Rentals, Big Lake Trail in City Park. www.wheelfunrentals.com. © **504/300-1289.** Pedal boat $26–$36/hr.; kayak $15–$22/hr. stand-up paddleboard $20/hr.; Surrey $26–$36/hr.; bike $8–$20/hr. (in-park use only). Mar to mid-Oct Mon–Fri 10am–sunset, Sat–Sun 9am–sunset; mid-Oct to Feb Thurs–Sun 10am–5pm. Hours change seasonally, so call ahead to verify.

City Putt Miniature Golf ★ We're partial to the two 18-hole miniature golf courses opened in 2013, and impressed with the design: On one course, each hole is designed around a New Orleans neighborhood, with iconic statues and signage and stuff; the other course keys off of statewide themes (learning is fun!).

On Victory Dr. in City Park, across from the entrance to Storyland and the Botanical Garden. www.neworleanscitypark.com/in-the-park/city-putt. © **504/483-9385.** $8 adults; $6 children 4–12; free for children 3 and under. Tues–Thurs 10am–10pm; Sat–Sun 10am–midnight; last rental 1 hour before closing. Hours may vary mid-Nov to New Year's Day when Celebration in the Oaks is under way in City Park.

French Quartour Kids Tour ★★ Believe it or not, this is the only tour in New Orleans designed specifically for kids. And it's super. The company's founder and regular guide is a former schoolteacher and an excellent kid-wrangler. She conducts the tour in costume and manages to maintain the

get the kids JAZZED

In such a musical town, there is a sorrowful lack of music options for the younger set. Parents who might be trying to indoctrinate their kids into the joys of jazz, brass bands, or zydeco (or who just want to enjoy it themselves) will be hard-pressed to find options. Blame it on the booze—most music venues serve alcohol and are legally prohibited from allowing anyone younger than 21 to enter. The street performers along **Royal Street** and in **Jackson Square** work well, but fear not, we've got a few other interesting ideas.

o **Frenchmen Street Clubs** Yes—you can make the Frenchmen Street scene with kids in tow. The **Maison** (p. 196) and **Three Muses** (p. 198) allow kids for the early shows, which usually start around 4 or 5pm (parents must be in attendance). Grab a table, order snacks, and let the little ones shake their miniature groove thangs. They may be asked to leave when the tables break down and the drinking crowd moves in, around 9 or 10pm.

o **Jazz National Historical Park** Occasional-fee family-oriented music workshops, concerts, and funnery, including monthly kids' concerts at the French Market. Get details at www.nps.gov/jazz/index.htm

o **Little Gem** This straightforward jazz club is accessible and welcoming, even making a few nods to the young'uns (as in crayons and chicken tenders). Most shows are all-ages, but do double-check; a dinner reservation gets you a table. See more on p. 200.

o **Mid-City Lanes Rock 'n' Bowl** Hey, you got cool music in our bowling! Wait, you got bowling in our nightclub! It's two

enthusiasm level going for the full 2 hours. The spiels (there's one tour for ages 4–7; another for 7–13) keep it relatable, with attention to what life was like for kids in the olden days. History is definitely being conveyed as sites are explored, but the lessons use props (which she totes around in a colorful wheeled cart), storytelling, play-acting, and enough gory details to hold most kids' focus. Emphasis on "most." Ask about seasonally themed tours.

www.frenchquartourkids.com. ℂ **504/975-5355.** $20 per person (includes kids and adults; 1 adult chaperone required). Tours daily 9:30am, 12:30pm, 3:30pm, 5pm (may be adjusted for season or weather). Reservations required. Meeting locations vary.

Louisiana Children's Museum ★★★ This interactive museum is really a playground in disguise that will keep kids occupied for a good couple of hours. The museum's hands-on, experiential exhibits furtively explore literacy, health, science, arts, and the environment—through fun. In summer 2019, it moves to a gorgeous new location in City Park, with extensive outdoor exhibits: an edible garden and a mock grocery store, as parts of a "food journey" exhibit; a lagoon-side exhibit with water play, as part of a wetlands and natural resource "lesson." *Note:* Children 15 and under must be accompanied by an adult.

420 Julia St., moving mid-2019 to 1 Roosevelt Mall, City Park. www.lcm.org. ℂ **504/523-1357.** Admission $10; free for children under 1. Sept–May Tues–Sat 9:30am–4:30pm,

in one, and both work. It's hard to go wrong with this one, although the music usually doesn't get started till 8:30ish, so bedtime might need to be pushed back some. There's usually an early zydeco music show on Sunday. Kids with parents are welcome. See p. 200.

o **Music Box Village** Kids (like adults) may or may not "get" the performances here—the eclectic music made in this "sonic village" isn't exactly mainstream. But curious minds of all ages will find the musical-instrument structures fascinating. During the hands-on public hours, visitors can explore them and create their own eclectic tunes. See more on p. 210.

o **Preservation Hall** The historic, inimitable traditional jazz venue is open to all ages. The earliest show starts at 8pm nightly; get there early so the young ones can see (if they're really young, sit by the door in case a boredom-induced quick exit is required). See p. 193.

o **Tipitina's** On most Sundays at 1pm the torch gets passed at the legendary Tip's. The **Youth Music Workshop** is a jam session/music lesson for aspiring players, where some of the city's best musicians give free lessons to kids (and also show off their chops). It's pretty free-form and largely attended by local kids, but anyone can come. Bring an instrument if you have one. See p. 201.

o **New Orleans Jazz Museum at the U.S. Mint** The gorgeous performance room upstairs in this museum has some form of free music nearly every day, and all ages are welcome. See p. 151.

Sun noon–4:30pm; June–Aug Mon–Sat 9:30am–5pm, Sun noon–5pm. Closed major holidays. The Julia St. location will be closed for about 2 months before the move; hours may change at new location. Check website or call for most current info.

GETTING SPORTY

Big Easy Rollergirls ★ Okay, it's a total goof, but a hoot of a goof. By definition, roller derby is going to be a bit wild (though the athleticism can't be denied). Mix in New Orleans, and the resulting outcome is pure wack. The Big Easy babes play it up for all it's worth, and the crowd action is equally rowdy. More of a hipster scene but with a smattering of families, it's all in fun, and worth the modest ticket price just to check out the cheerleaders, halftime entertainment, outfits, and the food trucks.

University of New Orleans' Human Performance Center, Elysian Fields and Leon C. Simon Dr. www.bigeasyrollergirls.com. Tickets $15 at door, $10 with advance online purchase. Kids $5; free for 6 and under.

New Orleans Pelicans ★★ Playing in the renovated **Smoothie King Center** (next door to the Superdome), the NBA Pelicans (formerly the Hornets) now command an exclusive area on the sidelines called "Hollywood" where seats can be had for some serious green. A few years ago that was not

BET YOU CAN FIND places to gamble

Harrah's Casino is quite like a Vegas casino (115,000 sq. ft., 1,700 slot machines, more than 100 tables, a steakhouse restaurant, and the Masquerade Lounge). It's located on Canal Street at the river (www.caesars.com/harrahs-new-orleans; *℗* **504/533-6000**). *Tip:* Locals know the voluminous buffet can satisfy the most serious munchies for not-so-serious cash (it's a good deal for an awful lot of food). There's also riverboat gambling in the area. Outside the city, the

Boomtown Casino (www.boomtown neworleans.com; *℗* **504-366-7711** for information and directions) is located on the West Bank, and the **Treasure Chest Casino** (www.treasurechest.com; *℗* **504-443-8000**) is docked on Lake Pontchartrain in Kenner. **Slot machines** can be found in every imaginable locale in the city, from bars to Laundromats to riverboats, separated (by law) from the main room by a door or curtain.

a possibility. Then Chris Paul and subsequently Anthony Davis came along to change everything by leading the team to playoffs and higher heights. The Pels put on a good b-ball show and remain a major attraction.

1501 Girod St. www.nba.com/pelicans. *℗* **504/525-4667.** Tickets $42 and up.

New Orleans Saints ★★★ Who dat won the Super Bowl? The Saints' incredible Super Bowl XLIV victory in 2010 was the culmination of the city's 43-year collective dream (to say nothing of the end of 43 years of frustration), in which the beloved 'Aints finally won the big one, becoming a metaphor for the city's post-Katrina comeback and a source of frenzied pride. A scandal here and there has barely dampened the enthusiasm for this team, and if you're the least bit of a football fan, try to get yourself inside the Superdome (p. 157) for a Saints game—there's really nothing like it. Your best bet is the **NFL Ticket Exchange** (www.ticketexchangebyticketmaster.com). Otherwise, the pregame party at **Champions Square,** outside the Superdome (or any sports bar, really), is an excellent place to start your game day.

Mercedes Benz Superdome, 1500 block of Poydras St. Saints home office: 5800 Airline Dr., Metairie. www.neworleanssaints.com. *℗* **504/733-0255.** Ticket info: *℗* **504/731-1700.** Tickets $60–astronomical, depending on the game.

New Orleans Baby Cakes ★★ A post-2016 season rebranding delivered a head-scratching moniker for the Florida Marlins' farm team, formerly the Zephyrs. But the experience is the same, and truly, there may be no better entertainment value in pro sports than AAA baseball. A few hours at the Shrine on Airline field out near the airport affirms that. Mascots Boudreaux D. and Clotile Nutria do their enthusiastic best to ensure that family fun is foremost, with various fan-participation promos and activities. There's a pool area behind right field (rentable for groups or parties) and, on weekends, a general-admission grass "levee" behind center field.

Shrine on Airline Field 6000 Airline Dr., Metairie. www.cakesbaseball.com. *℗* **504/734-5155.** Tickets $5–$10; family four-pack with dawgs and sodas $44.

NEW ORLEANS NIGHTLIFE

8

New Orleans works her wily exotic charms most effectively after dark, when the jazz singers and cocktail slingers ply their magic. It is impossible to imagine this city without a soundtrack of jazz, brass bands, R&B, hip-hop, blues, bounce, and funk. After all, this is the town that sends you to your grave with music and then dances back from the cemetery. It's the city that lets the good times roll and lets you take them to go (you can stroll the streets with a drink in hand, as long as it's in a plastic "go cup"—or "geaux," to use the faux-French). Here, some of the world's greatest musicians (no exaggeration) can be seen and heard with relative ease in remarkably intimate surroundings. And when the clubs get too full, no matter: The crowd spills into the street, where the talking, drinking, and dancing continue.

We'll help you wend your way through all the awesomeness, but don't forget that tomorrow beckons, with more of the city's enchantments to explore. First, a few things to know:

o **Club-hopping is easy.** The city is compact, so most clubs are within easy walking or taxi distance from your hotel or dinner locale. Many are closely clustered so you can hop from one to another. Club clusters can be found on Bourbon Street in the Quarter; Frenchmen Street in the Marigny; Tchoupitoulas Street in the Warehouse District; St. Claude Avenue in the Marigny and Bywater; Freret, Oak and Maple streets Uptown; and around Willow Street in the Riverbend.

o **Showtimes vary.** Posted start and end times range from strict to strictly a suggestion (and sometimes indicate door times, not show times). Call if your schedule depends on it. Shows often start later than promised. Except when they start on time.

o **Yes, they card.** Some clubs allow 18-year-olds, and a few allow kids to early shows when accompanied by a parent (like The Maison, p. 196). Mostly, though, it's 21+ and expect to be carded. Even you, grandpa. It's da law.

- **No cover doesn't mean free.** It means buy drinks (bottled water counts) and tip the band (and/or buy their CDs, merch, whatever).
- **Early shows rock.** Shows starting from 4 to 7pm are often no or low cover, mellower music, and a great way to avoid the crowds and the crazy.
- **Cover charges vary widely.** During big events and for big acts, they can be much higher than cited here. Crowd sizes also vary accordingly.
- **Music is everywhere.** A blurry line separates "clubs" from bars, restaurants, hotel lounges, streets, parks, and front stoops. All can showcase excellent music, so don't overlook them.
- **Smoking is nowhere.** All clubs, bars, and restaurants are nonsmoking. Take it to the streets, if you must (or courtyards, where allowed).
- **What's going on:** Check **Offbeat.com** and sign up for "Weekly Beats" e-mails or go to **WWOZ.org/livewire** (you can also tune in to 90.7; club lineups are announced at the top of every odd hour). Both have good apps, worthy of downloading for the duration of your visit (and after).

THE RHYTHMS OF NEW ORLEANS

New Orleans R&B legend Ernie K-Doe was once quoted as saying, "I'm not sure, but I think all music came from New Orleans." What might be a more accurate account—and relatively hyperbole-free—is that all music came *to* New Orleans. Any style you can name, from African field hollers to industrial techno-rock to classical, finds its way to the Crescent City. Paul McCartney, Led Zeppelin, Trent Reznor, and Beyoncé have recorded here. Pianist James Booker, an eye-patched eccentric even by New Orleans standards, could make a Bach chorale strut like a second-line umbrella twirler. Then it's blended, shaken, and stirred into a new, distinctive, and frothy concoction that could have come from nowhere else.

That sublime hybrid is what you'll likely find: jazz descended from Buddy Bolden, Louis Armstrong, and their Storyville compatriots. Head-bobbing R&B transmitted via Fats Domino and Professor Longhair. Hip hop incorporating rhythmic Mardi Gras Indian chants. Brass bands of the second lines, infused with funk exuberance. Soak it in.

The Jazz Life of New Orleans

—With thanks to jazz historian George Hocutt

Music was of great importance to the Louisiana settlers and their Creole offspring, and early on the city had a fascination with marching bands (records of parades go back to 1787). Bands became de rigueur at occasions from baptisms to funerals ad infinitum—as they still are today.

In the early 19th century, enslaved people were allowed to congregate in the area known as **Congo Square** (now part of Armstrong Park) for dancing and drumming to the rhythms of their African and Caribbean homelands.

Eventually these enslaved people and free people of color became accomplished instrumentalists. When blues, work songs, hollers, and spirituals were melded with their native-based rhythms and syncopations, the precursor to jazz was forming. The music was taking on a distinctly New Orleanian aura.

By the late 1890s, cornetist **Charles "Buddy" Bolden,** the "First Man of Jazz," and drummer **"Papa" Jack Laine** were taking the sounds to the next level, and to white audiences—helped along by black vaudeville crossing the color line. (In a part of the Central Business District once called **"Backatown,"** their original haunts still stand—barely—awaiting pending renovation. We hope. Check out the **Eagle Saloon** at 401-403 S. Rampart St., and the neighboring **Iroquois Theatre,** where an adolescent Louis Armstrong first played, at 413-415 S. Rampart St.).

Meanwhile, the Storyville brothel zone was flourishing on nearby Basin Street. The entertainment lineup at the better houses included a piano player in the parlor—the immortal Jelly Roll Morton among them. By the twenties, sleazy Storyville was folding. Its players took the new sounds on the road: Kid Ory to California; King Oliver and his protégé Louis Armstrong to Chicago; Papa Jack and his Original Dixieland Jazz Band to New York. Their shows drew hordes and their records sold wildly. After World War II, Sidney Bechet and horn set up shop in France, and jazz consumed the continent. The jazz genie was officially out of the bottle and the craze was on.

New Orleans is still producing jazz greats and pushing the form forward. Start with **Ellis Marsalis,** father to jazz-playing sons **Branford, Jason,** and Pulitzer Prize–winning trumpeter **Wynton. Jon Batiste. Christian Scott aTunde Adjuah, Terence Blanchard,** and brothers **Troy "Trombone Shorty" Andrews** and **James "Satchmo of the Ghetto" Andrews** (among others) blow their horns to ever-adventurous distances. Obviously, the city still abounds with creativity.

Meanwhile, the nouveau traditional jazz movement is mad hot. On any given night in any given club, players from their 20s to their 70s share the bandstand, covering Jelly Roll or Django—or playing originals straight outta their eras. The **Jazz Vipers, Moonshiners, Cottonmouth Kings, Smokin' Time Jazz Band, Palmetto Bug Stompers, Tuba Skinny, Little Big Horns,** and **Hot Club of New Orleans** start the long list.

Brass Bands

Today, there's way more to New Orleans brass bands than the post-funeral "second line" parade of "When the Saints Go Marching In." Now, brass is imbued with funk, R&B, reggae, and hip hop, and appearances on the HBO TV show *Tremé* have engendered a new crop of fans. Classics like the **Tremé** and **Olympia Brass Bands** still hold court, but the revival goes back to the late 1980s, when **Dirty Dozen Brass Band** and **Rebirth Brass Band** started mixing things up. Today this horn-heavy, booty-moving, New-Orleans-born-and-bred-style packs the clubs and the streets. Try to catch the sounds of Louis Armstrong–inspired and reigning king **Kermit Ruffins and his**

CAN'T-MISS NEW ORLEANS MUSICAL
experiences

o **Kermit Ruffins,** anywhere he and his rowdy trumpet show up (try Blue Nile, Little Gem, Bullets, or the iconic Mother-in-Law Lounge, which he now owns).

o The **Soul Rebels** brass band's roof-raising Thursday sets at Les Bon Temps Roulé.

o The soul-wrenching, party-starting early set of the sublime **John Boutté** at d.b.a.

o Multi-instrumentalist (and mad musical mastermind) **Aurora Nealand** with her Royal Roses or in other forms. Try to keep your toes from tapping. Just. Try.

o The mellow tones and vivid lyrics of folk-leaning **Paul Sanchez, Alexandra Scott,** or troubadour **Andrew Duhon.**

o Piano wizards **Tom McDermott, Josh Paxton,** or **Jon Cleary,** solo or not.

o **Swank hotel lounging.** Try the **Davenport Lounge** at the Ritz-Carlton, the Monteleone's **Carousel Bar,** or the Windsor Court's **Polo Club.**

o Catching someone huge like Pearl Jam or Bonnie Raitt at **Tipitina's** (give the 'Fess Head statue an extra rub for your good fortune).

o Brilliant singer-songwriter-guitarist and Death Valley dry wit **Alex McMurray** solo or in any of his many guises, like the Tin Men trio (or if you hit the jackpot, doing sea shanties with the Valparaiso Men's Chorus).

o **Rebirth Brass Band** at the Maple Leaf on a Tuesday. Or anywhere, any day.

o Bounce queen **Big Freedia** live at the **Republic.** Or anywhere, any day, also.

o Bowling and dancing at **Rock 'n' Bowl,** especially on zydeco night.

o Excellent modern jazz in a quality room, like **Snug Harbor, Little Gem,** or the **Jazz Playhouse.**

o Seeing the Stooges, Hot 8, Soul Rebels, TBC, or Rebirth and finally **getting what this brass band thing is all about**—and never wanting it to stop.

o **Dr. Michael White,** whose dulcet clarinet snake-charms even die-hard jazz cynics.

o **DJ Soul Sister,** whose rainbow flow jams the floor monthly at One Eyed Jacks.

o **Don Vappie** on banjo, perhaps the swingingest strumming you'll ever see.

o **The Wild Magnolias.** Just. See. Them. Or any Mardi Gras Indians band.

o **Corey Henry** ripping the roof off of Vaughan's in the storied Thursday-night slot.

o Catching **King James & Special Men, Flow Tribe,** or **Brass-a-Holics** before they get any huger. Later you can say you knew them when.

o A show at **Preservation Hall,** where the soul of traditional jazz oozes from the instruments as much as from the ancient-looking walls.

o Superstar **Trombone Shorty** if he happens to be back in town on his home turf.

Barbecue Swingers; Hot 8; New Birth; or the **Stooges.** Or newer arrivals like the blazing **TBC (To Be Continued) Brass Band,** eclectic Soul Brass, raging **Brass-a-Holics,** or the pumping street-corner Gods, **Young Fellaz.** Did we mention the ladies-only **Pinettes?** Yeah, see them.

Cajun & Zydeco

Cajun and zydeco don't come from New Orleans at all despite the soundtrack you hear blaring out of Bourbon Street T-shirt shops. Both genres originated in the bayous of southwest Louisiana, a good 3 hours away. Their foundations lie in the arrival of two different French-speaking peoples in the swamp country: the white Acadians (French migrants who were booted out of Nova Scotia by the English in 1755) and the black Creoles (who came from the Caribbean slave trade). Both oppressed groups took to the folksy button accordion, newly introduced from Germany and France, which added a richness and power to their fiddle and guitar music. Later, drums, amplifiers, and steel guitars filled out the sound.

The styles began to separate after WWII, with the Cajuns gravitating toward country-and-western swing and Creole musicians being heavily influenced by the urban blues. **D. L. Menard** (the Cajun Hank Williams) and **Clifton Chenier** (the King of Zydeco) pioneered exciting new strains in their respective directions. During the early 1960s folk-music boom, such figures as the **Balfa Brothers** and fiddler **Dennis McGee** performed at folk festivals. A turning point came when a Cajun group received a standing ovation at the 1964 Newport Festival, energizing the form and Cajun pride, and spawning a new generation of Cajun musicians.

The proud new generation was led by accordion guru Marc Savoy and his multi-instrumentalist/author wife **Ann,** and fiddler **Michael Doucet** and his band **Beausoleil**—with **Steve Riley** and **Zachary Richard** in quick-step. The next generation of ambassadors, like the Grammy-winning **Pine Leaf Boys, Feaufollet,** and intoxicating hybridists **Sweet Crude** and **Lost Bayou Ramblers,** are mixing in new styles while venerating old-timey music. (The **Ramblers** regularly cover the **Pogues,** scrambling Irish punk with Cajun French in a madcap, Mensa-level mash-up.)

As for zydeco, the late **Boozoo Chavis, John Delafose,** and **Rockin' Sidney** joined king Clifton Chenier and added their own embellishments. More recently, **Nathan Williams** and the late, great, stately **Beau Jocque** did the same. The form is thriving today thanks to some of their musical progeny, including Chenier's son **C. J.,** Delafose's son **Geno,** and various Dopsie kin (**Dwayne and Rockin' Dopsie, Jr.**); plus **Keith Frank** and girl powerhouses like "Zydeco Sweetheart" **Rosie Ledet** and **Amanda Shaw. Terrance Simien** won the first zydeco Grammy in 2008, and the latest crop of players, like **Corey Ledet** and **Jeffrey Broussard,** are blending in the influences du jour. Also see "Cajun Country," p. 256.

Rhythm & Blues (& Hip Hop & Bounce, Oh My)

The Delta isn't far, and the blues' gospel and African-Caribbean bloodlines took deep root in the Crescent City. In the 1950s, **Fats Domino** and his great producer-collaborator **Dave Bartholomew** fused those elements into the seminal hits "Blueberry Hill" and "Walkin' to New Orleans." Simultaneously, the unheralded **Professor Longhair** and **"Champion" Jack Dupree** were developing trailblazing piano sounds, contrasting mournful woe with party-time spirit. More piano genii followed, from **James Booker** to **Dr. John.** Crooners **Johnny Adams** and "Soul Queen" **Irma Thomas** kept it smooth (she still does—don't miss her if you get the chance).

The long-time keepers of the flame, the **Neville Brothers,** retired (R.I.P. saxophonist Charles, who died in 2018), but their funky offshoot the **Meters** are going strong in various guises. The genre has broadly evolved into funk, jam, and hip hop—with **Lil Wayne** and **Juvenile** and the beleaguered Cash Money label driving that end, not to mention the only-in-New-Orleans, proto-twerking bounce genre led by gender-tweaking post-rapper **Big Freedia.** And we gotta include funksters **Galactic** and **Dumpstaphunk** and breakout super-star **Troy "Trombone Shorty" Andrews.**

The bluesy end of the spectrum is well represented by late greats like **Snooks Eaglin** and **Earl King,** and current keepers of the acclaim, axe men **Tab Benoit, Anders Osborne,** and **Sonny Landreth; pianist Jon Cleary,** and harpist nonpareil **Johnny Sansone,** to name a few.

CLUB LISTINGS

The French Quarter

BB King's ★   We tend to eschew chains. With so many wonderfully individualistic choices, why go cookie-cutter? But there's comfort in familiarity, and if Frenchmen Street's crowds and scruffiness seem intimidating or overwhelming, BB King's won't. The multilevel room is spacious and accessible; the people-pleasin' burgers, barbecue, beers, and blues are reliable. Service isn't perfect, but live music almost all day is a hard-to-find plus. Overall, a worthy addition to this part of the French Quarter. 1104 Decatur St. www.bbkings. com/new-orleans. ✆ **504/934-5464.** No cover except for occasional concerts.

The Famous Door ★   Open since 1934, this is the oldest music club on Bourbon Street. Many luminaries have played here (including 13-year-old Harry Connick, Jr.). Great historic value, cheap drinks, no cover (usually), loud but solid cover bands. Drunken dancing might happen. 339 Bourbon St. ✆ **504/598-4334.** No cover.

Fritzel's European Jazz Pub ★★   From the open street front, this 1831 building looks sketchy, overlookable even. The pushy door folk will aggressively attempt to hustle you to a seat at the cramped picnic tables and rush you to order a drink. Let them: Some of the best traditional jazz is played on the teensy stage here, and the quasi-hofbrau atmosphere breeds community. 733 Bourbon St. www.fritzelsjazz.net. ✆ **504/586-4800.** 1-drink minimum per set.

Funky Pirate ★   The XXL attraction here is bluesman "Big" Al Carson, who holds court Tuesday through Saturday. It's popular, sometimes packed, always pirate-y. *Note:* If "Drink slime green liquid from a plastic weapon" is on your bucket list, the horrid, famously potent Hand Grenade is available here and next door at sister bar **Tropical Isle.** 727 Bourbon St. www.thefunky pirate.com. ✆ **504/523-1960.** 1-drink minimum per set. Big Al plays from 8:30pm on.

House of Blues ★   You can find this chain club elsewhere and you can find authentic (vs. ersatz) folk-art-laden roadhouses within a few miles (hello, Tipitina's). It's lost its domineering booking muscle, but when there is something worthy (George Clinton and Gary Clark, Jr., played here recently), the sightlines are good and the regionalized food is decent. We quite like the lesser-used non-main rooms: The upstairs **Parish** feels inviting and real; the **courtyard** is lovely and actually *is* real. 225 Decatur St. www.houseofblues/new orleans.com. ✆ **504/310-4999.** Cover varies.

The Jazz Playhouse ★★★   This Bourbon Street retreat is the go-to spot for ambitious, established, and on-the-rise local jazz artists. Talented regular performers include Gerald French, Joe Krown, and Germaine Bazzle. The excellent Friday midnight burlesque show is always a sassy good time. The draperied, midsize room is swank, and the well-prepared drinks aren't inexpensive (and service can be a bit snooty). 300 Bourbon St. in the Royal Sonesta Hotel. www.isonesta.com/jazzplayhouse. ✆ **504/553-2299.** Cover ranges from none to $20.

Maison Bourbon ★   Despite its location and the DEDICATED TO THE PRESERVATION OF JAZZ sign (an attempt to confuse tourists into thinking this is Preservation Hall?), Maison Bourbon isn't a tourist trap. The music is authentic, often superb Dixieland and traditional jazz, and the brick-lined room is a respite from the mayhem outside. If Kid Merv is on, get in there. 641 Bourbon St. www.maisonbourbon.com. ✆ **504/522-8818.** 1-drink minimum per set.

One Eyed Jacks ★★   With its bordello-flavored decor (swag curtains and red-flocked wallpaper), Jack's strikes a funky/retro/hip balance. A busy front bar leads to a tiered main-room floor that wraps around another crowded bar. The cool room full of cool people is booked with cool, alternative-leaning local and touring bands (tUnE-yArDs, Charles Bradley, Alabama Shakes, Kamasi Washington, White Denim), and the Thursday '80s nights are legendary. On super-busy evenings, the crowds and door situations can be off-putting. 615 Toulouse St. www.oneeyedjacks.net. ✆ **504/569-8361.** Cover $10–$20 or more.

Palm Court Jazz Cafe ★★   This stylish dinner club is a reliable, mature, comfortable venue for topnotch classic and traditional jazz Wednesday through Sunday. Table seating (make reservations), with a small back bar for non-diners. 1204 Decatur St. www.palmcourtjazzcafe.com. ✆ **504/525-0200.** Wed–Sun 7–11pm. Cover $5 and up; entrees $17–$28.

Preservation Hall ★★★   The decaying, ancient-looking building lends just the right air of consecration to this, an essential spot for traditional jazz fans and, well, everyone (Robert Plant and U2's Edge have sat in here). With little air, so-so sightlines, no bathrooms (you are warned), and constant crowds, the awesomeness is in the hallowed, intimate atmosphere and the superb musicianship. Shows start at 5, 6, 8, 9, and 10pm; the line starts forming about an hour before. Go early for bench seats (the line can be long—bring a go cup), or prepare to stand or sit on the floor. A few line-skipping, up-front "Big Shot" seats are sold online; get them well in advance. 726 St. Peter St. www.preservationhall.com. ✆ **504/522-2841.** Cover $20; Big Shot $40–$50.

New Orleans Nightlife

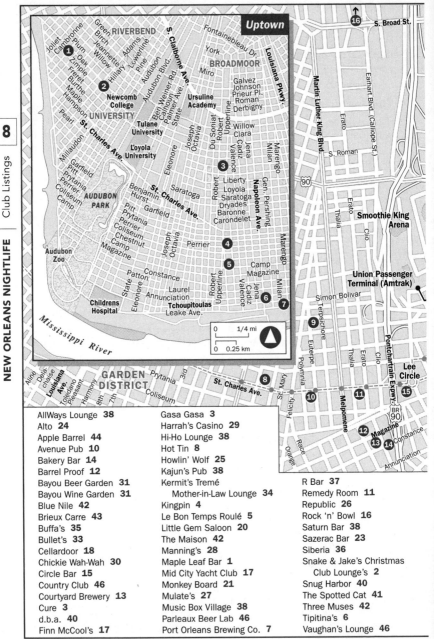

AllWays Lounge **38**
Alto **24**
Apple Barrel **44**
Avenue Pub **10**
Bakery Bar **14**
Barrel Proof **12**
Bayou Beer Garden **31**
Bayou Wine Garden **31**
Blue Nile **42**
Brieux Carre **43**
Buffa's **35**
Bullet's **33**
Cellardoor **18**
Chickie Wah-Wah **30**
Circle Bar **15**
Country Club **46**
Courtyard Brewery **13**
Cure **3**
d.b.a. **40**
Finn McCool's **17**

Gasa Gasa **3**
Harrah's Casino **29**
Hi-Ho Lounge **38**
Hot Tin **8**
Howlin' Wolf **25**
Kajun's Pub **38**
Kermit's Tremé
   Mother-in-Law Lounge **34**
Kingpin **4**
Le Bon Temps Roulé **5**
Little Gem Saloon **20**
The Maison **42**
Manning's **28**
Maple Leaf Bar **1**
Mid City Yacht Club **17**
Monkey Board **21**
Mulate's **27**
Music Box Village **38**
Parleaux Beer Lab **46**
Port Orleans Brewing Co. **7**

R Bar **37**
Remedy Room **11**
Republic **26**
Rock 'n' Bowl **16**
Saturn Bar **38**
Sazerac Bar **23**
Siberia **36**
Snake & Jake's Christmas
   Club Lounge's **2**
Snug Harbor **40**
The Spotted Cat **41**
Three Muses **42**
Tipitina's **6**
Vaughan's Lounge **46**

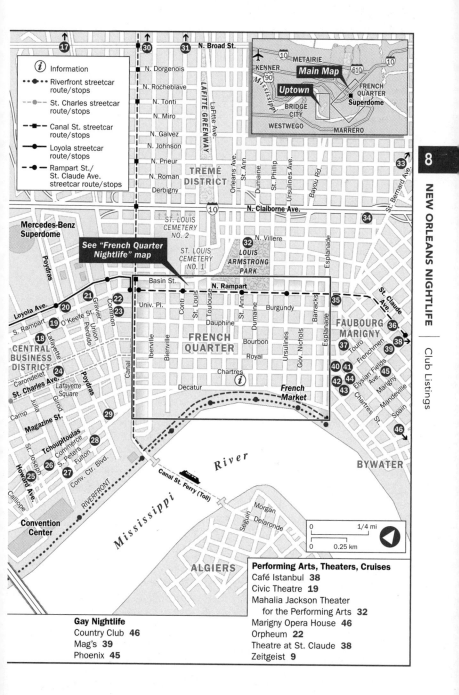

Performing Arts, Theaters, Cruises
Café Istanbul **38**
Civic Theatre **19**
Mahalia Jackson Theater
   for the Performing Arts **32**
Marigny Opera House **46**
Orpheum **22**
Theatre at St. Claude **38**
Zeitgeist **9**

Gay Nightlife
Country Club **46**
Mag's **39**
Phoenix **45**

Frenchmen Street & the Marigny

Apple Barrel ★ Time was, Frenchmen Street was a quiet little stretch where neighbors shopped, ate, and drank. They did the latter—and still do—right here, especially weeknights when they can fit into the dank shoebox of a room. Nowadays the Barrel is almost an afterthought, given the plethora of shinier nearby options. But for authenticity, divey-ness, and solid, low-key tunes, it shouldn't be. There's no cover, there's Sam Cammarata's unpredictable blues guitar on occasion, and there's **Adolfo's** upstairs for pretty darn good Creole Italian food (put your name on the list about an hour before you get hungry). 609 Frenchmen St.

Blue Nile ★★★ This chill, midsize club has a killer sound system and pretty much zero attitude, making it a fun hang for the local, reggae, and jam bands they book. Late-night DJs upstairs. 532 Frenchmen St. www.bluenilelive. com. ℂ **504/948-2583.** Cover free–$15.

Buffa's ★★ "Hey, let's throw some diner-style tables and chairs in our non-descript back room, book some top, local, jazz-leaning musicians, and create a friendly, laid-back scene." Okay, we're in. The burgers are juicy, the beer cold, and kids are welcome. Bonus worth bookmarking: Bar and kitchen are open 24 hours. 1001 Esplanade Ave. www.buffasbar.com. ℂ **504/949-0038.** Cover free–$12.

d.b.a. ★★★ A favorite bar/nightclub for its superb beer and spirits selections, laid-back vibe, and fine bookings. Shows (usually) start on time and feature an occasional, on-the-cusp national or Louisiana act and a wide variety of excellent local acts like magnificent crooner John Boutté, the tight blues of Walter Washington, and breakout bluesy rockers Honey Island Swamp Band. Mostly standing-room only, and the low stage doesn't help those in the back (maybe that's why they're so dang chatty). *Tip:* The 7pm shows, including Boutté's Monday residency, may command a small (and so worth it) cover during peak seasons, but most times this well-booked slot is free. 618 Frenchmen St. www.dbaneworleans.com. ℂ **504/942-3731.** Cover $5–$15, occasionally higher.

The Maison ★★ A brick-walled Frenchmen mainstay with always solid local musicians—there's jazz and table seating early, but later on the scene gets funkier, danceable, and well…it just gets down. The second-level wraparound balcony is a good hang when the main floor gets too packed. Drinks are average, food less so, but the scene is stellar. Under 18 okay early in evening. 508 Frenchmen St. www.maisonfrenchman.com. ℂ **504/371-5543.** Rarely a cover.

Snug Harbor ★★★ This sit-down, concert-style club and early Frenchmen Street settler is the city's premier showcase for contemporary jazz. Two levels provide mostly good viewing (beware the pillars upstairs—try to sit along the rail) for the attentive aud. The adjoining restaurant has great burgers and more, making for a one-stop date night. Monitors screen the concerts in the low-ceilinged bar—for the budget-minded, the next-best thing to live. Advance ticketing is wise. 626 Frenchmen St. www.snugjazz.com. ℂ **504/949-0696.** Cover $15–$40.

French Quarter Nightlife

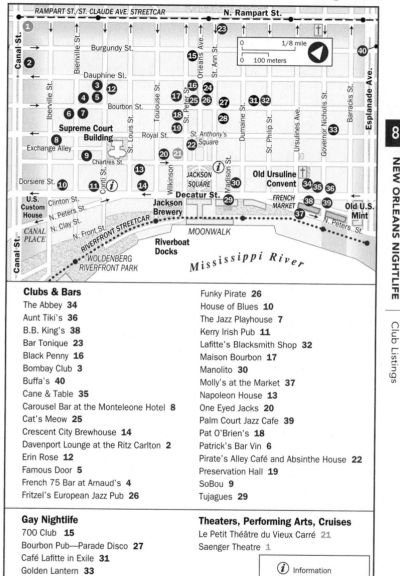

Clubs & Bars

The Abbey **34**
Aunt Tiki's **36**
B.B. King's **38**
Bar Tonique **23**
Black Penny **16**
Bombay Club **3**
Buffa's **40**
Cane & Table **35**
Carousel Bar at the Monteleone Hotel **8**
Cat's Meow **25**
Crescent City Brewhouse **14**
Davenport Lounge at the Ritz Carlton **2**
Erin Rose **12**
Famous Door **5**
French 75 Bar at Arnaud's **4**
Fritzel's European Jazz Pub **26**

Funky Pirate **26**
House of Blues **10**
The Jazz Playhouse **7**
Kerry Irish Pub **11**
Lafitte's Blacksmith Shop **32**
Maison Bourbon **17**
Manolito **30**
Molly's at the Market **37**
Napoleon House **13**
One Eyed Jacks **20**
Palm Court Jazz Cafe **39**
Pat O'Brien's **18**
Patrick's Bar Vin **6**
Pirate's Alley Café and Absinthe House **22**
Preservation Hall **19**
SoBou **9**
Tujagues **29**

Gay Nightlife

700 Club **15**
Bourbon Pub—Parade Disco **27**
Café Lafitte in Exile **31**
Golden Lantern **33**
Good Friends Bar & Queens Head Pub **24**
Oz **28**

Theaters, Performing Arts, Cruises

Le Petit Théâtre du Vieux Carré **21**
Saenger Theatre **1**

ⓘ Information

•••◆••• Riverfront streetcar route/stops

– –◆– Rampart St./ St. Claude Ave. streetcar route/stops

The Spotted Cat Music Club ★★★ Our aesthetic leans toward cramped rooms, little amplification, and scrappy bands with a fresh take on big-band, old timey, gypsy, hot—well, any type of swinging—jazz. So we adore the oft-crowded Cat. The scarce seats are hardly comfy, but the 100% reliably fine music is the real deal, as evidenced by the frenetic-footed jitter-buggers squeezed in front of the minute stage. We love the uncrowded early hours (music starts at 2pm) and scrappy local artwork. Cash only. 623 Frenchmen St. www.spottedcatmusicclub.com. No phone. No cover except special events. 1 drink per set. Tip the band!

Three Muses ★★★ Sophisticated modern lounge meets classic 1920s saloon, and we likey. It serves up beautifully balanced, new-timey cocktails and mouthwatering (quite) small plates to old-timey tunes, with no cover (but the food and drinks can add up; feta fries are best for value and sharing). The scant tables and stools go fast; call for a reservation or expect a line when the street is hopping. If they're here, don't miss Debbie Davies, Royal Roses, or muse Miss Sophie Lee. Closed Tuesdays, otherwise open 5pm; kids okay till 9-ish. 536 Frenchmen St. www.thethreemuses.com. ☎ **504/252-4801.** No cover. Tip the band!

Elsewhere Around the City

Bullet's Sports Bar ★ Situated on a residential street named for the civil rights attorney credited with fighting local Jim Crow laws, this gritty 7th Ward bar comes alive with a bullet on Fridays when the all-female Pinettes brass band plays, and on Thursdays when trumpeter Kermit Ruffins holds sway. The crowd is friendly, bartenders efficient, and the experience pure booty-shaking NOLA. There's often a barbecue truck outside for eats. Although it's only 2 miles and change from Bourbon Street, it's best to take a cab. 2441 A.P. Tureaud Ave. ☎ **504/948-4003.** Cover free to $10.

Chickie Wah-Wah ★★★ We're ever so fond of this Mid-City club, where the best of the local roots, rock, blues, and singer-songwriter acts draw reverent crowds. Cool old tin signs lend ambience to the clean, midsize, shotgun-style room, and food occasionally pops up inside or at food trucks. It's off the Canal Street streetcar at N. White Street, just past Broad. Try to catch Paul Sanchez, Tom McDermott, Jon Cleary, Susan Cowsill (yup, that one), or a rare appearance by Austinite Alejandro Escovedo. 2828 Canal St. www.chickiewahwah.com. ☎ **844/244-2543.** Cover $10–$20.

Circle Bar ★★ It's hard to believe this club was totally renovated a few years ago. The 1883 building maintains the quirky, elegant decay suitable to the laidback, Marlboro-loving clientele in this tiny dive. The jukebox feeds the idiosyncratic vibe with mood-enhancing selections from the Velvet Underground, Dusty Springfield, and Curtis Mayfield. Three of our favorites play regularly in the eponymous round alcove that's about the size of a family dinner table: Alex McMurray (Tues), Iguanas (Wed), and Micah McKee (Sun). It gets louder later. 1032 St. Charles Ave. at Lee Circle. www.circlebarnew orleans.com. ☎ **504/588-2616.** Cover $5–$12.

THE ST. CLAUDE scene

The scruffy local alternative types have carved out a pulsing, metal- and punk-infused scene (well, with just about every other genre thrown in for good measure) along a stretch of St. Claude Avenue in the Marigny. If this is what you're into (or if you think Frenchmen St. has jumped the shark), check out **Siberia**'s sundry bookings, which span the punk/funk/death metal/trivia/whatev realms (2227 St. Claude Ave.; www.siberianola.com; © 504/265-8855). At the spacious, comfortable **Hi-Ho Lounge,** we dig Monday night's BYOBanjo bluegrass jam and Saturdays for the Pink Project's genre-spanning, multi-culti house party (2239 St. Claude Ave.; www.hiholounge. net; © 504/945-4446). The loose, welcoming karaoke at 24-hour **Kajun's Pub** (2256 St. Claude Ave.; www.kajunpub.

com; © 504/947-3735 or 504/267-6108) and the friendly **AllWays Lounge** (2240 St. Claude Ave.; www.theallwayslounge. com; © 504/218-5778) round out the tatty, happening street scene. These clubs are just a few blocks from the Marigny and Frenchmen Street. Up the road a bit, **Saturn Bar** in Bywater falls somewhere between art project and junque-house, but the dive vibe is unfakeable; punk, surf, DJs, and metal rotate, with the blistering hot blues of King James and the Special Men most Monday nights (3067 St. Claude Ave.; © 504/949-7532). Do take a cab, and don't wander into the transitional bordering areas. Hungry? Hit **Kukhnya** in **Siberia** for delish, crazy-affordable "Slavic soul food." Also see p. 100 for other local food options.

8

NEW ORLEANS NIGHTLIFE | Club Listings

The Fillmore   We're anticipating good things from the NOLA outpost of this legendary San Francisco nightclub when it opens the doors in early 2019. Nationally known bands on tour are expected to play the 2,200-capacity, standing-only club inside Harrah's, above the casino. 8 Canal St. www.thefillmorenola.com. Cover TBD.

Gasa Gasa ★   Filling the eclectic, indie-rock niche in a single room, Gasa draws a Tulane-to-20-something crowd. Occasional readings, art exhibits, the hopping Freret Street scene, and the mind-blowing exterior mural by Berlin-based street artist MTO augment the allure. 4920 Freret St. www.gasagasa.com. © 504/304-7110. Cover free–$15.

The Howlin' Wolf ★★   The big (10,000-sq.-ft.), not-at-all-bad Wolf brings in leading local and occasional midlevel national acts focusing on rock, funk, and jam (Leftover Salmon, of Montreal; local faves like Galactic, Anders Osborne, and Dumpstaphunk). Good sound, good sightlines, good times—especially Sundays when the Hot 8 brass band plays the smaller "Den." *Fun fact:* The bar is from Al Capone's Chicago hotel. 907 S. Peters St., in the Warehouse District. www.thehowlinwolf.com. © 504/529-5844. Cover varies.

Kermit's Tremé Mother-in-Law Lounge ★   All aboard! Trumpeter and unofficial NOLA mayor Kermit Ruffins took over this brightly muraled, historic spot from dearly beloved Ernie K-Doe (decor no longer features his illustrious manikin, sadly). It mostly draws 7th Ward locals; entertainment is irregular and consists mostly of overamplified beats. But if Kermit happens to be blowing, or if the BBQ is fired up in the yard, it's worth stopping in for a bone, a brew, and the historic value. 1500 S. Claiborne Ave. www.facebook.com/ruffinsbbq. 🕿 **504/975-3955.** Cover varies.

Little Gem Saloon ★★★ This is jazz-history hallowed ground: The record books may be sketchy, but most agree that jazz began on this block, perhaps in this very building. The first greats, including Buddy Bolden and Jelly Roll Morton, played the 1906 Little Gem. They'd love this beautifully restored iteration. It books top local and visiting jazz acts in the brick-walled, velvet-curtained Ramp Room and the white-tile-floored, first-level saloon. The kitchen serves far-better-than-average modern Southern club food; advance reservations and tickets are available. All this means that drinks are pricey and the cover can be steep. 445 S. Rampart St. www.littlegemsaloon.com. 🕿 **504/267-4863.** Cover free–$30. All ages.

Maple Leaf Bar ★★★ This classic New Orleans club is a locals bar by day, a poetry hub on Sundays (3pm readings) and a medium-size, tin-ceilinged, twinkle-light-strung club at night. Personal space can become a wistful memory when the crowds pack in (usually by 11), and the drunk frat crowd can be maddening; seek temporary refuge on the back patio, at the back bar's junky pool table, or on the sidewalk where the overflow party goes. But it's got that magical, transformative vibe you can't manufacture, and when Rebirth rips it up on Tuesdays it's pretty much a must-do (but if you're only around on Thurs, see the Trio). Check out the 3pm Sunday poetry readings. 8316 Oak St. www.mapleleafbar.com. 🕿 **504/866-9359.** Cover $10–$20.

Republic ★ The converted produce warehouse dates to 1852 but features DJs that date to last week. Maybe the week before. It's our choice for dance music since, even with all the lighting, it still manages to feel like NOLA rather than SoBe. Frequent appearances by local bounce stars (Big Freedia, Sissy Red); worn-out murals; and plenty of distressed wood add vibe—just get up front or upstairs to avoid the view-blocking wood columns. Drinks are nothing great but easily accessed. 828 S. Peters St. 🕿 **504/528-8282.** www.republicnola.com.

Rock 'n' Bowl ★★★ Bowling. Bands. Beer. If you can't have fun here, we give up. There's swing most Wednesdays, zydeco on Thursdays, and local blues, rockabilly, rock, who cares on other nights. It's an utter hoot and an

---

Bender Mender

If the aftermath of clubbing leaves you with a morning-after case of the liquid flu, consider the **Remedy Room.** An actual M.D. hooks you up to an actual I.V. packed with fluids, vitamins, and various other restoratives, to get you upright and sharp for that 1pm swamp tour or conference call. Next time, remember: Try a glass of water with each cocktail (1224 St. Charles Ave.; www.theremedyroom.com; 🕿 **504/301-1670;** $139 and up).

Sunday School at Tipitina's

Besides its pedigree as one of the city's premier live-music venues, **Tipitina's foundation** also actively supports and enhances the local scene. At its Sunday-afternoon youth music workshops (1–3pm), music students can play and study with leading local luminaries. This low-key, free scene offers a cool opportunity to participate or observe as traditions are passed on. All ages okay, but recommended for 10- to 18-year-olds. Most but not all Sundays; do call.

unbeatable experience that draws all ages and types to the lanes and spacious, well air-conditioned dance floor. The custom-embroidered bowling shirts make splendid souvenirs. ***Fun fact:*** The hanging, vintage ball return is from the still-missed pre-Katrina location. ***Tip:*** Dine next door at **Ye Olde College Inn** (p. 106) and get an admission discount. 3000 S. Carrollton Ave. www.rockn bowl.com. ℭ **504/861-1700.** Private parties sometimes take over, so call ahead. Bowling $24/hr. per lane and a $1 shoe-rental fee; show admission $5–$25. Mon–Thurs 11:30am–midnight; Fri–Sat 11:30am–2am; Sun check calendar.

Tipitina's ★★★ Dedicated to the late piano master Professor Longhair (that's him in bronze just inside the entrance; rub his head for luck), Tip's is, if not *the* New Orleans club, a major musical touchstone and a reliable place for top local and out-of-town roots, brass, jam, and rock bands from Wilco to Willie Nelson. If you can catch locals like Troy "Trombone Shorty" Andrews, Galactic, the Funky Meters, or especially Dr. John here, do not waver for a sec. It's nothing fancy: four walls, buncha bars, wraparound balcony (often reserved for VIPs), and a stage (which, if you're under 6 feet, isn't easy to see from the back on crowded nights). This uptown (location, not atmosphere) institution has good (loud) sound and air-con, and there's usually some food truck action. Get advance tix for festival bookings and other big-name acts, and plan on cabbing. 501 Napoleon Ave. www.tipitinas.com. ℭ **504/895-8477.** Cover $5–$30.

Vaughan's Lounge ★ Most Thursdays, the massive grooves of trombonist Corey Henry's Tremé Funktet pump this rambling, shambling Bywater dive into the best kind of loud, hot, roadhouse mess. Most other nights it's just your classic, friendly bar. 4229 Dauphine St. ℭ **504/947-5562.** Thurs cover varies, usually $10–$15.

THE BAR SCENE

You won't have any trouble finding a place to drink in New Orleans. Heck, thanks to liberal laws and "go cups," you won't have to spend a minute *without* a drink in hand. But there's more to this town than bars (much), and more to bars than Bourbon Street (ditto), so as with all things, let moderation preside. There, that's our sermon. Our suggestions include some of the most convivial, quaint, or downright eccentric spots; also keep in mind that many restaurants and hotels have excellent bars; see chapters 5 and 6.

cajun & zydeco JOINTS

There are few of these here in the big city; then again Cajun and Zydeco music didn't originate in New Orleans. Dance halls are plentiful in Lafayette or beyond—see p. 257. You might catch the world-renowned Beausoleil, raucous Pine Leaf Boys, or Lost Bayou Ramblers at **d.b.a.** (p. 196) or **Tipitina's** (p. 201) while they're "in town." Tip's hosts a Fais do-do Sundays at 5pm, with live Cajun music and dancing; on Thursday nights at **Rock 'n' Bowl** (p. 200), Zydeco rules and dancers vie for "hottest." **Mulate's** (201 Julia St., at Convention Center Blvd. in the CBD; www.mulates.com; ℂ **800/854-9149** or 504/522-1492) is a tourist-friendly dinner-dancehall with patient instructors to help you become one of those dancing hotties (well, we can all aspire). The food is ordinary, but the dancing is folksy, all-ages fun. It's open 7pm nightly; call to make sure it's not closed for a private event.

The French Quarter & the Faubourg Marigny

Bar Tonique ★★ If we lived in this Quarter's-edge neighborhood, this would be our bar. Except we wouldn't be anti-hip service-industry locals, and we'd chat up the tourists more. Mostly we'd glow in the candlelight bouncing off the original brick walls, or cozy up with our honey in the smoochy booths in the offshoot alcove (a working fireplace adds a nice glow when it's chilly outside). We'd sip one of the prodigious punches like the Blanche Dubois, or a superbly poured cocktail from another era. You know they're serious about the drinks, because there is nothing—nothing—to eat. 820 N. Rampart St. www.bartonique.com. ℂ **504/324-6045.** Daily noon–2am.

Black Penny ★★ Red alert, beer aficionados: Here on the Quarter's upper edge lies mellow ambience and a killer selection of 75-plus canned craft and local brews. Also, some well-made cocktails. If you're not an aforementioned B.A., you might become one, thanks to the infinitely patient, helpful beertenders. So we'll forgive our snobbish companion who noted that the glassware wasn't quite on point. Sheesh. The darkly sophisticated decor—white leather booths and a dab of bronzer on the aged brick walls—befits the chill mix of locals and visitors and background tunes. No food but occasional pop-ups, or you can order in. 700 N. Rampart St. www.facebook.com/blackpenny-nola. ℂ **504/304-4779.**

The Bombay Club ★★ This grownup, wood-paneled bar/restaurant/British library is an oasis of civility just off Bourbon Street. We can't help but order something with gin from the long martini list, and a boudin Scotch egg from the $4 happy-hour menu (the food is quite good). We're supremely fond of the fetching curtained back booths, and any day when David Boeddinghaus is manning the upright piano. 830 Conti St., off-street in the Prince Conti Hotel. www.bombayclubneworleans.com. ℂ **504/577-2237.** Mon–Thurs 4pm–midnight, Fri 4pm–1am, Sat 10am–1am, Sun 10am–midnight.

Cane & Table ★★★   C&T's "sophisticated faded" decor is marked by distressed plaster and brick walls, sparkly chandeliers, a gleaming white-marble bar top, and a slim, sexy patio. But rum (that's the cane) is the star, mixed with housemade ingredients and squeezed-to-order juice by some of New Orleans' most revered craft cocktail revivalists. They call it proto-tiki; we call it high-culture colonialism. The complex flavors may not be for every-one, so start with the C&T Colada. Excellent small and large plates follow the Latin/Caribbean tide: Share the brussels sprouts, but bogart the pepper-jelly ribs. Love. 1113 Decatur St. (no sign; it's next to Coop's). www.caneandtablenola.com. ✆ **504/581-1112.** Sun–Thurs 5–11pm, Fri–Sat 5pm–midnight.

Carousel Bar at the Monteleone Hotel ★★   No, you're not drunk (or maybe you are). The bar *is* spinning (one drink per rotation is the pur-ported ratio—don't worry, its slo-o-o-w). There's plenty of soignee sofa seat-ing and fine piano-based entertainment, but the classic experience requires a coveted seat at one of the 25 barstools ringing the Carousel and a Vieux Carré Cocktail, invented here some 70 years ago. 214 Royal St. www.hotelmonteleone.com/carouselbar. ✆ **504/523-3341.**

Cat's Meow ★   The drinks and drink specials flow aplenty—the better to loosen the larynx at this Bourbon Street karaoke mecca. Whether or not you take the mic, the scene is entertaining and the crowds get thick. Then they get drunk. The action starts at 4pm Monday through Thursday, and 2pm Friday through Sunday. 701 Bourbon St. www.catskaraoke.com. ✆ **504/523-2788.**

Crescent City Brewhouse ★★   When it was opened by a world-renowned master brewer in 1991, CCB was the first new brewery in New Orleans in more than 70 years. Its German-style beers still hold up, and come with a full menu, an excellent balcony view, and live jazz. 527 Decatur St. www.crescentcitybrewhouse.com. ✆ **888/819-9330** or 504/522-0571. Sun–Thurs 11:30am–10pm, Fri–Sat 11:30am–11pm.

Pat O'Brien's & the Mighty Hurricane

Pat O'Brien's, 718 St. Peter St. (www.patobriens.com; ✆ **504/525-4823**), is world-famous for the hefty, vivid red drink with the big-wind name. The bar's owners created the Hurricane's rum-heavy formula during a 1940s whiskey shortage. It's served in signature hurri-cane-lamp-style glasses, or in a 3-gallon magnum, taller than many small children and shared (one profoundly hopes) through long straws, while standing up. Naturally, this attracts drinkers in droves. The line can stretch down the street, despite the plethora of nearby drinking options…and the fact that the Hurricane is kinda sickly sweet.

Pat O's is still a reliable, rowdy, friendly introduction to New Orleans. The large, dueling-pianos lounge is awfully fun (music 6pm; 2pm weekends), and locals populate the main bar up front, but when weather permits, the often boisterous tropical patio with the flaming fountain is the place to be. Your Hurricane comes with a $3 charge for the glass. Return it for a refund or ask for packing materials.

Erin Rose ★★★   Triple threat: friendly, unassuming Irish Pub, craft cocktail bar, and **Killer PoBoys** in the back room. That's the name *and* the bold-but-accurate description of the enterprise. Try the rum-marinated pork-belly po' boy with citrus lime slaw. Killer, indeed (so good they opened another location, **Big Killer PoBoys**, at 219 Dauphine St.). Good drinks, too, including the signature frozen Irish coffee. 811 Conti St. www.erinrosebar.com. ✆ **504/522-3573.**

French 75 Bar at Arnaud's ★★★   A beautiful, intimate bar space in one of the Quarter's most venerable restaurants (p. 84), French 75 won a 2017 James Beard Award for Outstanding Bar Program. It feels like drinking in New Orleans should: classic and classy. Acclaimed bartender Chris Hannah and others are equally adept at vintage mixes (including a perfect Ramos Gin Fizz and the namesake French 75 champagne cocktail) and original concoctions. Order a side of Arnaud's dreamy soufflé potatoes to munch on. Perfection. 813 Bienville St. www.arnaudsrestaurant.com/bars/french-75. ✆ **504/523-5433.** Sun 10am–2:30pm, 6–10pm; Mon–Thurs 6–10pm; Fri–Sat 6–10:30pm.

Kerry Irish Pub ★   This pub has darts, pool, a proper pint of Guinness, and, occasionally, Beth Patterson, who mashes traditional Celtic folk, honeyed originals, metal-to-acoustic conversions, and hilariously filthy knockoffs. The Kerry specializes in very-late-night drinking. Nightcap, anyone? 331 Decatur St. www.facebook.com/Kerry-Irish-Pub-163926209622. ✆ **504/527-5954.**

Lafitte's Blacksmith Shop ★★   Even if it wasn't the oldest bar (and maybe building) in the Quarter or a legendary pirate's lair, Lafitte's would merit a visit. It's ancient and ultra-atmospheric, so even amid the crowd chatter and anachronistically blaring jukebox, sipping an ale in the crumbling, cavernlike, candlelit interior is nearly akin to time traveling. Avoid the vaunted VooDoo daiquiri, aka Purple Drank, and stick with beer and ambience instead (although some swear by their Hurricane). 941 Bourbon St. www.lafittes blacksmithshop.com. ✆ **504/593-9761.**

Manolito ★★   This teensy divot just off Decatur Street, helmed by some of the city's shiniest bar luminaries, will likely be populated by cocktail nerds geeking out on the Cuban-inspired craft cocktails. Nerd or not, join them. These are serious, good, seriously good drinks. And get the tortilla española. 508 Dumaine St. Ave. www.manolitonola.com. ✆ **504/603-2740.** Daily 5–11pm.

Molly's at the Market ★   The hangout for bohos and literary locals, who chew over the state of their world and their city in this casual, comfortable, East Village–feeling bar. A kind of platonic-ideal locals' bar, it's perpetually popular. **Junction** (p. 100) does a pop-up here, ably tending to the puckish with burgers and wings out of the back patio kitchen. 1107 Decatur St. www.mollysatthemarket.net. ✆ **504/525-5169.** Daily 10am–6am.

Napoleon House ★★★   Set in a landmark building, the cave-dark barroom and romantically faded courtyard seem almost too perfectly aged. No plastic surgery here (when it sold in 2015 after 101 years in the same family,

GAME on

Pretty much every bar and club in town, no matter how unsporty, becomes a **sports bar** on Saints game days. So if you're looking for a place to watch the game, try anywhere. We'll single out **Manning's** for its wall-size screen and fully reclining leather lounge chairs—reserve them well in advance and expect to pay a hefty bounty: from $25 in food and drink for an average Red Wings game to $100+ for a Saints games, chair and beer bucket only. Yes, Manning's is named for its co-owner (with Harrah's Casino), the legendary NFL quarterback and longtime New Orleanian Archie Manning (519 Fulton St.; www.facebook.com/ManningsNOLA; ℂ **504/593-8118**). To hang with masses of locals, taxi to Mid-City's **Finn McCool's** (3701 Banks St.; www.finnmccools.com; ℂ **504/486-9080**) or stroll from the FQ to the **R Bar** in the Marigny (1431 Royal St.; www.royalstreetinn.com; ℂ **504/948-7499**).

new owners swore not to change a thing). Even locals come for the toasty muffuletta and signature Pimm's Cup, a cucumber-infused glass of summer that's divine year-round. 500 Chartres St. www.napoleonhouse.com. ℂ **504/524-9752.** Sun–Thurs 11am–10pm; Fri–Sat 11am–11pm.

NOLA Brewing Taproom ★★★   See p. 179.

Patrick's Bar Vin ★★   Half a block and a million miles from Bourbon Street, Patrick Van Voorhees, one of the city's premier sommeliers, serves conviviality and an excellent selection of wines by the glass (and other spirits). The bar feels like your great uncle's decorous but restful library; the sweet courtyard screams for something bubbly. 730 Bienville St., in the Hotel Mazarin. www.patricksbarvin.com. ℂ **504/200-3180.** Mon–Thurs 4pm–midnight, Fri noon–1am, Sat 2pm–1am, Sun 2pm–midnight.

Pirate's Alley Café and Absinthe House ★   Its tucked-away locale behind St. Louis Cathedral has outdoor alleyway tables. Purists will balk at its absinthe service, but it's fun for others—flaming sugar cube and all. The food's handy but nothing more. 622 Pirate's Alley. www.piratesalleycafe.com. ℂ **504/524-9332.**

SoBou ★   At a self-service gastropub, do you self-tip? The fun here includes tables with beer taps, wine-dispensing machines (think soda fountains, but grapier), and pitcher-sized flasks. It's less kitschy and more full-service than it sounds—it's by the Commander's Palace folks, after all. A second room is highlighted (literally—and strikingly) by a wall of white LED-lit bottles. Drinks are pedigreed and skillfully composed; food can be hit-or-miss (shrimp *pinchos* are a hit). Good happy-hour deals and burlesque-themed Legs and Eggs brunch. 310 Chartres St., in the W Hotel. www.sobounola.com. ℂ **504/522-4095.** Daily 7am–10pm.

Hot Tin ★★★   Leading the pack among the explosion of rooftop bars (**Alto** at the Ace Hotel, p. 69; **Monkey Board** at the Troubadour, p. 74), the Tin Roof has the vintage feel of a 1940s writer's studio, and the cocktails are

dive RIGHT IN

If you'd rather drink with Tom Waits than Tom Cruise, you'll appreciate New Orleans' fine dive bars—and by fine, we mean down-and-dirty, neighborhood holes-in-the-wall with regulars straight out of a Jim Jarmusch casting call. **Snake & Jake's Christmas Club Lounge**'s only illumination comes from dwindling Christmas lights, which doesn't make it easier to find this crowded, sweat-soaked, off-the-beaten-path shack. It's BYOD (dog), so you know it's friendly (7612 Oak St., Uptown; www. snakeandjakes.com. ✆ **504/861-2802**). **Aunt Tiki's,** in the depths of Decatur Street, is laden with stickers, Halloween dreck, and affable, slouching degenerates. As if that's not draw enough, drinks are strong and cheap (1207 Decatur St., French Quarter; ✆ **504/680-8454**). At the Elvis-themed **Kingpin,** 20-somethings in CBGB tees come for shuffleboard and cheap drink specials (1307 Lyons St., Uptown; ✆ **504/891-2373**). **The Abbey** has a few motley stained-glass windows, but everything else is the antithesis of church. Yet the David Lynchian clientele pray at their bar 24/7, and any jukebox offering both classic country and the Cramps is worthy of worship (1123 Decatur St., French Quarter; ✆ **504/523-7177**).

just fine. But the main draw is THE VIEW. Probably the best in the city, day or night. Be sure to seek out the less astounding back terrace for an alternate perspective. 2301 St. Charles Ave. (take the lobby elevator on the right). www.hottin bar.com. ✆ **504/323-1500.** Mon–Thurs 4pm–midnight; Fri–Sat 2pm–2am; Sun noon–midnight.

Tujague's ★★ The attraction here is the centuries-old bar with the wall-size mirror, which was hand-carried—whole—from France to New Orleans (a boat was involved). The bartenders tell the tale while pouring a grasshopper (invented here) or one of the better Sazeracs in town. There are few seats but usually some colorful characters worth sidling up to. 823 Decatur St. www. tujaguesrestaurant.com. ✆ **504/525-8676.** Mon–Thurs 5pm–9pm; Fri 11am–2:30pm, 5–10pm; Sat 10am–2:30pm, 5pm–10pm; Sun 10am–2:30pm, 5pm–9pm.

Elsewhere Around the City

Avenue Pub ★★ This is beer-geek heaven, what with 40+ options on tap and many more in bottles. Proper glassware and weekly cask ales show they're serious about their suds, but even the PBR crowd enjoys the upstairs balcony overlooking St. Charles Boulevard (and the currywurst and fries). 1732 St. Charles Ave. www.theavenuepub.com. ✆ **504/586-9243.** Open daily 24 hours.

Bakery Bar ★★ There are two important reasons to recommend this comfy, oddly located spot tucked in the shadows of the Pontchartrain Expressway: 1) It is a bar. 2) It is a bakery. Featuring the elusive, exceptional Debbie Does Doberge cakes: moist, multi-layered mouthgasms worth a taxi ride. There's food and games too. But ultimately, it's a bar. With cake. Just. Say. Franchise. 1179 Annunciation St. www.bakery.bar. ✆ **504/265-8884.** Tues–Fri 11am–midnight, Sat–Sun 10am–midnight.

Barrel Proof ★★   As the name implied, whiskey is the leading man at this shadowy, wood and tin-walled room in the Lower Garden District. And beer, for the beer-and-a-shot specials. If you know and love your brown liquor, the substantive selection, primarily American, Japanese, and Scottish, will blow your hair back. If you don't, the bartenders will share their expertise. Customized flights work well for both scenarios. Reliable pop-up restaurants rotate through the kitchen. 1201 Magazine St. www.barrelproofnola.com. ✆ **504/299-1888.** Daily 4pm–close.

Bayou Beer Garden and Bayou Wine Garden ★★   For visitors looking for the "real" New Orleans, here's a taste. Two, actually. Bayou Beer Garden is a neighborhood bar with a big, covered backyard deck, big screens, and a big beer list. The sister wine bar, connected by a walkway, has a slightly upper-scaler atmosphere and food (Beer Garden = wings and jalapeño poppers; Wine Garden = charcuterie and popcorn escargots). Either is a hang with the locals, perhaps before or after a visit to nearby City Park. When the **Piece of Meat** charcuterie and sandwich shop opens in the same complex, they'll be a destination. Beer: 326 N. Jefferson Davis Pkwy. www.bayoubeergarden.com. ✆ **504/302-9357.** Wine: 315 N. Rendon St. www.bayouwinegarden.com. ✆ **504/826-2925.** Mon–Sun 11am–2am.

Cellardoor ★★   This supermodel—a near-hidden, converted brothel—is one of the most stunning, sexy bars in the city, so it has some airs about it. It's still approachable and worth it for the look, the drinks made with care, and good bar snacks. Dressed-up date-nighters and young professionals mix quietly on the seductive patio or in the sleek brick interior. 916 Lafayette St. www. cellardoornola.com. ✆ **504/265-8392.** Mon–Thurs 4–11pm, Fri 4pm–1am; Sat 5pm–1am.

Cure ★★★   This mixologist mecca helped instigate the resurgence of craft cocktails in New Orleans as well as now-booming Freret Street. It's an oasis of sleek, boasting great small plates and some of the most knowledgeable bar chefs in town, who blend exceptional ingredients with personable chat. Avoid the late crowds and go at happy hour. 4905 Freret St. www.curenola.com. ✆ **504/302-2357.** Mon–Thurs 5pm–midnight; Fri–Sat 3pm–2am; Sun 3pm–midnight.

Le Bon Temps Roulé ★   Another way-uptown, rundown shack with a cramped bar and decent beer list. So? So schedule your visit for a Thursday, when the Soul Rebels brass band blows this here roof off. The archetypal local characters are quite welcoming the other 6 nights of the week, too. 4801 Magazine St. www.lbtrnola.com. ✆ **504/895-8117.** Daily 24 hours.

Polo Club Lounge ★★   Upstairs in the Windsor Court Hotel (p. 71), the Sazerac-and-cigar crowd lounges on velvet sofas and leather armchairs to a cool piano combo, as big-money deals and serious romances discreetly work themselves out. In the columned lobby's **Cocktail Bar,** local professionals who prefer a refined hipness enjoy the updated cocktail program and mellow jazz. 300 Gravier St. www.windsorcourthotel.com/polo-club-lounge. ✆ **504/523-6000.** Sun–Thurs 11:30am–midnight, Fri–Sat 11:30am–1am.

getting crafty: MAKING THE BREWERY SCENE

Craft brewing got a slow start in New Orleans, but now we're up to speed (well, we'll never be Portland. But they've got donuts and we've got actual Voodoo). Here are a few worth the Uber.

o **Courtyard Brewery:** Beer-wise, this small, funky converted warehouse in the Lower Garden District offers the best of the local IPA lot. 1020 Erato St. www.courtyardbrewing.com.

o **Parleaux Beer Lab:** Deep in the Bywater, the Beer Lab's backyard beer garden is full of charm—and fruit trees and herbs, which sometimes turn up in their creative brews. Also, standout stouts and proximity to **The Joint** barbecue (p. 101). 634 Lesseps St.

www.parleauxbeerlab.com. ℂ 504/702-8433.

o **Port Orleans Brewing Co.:** Way uptown, the beer at Port Orleans is just fine. The large brewery is notable for its better-than-average taproom restaurant, **Stokehold**. Go for both. 4124 Tchoupitoulas St. www.portorleansbrewingco.com. ℂ 504/266-2332.

o **Brieux Carre:** They're having fun with beer here, an experimental oasis of hops steps from the Frenchmen Street madness. 2115 Decatur St., www.brieuxcarre.com. ℂ 504/303-4242.

o **Crescent City Brewhouse** (p. 203) and **NOLA Brewing** (p. 179): Don't forget the originals.

Sazerac Bar at the Roosevelt ★★ If the New Orleans bar scene were a monarchy, the historic Sazerac Bar in the glamorous Roosevelt Hotel might be queen. The sinuous wood walls and Deco-era murals here have borne witness to movie stars, political scandals, and we don't want to know what (check the bullet hole in the paneling to the left of the bar). You're here for all that panache as much as the namesake cocktail. Bar service could be friendlier, but nevermind, the ambience is stellar. 123 Baronne St. www.therooseveltneworleans. com. ℂ **504/529-4733.** Mon–Thurs noon–midnight; Fri–Sat 11am–2am; Sun 11am–midnight.

GAY NIGHTLIFE

Most of these bars catering to New Orleans' thriving LBGTQ community are along the French Quarter's illustrious 4-block "fruit loop." Expect late hours, friendly folk, and *insane* crowds during Southern Decadence (p. 26), Mardi Gras, Halloween, Easter (yes)—basically at the drop of any quasi-celebratory hat. Also see the resources on p. 273.

Bars & Clubs

In addition to those reviewed below, you might try the long-running **Golden Lantern,** 1239 Royal St. (ℂ **504/529-2860**), the über-diverse Cheers of NOLA. It typically has one of everything—one drag queen, one leather boy, one guy in a suit, one beer-drinking dog at the bar. Everybody is friendly and it's open 24/7 (℃ **504/945-9264**). For drag, there's the neighborly neighboring **Mag's** at 940 Elysian Fields Ave. (℃ **504/948-1888**).

If your proclivities lean in any other direction, you probably know how to find what you're looking for. It's out there.

The Bourbon Pub—Parade Disco ★★
Of the two hyper-popular bars, the downstairs pub is a bit calmer for most of its 24 hours. Upstairs, Parade Disco's high-tech dance setup comes alive on weekend nights. Sunday eve is also big, with glam drag at 10:30 for $15, which includes a cocktail. 801 Bourbon St. www.bourbonpub.com. ℃ **504/529-2107.** Downstairs open 24/7; upstairs closed Mon and Wed.

Café Lafitte in Exile ★★
One of the oldest gay bars in the U.S., this was established in 1933 and claims Tennessee Williams as a patron. It's got a theme-night cruise bar downstairs (not so much for teeny-boppers or twinks), and a friendly, publike atmosphere upstairs. We don't really get the famous Sunday-night "Love is in the Air" napkin toss, but we love it. 901 Bourbon St. www.lafittes. com. ℃ **504/522-8397.** Downstairs open 24/7; upstairs Thurs–Sun 1pm–till close.

Country Club ★★
We still miss the days when this bar, pool, restaurant, club was an anything-goes, clothing-optional, locals retreat. But we'll admit that the new and much-improved version is quite delightful (and tastier, with the former Commander's Palace chef now handling kitchen duties). The converted Creole cottage tucked away in the residential Bywater offers a staycation for locals and visitors of all persuasions, with a pretty veranda, airy dining room, pool, and Jacuzzi. Fair warning: The hilarious, ultra-popular drag brunch books up months in advance. 634 Louisa St. www.thecountryclubnew orleans.com. ℃ **504/945-0742.** Day pass for the pool $10–$15; more for events.

Good Friends Bar & Queens Head Pub ★★
This truly is a friendly spot, drawing mixed genders, types, and ages. We like that the decor and music aren't generically techno'ed out—it at least tries to maintain some NOLA feel—and that the straight-welcoming local denizens will gladly chat you up. The upstairs Queens Head Pub is most entertaining during the Sunday 3pm singalong. On a hot day, the frozen concoction called the Separator goes down easy. 740 Dauphine St. www.goodfriendsbar.com. ℃ **504/566-7191.** Open 24 hr. on weekends (till 2am weekdays); upstairs Thurs–Sun only.

Oz ★★
This world-renowned, bass-heavy dance club might be overrated, but it still has an incredible light show, go-go boys atop the bar (usually), and drag on Wednesdays. It's a see-and-be-seen spot for a mostly young crowd including plenty of straights. The dance-floor view from the upstairs balcony is worth it alone. 800 Bourbon St. www.oznweorleans.com. ℃ **504/593-9491.** Cover varies.

700 Club ★
No, not *that* 700 Club. Just a low-key, chandelier-lit bar you can wander into, get a decent drink and—as locals know—something from the surprisingly good **Faubourg Bistro** kitchen (food served noon–2am daily). The scene here is *no* scene. Sometimes that's perfect. 700 Burgundy St. www.700clubneworleans.com. ℃ **504/561-1095.**

PERFORMING ARTS, THEATERS & CONCERT HALLS

Culture vultures may also want to see what's on tap at local colleges, including **Tulane University** (www2.tulane.edu/calendar), and several eclectic, occasional performance spaces: **Zeitgeist** (1618 Oretha Castle Haley Blvd.; www.zeitgeistinc.net; ✆ **504/352-1150**); **Marigny Opera House** (725 St. Ferdinand St.; www.marignyoperahouse.org; ✆ **504/948-9998**); the **Theatre at St. Claude** (2240 St. Claude Ave.; www.thetheatreatstclaude.com; ✆ **504/638-6326**; and **Café Istanbul** (2372 St. Claude Ave.; www.cafe istanbulnola.com; ✆ **504/975-0286**).

Civic Theatre ★★ Before 2013 there was nothing in here but the exquisite Deco chandelier and a flock of pigeons. Little was spared in restoring the original 1906 architecture and plasterwork in this triple-tiered, midsize theater. The lineup has stretched from John Prine to Slayer to Belle and Sebastian and Trey Anastasio. 510 O'Keefe St. www.civicnola.com. ✆ **504/272-0865.** Ticket prices vary by event.

Le Petit Théâtre du Vieux Carré ★★ One of the oldest community theaters in the U.S., Le Petit has occupied this building since 1923, save for a scary 2011 shutdown. Fortunately, the opening of restaurant Tableau (p. 92) in the shared building enabled the 350-seat theater to reopen, and patrons to enjoy a dinner-and-a-play night out. Local productions of classic dramas, musicals, and comedies vary from very good to stellar. 616 St. Peter St. www. lepetittheatre.com. ✆ **504/522-2081.** Tickets $10–$50.

Mahalia Jackson Theater for the Performing Arts ★ This cultural hub (located in Armstrong Park bordering the French Quarter) has been home to the local Philharmonic, opera, and ballet companies. The handsome midcentury theater is spacious but not big, so every seat is decent. It also hosts theater, dance troupes, rock concerts, and other live acts. 1419 Basin St. www. mahaliajacksontheater.com. ✆ **504/287-0350.** Ticket prices vary according to event.

Music Box Village ★★★ We haven't been *every*where, but we're pretty sure there's nothing like the Music Box Village *any*where else. It's an enchanted collection of artisan-fabricated structures. Each is at once an edifice, an artwork, and a musical instrument—the love child of Burning Man and the London Philharmonic, born and being raised in Bywater. A performance in, on, and around these magical musical houses is a mesmerizing experience that should not be missed. Dress for outdoor conditions; seating is rustic, so come early to snag a bench or a hay bale, or bring a folding chair or blanket. If there are no performances while you're in town, try to check it out during public hours. 4557 N. Rampart St. www.musicboxvillage.com. $10–$20.

The NOLA Project ★★ This excellent ensemble presents boldly conceived and staged productions in a variety of places and settings (think "Alice in Wonderland" in NOMA's Sculpture Garden). Location varies. www.nolaproject. com. ✆ **504/302-9117.** Ticket prices vary by production, but usually $18–$25.

Orpheum ★★★   It took $15 million and a lot of elbow grease to restore this drop-dead-stunning, 1,500-seat Beaux Arts theater to its original 1908 glory, after it languished in post-Katrina ruin. Finally reopened in late 2015, it now hosts the Louisiana Philharmonic and all manner of comedy, plays, film, and music, ranging from Wilco to Kraftwerk to Charlie Puth. 129 Roosevelt Way. www.orpheumnola.com. ✆ **504/592-7854.** Ticket prices vary according to event.

Saenger Theatre ★★★   Following an extensive, gajillion-dollar, post-Katrina renovation, this magnificent 1927 stunner from the glory movie-house days is now technologically state of the art. The Saenger hosts concerts, comedy shows, Broadway shows, and more. 1111 Canal St. www.saengernola.com. ✆ **504/287-0351.** Ticket prices vary according to event.

Southern Repertory Theatre ★★   Focusing (mostly) on Southern playwrights and themes, Southern Rep's productions are consistently high quality, if not always high budget. Anything written by or starring the hyper-talented Ricky Graham is worth catching. Location varies. www.southernrep.com. ✆ **504/522-6545.** Ticket prices vary by production, but usually $20–$40.

SHOPPING NEW ORLEANS

Shopping in New Orleans is a highly evolved leisure activity, with a shop for every strategy and a fix for every shopaholic—at every budget. Think of the endless souvenir shops on Bourbon Street and swanky antiques stores on Royal Street as the bookends for all the shopping New Orleans has to offer. There are sweet deals to be had, lavish riches to be spent, artworks to be admired. But as all shoppers know, the fun is in the hunt. And New Orleans has some smashing hunting grounds.

MAJOR HUNTING GROUNDS

ART MARKETS   If you're in town between March and December on the last Saturday of the month, consider a trip to the **Palmer Park Arts Market** (S. Carrollton and S. Claiborne Aves., last stop on the St. Charles streetcar line; www.artscouncilofneworleans.org; ✆ **504/523-1465**). From 10am to 4pm you'll find paintings, pottery, glass, mosaics, jewelry, handmade frames, and more from quality, juried artists. At the Marigny's hip **Art Garden** and **Palace Art Market** (http://palaceartmarket.com)**,** we like the cool leather jewelry, music photography, and vintage box cameras upcycled as lamps. Both neighboring markets are open Thursday to Saturday 7pm to midnight (Palace till 1am); Palace adds Saturday noon to 4pm and Sunday to Wednesday 7am to noon (619 and 613 Frenchmen St.; www.frenchmenartmarket.com). The browsing is free; goods are original, local, and affordable.

SHOPS AT CANAL PLACE   At the foot of Canal Street (333 Canal St.) near the Mississippi River, this sophisticated shopping mall holds more than 30 shops, many of them elegant retail chains like Michael Kors, Brooks Brothers, Saks Fifth Avenue, Armani, and a sparkling Tiffany & Co. There's also a two-story Anthropologie, a recently expanded branch of local jeweler **Mignon Faget** (p. 223), and the **Guild** gallery of (mostly) locally made goods. It's open Monday to Friday 10am to 7pm, Saturday 10am to 8pm, and Sunday noon to 7pm (www.canalplacestyle.com).

THE FRENCH MARKET These historic shops begin in the colonnade along Decatur Street across from Jackson Square. Offerings include candy, housewares, fashion, crafts, and toys. The open-air section (the oldest continuously operated open-air market in the country) begins at Ursulines Avenue and N. Peters Street. There's a stage for live music and cooking demos, and food booths including an oyster bar, a terrific fresh juice bar, and tasty **Meals from the Heart.** The farmer's market and foodstuff stalls—including local seafood, meats, and spices—will pack your purchases for travel or shipping. The flea market section has low-end souvenirs (good buys, if not good quality) and a smattering of actual art and handmade goods. It's a fun stroll. Open daily 10am to 6pm (www.frenchmarket.org). See also p. 227.

JAX BREWERY Just across from Jackson Square at 600–620 Decatur St., the old brewery building is now a jumble of shops and cafes (and good bathrooms). It's a good stop for clothing and souvenirs, particularly the crawfish logo'd polo shirts and other preppie wear at **Perlis.** Open daily 10am to 7pm (www.jaxnola.com; ✆ **504/566-7245**).

JULIA STREET Some of the city's best contemporary art galleries (many listed below under "Art Galleries") line Julia Street from Camp Street to the river (and fork off into surrounding side streets). The quality of talent exhibited here—among both creators and curators—is quite astounding.

MAGAZINE STREET The Garden District's premier shopping drag, 6 miles of antiques, boutiques, galleries, and all manner of restaurants in 19th-century brick storefronts and quaint Creole cottages, from Washington Street to Audubon Park. Prime sections are, roughly, the 3700 to 4300 blocks (with the odd block or so of nothing); 1900 to 2100; and 5400 to 5700 blocks. A car or JazzyPass (p. 269) will help you browse the lengthy avenue.

THE OUTLET COLLECTION AT RIVERWALK Whoa. **Neiman Marcus Last Call, Coach, Nordstrom Rack, Le Crueset,** and 75 other outlet stores fill this sprawling, three-story mall. Bargains are a bonus when you can walk from the French Quarter, shop with a daiquiri in hand, and enjoy the best view from a mall food court in existence at tables overlooking the Mississippi. It's behind the Hilton at 500 Port of New Orleans Place just steps from the ferry and cruise terminals. Open Monday to Saturday 10am to 9pm; Sunday 10am to 7pm (www.riverwalknewworleans.com; ✆ **504/522-1555**).

RIVERBEND, MAPLE & OAK STREET To reach these fetching Carrollton-area shops, ride the St. Charles Avenue streetcar to stop no. 44, then walk a block down Maple Street. There, cool local designs at **Sarah Ott** and the delectable **Maple Street Patisserie** inhabit renovated Creole cottages and old buildings. Four blocks up Dublin Street is the happening Oak Street shopping and dining district. Check out the excellent **Blue Cypress Books,** high-end knives at **Coutelier,** and weird and wacky **Rabbit Ears** vintage-goods gallery. For refreshments, try famed restaurant **Jacques-Imo's** (p. 120), **Breads on Oak,** something chill from **Ale on Oak,** or icy **Plum Street Snoball** a block away.

SHOPPING NEW ORLEANS | Major Hunting Grounds

SHOPPING A TO Z

Antiques

Cohen & Sons ★★ Specializing in antique weapons, coins, and currency from points near and far, dating back to B.C. They're not the friendliest folk (unless you're a serious collector), but it's worth a look, and a locally minted antique coin or doubloon from actual sunken treasure makes a fine souvenir. 437 Royal St. www.cohenantiques.com. ℂ **504/522-3305.** Mon–Sat 9:30am–5pm.

Collectible Antiques ★★ One of our favorites of the dusty, jumbled, and eclectic antiques/junk stores on the Esplanade end of Decatur. Its stock runs from Art Deco to 1960s collectibles. 1232 Decatur St. http://shop.cohen antiques.com. ℂ **504/566-0399.** Daily noon–6pm.

Keil's Antiques ★★ Established in 1899 and currently run by the fourth generation of the founding family, Keil's has a considerable collection of 18th- and 19th-century French and English furniture, chandeliers, jewelry, and decorative items spanning three crowded floors. Ask a member of the family or staff about the doorman who worked his spot here for 78 years, and coax out some other stories from them. They've got plenty. 325 Royal St. www. keilsantiques.com. ℂ **504/522-4552.** Mon–Sat 9am–5pm.

Lucullus ★★★ A wonderful collection of culinary antiques as well as 17th- through 19th-century furnishings to "complement the grand pursuits of cooking, dining, and imbibing." You'll find all manner of china, Art Deco silverware, oyster plates, and rare absinthe accoutrements. 610 Chartres St. www. lucullusantiques.com. ℂ **504/528-9620.** Mon–Sat 9am–5pm (closed Mon late spring to summer).

Magazine Antique Mall ★ Diggers will dig the superb browsing and many good deals found among the 50-plus variegated stalls here. 3017 Magazine St. www.magazinestreet.com/merchant/magazine-antique-mall. ℂ **504/896-9994.** Mon–Sat 10am–5pm, Sun 11:30am–5pm.

M.S. Rau ★★★ The sheer scale and absurdity of the inventory makes century-old Rau a must-see for everyone and a destination for serious buyers. Every opulent item that could possibly be crafted from fine metals, gems, crystal, wood, china, and marble, plus articles made by every name known to the antique world, is here for the ogling or the investing, filling room after jaw-dropping room. We particularly like the selection of walking canes and the 8-foot attack-mode cave bear skeleton, circa 150,000 B.C. Most every item has a story to tell, and the knowledgeable sales reps pleasantly indulge your curiosity, even if you're just wool-gathering (ask them to show you the back room). 630 Royal St. www.rauantiques.com. ℂ **888/557-2406**. Mon–Sat 9am–5:15pm.

Art Galleries

Galleries share the **Royal** and **Magazine Street** landscapes with the afore-mentioned antiques shops; while in the Warehouse District, the 300 to 700 blocks of **Julia Street** house some 20 contemporary fine-arts galleries, anchored by the **Contemporary Arts Center** and **Ogden Museum of Southern Art** (p. 152). For the more intrepid, explore the burgeoning lowbrow and outsider art movement around **St. Claude Avenue** (no current collective website, but hit Barrister's, UNO St. Claude, Good Children, and The Front Galleries (2331, 2429, 4037, and 4100 St. Claude Ave. respectively).

Don't miss **Studio BE ★★★**, at 2941 Royal Street, home to the astounding works of artist, activist, and educator Brandon "BMike" Odums. For more on Studio BE, see p. 154.

Angela King Gallery ★★★ Opened in 2007 in a show of much-needed post-Katrina solidarity, this is still one of the best contemporary art galleries in the city. King shows works by significant artists such as Peter Max, Andrew Baird, Richard Currier, Steve Taylor, Raymond Douillet, Patterson & Barnes, and Michelle Gagliano . . . *and* has a lagniappe mini-gallery, the **Striped Hat,** dedicated to the art of Dr. Seuss. 241 Royal St. www.angelakinggallery.com. ✆ **504/524-8211.** Mon–Sat 10am–5pm; Sun 11am–5pm.

Antieau Gallery ★★★ We adore the supremely clever Chris Roberts-Antieau's whimsical side (sewn works that riff on current events and social mores) and her dark side (macabre snow globes and a dollhouse re-creation of the *In Cold Blood* crime scene). 927 Royal St. www.antieaugallery.com. ✆ **504/304-0849.** Daily 10am–8pm. Uptown: 4532 Magazine St. ✆ 504/510-4148. Mon–Sat 10am–6pm.

Arthur Roger Gallery ★★ Arthur Roger pioneered the Warehouse District and fine-arts scene when he opened in New Orleans some 30 years ago, tying the local community to the New York art world. Still blazing trails with shows that range from strongly regional to far-flung, the gallery represents Francis X. Pavy, Ida Kohlmeyer, Dawn DeDeaux, Dale Chihuly, and the stunning, brazen figurative photographs of the late George Dureau. 432-434 Julia St. www.arthurrogergallery.com. ✆ **504/522-1999.** Tues–Sat 10am–5pm.

Ashley Longshore ★★★ Not for the faint of heart or wallet, Ashley's clever, crass art riffs on pop culture and wealth-worship in bright hues and high-gloss. She slams (or glorifies?) materialism and winks at celebrity on pillows and paintings, but they're flower-strewn and alit with butterflies, so hey, it's all good. We were smitten with the fanciful, Crest-white armchairs with lipstick-red, metallic auto upholstery emblazoned with "No F**ks Given." Then some 14-year-old girl bought them for $6,000/pair. 4Realz. 4537 Magazine St. www.ashleylongshore.com. ✆ **504/333-6951.** Tues–Fri 9am–5pm; Sat noon–4pm or by appt.

Carol Robinson Gallery ★★ The grande dame of the local contemporary Southern arts scene, Robinson still shows accessible but surprisingly affordable works, including the stunning pastels of Sandra Burshell, Jere Allen's mysterious milky-white figures, James King's haunting oils, and Christina Goodman's exquisite, minute tableaus. 840 Napoleon Ave. https://carol robinsongallery.net. ℂ **504/895-6130.** Tues and Thurs–Sat 10am–5pm; Mon by appt.

Christopher Porche-West ★★★ Porche-West's stunning portrait photographs are themselves works of art, but when he sculpts and frames them within magnificent assemblages of architectural remnants, mechanical parts, natural materials, and found oddities, he creates highly collectible, singular statement pieces in what he calls the **Bank of Soul** studio. 3201 Burgundy St. www.porche-west.com or www.facebook.com/The-Bank-Of-Soul-148879701855987. ℂ **504/947-3880.** Irregular hours; call for appt. or drop by and get lucky.

Derby Pottery ★★ One of Mark Derby's hand-pressed tiles, glazed in gleaming single hues, makes for a lovely keepsake (particularly the New Orleans street-name tile reproductions). One hundred make for a stunning backsplash or fireplace surround. Ceramic mugs and water meter clocks make excellent, handmade souvenirs. 2029 Magazine St. www.derbypottery.com. ℂ **504/586-9003.** Mon–Sat 10am–5pm.

Dr. Bob ★★★ He of the now-iconic "BE NICE OR LEAVE" folk-art signs. See p. 7.

Frank Relle Gallery ★★ Sometimes spooky, sometimes serene, Relle's nightscapes of the local swamps and architecture are undeniably stunning. 910 Royal St. www.frankrelle.com. ℂ **504/265-8564.** Sun–Thurs 10am–6pm; Fri–Sat 10am–8pm.

A Gallery for Fine Photography ★★★ This incredibly well-stocked photography gallery emphasizes the historic and contemporary culture of New Orleans and the South, music, and black culture. The stunning investment images include Ernest Bellocq's legendary Storyville photos; Herman Leonard's jazz images; the haunting work of Sebastião Salgado; and something from just about every period, style, or noted photographer (including books, if photos aren't in your budget). 241 Chartres St. www.agallery.com. ℂ **504/568-1313.** Thurs–Mon 10:30am–5:30pm; Tues and Wed by appt.

Jonathan Ferrara Gallery ★★★ Since 1998, Ferrara has been showing emerging cross-media artists in thought-provoking exhibitions that lean toward playfulness and irony. Skylar Fein's pop-pundit pieces are both hilarious and horrifying in their truth; the G.A.S. Caravaggio photobombs are equally stunning and silly. 400a Julia St. www.jonathanferraragallery.com. ℂ **504/522-5471.** Mon–Sat 11am–5pm or by appt.

Kurt E. Schon, Ltd. ★★ Behold the country's largest inventory of 19th-century European paintings. The stunning collection, rivaling or exceeding that in many museums, includes French and British Impressionist and post-Impressionist paintings as well as art from the Royal Academy and the French

Salon. 510 St. Louis St. www.kurteschonltd.com. ✆ **504/524-5462.** Mon–Fri 10am–5pm; Sat 10am–3pm.

Martine Chaisson Gallery ★★ The stark, sweeping space screams for high-impact, highly saturated imagery, and Martine delivers, particularly with Herman Mhire's manipulated portraiture, J. T. Blatty's striking photography of nudes with fossils, and Norman Mooney's frisson-inducing carbon-on-paper imagery. 727 Camp St. www.martinechaissongallery.com. ✆ **504/302-7942.** Wed–Sat 11am–5pm; Mon–Tues by appt.

Modernist Cuisine Gallery ★ Those familiar with the game-changing *Modernist Cuisine* cookbooks may recognize Nathan Myhrvold's vibrant food photos. They look great on the page and online, but up close and personal, the large-format, resin-coated prints are even yummier. Bean sprouts were never more enticing. 305 Royal St. modernistcuisinegallery.com. ✆ **504/571-5157.** Sun–Wed 10am–6pm; Thurs–Fri 10am–8pm.

New Orleans School of GlassWorks & Printmaking Studio ★★★ This institution, with 25,000 square feet of studio space, houses a 550-pound tank of hot molten glass and a pre–Civil War press. At this sister school to the Louvre Museum of Decorative Arts, glasswork artists, bookbinders, and master printmakers display their work, demonstrate glass-blowing, and teach classes, including the popular "Wine & Design" gatherings. 727 Magazine St. www.neworleansglassworks.com. ✆ **504/529-7279.** Mon–Sat 10am–5pm.

OMG! ★ New and reclaimed religious folk art, anchored by Jan Keels' stirring gossamer, oil-on-wood angels and dancers and Jeff Passage's comely watercolor cemeteries. Fab Virgins Saints & Angels jewelry and hand-poured candles. 542 St. Peter St. www.OMG-NOLA.com. ✆ **504/522-8443.** Daily 10am–6pm.

Photo Works ★★ Photographer Louis Sahuc's family has been in New Orleans "since day one," and his life's work has been photo-documenting iconic New Orleans imagery, such as Jackson Square swathed in fog, or fragments of ironwork. 521 St. Ann St. www.photoworksneworleans.com. ✆ **504/593-9090.** Thurs–Tues 10am–5:30pm.

Red Truck Gallery ★★ The mad, sharp sensibility here plays out in conceptual art that is sometimes bizarre, often brilliant, and utterly covetous. We'd take any of Dennis McNett's sly, carved portraits on wood; Bryan Cunningham's whack folk assemblages; or Adam Wallacavage's sea-creature chandeliers. 938 Royal St. www.redtruckgallery.com. ✆ **504/522-3630.** Sun–Thurs 10am–9pm; Fri–Sat 10am–10pm.

Rodrigue Studio New Orleans ★ The late Cajun artist George Rodrigue's ubiquitous Blue Dog is the Zelig of New Orleans art: The cobalt kitsch canine appears in every imaginable pose and setting and invades your consciousness. Adorable? Obnoxious? You be the judge. The gallery also displays Rodrigue's considerable classical talents. 730 Royal St. www.george rodrigue.com. ✆ **504/581-4244.** Mon–Sat 10am–6pm; Sun 10am–5pm.

Books

Arcadian Books ★★ Bibliophiles will bask in these wondrous, dusty stacks, especially lovers of the classics (in English and Latin); the history inquisitive (local and far beyond); and seekers of French, German, or Russian literature in their native tongue. Proprietor Russell Desmond is ridiculously knowledgeable and nearly as personable, and knows every item in this gloriously decrepit grotto. 714 Orleans Ave. ℂ **504/523-4138.** Mon–Sat 9:30am–5:30pm.

Beckham's Bookshop ★★ More than 50,000 volumes carefully collected by the store's owners (and one cat) jam the two floors at beloved Beckham's—a pillar of the Quarter's thriving indie bookshop scene since 1967. It has used books for all interests (browse the glass cases for rare gems) and a fine small selection of new, locally focused titles. 228 Decatur St. www.beckhamsbookshop.com. ℂ **504/522-9875.** Daily 10am–5pm.

Books-a-Million ★ Hand it to the chains that are still committed to book-selling; this one stocks a good selection of local titles. If you're passing through, it's a good place to pick up New Orleans–related books on your way to or from the city. Fremaux Town Center, 360 Town Center Pkwy., Slidell. www.booksamillion.com. ℂ **985/847-9676.** Mon–Sat 10am–9pm; Sun noon–6pm.

Crescent City Books ★★ Rooms and shelves and more rooms and shelves cradle easily browsable, serious literature for the seriously literate, with an emphasis on rare history, local interest, literary criticism, philosophy, and art. It's also a general hub of info about literary events, and has a small but good selection of maps and art prints (and one cat). 124 Baronne St. www.crescentcitybooks.com. ℂ **504/524-4997**. Mon–Sat 10am–7pm; Sun 10am–5pm.

Faulkner House Books ★★★ That Nobel prize–winner William Faulkner lived here while writing his early works is but one literary morsel in this winning recipe for a perfect, small bookshop. Shelf after high shelf is occupied by decidedly desirable titles, from stunning first editions to Southern authors and current bestsellers. Just one room and a hallway, Faulkner House feels like somebody's private home (it is)—but the gracious advice and judicious selection make manifest the art of bookselling. Dogs. 624 Pirate's Alley. www.faulknerhousebooks.com. ℂ **504/524-2940.** Daily 10am–5:30pm.

Garden District Book Shop ★★★ This sweet, medium-size shop is stocked with just about every New Orleans– or Louisiana-themed book you can think of, no matter what the focus: interiors, exteriors, food, Creoles, fiction, poetry, you name it—including many signed copies. Best-sellers, too. Currently catless. 2727 Prytania St. (in the Rink). www.gardendistrictbookshop.com. ℂ **504/895-2266.** Mon–Sat 10am–6pm; Sun 10am–5pm.

Kitchen Witch ★★★ In a town of foodies, chefs, cooks, and eaters of all interests and proficiencies, this quirky used-cookbook store is the rainbow's end. It's chockablock with nearly 10,000 volumes, from the ultra-rare to the just-released—and if the delightful owners don't have it, they'll find it. Set the egg timer or you could spend way too much time browsing, chatting, and petting the cat and dog. 1452 N. Broad St., Ste. C. www.kwcookbooks.com. © **504/528-8382.** Mon–Fri 10am–5pm; Sat–Sun 10am–6pm. Closed occasional Tues, call to confirm.

Octavia Books ★★★ For those who adore independent bookstores, this far-uptown beauty with its sweet, tiny patio (complete with waterfall, but no cat) is worth the detour. There is much to savor here, in the extensive, well-selected stock, and in the frequent signings and readings. 513 Octavia St. (at Laurel St.). www.octaviabooks.com. © **504/899-7323.** Mon–Sat 10am–6pm; Sun 10am–5pm.

Candies, Pralines & Pastries

Bittersweet Confections ★ Ideal for the fortification of caffeine and sweetness after (or before) a tough gallery- or museum-hopping stint. Chocolates are their forte, but the cupcakes are hard to resist. Wish it was open later for a little something after a Warehouse District dinner; weekend waffles make up for it. 725 Magazine St. www.bittersweetconfections.com. © **504/523-2626.** Mon–Fri 7am–5:30pm; Sat 7am–4pm; Sun 7:30am–2pm.

Laura's Candies ★ Charming Laura's is said to be the city's oldest candy store, established in 1913. The pralines are fabulous, but the rich, delectable (if pricey) golf-ball-size truffles are a personal favorite indulgence. 331 Chartres St. www.laurascandies.com. © **504/525-3880.** Daily 10am–9pm.

Southern Candymakers ★★★ Our top choice for pralines, it offers the usual suspects and some non-traditionals (coconut and sweet potato!), and all are just extra creamylicious (and made fresh right in front of you—if the display doesn't reel you in, the aroma will). We swoon for the pecan-laden *tortues*; the boxed chocolate crawfish and gator pops make fine gifts. 334 Decatur St. (factory). www.southerncandymakers.com. © **504/523-5544.** Daily 9am–7pm. 1010 Decatur St. © **504/525-6170.** Daily 10am–6pm.

Sucré ★★★ The beautiful, high-end confections at these stylish cafes—sherbet-hued macarons, gold-dusted chocolates—are ideal for an afternoon indulgence or gifts (they're as pretty as they are pricey, and not overly sweet, so opinions vary from bland to brilliant). But we're partial to the minicakes, like the luscious "Tiffany." The gorgeous inside-and-out French Quarter location has a high-level coffee program with a swank Modbar system, and upstairs café **Salon** serving high tea, wine, and brunch (Thurs–Mon 10am–7pm). The balcony is perfect for sipping. 3025 Magazine St. www.shopsucre.com. © **504/520-8311.** 622 Conti St. © 504/267-7098. Both Sun–Thurs 9am–10pm; Fri–Sat 9am–11pm.

Costumes & Masks

Costumery is big business and big fun in New Orleans, and not just for Mardi Gras. Playing dress-up needs no event, and nothing is too elaborate. In addition to these shops, try thrift stores, where slightly used outfits can sometimes be found at a fraction of their original cost. Troll lower Decatur and Dauphine in the Bywater (especially **Le Garage,** 1234 Decatur St.; © **504/522-6639**). Also check **Uptown Costume & Dancewear** (4326 Magazine St.; www.uptowncostume.com; © **504/895-7969;** Tues–Thurs and Sat 11am–6pm, Fri 11am–7pm).

Carl Mack Presents ★★ Mack, doyen of Mardi Gras entertainment, rents or creates ornate costumes for Fat Tuesday or any day. This is high-production-value stuff—no naughty nurses here. 318 N. Rampart St. www.carlmack.com. ☏ **504/949-4009.** Mon–Fri 9am–5pm or by appt.

Fifi Mahony's ★★ Wig wackiness, why not? Have the hair you've always wanted (even if just for the day). Worth visiting to see (or get) their outrageous custom pieces. Salon and makeup services, too. 934 Royal St. www.fifimahonys.com. ☏ **504/525-4343.** Sun–Fri noon–6pm; Sat 11am–7pm.

Southern Costume Company ★★ They rent, they design, they alter, they'll get you dressed. Enormous stock, reasonable prices and helpful service. 951 Lafayette St. www.sccnola.com. ☏ **504/523-4333.** Mon–Fri 9am–6pm.

Fashion, Vintage Clothing, Hats & Accessories

Art and Eyes ★★★ Eyeglass wearers who demand something above average: For a souvenir you'll use daily, consider something from this extensive assortment of fabulous frames for discerning heads. Artisan-made, unusual materials, vintage, designer, imported…too much gorgeousness to pick just one. 3708 Magazine St. www.artandeyesneworleansla.com. ☏ **504/891-4494.** Tues–Thurs 11am–7pm; Mon 11am–5pm; Sat 10am–6pm; Sun noon–5pm.

Dollz & Dames ★★ If the Frenchmen Street jitterbugging scene has released your inner pin-up gal, this is your store. The vintage-y frocks make for darling datewear, but we'd don them any time. Tops cost $60 to $130, and dresses are under $200. Cute accessories, custom T-strap dance shoes, and helpful help. 216 Decatur St. www.dollzanddames.com. ☏ **504/522-5472.** Daily noon–6pm.

Fleur de Paris ★★★ The 1920s and 1930s elegance on display here is positively swoonworthy. The hand-blocked, stylishly trimmed hats are expensive, but these are works of art. They also have luscious stockings and scarves, an ever-changing collection of vintage gowns, and custom design services. 523 Royal St. www.fleurdeparis.net. ☏ **504/525-1899.** Daily 10am–6pm.

Lili Vintage ★★★ Lili is the utopian women's vintage clothing boutique, because of Laura Hourguettes. Everything in this dollhouse—from crinolines to cardigans and Victoriana to Audreyana—is pristinely selected, beautifully merchandised, in good condition, and, OMG, well-priced (not thrift-store level, but almost everything's $35–$100). It's girly stuff to be sure, and you have to hit it when that just-right-for-you item is in, but if the perfect beaded purse or Pucci print gives you that tingly shopping feeling, come. 3329 Magazine St. www.lilivintage.com. ☏ **504/931-6848.** Mon–Sat 10am–6pm.

Love It ★★ Charming owner Danna Lea's restyled vintage clothes and exquisite, hand-crafted hats, purses, and accessories made from found leathers, feathers, and other adornments are worth the hunt and the splurge. A few well-selected new dresses at this jewel box of a shop, too. 2028 Magazine St. www.facebook.com/pages/Love-It/250712024957567. ☏ **504/523-7888.** Mon–Fri noon–5pm (hours sometimes vary).

Meyer the Hatter ★★★   Family-owned for more than 100 years, this haberdashery has one of the largest selections of fine hats and caps in the South. Men will find distinguished international labels such as Bailey, Stetson, Kangol, Dobbs, and Biltmore (the women's collection is smaller). Let them fuss over you and pick out the proper feather for your new chapeau—these hat whisperers know just how to top every head. 120 St. Charles Ave. www.meyerthehatter.com. ✆ **504/525-1048.** Mon–Sat 10am–5:45pm.

Muse ★★   Gentlemen, should the city and the spirit induce an undeniable need for a metallic paisley, madras plaid, or seersucker sport jacket, Muse will fix you right up (seasonally, and starting at about $250). The Jackson Square boutique also dishes fab accessories and girly fashion. 532 St. Peter St. (on Jackson Sq.). www.museinspiredfashion.com. ✆ **504/522-8738.** Daily 10am–6pm.

odAOMO ★★   Owner/designer Dr. Sophia Aomo Omoro designs dresses, bags, and accessories that are hand-crafted in Kenya by her own small team. The looks are breezy, exotic, fashion-forward and eminently wearable. The real standouts are the statement neckpieces, belts, and bags of leather, beading, and metals. Fair wages and eco-friendly materials are preeminent to the odAOMO philosophy. 839 Chartres St. www.odaomo.com. ✆ **504/460-5730.** Mon–Sun 10am–6pm.

Rubenstein's ★★★   Many a proper young New Orleans man learned the art of attire here. For more than 90 years the hallowed haberdasher has outfitted gents in custom suits, fine menswear, and perfect prepwear. Their pros will dress you to the nines and fit you to a T. Quick-turnaround tailoring gets you Galatoire's-ready. 102 St. Charles Ave. www.rubensteinsneworleans.com. ✆ **504/581-6666.** Mon–Thurs 10am–5:45pm; Fri–Sat 10am–6pm.

ShoeBeDo ★★   As much a gallery as a shoe store, it's worth a visit just to gawk at the outrageousness. More power to you if you can actually pull off this crazy glam footwear. 324 Chartres St. www.shoebedousa.com. ✆ **504/523-7463.** Mon–Sat 10am–6pm; Sun 11am–6pm.

Tchoup Industries ★★   Stylish, sturdy messenger bags, backpacks, dop kits, and purses made on-site from sustainable, repurposed, and locally sourced or made materials. Think waxed canvas, sailcloth, burlap, alligator skins nutria fur. Good for the environment *and* the community—and good-looking to boot. 1115 Saint Mary St. www.tchoupindustries.com. ✆ **504/872-0726.** Mon, Tues, Thurs–Sat 11am–6pm; Sun noon–5pm.

Trashy Diva ★★★   There's actually nothing trashy about the 1940s and '50s vintage-inspired clothes here. The flirty, curve-flattering numbers in silks and velvets appeal to both Bettys and Goths, as do the similar-era shoes and va-va-voom corsets and lingerie. Check the sales racks for good bargains. All shops open daily, but hours vary, so give a ring. Boutiques: 537 Royal St. (www.trashydiva.com; ✆ **504/522-423**) and 2048 Magazine St. (✆ 504/299-8777). Lingerie: 712 Royal St. (✆ 504/522-8861). Royal St. daily 11am–7pm; Magazine St. Mon–Fri noon–6pm, Sat 11am–6pm, Sun 1–5pm.

UAL ★   This destination for local and visiting fashionistas offers incredible deals on discontinued and leftover designer goods (McQueen, McCartney, Jason Wu, Chanel). Major markdowns and one-off stock can lead to fiercely competitive (but utterly satisfying) hit-or-miss guerilla shopping. 518 Chartres St. https://shopual.com. ☏ **504/301-4437.** Daily 10am–8pm.

Food, Wine & Liquor

Every souvenir shop in town stocks spices, hot sauce, coffee, and beignet mix. The French Market vendors do too, along with meat and seafood, and they're set up to ship it home or pack it for travel. If you get a hankering from home, try **www.cajungrocer.com**.

Keife & Co ★★   If you just can't get out the door, Keife & Co. will deliver a basket with gourmet meats, cheeses, and wine to your Central Business District hotel room. If you *can* get out, grab a bottle on your way to the restaurant or to take home. Great selection; even better service. 801 Howard Ave. www.keifeandco.com. ☏ **504/523-7272.** Tues–Sat 10am–8pm.

Martin Wine Cellar ★★   Massive Martin carries an eye-popping selection of wines, beers, and spirits for the connoisseur, the casual imbiber, or the BYOer, many at surprisingly reasonable prices. A terrific, full-service deli and good selection of cheeses, cookies, and such make for a fine picnic, in your hotel room or Audubon Park. 3827 Baronne St. www.martinwine.com. ☏ **504/899-7411.** Mon–Fri 10am–7pm; Fri 10am–6:30pm; Sat 9am–7pm; Sun 10am–3pm.

Vieux Carré Wine and Spirits ★★   If you're looking for Herbsaint, absinthe, or Sazerac rye, are a serious wine buyer, or just want a bottle for your hotel room or dinner, this densely packed French Quarter shop will fit the bill. 422 Chartres St. ☏ **504/568-9463.** Mon–Sat 9:30am–8pm.

W.I.N.O. ★   Try before you buy with the Wine Institute of New Orleans' enomatic system. Top up a debit card and set to dispensing 1-, 2-, or 3-ounce pours of some 120 wines, covering many regions and varietals. Cheese, charcuterie, and tapas plates round out the experience; then grab a bottle or three to go. Classes also offered if self-study isn't your pace. 610 Tchoupitoulas St. www.winoschool.com. ☏ **504/324-8000.** Sun–Tues 2–10pm; Wed–Sat 2pm–midnight.

Gifts, Home Decor & Bath

Aidan Gill for Men ★★★   Long before the facial-hair frenzy begot the male grooming renaissance, Aidan Gill championed the art of gentlemanliness. Sharp-dressed men and those in need of gifts for same will find fine accessories and old-fashioned grooming implements brought thoroughly up to date: elegant shaving brushes, hand-held razors, colognes, and top-shelf skin and hair products. Their superb services start with a hot towel and finish with a whiskey (no less authority than *Playboy* dubbed its $40 Shave at the End of the Galaxy the best in America). 2026 Magazine St. www.aidangillformen.com. ☏ **504/587-9090.** Mon–Fri 10am–6pm; Sat 9am–6pm; Sun noon–6pm.

Bevolo ★★★ Even if you're not planning to take home a handmade copper gaslight lantern as your vacation souvenir, you should check out Bevolo because a) the lanterns are a gorgeous local tradition; b) master craftsmen fabricate them right in front of you at the onsite workshop; and c) you might change your mind about your souvenir choice. 316 Royal St. www.bevolo.com. ℂ **504/552-9485.** Mon–Fri 8am–5pm; Sat 9am–4pm.

Hazelnut ★ The housewares and gifts here are generally cute with one dazzling standout: the line of toile items with a customized pattern of iconic New Orleans scenes—the St. Charles streetcar, a live oak tree, St. Louis Cathedral, and such. It's desperately darling and we want it all—the bedding, tote bag, and picture frame. Sigh. *Fun fact: Mad Men*'s Bryan Batt is part owner. 5515 Magazine St. www.hazelnutneworleans.com. ℂ **504/891-2424.** Mon–Sat 10am–6pm (till 5pm in summer).

Hové ★★★ The oldest perfumery in the city, Hové features a fabulous selection of all-natural scents for men and women. Original creations ("Kiss in the Dark") and Southern smells such as vetivert and tea olive, available in many forms, make lovely presents—even for yourself. Literature buffs will appreciate the letter from author Tom Robbins confirming that his *Jitterbug Perfume* shop was roughly based on Hové. 434 Chartres St. www.hoveparfumeur.com. ℂ **504/525-7827.** Mon–Sat 9:30am–6pm; Sun 11am–6pm.

Queork ★★ All-cork merchandise seems a strange concept, till you spy that want-want-want $39 iPhone case. Then it's a slippery slope to a cork belt and surprisingly durable cork-upholstered furniture and the shoes, oh, the shoes. 838 Chartres St. ℂ **504/481-4910.** 3005 Magazine St. ℂ 504/388-6803. www.queork.com. Daily 10am–6pm.

Simon of New Orleans/Antiques on Jackson ★★ Folk artist Simon, whose brightly painted signs are seen throughout New Orleans in homes and businesses, will paint-to-order your own personal sign and ship it to you. The studio also has a particularly good collection of primitive furniture, antiques, and hodgepodgery. 1028 Jackson Ave. www.facebook.com/simonofneworleans. ℂ **504/524-8201.** Mon–Sat 10am–5pm.

Jewelry

GoGo ★★ Designer GoGo's own colorful silver cuffs, necklaces, and belt buckles in attention-getting designs like a cartoon-punchy "POW!" burst are just plain funwear. But her selection of other artist-made jewelry (and taxidermy and paint-by-number art) make a visit to this itty-bitty boutique a gottago. Loves: Hypnovamp 3-D printed spider web necklace and Stephanie Lyman's purses made from vintage cowboy boots. 2036 Magazine St. www.ilovegogojewelry.com. ℂ **504/529-8868.** Mon–Sat 11am–6pm; Sun noon–5pm.

Marion Cage ★★★ Cage's ultrafine, exquisitely wrought work is popular with collectors in Paris and New York, where she worked before opening this gallery in her native New Orleans. Clean lines of matte rose and yellow gold, rhodium, and leather hardwoods start around $95, like the slender initial pendants. A delicate sterling talon runs $245. 3807 Magazine St. www.marioncage.com. ✆ **504/891-8848.** Mon–Sat 10am–5pm.

Mignon Faget, Ltd. ★★   Faget, a New Orleans native, lends her signature style to New Orleans–specific designs in gold, silver, and bronze d'oré (and housewares)—all superb souvenirs or gifts. 3801 Magazine St. www.mignonfaget.com. ✆ **504/891-2005.** Mon–Sat 10am–6pm. Canal Place, Level 1. ✆ 504/524-2973. Mon–Fri 10am–7pm; Sat 10am–8pm; Sun noon–7pm.

Music

Domino Sound Record Shack ★★   A one-room beats shop off the beaten track. Stellar ska, rock steady, and R&B collections; world music from countries you've never heard of; local weirdness; and pretty much everything Sun Ra ever put out. All vinyl except for about 37 cassettes. Bonus points for proximity to McHardy's Chicken (p. 103). 2557 Bayou Rd. www.dominosoundrecords.com. ✆ **504/309-0871.** Wed–Mon noon–6pm (till 7:30 Fri).

Euclid Records ★★   If you love the smell of vinyl in the morning, or any time, Euclid will fire your pheromones. This younger-than-it-feels Bywater shop (sistah of the iconic St. Louis shop) stocks vintage platters from every era and gobs of local goods. Look for occasional in-store performances. 3301 Chartres St. www.euclidnola.com. ✆ **504/947-4348.** Daily 11am–7pm.

Louisiana Music Factory ★★★   *The* place to get yourself stocked with New Orleans music, with helpful staff and a large selection of regional music—including Cajun, zydeco, R&B, jazz, blues, and gospel—plus books, posters, and T-shirts. Live performances most Saturdays. It's especially hopping during Jazz Fest. 421 Frenchmen St. www.louisianamusicfactory.com. ✆ **504/586-1094.** Daily 10am–7pm.

Peaches Records ★   Peaches' first store (circa 1975) was a stop-off for R&B royalty (Stevie Wonder!) and helped launch local hip-hop artists like Juvenile and Lil Wayne. Still family-owned and a hip-hop hub, the spacious store stocks a broad swath of locally focused CDs, vinyl, books, DVDs, and one of the better logo'd T-shirts in town. 4318 Magazine St. www.peachesrecordsneworleans.com. ✆ **504/282-3322.** Daily 10am–8pm.

The Occult

Also see p. 167 for Voodoo temples and practitioners.

Bottom of the Cup Tearoom ★   Open since 1929, it bills itself as the "oldest tearoom in the United States," so a reading with Otis, its premier psychic, is a pretty classic experience. The tearoom psychics can read palms, tarot cards, tea leaves, and crystals, and your experience is guaranteed to be quirky. Great selection of teas for purchase and various psychic-y goods. 327 Chartres St. www.bottomofthecup.com. ✆ **800/729-7148** or 504/524-1997. Daily 10am–6pm.

Boutique du Vampyre ★   Of course the only brick-and-mortar vampire shop in America is in New Orleans. Proprietress Marita Jaeger showcases local artisans, custom-made fangs, coffin-shaped backpacks . . . and for the

faint of heart, temporary bite tattoos. 709½ St. Ann St. http://feelthebite.com.
℃ **504/561-8267.** Daily 10am–9pm.

F&F Botanica ★★   This unassuming, jam-packed Tremé shop is among
the largest suppliers anywhere of candles, herbs, icons, and elixirs for the serious practitioner. Mr. Felix (Figueroa) and son will kindly assist new or non-
believers. While you're there, check out the Zulu Social Aid & Pleasure Club
store across the street. 5801 N. Broad St. www.fandfbotanica.com. ℃ **504/482-5400.**
Mon, Tues & Thurs–Sat 8am–5pm.

Marie Laveau's House of Voodoo ★   This is tourist Voodoo, to be
sure, but the Voodoo dolls and gris-gris bags make great souvenirs for the
right friends. 739 Bourbon St. www.voodooneworleans.com. ℃ **504/581-3751.** Sun–
Thurs 10am–11:30pm; Fri–Sat 10am–1:30am.

Voodoo Authentica ★★   With two big rooms of Voodoo paraphernalia,
it feels like a real retail establishment, and the merchandise feels authentic.
The locally made Voodoo dolls, potions, spell candles, and daubs range from
cheap to costly, and there are simple souvenirs as well as serious works of art.
612 Dumaine St. www.voodooshop.com. ℃ **504/522-2111.** Daily 11am–7pm.

T-Shirts & More

If crass and mass market suits your style, by all means buy up the Bourbon
Street goods. But for garments with local flavor that are also clever and maybe
even have a decent design aesthetic, there are a plethora of superior options.
Shirts (and hats, hoodies, and so forth) in these shops will probably run $5 to
$10 more than your average show-me-your-whatever tops, but they're softer.
And smarter.

DNO (Defend New Orleans) ★★   Small shops with smart and stylish
locally inspired goods, comfy shirts and hoodies, caps, home décor, plus some
lesser-known NOLA-related books. We dig the "n.o." caps and the T-shirts
lettered with iconic corner grocery signage: "Fresh Meat Cold Beer *
Wine Liquor Po-Boys." 1101 First St. www.dno.la. ℃ **504/941-7010.** Daily 11am–
6pm. 600 Carondelet St. ℃ 504/324-7463. Mon–Sat 11am–8pm; Sun 11am–7pm.

Dirty Coast ★★   Utterly witty, eye-catching, and original T-shirt designs
(painted in the city), like the "Crawfish Pi," with the Greek symbol composed
of a tasty pile of mudbugs, and "504Ever." Way uptown or in the French
Quarter. 5631 Magazine St. www.dirtycoast.com. ℃ **504/324-3745.** Daily 10am–6pm.
713 Royal ℃ **504/324-6730.** Daily 11am–7pm.

Fleurty Girl ★★★   It's hard to leave here without one (or more) of its
pithy and near-perfect NOLA-centric T-shirts, even if some need a NOLA-to-
English translation. Dig the cocktail-related tees, like "Keep Calm and
Carry a Go-Cup" and the Mardi Gras–inspired "Everywhere Else it's
Just Tuesday." Also excellent jewelry, housewares, accessories, and $5
NOLA-themed tea towels—a fave gift. 632 St. Peter St. www.fleurtygirl.net.
℃ **504/304-5529.** Sun–Thurs 10am–6pm; Sat 10am–7pm. 3117 Magazine St.
℃ **504/301-2557.** Mon–Thurs 11am–6pm; Sat 10am–7pm; Sun 11am–5pm.

WALKING TOURS OF NEW ORLEANS

W e've said it before, and we'll keep saying it: This town was made for walking. Even at the height of the humid summer months, when everyone's main motivation is to laze in the shade and sip cool drinks, you can still flit between air-conditioned restaurant and air-conditioned museum.

With every step in undeniably unique New Orleans, there is something extraordinary to marvel at and commit to memory, in your mind's eye or on your phone: a gorgeous building more interesting than the last, a "colorful" character, a tuba-lugging musician in formal wear.

10

Stroll along the city streets, or the banks of Bayou St. John, turning when it strikes your fancy. You might have a street to yourself—or share it with a fleeting ghost? Imagine it 100 years ago, without the cars and overhead wires: It wouldn't have looked much different than it does now.

The French Quarter, Garden District, and Bayou St. John—each has its own distinct appearance, fascinating history, and a bit of mystery—and all are easily manageable on foot. So put on some good walking shoes, breathe in that Southern breeze, and mosey. Go slow. Take it (big) easy. Admire the lacy ironwork. Peek through French Quarter gateways, where simple facades hide exquisite courtyards with elaborate fountains and thick foliage. Gawk at the mighty oaks, some dripping with swaying Spanish moss.

These self-guided walking tours provide a solid introduction to what is simply one of the most beautiful cities anywhere, and answer some "That looks interesting—what the heck *is* it?" queries. For professional, guided tours, see p. 171.

START:	**The intersection of Royal and Bienville streets.**
FINISH:	**Jackson Square.**
TIME:	**Allow approximately 2 hours, not including time spent in shops or historic homes.**
BEST TIMES:	**Any day between 8am and 10am (the quiet hours).**
WORST TIME:	**At night. Some attractions won't be open, and you won't be able to get a good look at the architecture.**

If you only spend a few hours in New Orleans, do it in the exquisitely pictur-esque French Quarter. In these 80 city blocks, the colonial empires of Franc and Spain intersected with the emerging American nation. It's called the Vieux Carré or "old square," but somehow it's timeless—venerable yet vibrantly alive. Today's residents and merchants are stewards of a rich tradi-tion of individuality and creativity. This tour will introduce you to its style, history, and landmarks.

Start at the corner of Royal and Bienville streets, heading into the Quarter (away from Canal St.). That streetcar named Desire rattled along Royal Street until 1948 (then came the bus named Desire. Really). Imagine how noisy these narrow streets were when the streetcars ran here. Your first stop is:

1 337–343 Royal St., Rillieux-Waldhorn House
Now the home of Waldhorn and Adler Antiques (est. 1881), the place was built between 1795 and 1800 for Vincent Rillieux, the great-grandfather of the French Impressionist artist Edgar Degas. The wrought-iron balco-nies are an example of excellent Spanish colonial workmanship.

2 334 Royal St., Bank of Louisiana (Police Station)
Across the street, this old bank was erected in 1826, and its columned, Greek Revival edifice followed in the early 1860s. It suffered fires in 1840, 1861, and 1931, and has served as the Louisiana State Capitol, an auction exchange, a criminal court, a juvenile court, and an American Legion social hall. Now a pretty yellow, it houses the Vieux Carré police station.

Cross Conti Street to:

3 403 Royal St., Latrobe's
Benjamin H. B. Latrobe died of yellow fever shortly after completing designs for the Louisiana State Bank, which opened here in 1821. One of the nation's most eminent architects, he contributed to the design of the U.S. Capitol and the White House. Note the monogram "LSB" on the Creole-style railing. It's now an elegant banquet hall named for the archi-tect. Peek inside if you can.

4 417 Royal St., Brennan's Restaurant

The famed, bright-pink Brennan's opened in this building in 1955 and was crowned restaurant royalty almost immediately. Shuttered in 2013 following a sad financial, legal, and family squabble, it changed hands (but stayed in the family) and was gloriously restored and reopened in 2014. One of 200 buildings destroyed in the 1794 fire and rebuilt (also by Vincent Rillieux) in 1855, it has been home to the Banque de la Louisiane, the world-famous chess champion Paul Charles Morphy, and the parents of Edgar Degas. If it's open, take a gander at the elegant center staircase and pretty courtyard, with the turtle-stocked fountain.

5 437 Royal St., Peychaud's Drug Store

When Masons held lodge meetings here in the early 1800s, proprietor and druggist Antoine A. Peychaud served after-meeting drinks of bitters and cognac to lodge members in small egg cups, called *coquetier*—later Americanized to "cocktails." And so it began (the cocktail and the much-debated legend).

6 400 Royal St., Louisiana Supreme Court

Built in 1909, this was and still is a courthouse, covering the length of the block. The ostentatious baroque edifice laden with Georgia marble seems out of scale here. Sadly, many original Spanish-era structures were demolished to pave its way. Granted, those original buildings were indeed rundown; the new construction was positioned as slum-clearing. But all this was well before the Vieux Carré Commission formed in the early 1930s to protect the historic French Quarter buildings. Ironically, rulings in this very courthouse upheld the preservation regulations fueled by the Vieux Carré Commission.

7 519-521 Royal St., Antoine's Wine Cellar

See the little barred window between these buildings? Watch how many people walk right by this hidden marvel. Peer inside to spy the 165-foot-long, wow-factor wine cellar belonging to **Antoine's Restaurant** (p. 81), around the corner. The 25,000-bottle capacity leaves oenophiles envious.

Cross St. Louis Street to:

8 533 Royal St., The Merieult House

Built for the merchant Jean François Merieult in 1792, this house was the only building in the area left standing after the 1794 fire. Legend has it that Napoleon offered Madame Merieult great riches in exchange for her hair, to create a wig to present to a Turkish sultan (she refused). Nowadays, it's home to the excellent **Historic New Orleans Collection** (see p. 143).

Walking Tour 1: The French Quarter

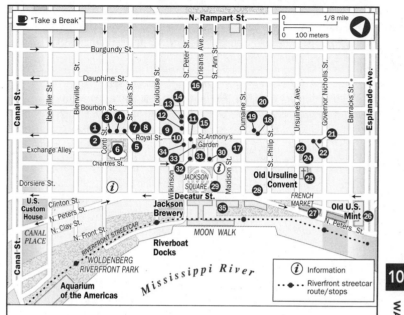

"Take a Break"

N. Rampart St.

0   1/8 mile
0   100 meters

Burgundy St.
Dauphine St.
Bourbon St.
Royal
Chartres St.
Dorsiere St.
Clinton St.
N. Peters St.
N. Clay St.
N. Front St.

Canal St.
Iberville St.
Bienville St.
St. Louis St.
Conti St.
Toulouse St.
St. Peter St.
St. Ann St.
Orleans Ave.
Dumaine St.
St. Philip St.
Ursulines Ave.
Governor Nicholls St.
Barracks St.
Esplanade Ave.
Madison St.
Wilkinson

Exchange Alley

St. Anthony's Garden

U.S. Custom House

CANAL PLACE

Jackson Brewery

JACKSON SQUARE

Decatur St.

Old Ursuline Convent

FRENCH MARKET

Old U.S. Mint

MOON WALK

Riverboat Docks

RIVERFRONT STREETCAR

WOLDENBERG RIVERFRONT PARK

Mississippi River

Aquarium of the Americas

(i) Information

- - ◆ - - Riverfront streetcar route/stops

10

WALKING TOURS

The French Quarter

1 Rillieux-Waldhorn House	18 Cornstalk Hotel
2 Bank of Louisiana (Police Station)	19 Andrew Jackson Hotel
3 Latrobe's	20 Lafitte's Blacksmith Shop
4 Brennan's Restaurant	21 The Lalaurie Home
5 Peychaud's Drug Store	22 Gallier House Museum
6 New Orleans Court Building	23 Croissant D'Or
7 Antoine's Wine Cellar	24 Beauregard-Keyes House
8 The Merieult House	25 Old Ursuline Convent
9 The Court of Two Sisters	26 The Old U.S. Mint
10 Le Monnier Mansion	27 The Historic French Market
11 The LaBranche House	28 Central Grocery
12 Lacoul House (Old Coffee Pot)	29 The Pontalba Buildings
13 Pat O'Brien's	30 The Presbytère
14 Preservation Hall	31 St. Louis Cathedral
15 Bourbon Orleans Hotel	32 The Cabildo
16 Le Pretre Mansion	33 Faulkner House Books
17 Madame John's Legacy	34 Tennessee Williams House
	35 Café du Monde

Cross Toulouse Street to:

9 613 Royal St., The Court of Two Sisters

This structure was built in 1832 for a local bank president on the site of the 18th-century home of a French governor. The two sisters were Emma and Bertha Camors, whose father owned the building; from 1886 to 1906, they ran a curio store here.

10 640 Royal St., Le Monnier Mansion

No one thought the 1811 building would survive a fourth-floor addition in 1876, creating the city's first "skyscraper." 'Sieur George, fictional hero of George W. Cable's scandalous *Old Creole Days,* "lived" here.

Cross St. Peter Street to:

11 700 Royal St., The LaBranche House

The lacy cast-iron grillwork, with its delicate oak leaf and acorn design, makes this one of the most photographed buildings in the Quarter. This is one of 11 three-story brick row houses built from 1835 to 1840 for the widow of wealthy sugar planter Jean Baptiste LaBranche.

Turn left at St. Peter Street and continue to:

12 714 St. Peter St., Lacoul House (Old Coffee Pot)

Built in 1829 by prominent physician Dr. Yves LeMonnier, this was a boardinghouse run by Antoine Alciatore in the 1860s. His cooking became so popular that he eventually gave up catering to open the famous Antoine's restaurant (p. 81), 2 blocks away and still operated by his descendants. The Old Coffee Pot restaurant has operated in this space since 1894; check out the gorgeous arched ceilings and the tasty calas cakes.

13 718 St. Peter St., Pat O'Brien's

Now the de facto home to the famed Hurricane cocktail (p. 203), this building was completed in 1790. Later, Louis Tabary put on popular plays here including, purportedly, the first grand opera in America. The popular courtyard is well worth a look, maybe even a refreshment.

14 726 St. Peter St., Preservation Hall

Scores of people descend here nightly for traditional New Orleans jazz (p. 193). A daytime stop affords a glimpse, through the ornate iron gate, of a lush tropical courtyard in back. Author Erle Stanley Gardner, of Perry Mason fame, lived upstairs.

Continue up St. Peter Street until you reach Bourbon Street, and turn right: Walk 1 block to Orleans Street and **stop at the corner**. The beige, three-story hotel with the wraparound balcony is the:

15 Bourbon Orleans Hotel

Site of the notorious quadroon balls, where wealthy white men were introduced to potential mistresses: free women (and girls) of color who were one-fourth black (quadroon) or one-eighth (octoroon). During these balls, the men and the young women's mothers would carefully negotiate *placage* arrangements, which often included financial, educational, housing, and child support for the mistresses. Imagine the discussions on those balconies....The building later became a convent for the Sisters of the Holy Family, the second-oldest order of black nuns in the country. Their founder (whose mother was a quadroon mistress!), Henriette De-Lille, has been presented to the Vatican for consideration for sainthood.

Continue along Bourbon Street. We're not stopping you along Bourbon Street, but look up and down the block and try to imagine what it was like in the 1950s and '60s during that particular heyday of jazz and burlesque. Ahead of you, clarinetist Pete Fountain held court over the wild, swinging scene at his club; a few blocks behind you Blaze Starr stripped her way into the limelight and the hearts of tens of thousands of men.

Stay on Orleans, heading lakeside (away from the Bourbon Orleans Hotel). Turn left onto Orleans and follow it a block to Dauphine (pronounced Daw-*feen*) Street. On the corner is:

16 716 Dauphine St., Le Pretre Mansion

In 1839, Jean Baptiste Le Pretre bought this 1836 Greek Revival house and added the romantic cast-iron galleries. The house is the subject of an oft-told horror story: In the 19th century, a conspicuously wealthy Turk, supposedly the exiled brother of a sultan, rented the house. He brought an entourage of servants and beautiful young girls—all thought to have been stolen from the sultan—and threw lavish parties. One night screams came from inside; the next morning, neighbors found the tenant and the young beauties lying dead in a pool of blood. The mystery remains unsolved. Local ghost experts say you can sometimes hear exotic music and piercing shrieks. This story is strangely similar to "The Brother of the Sultan," a 1922 fictional tale by Helen Pitkin Schertz. Draw your own conclusions.

Turn right on Dauphine Street and go 2 blocks to Dumaine Street. Hydrate at the **Good Friends Bar** (p. 209) along the way if necessary. Turn right on Dumaine and walk 2 blocks to:

17 632 Dumaine St., Madame John's Legacy

This structure was once thought to be the oldest building on the Mississippi River, originally erected in 1726, 8 years after the founding of New Orleans. Recent research suggests, however, that only a few parts of the original building survived the 1788 fire. Its first owner was a ship captain who died in the 1729 Natchez Massacre; upon his death, the house passed to the captain of a Lafitte-era smuggling ship—and 21 subsequent owners. The structure is a rare example of the original French "raised cottage." The above-ground basement is of brick-between-posts construction (locally made bricks were too soft to be the primary building material). The hipped, dormered roof extends out over the veranda. Its name comes from George W. Cable's fictional character who was bequeathed the house in the short story *'Tite Poulette.* Now part of the Louisiana State Museum complex, it's open to visitors Tuesday to Sunday 10am to 4:30pm; admission is free.

10

WALKING TOURS | The French Quarter

Turn around and double-back to Royal Street. Turn right.

18 915 Royal St., Cornstalk Hotel

Legend persists that the fence surrounding this sweet Victorian was ordered by the home's owner to ease his wife's homesickness for her native Iowa. Oddly, the same story is told about a house in the Garden District with a similar fence. It was forged in Philadelphia, and only one more exists (at the Banning Museum in California, but from New Orleans). In any case, it's awfully pretty, isn't it? Enough so that Bill and Hillary Clinton and Elvis himself have walked the supposedly haunted halls here.

19 919 Royal St., Andrew Jackson Hotel (Old Federal Courthouse)

Just after General Andrew Jackson slammed the British in the 1815 Battle of New Orleans, Louis Louaillier, a member of the legislature, criticized the popular general. Stonewall responded by tossing Louis into jail, ditto the judge who ordered Louis' release. When the wartime prisoners were released, the judge hauled Jackson back into this here courthouse, citing him for contempt of court and fining him $1,000. Twenty-nine years later, Congress ordered Jackson to be repaid with interest (his impeachment trial came 24 years after that). The courthouse survived until 1990, when this hotel was built.

Continue down Royal Street for half a block (good gallery browsing here). Turn left on St. Philip. Go 1 block to:

20 941 Bourbon St., Lafitte's Blacksmith Shop

This National Historic Landmark claims to be the oldest continually operating bar in the country (see p. 204), and the legend is that it was the headquarters of Jean Lafitte and his pirates, who posed as blacksmiths and used it to fence goods they'd plundered on the high seas. It still reflects the architectural influence of late-1700s French colonists. It may also be the oldest building in the Mississippi Valley, but that has not been documented. An unfortunate exterior renovation trying to replicate the original brick and plaster makes it look fake (it's actually not), but the candlelit interior is still an excellent place to imagine 19th-century Quarter life and swill some grog.

Turn right onto Bourbon Street and follow it 2 blocks to Governor Nicholls Street. Turn right and go 1 block to the corner of Royal Street:

21 1140 Royal St., The Lalaurie Home

Two-time widow Madame Delphine Macarty de Lopez Blanque wed Dr. Louis Lalaurie and moved into this residence in 1832, where the couple impressed the city with extravagant parties. When a fire broke out, neighbors crashed through a locked door to find seven starving slaves chained in painful positions. The sight, combined with Delphine's stories of past slaves having "committed suicide" and rumors of hideous live-subject medical experiments conducted within, enraged her neighbors. Madame Lalaurie and her family escaped a mob's wrath and fled to Paris. After her death, her body was secretly returned to New Orleans for burial. Tales of hauntings persist, especially that of a slave child who fell from the roof trying to escape Delphine's cruelties. The building was a Union headquarters during the Civil War, a gambling house, and home to actor Nicolas Cage. Haunted himself by financial difficulties, Cage returned the house to the bank in 2009. It's luxury condos now.

22 1132 Royal St., Gallier House Museum

James Gallier, Jr., built this house as his residence in 1857. He and his father were two of the city's leading architects (p. 142). Anne Rice based Lestat and Louis's home in *Interview with the Vampire* on this house.

Continue on Royal Street to Ursulines Street and turn left, toward the river.

23 617 Ursulines Ave., Croissant D'Or 🍵

For a little rest or sustenance, stop in the popular **Croissant D'Or,** 617 Ursulines St. (www.croissantdornola.com; ☏ **504/524-4663;** p. 131). The pastries here are very good, as is the ambience—inside or out.

At the corner of Ursulines, turn left onto Chartres Street. You'll be in front of:

24 1113 Chartres St., Beauregard-Keyes House

This raised cottage was built as a residence in 1826 by Joseph Le Carpentier, though it has other important claims to fame (detailed on p. 139). Notice the Doric columns and handsome twin staircases.

Across the street is the imposing:

25 1100 Chartres St., Old Ursuline Convent

Built in 1752, this is the oldest building in the Mississippi River Valley. It was home to the hearty French nuns of Ursula, who helped raise young girls into marriageable prospects for the lonely men settling this new territory (more on p. 141). Many locals claim to be direct descendants of those proper young girls—so many, in fact, that the math doesn't add up. But it beats the alternate ancestry of criminals and other heathens.

Continue along Chartres until you get to Esplanade Avenue and turn right. This is one of the city's most picturesque historic thoroughfares, with grand 1800s townhouses gracing the tree-lined avenue. At Decatur Street, you'll see:

26 400 Esplanade Ave., The New Orleans Jazz Museum at the Old U.S. Mint

This was the site of Fort St. Charles, built to protect New Orleans in 1792. Andrew Jackson reviewed the "troops" here—pirates, ragtag volunteers, and a nucleus of actual trained soldiers—whom he later led in the Battle of New Orleans. It's now a Louisiana State Museum housing coin and jazz collections (p. 151).

Follow Esplanade toward the river and turn right at the corner of North Peters Street. Follow North Peters until it intersects with Barracks Street. This is the back end of:

27 The Historic French Market

This European-style market (p. 138) has been here for well over 200 years, and today it has a farmer's market, food booths, arty-crafty goods, and flea-market stalls with souvenirs. Do stop to shop or nosh.

When you leave the French Market, exit on the side away from the river onto Decatur Street toward St. Ann Street. You'll see 923 and 919 Decatur St., where the Café de Refugies and Hôtel de la Marine stood. In the 1700s and early 1800s these were gathering places for pirates, smugglers, European refugees, and outlaws. Today, it's muffuletta time:

28 923 Decatur St., Central Grocery 🐷

If it's lunchtime, pop into **Central Grocery** (✆ **504/523-1620;** p. 96), and pick up a famed muffuletta sandwich. Eat inside at the little tables, or take it with you and dine alfresco in Jackson Square, near your next stop.

Decatur Street will take you to Jackson Square. Turn right onto St. Ann Street; the twin four-story, redbrick buildings here and on the St. Peter Street side of the square are:

29 The Pontalba Buildings

These highly coveted buildings sport some of the most impressive cast-iron balcony railings in the French Quarter. They also represent early French Quarter urban revitalization—and early girl power. In the mid-1800s, Baroness Micaela Almonester de Pontalba inherited rows of buildings along both sides of the Place d'Armes from her father, the wealthy Spanish nobleman-turned-magnate Don Almonester (who rebuilt St. Louis Cathedral, p. 139, among other developments). In an effort to counteract the emerging American sector across Canal Street, Baroness Pontalba had the structures razed, and under her supervision the Pontalba Buildings were begun in 1849 (you can see her mark today in the entwined initials "A.P." in the ironwork). These high-end apartments were built in the traditional Creole-European style, with commercial space at street level, housing above, and courtyards in the rear. The Baroness also had Jackson Square built, including the cast-iron fence and the equestrian statue of Andrew Jackson. Her scandalous personal story (see p. 143) is equally fascinating.

At the corner of St. Ann and Chartres streets, turn left and continue around Jackson Square; you will see:

30 751 Chartres St., The Presbytère

This, the Cabildo, and the St. Louis Cathedral—all designed by Gilberto Guillemard—were the first major public buildings in the Louisiana Territory. The Presbytère was originally designed as the cathedral's rectory. Baroness Pontalba's father financed the building's beginnings, but he died in 1798, leaving only the first floor done. It was finally completed in 1813. Never used as a rectory, it became a city courthouse and now houses the excellent **Louisiana State Museum** (p. 140).

The French Quarter

WALKING TOURS

Next you'll come to:

31 St. Louis Cathedral

Although it is the oldest Catholic cathedral in the U.S., this is actually the third building erected on this spot—the first was destroyed by a hurricane in 1722, the second by fire in 1788. The cathedral was rebuilt in 1794; the central tower was later designed by Henry S. Boneval Latrobe, again remodeled and enlarged between 1845 and 1851 under the direction of Baroness Pontalba. The bell and stately clock (note the nonstandard Roman numeral 4) were imported from France (p. 139).

The building on the cathedral's right is:

32 701 Chartres St., The Cabildo

In the 1750s, this was the site of a French police station and guardhouse. Part of that building was incorporated into the Spanish government state-house (known as the "Very Illustrious Cabildo"). It was still under recon-struction when the transfer papers for the Louisiana Purchase were signed in a room on the second floor in 1803. Since then, it has served as New Orleans' City Hall, the Louisiana State Supreme Court, and, since 1911, a Louisiana State Museum (p. 142).

Think those old Civil War cannons out front look pitifully obsolete? Think again. In 1921, in a near-deadly prank, one was loaded and fired. That missile traveled across the wide expanse of the Mississippi and 6 blocks inland, landing in a house in Algiers and narrowly missing its occupants.

Walk down the narrow alley between the Cabildo and the St. Louis Cathedral. You'll come to Pirate's Alley:

33 624 Pirate's Alley, Faulkner House Books

In 1925, William Faulkner lived here. He contributed to the *Times-Pica-yune* and worked on his first novels, *Mosquitoes* and *Soldiers' Pay* (soon to be a major motion picture), making this lovely store a requisite stop for literature lovers and book buyers of any persuasion (p. 218).

To the left of the bookstore is a small alley that takes you to St. Peter Street.

34 632 St. Peter St., Tennessee Williams House

Have a sudden urge to scream "Stella!!!" at that second-story wrought-iron balcony? No wonder. This is where Tennessee Williams wrote *A Streetcar Named Desire,* one of the greatest pieces of American theater. He remarked that he could hear "that rattle-trap streetcar named Desire running along Royal and the one named Cemeteries running along Canal and it seemed the perfect metaphor for the human condition."

Backtrack toward Jackson Square. Walk toward the river on St. Peter Street to Decatur Street. Make a left on Decatur, and pass the carriages and artists in front of Jackson Square. Cross Decatur at St. Ann to get to:

35 800 Decatur St., Café du Monde 🚋

You've finished! At **Café du Monde** (*©* **504/525-4544;** p. 130), get beig-nets and café au lait. Do climb the stairs up to the "Moonwalk" atop the levee. Relax on a bench and watch the river roll.

START:	**Prytania Street and Washington Avenue.**
FINISH:	**Lafayette Cemetery.**
TIME:	**45 minutes to 2 hours.**
BEST TIME:	**Daylight.**
WORST TIME:	**Night, when you won't be able to get a good look at the architecture.**

Walking around the architecturally astounding Garden District, you may get the impression that you've entered an entirely separate city—or time period—from the French Quarter. Although the Garden District was indeed once a separate city (Lafayette) from the Vieux Carré and established later, their development by two different groups is what most profoundly distinguishes the two.

The French Quarter was settled by Creoles during the French and Spanish colonial periods, and the Garden District was created by Americans after the 1803 Louisiana Purchase. The lucrative combination of Mississippi River commerce, abundant slave trade, and national banks fueled the local economy, resulting in the remarkable antebellum building boom still seen here.

Thousands of Americans moved here after the Louisiana Purchase. Friction arose between these new residents and the Creoles around language barriers, religious division, competition over burgeoning commerce, and mutual snobbery. With inferior business experience, education, and organizational skills, the Creoles worried that *les Americains* would drive them out of business. Americans were thus barred from the already overcrowded French Quarter. The snubbed Americans moved upriver and created a residential district of astounding, in-your-face opulence: the Garden District. It is, therefore, a culture clash reflected through architecture, with Americans creating an identity by introducing bold, new styles.

Note: With few exceptions, houses on this tour are occupied, private homes and are not open to the public. Several are owned by celebrities (names are omitted for privacy). Please be respectful of the residents.

To reach the Garden District, take the St. Charles streetcar to Washington Avenue (stop no. 16) and walk 1 block toward the river to:

1 2727 Prytania St., The Garden District Book Shop

A stellar collection of national and regional titles, with many signed editions, makes this bookshop (p. 218) an appropriate kickoff for a Garden District tour. The historic property was built in 1884 as the Crescent City Skating Rink, and subsequently acted as a livery stable, mortuary, grocery, and gas station. Today "the Rink" also offers a coffee shop, restrooms, and air-conditioning (appreciated if you're doing this tour in summer).

Walking Tour 2: The Garden District

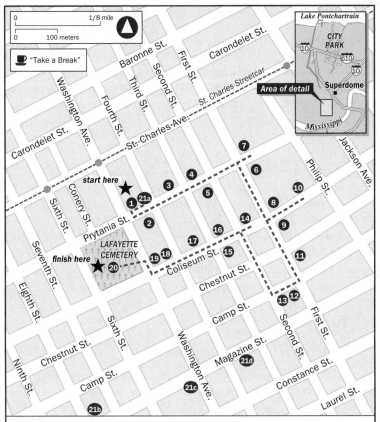

1 The Garden District Book Shop

2 Colonel Short's Villa

3 Briggs-Staub House

4 Our Mother of Perpetual Help

5 Women's Opera Guild Home

6 Toby's Corner

7 Bradish Johnson House
    & Louise S. McGehee School

8 Pritchard-Pigott House

9 Morris-Israel House

10 The Seven Sisters

11 Brevard-Mahat-Rice House

12 Payne-Strachan House

13 1137 Second St.

14 Joseph Merrick Jones House

15 Musson-Bell House

16 Robinson House

17 Koch-Mays House

18 Benjamin Button House

19 Commander's Palace

20 Lafayette Cemetery

21a Still Perkin' 🍵

21b Sucré 🍵

21c Coquette 🍵

21d Tracey's 🍵

Across Prytania Street, you'll find:

2 1448 Fourth St., Colonel Short's Villa

This house was built by architect Henry Howard for Kentucky Colonel Robert Short. The story goes that Short's wife missed the cornfields in her native Iowa, so he bought her the cornstalk fence (for a laugh, see Cornstalk Hotel, p. 232). But a revised explanation has the wife requesting it because it was the most expensive, showy fence in the building catalog. Second Civil War occupational governor Nathaniel Banks was quartered in this 9,800-square-foot beauty, which has been on the market for a while. At press time, it could be yours for $4.3 million.

Continuing down Prytania, you'll find:

3 2605 Prytania St., Briggs-Staub House

This is the Garden District's only example of Gothic Revival architecture (unpopular among Protestant Americans because it reminded them of their Roman Catholic Creole antagonists). Original owner Charles Briggs built the relatively large adjacent servant quarters for his Irish slaves. Irish immigrants were starting to create the nearby Irish Channel neighborhood across Magazine Street from the Garden District.

4 2523 Prytania St., Our Mother of Perpetual Help

The original owner, Henry Lonsdale, made his fortune selling burlap sacks, and was the first to add chicory to coffee. Once an active Catholic chapel, this site was one of several in the area owned by novelist Anne Rice and the setting for her novel *Violin*. The author's childhood home is down the street at 2301 St. Charles Ave.

5 2504 Prytania St., Women's Opera Guild Home

Some of the Garden District's most memorable homes incorporate more than one style. Designed by William Freret in 1858, this one combines his Greek Revival design with Queen Anne–style additions. It's now owned by the Women's Opera Guild. Tours ($15 per person) are offered Monday 10:30am to 4pm between Labor Day and Memorial Day (but not holiday Mon) (*©* **504/914-2591;** www.operaguildhome.org; or at 9:30am daily year-round through Gray Line New Orleans, p. 172).

6 2340 Prytania St., Toby's Corner

The Garden District's oldest known home was built in 1838 for Philadelphia wheelwright Thomas Toby in the then-popular Greek Revival style—by way of the West Indies. The "non-Creole" style still followed Creole building techniques, such as raising the house up on brick piers to combat flooding and encourage air circulation. The house changed hands in 1858 to a family whose descendants still live here, six generations and many renovations and expansions later.

7 2343 Prytania St., Bradish Johnson House & Louise S. McGehee School

Paris-trained architect James Freret (cousin of William; see stop #5 above) designed this French Second Empire–style mansion for sugar factor Bradish Johnson in 1872 at a cost of $100,000 ($2 million plus today). Contrast the house's awesome detail with the stark, classical simplicity of Toby's Corner across the street—illustrating the effect that one generation of outrageous fortune had on Garden District architecture. Since 1929 it has been the private Louise S. McGehee School for girls.

Turn down First Street (away from St. Charles), and it's a short block to:

8 1407 First St., Pritchard-Pigott House

This grand Greek Revival double-galleried townhouse shows how, as fortunes grew, so did Garden District home sizes.

Note the marble carriage block in front of the house across the street. Past residents used these like a step-stool when mounting their horses and carriages.

9 1331 First St., Morris-Israel House

As time passed, the trend toward the formal Greek Revival style took a playful turn. By the 1860s, Italianate was popular, as seen in this (reputedly haunted) double-galleried townhouse. Architect Samuel Jamison designed this house and the **Carroll-Crawford House** on the next corner (1315 First St.); note the identical ornate cast-iron galleries.

Follow Coliseum Street to the left, less than half a block to:

10 2329–2305 Coliseum St., The Seven Sisters

This row of "shotgun" houses gets its nickname from a (false) story that a 19th-century Garden District resident built these homes as wedding gifts for his seven daughters. Actually, there are eight "Seven Sisters," and they were built on speculation (the eighth looks somewhat different). "Shotgun"-style homes are so named because, theoretically, if one fired a gun through the front door, the bullet would pass unhindered through a series of rooms and out the back. (Also, a West African word for this native African house form sounds like "shotgun.") Common in hot climates, the shotgun style effectively circulates air. The relatively small homes are popular in New Orleans, but rare along the imposing Garden District streets.

Now turn around and go back to First Street and turn left. At the corner of First and Chestnut, you'll see:

11 1239 First St., Brevard-Mahat-Rice House

This 1857 Greek Revival townhouse was later augmented with an Italianate bay, in a fine example of "transitional" architecture. The fence's rosettes begat the house's name, "Rosegate," and its woven diamond pattern is said to be the precursor to the chain-link fence. This was novelist Anne Rice's home and a setting in her *Witching Hour* novels.

12 1134 First St., Payne-Strachan House

As the stone marker out front notes, Jefferson Davis, president of the Confederate States of America, died in this classic Greek Revival antebellum home, that of his friend Judge Charles Fenner. The sky-blue ceiling of the gallery is believed to keep winged insects from nesting there and to ward off evil spirits. Many local homes adhere to this tradition (now that you're aware of it, you'll notice it everywhere).

Turn right on Camp and go less than a block to:

13 1137 Second St., Stained Glass House

This house exemplifies the Victorian architecture popularized in uptown New Orleans toward the end of the 19th century. Many who built such homes were from the Northeast and left New Orleans in the summer; otherwise, it would be odd to see this claustrophobic, "cool climate"–style house. Note the exquisite stained glass and rounded railing on the gallery.

Turn right onto Second Street and go 2 blocks to the corner of Coliseum:

14 2425 Coliseum St., Joseph Merrick Jones House

When previous owner Trent Reznor of the band Nine Inch Nails moved in, new anti-noise ordinances were introduced at city council. His next-door neighbor was Councilwoman Peggy Wilson. Coincidence?

Turn left onto Coliseum Street and go 1 block to Third Street. Turn left to get to:

15 1331 Third St., Musson-Bell House

This is the 1853 home of Michel Musson, one of the few French Creoles then living in the Garden District and the uncle of artist Edgar Degas, who lived with Musson on Esplanade Avenue during a visit to New Orleans. On the Coliseum Street side of the house is the foundation of a cistern. Most of these once-common water tanks (Mark Twain commented that it looked as if everybody in the neighborhood had a private brewery) were destroyed at the turn of the 20th century when mosquitoes, which breed in standing water, were found to be carriers of yellow fever. Yellow-fever epidemics infamously killed 41,000 New Orleanians between 1817 and 1905.

Turn around and cross Coliseum to see:

16 1415 Third St., Robinson House

This striking Italianate villa was built between 1859 and 1865 by architect Henry Howard for tobacco grower Walter Robinson. Walk past the house to appreciate its scale—the outbuildings, visible from the front, are actually connected to the side of the main house. The entire roof is a large vat that once collected water. Add gravity and water pressure: thus begat the Garden District's earliest indoor plumbing. The lavish 11,000-square-foot interior features a dining table seating 26 guests and a grand, curving staircase with 28 stairs each covered in their own design. Hard to believe that, in sorrier, post-depression times, it was sold for just $500…especially considering that the seven-bedroom home was on the market recently for $12 million (it sold for $4 million).

Continue down Coliseum Street a half block to the corner of Washington Avenue:

17 2627 Coliseum St., Koch-Mays House

This picturesque chalet-style dollhouse (well, for a large family of dolls) was built in 1876 by noted architect William Freret for James Eustis, a U.S. senator and ambassador to France (perhaps justifying the full-size ballroom). It and four other spec homes he built on the block were referred to as Freret's Folly. No detail was left unfrilled, from the ironwork to the gables and finials.

18 2707 Coliseum St., Benjamin Button House

This 8,000-square-footer is best known as the title character's home in the film *The Curious Case of Benjamin Button*. Ergo Brad Pitt slept here, fictionally (he bought his own French Quarter home soon after filming). The house was owned by the same family from 1870 until its 2009 sale. Thus when the "Button" location scouts came calling, they dealt with the family's 90-year-old matriarch, who had raised seven kids under this roof. Or *roofs*, since it's actually two houses combined: The original 1832 cottage was raised atop the columned Colonial number built in 1908. Both were renovated in 1872.

19 1403 Washington Ave., Commander's Palace

Established in 1883 by Emile Commander, this turreted Victorian (a bordello in the 1920s) is now the pride of the Brennan family, the most respected restaurateurs in New Orleans. Commander's Palace has long reigned as one of the city's—nay, the country's—top restaurants (p. 118).

20 1400 Washington Ave., Lafayette Cemetery

Established in 1833, this "city of the dead" is one of New Orleans' oldest cemeteries. It has examples of all the classic above-ground, multiple-burial techniques. These tombs typically house numerous corpses from an extended family—one here lists 37 entrants; others are designated for members of specific fire departments or fraternal organizations. More cemetery info and tour options on p. 165.

Walk to St. Charles Avenue to pick up the streetcar (there is a stop right there) or flag down a cab to return to the French Quarter.

21 Wind Down at Still Perkin', Tracey's, Coquette, or Sucré 🍽

Now go back to your first stop, the Rink, where you can enjoy a cup of coffee and some light refreshments at Still Perkin'. Or head south on Washington to Magazine Street, where a po' boy at Tracey's, lunch at Coquette, or a sweet from Sucré (p. 132) will satisfy other appetites.

10

WALKING TOURS | The Garden District

241

START:	**Esplanade Avenue and Johnson Street.**
FINISH:	**City Park.**
TIME:	**Allow approximately 2 hours, not including museum, cemetery, and lunch stops.**
BEST TIMES:	**Monday through Saturday, early or late morning.**
WORST TIMES:	**Sunday, when attractions are closed, or after dark. If you decide to stay in City Park or in the upper Esplanade area until early evening, plan to return on the bus, streetcar, or by taxi.**

If you're heading to City Park, the New Orleans Museum of Art, or the Jazz & Heritage Festival, consider some sightseeing in this overlooked region. We particularly enjoy the quiet, meandering stretch along Bayou St. John. Historically, Esplanade Ridge was Creole society's answer to St. Charles Avenue—another lush boulevard of stately homes and seemingly ancient trees stretching overhead. The lots are not quite as expansive as along St. Charles, so the grand front lawns are not in evidence. Originally home to the descendants of the earliest settlers, the avenue had its finest days toward the end of the 19th century, and some of the neighborhoods along its path have seen better days. Still, it's closer to the soul of the city than St. Charles Avenue (read: regular people live here, whereas St. Charles always was and is for the well-heeled).

You can catch a bus on Esplanade Avenue at Rampart Street, headed toward the park and your starting point. Otherwise, stroll (about 15 min.) up Esplanade Avenue to:

1 2023 Esplanade Ave., Charpentier House

Originally a plantation home, this elegant Greek Revival house was built in 1861 for businessman and railroadman A. B. Charpentier. It's now Ashton's Bed & Breakfast (p. 66), which maintains a Charpentier room.

2 2033–2035 Esplanade Ave., Widow Castanedo's House

Juan Rodriguez purchased this land in the 1780s, and his granddaughter, Widow Castanedo, lived here until her death in 1861 (when it was a smaller, Spanish colonial–style plantation home). Before Esplanade Avenue extended this far from the river, the house was located in what is now the middle of the street. The widow tried and failed to block the extension of the street. The late-Italianate house was moved to its present site and enlarged sometime around the 1890s. It's been split down the middle and is inhabited today by two sisters.

3 2139 Esplanade Ave.

A great example of the typical Esplanade Ridge style. Note the Ionic columns on the upper level.

Walking Tour 3: The Esplanade Ridge

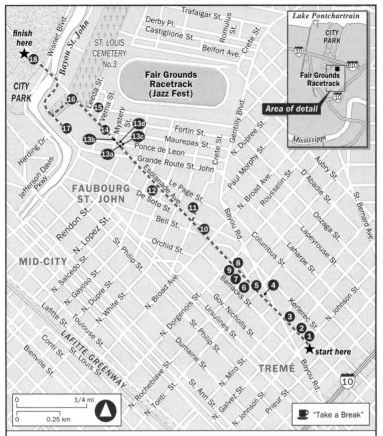

1 Charpentier House (Ashton's)
2 Widow Castanedo's House
3 2139 Esplanade Ave.
4 Goddess of History—
   Genius of Peace Statue
5 Degas House
6 2212, 2216 & 2222 Esplanade Ave.
7 Reuther House
8 2337 & 2341 Esplanade Ave.
9 2453 Esplanade Ave.
10 2623 Esplanade Ave.

11 2809–2911 Esplanade Ave
12 2936 Esplanade Ave.
13a Café Degas
13b Terranova's
13c Fair Grinds
13d 1000 Figs
14 3330 Esplanade Ave.
15 Luling Mansion
16 St. Louis Cemetery No. 3
17 Pitot House
18 City Park

After you cross North Miro Street, Esplanade Avenue crosses the diagonal Bayou Road, which was the route to the French-Canadian settlements at St. John's Bayou in the late 17th century. Veer left at the fork to stay on Esplanade Avenue and look for:

4 Goddess of History—Genius of Peace Statue

In 1886, this triangular plot was given to the city by Charles Gayarre. George H. Dunbar donated the terra-cotta statue, a victory monument. It was destroyed in 1938 and replaced with this cement-and-marble model.

5 2306 Esplanade Ave., Degas House

The Musson family rented this house for many years. Estelle Musson married René Degas, brother of Edgar Degas, the French Impressionist artist. (She and her descendants dropped his last name after he ran off with a neighbor's wife.) Degas is said to have painted the portrait of Estelle, now in the New Orleans Museum of Art, during his brief time living here. The house was built in 1854, and the Italianate decorations were added later when it was split into two buildings. It's now a B&B, event venue, and museum (tours are offered).

6 2212, 2216, 2222 Esplanade Ave.

Originally built as spec townhomes in 1883, these three Candy Crush–colored Italianate houses now comprise Le Belle Esplanade B&B inn. Although they look like triplets, each has its own architectural identity, and the intricate millwork and detailing surely stood on its own stead long before the eye-catching paint job was applied.

7 2326 Esplanade Ave., Reuther House

Check out the collection of metal and cinder-block sculptures in this front yard. The current resident is an artist, co-founder of the Contemporary Arts Center, and a major figure in the city's arts community.

In passing, take a look at nos. 2325, 2327, 2329, and 2331—all interesting examples of Creole cottages. Then, continue to:

8 2337 & 2341 Esplanade Ave.

These houses were identical structures when they were built in 1862 for John Budd Slawson, owner of a horse-drawn-streetcar company that operated along Bayou Road. Back then, both were single-story shotgun-style houses. Notice the unusual ironwork beneath the front roof overhang.

Cross North Rocheblave Street to:

9 2453 Esplanade Ave.

This house was one of a matching pair at the corner of Dorgenois Street; the other was demolished. Though its architecture has been greatly altered, it's one of the few remaining mansard-roofed homes on Esplanade Ridge.

Cross North Broad Street to:

10 2623 Esplanade Ave.

The Corinthian columns denote the classical revival style of this home, built in 1896 by Louis A. Jung. The Jungs donated the triangular piece of land at Esplanade Avenue, Crete Street, and DeSoto Street to the city on the condition that it remain public property. The pretty pocket park features a fountain (well, planter) and is graced by an unusual Art Nouveau fence.

11 2809-2911 Esplanade Ave.

This decorative, Queen Anne–style center-hall Victorian is just one of many pretty houses on Esplanade Ridge.

12 2936 Esplanade Ave.

This Gothic villa–style house is now an ISKCON (Hare Krishna) center (free vegetarian dinners on Sunday eves!).

13 Take a Break at Café Degas, Terranova's, 1000 Figs, or Fair Grinds ♨

The shops and restaurants at the intersection of Mystery Street and Esplanade Avenue offer fine lunchtime options. If the weather is nice, the semi-outdoor setting is exceedingly pleasant at **Café Degas** (p. 104). For snacks or picnic food for City Park, try the family-run **Terranova's Italian Grocery,** 3308 Esplanade Ave. (© **504/482-4131**), across the street. **1000 Figs** offers very good Mediterranean fare (© **504/301-0848**), or opt for the quirky **Fair Grinds** coffeehouse (© **504/913-9072**), both behind Café Degas at 3141 and 3133 Ponce De Leon St. respectively.

Continue to:

14 3330 Esplanade Ave.

A galleried frame home built in the Creole-cottage style. Also note the orientation of this stretch (and many of the houses along Esplanade Avenue). The lots are on a diagonal, so houses face Esplanade at a slight angle—a remnant from either the original plantation plots, or from fortifications built at strategic angles to protect the city from attack.

Continue along Esplanade until Leda Street; turn right for a ½-block detour off Esplanade to:

15 1436 Leda Ct., Luling Mansion

Florence Luling, a German sugar and cotton baron, purchased 80 acres and commissioned famed architect James Gallier, Jr., to build this elaborate, three-story Italianate mansion in 1865. Built with a full moat, the mansion had ornate formal gardens that once stretched all the way to Esplanade Avenue. Later it served as the Louisiana Jockey Club (it backs up to the Fair Grounds Race Track). Unfortunate modern adjustments have taken a toll, but its original magnificence is still apparent. It's a popular film site.

Return to Esplanade Avenue and turn right. On your right is:

16 3421 Esplanade Ave., St. Louis Cemetery No. 3

The public Bayou Cemetery, established in 1835, was purchased and expanded by the St. Louis diocese in 1856. It contains the burial monuments of many of the diocese's priests and religious orders. It might also be called "Restaurateurs' Rest": the tombs for the Galatoire, Tujague, and Prudhomme families are here. If you've been squeamish about going into the cemeteries because of safety concerns, you can comfortably explore this one on your own—though as always, stay alert.

From the cemetery, head back out to Esplanade Avenue and continue walking toward City Park. When you get to the bridge, go straight to continue to City Park, or left for a ¼-mile detour, following the signs, along Bayou St. John to:

17 1440 Moss St., Pitot House

This Creole country house overlooking the historic Bayou was home to the city's first mayor. It's open to the public (p. 158), with docents offering a window onto life when Bayou St. John was the city's main trade route.

Double back to Esplanade Avenue, turn left, cross the bridge, and walk straight into:

18 Esplanade & City Park Aves., City Park

In the middle of the traffic circle at Esplanade and Wisner, just outside City Park, a stately equestrian statue of P.G.T. Beauregard stood from 1915 until 2017, when the monument to the Confederate Army General was removed. Now, an empty platform awaiting its fate greets entrants to glorious, expansive City Park (p. 160)—the sculpture garden, museum, lakes, and more. Not to mention fresh beignets at **Morning Call** (p. 132).

SIDE TRIPS: PLANTATION HOMES & CAJUN COUNTRY

I f you have time (say, 3 days), you should strongly consider a sojourn into the countryside outlying New Orleans. It makes for an interesting cultural and visual contrast to the big city. This chapter starts off by following River Road along the banks of the Mississippi, and the plantation homes that line it, heading upriver from New Orleans. The second part takes you 150 miles west of New Orleans to the heart of the prairie Cajun Country.

The River Road trip can be done as a day trip, or you could keep rambling north to visit the plantation homes in the St. Francisville area and stay overnight. The Cajun Country trip requires a 1- or 2-night stay, more if you can. A GPS will be your friend for either jaunt.

PLANTATIONS ALONG THE GREAT RIVER ROAD

If your image of plantation homes comes strictly from Tara in *Gone with the Wind,* you can see something reasonably close to that Hollywood creation by touring these parts. You'll also see humbler but realistic plantation homes, and get an idea of plantation life and its legacy—for better and worse.

THE EARLY PLANTERS Creole plantation houses are low-slung, simple affairs; the showier American style is closer to Hollywood's antebellum grandeur (they got grander after 1850, which most of these predate). They're smaller than you might expect, even cramped compared with the lavish mansions of the Gatsby-era oil barons and today's nouveau riche. If your fantasies would be dashed without pillars and porticos, stick to Destrehan, San Francisco, Oak Alley, and Madewood.

The early planters of Louisiana were rugged frontier people. As they spread out along the Mississippi from New Orleans, they cleared vast swamplands to create unhindered waterways for transporting indigo and other crops. Rough flatboats moving produce to market could be capsized by rapids, sandbars, and floating debris, or captured by river pirates. If they made it to New Orleans, these farming men (and a few extraordinary women) collected their pay and went on wild drinking, gambling, and brawling sprees—earning them a reputation as barbarians among the French Quarter Creoles.

By the 1800s, Louisiana planters (and their slaves) had introduced large-scale farming and brought more acreage under cultivation. King cotton, rice, and sugarcane were popularized around this time, bringing huge monetary returns. But natural dangers, a hurricane, or a swift change in the course of the capricious Mississippi could wipe out entire plantations and fortunes.

THE RIVERBOATS   After 1812, the planters turned to speedier, and ostensibly safer, new steamboats to transport their crops. When the first steamboat (the *New Orleans,* built in Pittsburgh) chugged downriver belching sooty smoke, it was so dirty and potentially explosive that it was dubbed a "floating volcano."

As vast improvements were made, the steamboats became more than a means to move goods to market. Families and slaves could now travel in lavish staterooms amid ornate "grand salons" in these floating pleasure palaces. Some set up dual residences, spending the social season and winters in swank New Orleans townhouses. They fashioned more elegant lifestyles back in their upriver homes as well, where they shipped fine furnishings and luxury goods.

On the darker side, the boats were the realm of riverboat gamblers and confidence, or "con," men. Huge fortunes and no doubt a few deeds to plantations were lost to (and perhaps won back from) these silver-tongued professional gamers and crooks.

BUILDING THE PLANTATION HOUSES   During this prosperous period from the 1820s until the beginning of the Civil War, most of the impressive plantation homes were built, as were grand New Orleans townhouses.

Generally located near the riverfront, the plantation home was the focal point of a self-sustaining community. Most were modest, but some had wide, oak-lined avenues leading from its entrance to a wharf. On either side of the avenue would frequently be *garçonnières* (small guesthouses, sometimes used by adolescent sons and their friends). The kitchen was separated from the house because of fire danger. Close by was the overseer's office. Some plantations had pigeon houses or dovecotes—and all had the inevitable slave quarters lining the lane to the crops or across the fields and out of sight. The first houses were simple "raised cottages," with long, sloping roofs, cement-covered brick walls on the ground floor, and wood-and-brick (brick between posts) construction in the living quarters on the second floor. Influenced by West Indian styles, these colonial structures suited the sultry Louisiana climate and swampy building sites, and made use of native materials.

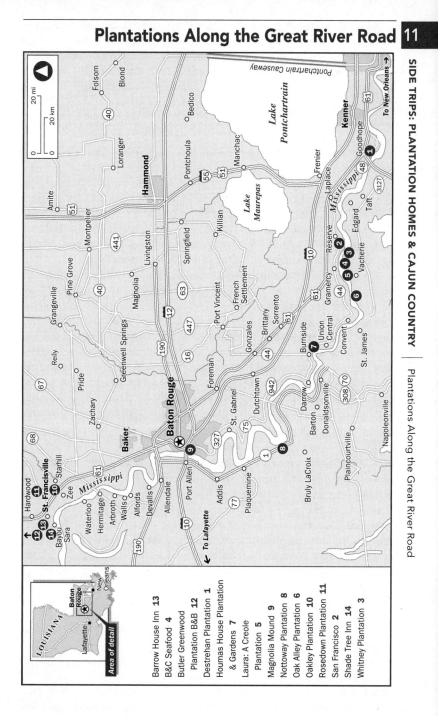

Barrow House Inn **13**
B&C Seafood **4**
Butler Greenwood
 Plantation B&B **12**
Destrehan Plantation **1**
Houmas House Plantation
 & Gardens **7**
Laura: A Creole
 Plantation **5**
Magnolia Mound **9**
Nottoway Plantation **8**
Oak Alley Plantation **6**
Oakley Plantation **10**
Rosedown Plantation **11**
San Francisco **2**
Shade Tree Inn **14**
Whitney Plantation **3**

In the 1820s, they began to add Greek Revival and Georgian influences—creating a style dubbed Louisiana Classic. Large, rounded columns and wide galleries surrounded the main body of the house, and the roof was dormered. Inside, rooms flanked an expansive central hall. They had few imported details like fireplace mantels, and were constructed of native materials, like cypress and bricks of cement-sealed river clay.

GRAND & GRANDER   By the 1850s, homes grew in tandem with prosperity and became more grandiose. Many embraced the styles of extravagant Victorian architecture, northern Italian villas, or Gothic lines (notably the fantastic San Francisco plantation, sometimes called "steamboat Gothic"; p. 252). Planters and their families brought back ornate furnishings and skilled artisans from their European travels. Glittering crystal chandeliers and *faux marbre* (false marble) mantels appeared.

Social lives, families, and egos also grew. The **Madewood house** on Bayou Lafourche was built explicitly to outshine Woodlawn, the beautiful home of the builder's brother (not open to the public, unfortunately).

But the enormous wealth stemmed from an economy based on human servitude. The injustice and cruelty of slavery became the seeds of its own demise. After the Civil War, large-scale farming became impossible without that labor base. During Reconstruction, lands were confiscated and turned over to people who proved unable to run them; many were subdivided. Increasing international competition began to erode the cotton and sugar markets. The culture represented by the plantation houses you'll see emerged and died in a span of less than 100 years.

THE PLANTATION HOUSES TODAY   Where scores of grand homes once dotted the riverfront, few remain. Several that survived the Civil War fell victim to fires, floods, or industrial development. Others, too costly to be maintained, were left to the ravages of dampness and decay. But a few have been saved, preserved, and upgraded with electricity and plumbing. Most are private residences, but some are open to visitors, the admission fees supplementing upkeep.

Tours of plantations are hit-or-miss—much depends on your guide. We've listed our favorite choices here. After you visit several, you'll begin to hear many of the same facts about plantation life, sometimes as infill for missing or boring history. It can also be easy to romanticize the era, while giving short shrift to the fact that these plantations would not exist were it not for unthinkably savage, yet unimaginably real, human cruelty.

Planning Your Trip

All the plantation homes shown on the map on p. 249 are within easy driving distance of New Orleans. How many you can tour in a day will depend on your endurance (in the car and on your feet) and time allotment. If returning late, the small highways can be a little intimidating after dark. Don't expect broad river views along the Great River Road (the roadway's name on *both* sides of the Mississippi); it's obscured by tall levees. You'll see sugarcane fields and plenty of evidence of Louisiana's petrochemical industry. But spontaneous detours through little, centuries-old towns might result in finding a choice resale shop or good road food.

If you have minimal time, **Laura,** the **Whitney,** and **Oak Alley** are 15 minutes apart, and each offers a different perspective on plantation life and the tourism industry. Try to visit two. Laura is classic understated Creole and has a low-key but superb presentation. Tara-esque Oak Alley represents the showy Americans and is slicker and glitzier (one could even do an Oak Alley drive-by). The Whitney's tour is told from the perspective of the enslaved. All are approximately an hour from New Orleans. Alternately, a day is well spent on the magnificent grounds of the **Houmas House.**

If you're in town on **Christmas Eve,** consider driving along the River Road to see the huge bonfires residents build on the levees to light the way for the Christ child and Papa Noël (who rides in a sleigh drawn by—what else?—eight alligators!).

Organized Tours

Seeing plantation houses via a bus tour is a comfortable, planning-free option, and you get some bonus narration along the route. Almost every New Orleans tour company operates a tour to one or two plantations; most offer pickup at hotels or a central French Quarter locale. Costs include transportation and admission, and the offerings are always subject to change.

The reliable 5- to 7-hour tours (including travel time) given by mainstay **Gray Line** (www.graylineneworleans.com; © **800/233-2628** or 504/569-1401) offer a choice of two of three plantations: Laura, Oak Alley, or Whitney Plantation. Daily tours depart Gray Line's Toulouse Street station (near Jax Brewery in the French Quarter). Times vary, so call ahead (adults $88, children 6–12 $60). They also offer a combo Destrehan Plantation (see next page) and swamp tour ($89 and $48).

Legendary Tours (www.legendarytoursnola.com; © **504/471-1499**) visits the Whitney and Oak Alley for $85 (Whitney only $65). For smaller groups, we like **Tours by Isabelle** (www.toursbyisabelle.com; © **877/665-8687** or 504/398-0365). Isabelle Cossart takes groups of 6 to 13 people in a comfortable van on a half-day expedition to Oak Alley and Laura (Whitney and others by arrangement) or Houmas House and St. Joseph plantation ($115).

Plantations Between New Orleans & Baton Rouge

The plantations below are listed in the order in which they appear on the map, running north along the Mississippi from New Orleans. Tours of these homes range from 1½ to 2½ hours; most people do one or two in a day (and may drive past others). Depending on your choices, you may have to cross the Mississippi River by bridge a few times. The winding river makes distances deceiving; give yourself more time than you think you'll need. The plantations discussed here are roughly 1 hour from New Orleans (the most accessible for visitors to the city) and about 15 minutes apart.

Destrehan Plantation ★★ Its proximity (just 30 min. from New Orleans), in-character docents (better than it sounds), and role in *Interview with the Vampire* have made Destrehan Manor a popular plantation jaunt. It's the oldest intact plantation home in the lower Mississippi Valley open to the public. Built in 1787 by a free person of color for a wealthy Frenchman, it was modified from its "dated" French colonial style to Greek Revival in the 1830s. Its warmly colored, graceful lines are aesthetically pleasing, and some original furnishings remain. One room has been left un-renovated, to show the humble rawness beneath the usual public grandeur. Unlike most plantation homes, Destrehan has ramps and an elevator.

13034 River Rd., La. 48, Destrehan. www.destrehanplantation.org. ⓒ **877/453-2095** or 985/764-9315. Admission $20 adults; $16 military; $15 seniors; $7 children 7–17; free for children 6 and under. Daily 9am–4pm. Closed Jan 1, Mardi Gras, Easter, Thanksgiving, and Dec 24–25.

San Francisco ★★ This brightly colored "steamboat Gothic" mansion was completed in 1856 by Edmond B. Marmillion, who died before he could occupy the home. He willed it to his two sons, one of whom married in 1855 while on a grand tour of Europe. The new wife undertook elaborate redecorations, leaving the son *sans fruscin*, or "without a cent." Thus its first name, St. Frusquin . . . later changed to San Francisco.

The fanciful three-story house, which underwent a $1.3-million freshening in 2014, has wide galleries resembling a ship's double decks, and twin stairs leading to a broad main portal. Inside are beautiful carved woodwork, cypress ceilings, and walls gloriously painted with flowers, birds, nymphs, and cherubs.

2646 Hwy. 44, Garyville. www.sanfranciscoplantation.org. ⓒ **888/509-1756** or 985/535-2341. Admission $20 adults; $16 military with ID; $19 AAA members; $10 students 6–17; free for children 5 and under. Daily 9:30am–4pm. Closed Jan 1, Mardi Gras, Easter, Thanksgiving Day, and Dec 24–25.

Whitney Plantation ★★★ Slavery, the plantation-tour elephant in the room, may get meager mention or a thorough telling. Here at the first museum of its kind in the U.S., history comes from the perspective of the enslaved. Visitors receive a name tag with a slave's biography, immediately personalizing the experience, and begin the 90-minute, guided walking tour with a short film shown in a church. They share the pews with life-size sculptures of slave children, which are beautiful, spiritual, and heartrending. The tour moves to expansive gardens of somber monuments etched with personal testimonials and 107,000 names; a separate "Field of Angels" remembers child slaves (40 perished on this very land). These contemplative spaces lay the emotional foundation as the tour moves to sparse cabin homes; the historic kitchen; endless fields; murky creeks that gave cover during escape attempts; the blacksmith cabin where men toiled over the instruments of their own confinement.

Among the most affecting is the three-cell jail, a crude, iron cage positioned with cruel irony such that, now twice confined, the prisoner's barred view is

River Road Pit Stop

Restaurants are in short supply along the River Road. Houmas House and a cafe at Oak Alley are the best of the mostly so-so eateries at the plantations. Instead, stop at down-home **B&C Seafood,** just east of Laura Plantation. Join the locals digging into steaming trays of boiled seafood and Cajun standards (2155 Hwy. 18, Vacherie; ℘ **225/265-8356;** all items $7–$25; Mon–Sat 11am–4:30pm).

of the gleaming "big house" (where appropriately scant tour time is spent). Elsewhere, 60 ceramic heads on spikes pay noble, resonant tribute to slaves decapitated during an 1811 uprising. Not everything is original (much was razed), but it's all harshly authentic, haunting, and vital.

5099 Hwy. 18, Wallace. www.whitneyplantation.com. ℘ **225/265-3300.** Admission $22 adults; $17 seniors, students, active military; $10 kids 6–12; free for children 12 and under. Wed–Mon 9:30am–4:30pm. Tours hourly. Closed Jan 1, Mardi Gras Day, July 4, Thanksgiving Day, Dec 25. Bulk of tour is outdoors, rain or shine; paths are wheelchair-accessible, but parts are a bit rough. Second floor of house not wheelchair-accessible. Tours sell out and there is no self-guided option. Book in advance.

Laura: A Creole Plantation ★★★ If you see only one plantation, make it Laura, simple on the outside but utterly absorbing within. It has no hoop-skirted guides, offering instead a thorough view of daily life on an 18th- and 19th-century sugar plantation, a cultural history of Louisiana's Creole population, and a mesmerizing, in-depth examination of one Creole family. Much is known about this house and its residents thanks to extensive records (more than 5,000 documents researched in France), including the detailed memoirs of its namesake, proto-feminist head-of-household Laura Locoul. Many of the original artifacts on display—from cookware to jewelry—were saved by employees in a devastating 2004 fire, after which the main house and a slave cabin were accurately restored to the 1805 period. Tours are offered in French daily. *Fun fact #1:* The beloved Br'er Rabbit stories were first collected here by a folklorist in the 1870s. *Fun fact #2:* Fats Domino's parents lived on this plantation.

2247 Hwy. 18, Vacherie. www.lauraplantation.com. ℘ **888/799-7690** or 225/265-7690. Admission $25 adults; $23 military and AAA members; $15 teens 13–17; $10 children 6–12; free for children 5 and under. Tours run every 40 min. Daily 10am–4pm; last tour begins at 4pm. Tours in French available Tues and Sat; special-interest tours on Creole architecture, folklore, gardens, or Creole women available with advance notice. Closed Jan 1, Mardi Gras, Easter, Thanksgiving, and Dec 25.

Oak Alley Plantation ★★★ This is precisely what comes to mind when most people think "plantation." A splendid white house, its porch lined with giant columns, approached by a magnificent quarter-mile drive lined with stately oak trees (the 1839 house has 28 fluted Doric columns to match the 28 trees)—yep, it's all here. Consequently, this Hollywood honey is the most famous plantation house in Louisiana. It's also the slickest operation, with hoop-skirted guides and golf carts traversing the blacktopped property.

St. Francisville doesn't look like much on approach, but by the time you get to the town center, you are utterly charmed. This is not Cajun Country—this area has American plantations only and no French history, but if you're interested in plantations from an architectural, historical, or cultural perspective, you can do well by planting yourself here for an overnighter. It's 30 miles northwest of Baton Rouge and 2 hours by car from New Orleans. Contact the **St. Francisville tourism office** (www. stfrancisville.us; ⓒ **800/789-4221** or 225/635-4224; Mon–Sun 9am–5pm).

Recommended places to stay include the **Barrow House Inn**, at 9779 Royal St. (www.topteninn.com; ⓒ **225/635-4791;** $135–$160), with beautifully restored antiques-laden rooms; **Butler Greenwood Plantation B&B**, at 8345 U.S. 61 (www.butlergreenwood.com;

ⓒ **225/635-6312;** doubles $150-$250), with modest but sweet guest cottages, some with Jacuzzis or fireplaces, on oak-laden plantation grounds; and **Shade Tree,** 9704 Royal St. (www.shadetreeinn. com; ⓒ **225/635-6116;** $165–$215), a peaceful, romantic aerie with a slight hippie bent.

Area attractions include:

o **Magnolia Mound ★** This late-1700s, single-story plantation home was built as a small settler's house and vastly enlarged later. Costumed guides take you through the slave cabins and authentically furnished house, one of the oldest wooden structures in the state (2161 Nicholson Dr., Baton Rouge; www. friendsofmagnoliamound.org; ⓒ **225/343-4955;** $10 adults, $8

Oak Alley lay disintegrating until 1914; new owners and restorers were responsible for its National Historic Landmark designation. The tour provides fewer details about the families who lived here than about general plantation life. In 2013 a row of re-created slave quarters was added; they need a few years (or centuries) to feel authentic, but the well-researched displays do a good job of illuminating slave life and the means by which this plantation survived. Our favorite feature (besides the truly impressive row of mighty oaks) may just be the scholarly "Confederate soldier" in the rustic tent out back, who converses with visitors in full character as he polishes his boots or goes about other business of being a soldier (he's not always here; call ahead to check). A sit-down restaurant and casual cafe are on-site, and you can also stay in one of five pretty, century-old Creole cottages, now bed-and-breakfast rooms.

3645 La. 18, Vacherie. www.oakalleyplantation.com. ⓒ **800/442-5539** or 225/265-2151. Admission $22 adults; $8 students 13–18; $5 children 6–12; free for children 5 and under. Discounts for 65 and over, AAA members, and active military. Grounds open daily at 9am; tours begin every half-hour at 9:30am; Mon–Fri last tour at 4pm; Sat–Sun tours till 5pm. Restaurant hours 8:30am–3pm; casual cafe 9am–5pm. Closed Jan 1, Thanksgiving, and Dec 25.

Houmas House Plantation & Gardens ★★★ Houmas is actually two houses joined together under one roof: the original, 1775 four-room structure and the larger, Greek Revival–style house, completed in 1828 after 17 seniors, military, AAA, and students 18–22, $4 children 3–17, free ages 2 and under; Mon–Sat 10am–4pm, Sun 1–4pm; tours begin on the hour with last tour at 3pm).

o **Oakley Plantation at Audubon State Historic Site** ★ John James Audubon received room and board in exchange for giving art lessons to the young resident of this 1801 plantation home. After class, he painted 32 of his "Birds of America" series (those lessons helped finance the books' publication). A tour of the just-restored, 17-room colonial is worthwhile, and leave time to walk among the gardens and nature trails, part of a 100-acre wildlife sanctuary. (11788 Hwy

965, St. Francisville; www.crt. state.la.us/louisiana-state-parks/ historic-sites; *C* **225/635-3739;** $10 adults, $8 seniors; $5 students 6–17, free 3 and under; Wed–Sun 9am–5pm.

o **Rosedown Plantation** ★★ Rosedown is by far the most impressive and historic of the more far-flung plantations, starting with its wide avenue of ancient oaks and dramatic gardens (12501 Hwy. 10, at La. 10 and U.S. 61, St. Francisville; www.lastateparks.com; *C* **888/376-1867** or 225/635-3332; house tour and historic gardens $12 adults, $10 seniors, $6 students 6–17, free children 5 and under; daily 9am–5pm; tours begin at 10am).

years of construction. The former sugar plantation has been restored several times since then, including by the current owner, who invested millions in turning it into a fabulous showcase inside and out, a popular event venue, and his home. It's filled with stunning art and antiques and surrounded by elegant formal gardens. He also installed a lovely cafe, a pleasant bar, and a fine-dining restaurant amid these splendid environs, so one can make a day of it (or 2 days, if you stay in the fetching cottages, outfitted with antiques and modern amenities.). Note that the **upscale restaurant** is "event" dining, requiring reservations and proper dress (and a thick wallet).

40136 La. 942, Darrow. www.houmashouse.com. *C* **888/323-8314** or 225/473-9830. Admission (including guided tour) $24 adults; $15 children 13–18; $10 children 6–12; free for children 5 and under. Gardens and grounds only $10. Daily 9am–7pm. Closed Dec 25 and Jan 1.

Nottoway Plantation ★★ Nottoway is everything you want in a dazzling Old South mansion. Dating from 1858, it's the largest existing plantation house in the South, a mammoth structure with 64 rooms (covering 53,000 sq. ft.) and pillars to rival the White House's. Saved from Civil War destruction by a Northern gunboat officer who had once been a guest here, Nottaway has still-handsome interiors featuring marvelous curlicue plasterwork, hand-carved Corinthian columns of cypress wood in the ballroom, beautiful archways, and original crystal chandeliers. You can also stay here, in rooms with period furnishings and luxurious bathrooms ($174–$320 per night including breakfast and tour; check website for online deals).

31025 La. 1, White Castle. www.nottoway.com. © **866/527-6884** or 225/545-2730. Admission $20 adults; $6 children 6–12; free for children 5 and under. Daily 9am–4pm; tours begin on the hour. Closed Dec 25.

CAJUN COUNTRY

This area, also called Acadiana (though you won't find that on the maps) has a history and culture unique in America. It consists of a rough triangle of Louisiana made up of 22 parishes (counties), from St. Landry at the top of the triangle to the Gulf of Mexico at its base. Lafayette is the unofficial capital of Acadiana.

Meet the Cajuns

The Cajun's history is a sad one, but it produced a people and a culture well worth knowing. In the early 1600s, colonists from France began settling the southeastern coast of Canada in a region of Nova Scotia they named Acadia. They developed a peaceful agricultural society based on the values of a strong Catholic faith, deep love of family, and respect for their relatively small landholdings.

This pastoral existence was isolated from Europe for nearly 150 years, until Acadia became the property of the British. The king's representatives tried to force the Acadians to pledge allegiance to the British Crown, renounce Catholicism, and embrace the king's Protestantism, but for decades they steadfastly refused. Finally, the British governor of the region sent in troops. Villages were burned and families separated as ships were loaded to deport them. A 10-year diaspora began, scattering them to France, England, America's East Coast, and the West Indies. Hundreds of lives were lost to the terrible conditions onboard.

In 1765, Bernard Andry brought 231 men, women, and children to reestablish a permanent home in Louisiana, a natural destination thanks to its strong French background. These industrious settlers worked the swampy, wildlife-infested lands, building levees, draining fields, and planting many of the farms you still see here.

Cajun Language

Much of this essay was provided by author, historian, and two-time Grammy nominee Ann Allen Savoy, who, along with her husband, Marc (an acclaimed accordion maker) are members of the Savoy-Doucet Cajun Band and several other groups. The Savoys are celebrated keepers of the culture, not least for having spawned a musical dynasty. All four of their talented children are carrying the cultural torch through their own music and art.

The French influence in Louisiana is one of the things that sets the state apart from the rest of the United States. Although French is spoken by many of the

Our standard soundtrack for the drive from New Orleans to Cajun Country begins with the excellent **WWOZ 90.7 FM** (to which we're assiduously tuned while in the city). After an hour on the road, static takes over, signaling the unwrapping of whatever new music we've recently purchased from **Louisiana Music Factory** (p. 224). In about half a CD's time, we can usually pull in **KBON 101.1 FM** for some rollickin' Cajun and zydeco tunes. At that point we know we've arrived, as much in geography as mood.

older Cajuns (ages 60 and up), most middle-aged Louisianans don't speak the language. This is partially because knowledge of the French language, from the 1930s on, became associated with a lack of business success or education. Cajun music was considered hokey, and Cajun culture on the whole was denigrated and stigmatized.

Today, Cajun culture has experienced a resurgence of popularity and respect. The young people are emphatically adopting their ancestors' language, music, recipes, and other traditions, and proudly speak with the sharp, bright Cajun accent.

Cajun French is peppered with beautiful old words dating from Louis XIV, unused in France and historically intriguing. It is not a dialect of French, however; many words have been localized (a mosquito can be called a *marougouin* in one area, a *moustique* in another, a *cousin* elsewhere), and "Franglish" is common (*"On va revenir right back"*—We'll be right back).

Additionally, the fascinating Creole language is still spoken by many black Louisianans. A compilation of French and African dialects, it is quite different from standard French, though Cajuns and black Creoles can speak and understand both languages.

Cajun Music

It's hard to decide which is more important to a Cajun: food or music. In the early days when instruments were scarce, Cajuns held dances to a cappella voices. With roots probably found in medieval France, the strains came in the form of a brisk two-step or a waltz. Traditional groups still play mostly acoustic instruments—a fiddle, an accordion, a triangle, maybe a guitar, and the traditional high, loud vocal wail.

The best place to hear real Cajun music is on someone's back porch, the time-honored spot for eating some gumbo and listening to several generations of players jamming. If you can't wrangle an invitation, the local dance halls on any weekend will do just fine. It's quite the social scene, and there are usually willing dance coaches for newbies (don't be shy—everyone will be watching the really good dancers; you should, too). The following 3-day Cajun weekend takes you on a well-rounded musical introduction to this region. For Cajun music clubs in New Orleans, see p. 191.

Boudin (boo-*dan*) is a Cajun sausage link made of pork, pork liver, rice, onions, and spices and stuffed inside a casing. If it's done right, it's spicy and sublime. In these parts, you can get this inexpensive (about $4 per lb.) snack at just about any grocery store or gas station. Disputes rage about whose reigns supreme (**www.boudinlink.com** has digitized the argument). It's best eaten while leaning against a car, chased with a Barq's root beer. Conducting a comparison test is great fun, but the singular choice in these parts is the **Best Stop** (615 Hwy. 93 N., Scott, exit 97 off the I-10; www.beststopinscott.com; ✆ **337/233-5805**). It's always busy, so the links and crunchy pig-fat cracklins (aka *chicharones*) are always fresh. Did we mention that they ship? Send us some *now*, please. Best Stop is open Monday to Saturday 6am to 8pm and Sunday 6am to 6pm.

Planning Your Trip

You'll see and do a lot during this 3-day weekend, which includes options to customize the trip based on your own interests. A bit of adventurous meandering on your own will most definitely reward you with more finds.

It's awfully fun to visit Acadiana during **Cajun Mardi Gras** (p. 50), **Festival International de Louisiane** (p. 25), **Festivals Acadiens et Creoles** (p. 27), or the **Breaux Bridge Crawfish Festival**—but any weekend will do. There's plenty of music throughout the year and often a small festival somewhere in the area. If you find one, you simply have to go: they're almost guaranteed to be a memorable social, cultural, and musical experience. (We'll never forget our first Yambilee.)

For tons of good, detailed information, contact the **Lafayette Convention and Visitors Commission** (www.lafayettetravel.com; ✆ **800/346-1958** in the U.S., 800/543-5340 in Canada, or 337/232-3737).

Organized Tours

If you drive to Lafayette, **Cajun Food Tours** (www.cajunfoodtours.com; ✆ **337/230-6169**) will save you from additional driving by shuttling you to six Cajun food stops in a comfy 14-seater bus. They're not all the little down-home holes-in-the-walls you might stumble onto yourself, but it's convenient, fairly priced, and you'll get plenty of variety 59; kids 12 and under $35; reservations required). Plan in advance, because they may not be offered every day. Each year, **Festival Tours International** (p. 53) offers a stellar music-focused tour of the area during the 3 days between Jazz Fest weekends. Also see "Organized Tours," p. 170.

A CAJUN 3-DAY WEEKEND

The suggested itinerary for a 3-day side trip from New Orleans to Cajun Country is designed to introduce you to this marvelous, singular culture. The drive from New Orleans is about 2½ to 3 hours, mostly via I-10 (140 miles from New Orleans). If you opt to drive back via U.S. 90, it's about 170 miles. You'll be based in Lafayette and going to the smaller towns of Eunice, Mamou, and St. Martinville for a thorough immersion in real Cajun culture. We've provided main highway directions; some form of GPS is recommended to help get you to the in-town destinations.

Friday, Day 1: Lafayette ★★★

Leave New Orleans early in the day and head for the River Road (Hwy. 18) plantations to tour a plantation (p.174). Or head directly to Lafayette. *Tip:* Try to avoid going through Baton Rouge at afternoon rush hour.

Lafayette is a midsize city of 120,000, with a university (University of Louisiana Lafayette) and plenty of hotel options. But we recommend you opt for an atmospheric B&B instead. Check in at the newly renovated **Aaah! T'Frere's Bed & Breakfast** (1905 Verot School Rd., Lafayette; www.tfrereshouse.com; ✆ **800/984-9347** or 337/984-9347; doubles $135) or **Mouton Plantation Bed & Breakfast** (338 N. Sterling St., Lafayette; www.moutonplantation.com; ✆ **337/233-7816;** doubles $125–$175). For a more freewheeling, downtown experience, **Blue Moon Saloon & Guesthouse** offers en suite rooms or cottage and dorm-style accommodations in the main house, with shared kitchen and public areas adjacent to the storied outdoor live music venue (215 East Convent St., Lafayette; http://bluemoonpresents.com; ✆ **337/234-2422;** $23 dorm rooms, doubles from $80, bungalow $250)

Plan to arrive in time for lunch and go directly to **Creole Lunch House** (713 12th St., Lafayette, in a residential area; www.facebook.com/creoles stuffedbread; ✆ **337/232-9929;** Mon–Fri 10am–2pm). Get a couple of stuffed breads and whatever's been smothered that day (chicken thighs, pork chop, shoe, it's all gonna be ridiculously good home cooking). We'll toss out two other casual, worthy eatin' options to bookmark during your Lafayette stay: **Johnson's Boucaniere** (1111 St. John St.; www.johnsons boucaniere.com; ✆ **337/269-8878;** Tues–Fri 7am–3pm; Sat 7am–5:30pm), especially the sublime pulled pork; and **Olde Tyme Grocery** for poor boys (218 West Saint Mary Blvd.; www.oldetymegrocery.com; ✆ **337/235-8165;** Mon–Fri 8am–10pm; Sat 9am–7pm).

Relax or take a drive around town. Visit the **Church of St. John the Evangelist** (914 St. John St., Lafayette; www.saintjohncathedral.org; ✆ **337/232-1322**), a splendid Dutch Romanesque edifice done in red and white brick, with fine stained glass dating to 1916.

For dinner, head to **Mandez's** (110 Doucet Rd., Lafayette; www.mandez grill.com; ✆ **337/769-3917**). It's nothing fancy, but the redfish and fried oysters are spot-on and the burger's even better. If you have room, flip the time-travel clock back and squeeze in a sundae from **Borden's** (1103 Jefferson St., Lafayette; www.bordensicecreamshoppe.com; ✆ **337/235-9291**), the last retail Borden's shop in the world, and hardly changed since it scooped its first cone of creamy goodness back in 1940. Otherwise, head back and hit your relaxing veranda and cushy bed—Saturday is a full day.

Saturday, Day 2: Eunice & Mamou ★★

Grab a quick B from your B&B before heading out to supplement it. If you haven't already stopped for boudin, now's a good time, because a) pork sausage for breakfast = yes, always; b) you might want to stop here again tomorrow; and c) you'll instantly become more welcome at your next stop. Choose the **Best Stop** (p. 258), but if you require a little egg or biscuit action with your sausage, head across Highway 10 to **Don's** (730 I-10 S. Frontage Rd., Scott; www.donsspecialtymeats.com; ✆ **337/234-2528**). A half-link per person is a minimal sampling of boudin; get a few more links to take to the **Savoy Music Center**, 3 miles east of downtown Eunice (about a 35-min. drive; 4413 U.S. Hwy. 190 E.; www.savoymusic center.com; ✆ **337/457-9563**; Tues–Fri 9am–5pm, closed for lunch noon–1:30pm; Sat jam 9am–noon). On weekdays this working music store sells instruments, equipment, and Marc Savoy's exquisite, world-renowned, hand-crafted accordions (check out the folk-art aphorisms scrawled on his workshop cabinets, if you can). At the Saturday-morning jam sessions, this nondescript, faded-green building becomes the spiritual center of Cajun music, and an experience not to be missed. Local and visiting musicians young and old gather to savor this unpretentious, unparalleled music and culture. It's probably the closest thing to that back-porch experience you'll find.

Stay and savor this utter authenticity, or cut out (no later than 11:30am; it ends at noon) to head for the alternate universe known as **Fred's Lounge** in Mamou, about 20 minutes north (west on U.S. 190, then right on LA 13; 420 6th St.; ✆ **337/468-5411;** Sat 8am–2pm; music starts at 9am). This is the other end of the Cajun music spectrum, a small-town bar that for half a century has hosted Saturday daytime dances starting in the early morn. Couples waltz and two-step around the midfloor bandstand, while 80-something matriarch Tante Sue drinks shots and otherwise presides. It's pure dance-hall stuff (leaning toward the country-western side of Cajun, but much of it in French), where hard-working locals let loose. And we do mean loose (remember, they started with Coors while you were still on coffee).

Back to Eunice, sample a down-home lunch at **Ruby's Courtyard** (123 S. 2nd St., Eunice; ✆ **337/550-7665**), where the daily specials are your best bet, especially if the thick, crisp-fried pork chops with stewed okra are on. Revise all that if the crawfish étouffée is on (or just get both; it's a long time till dinner).

Take in some mellow museum time at the **Prairie Acadian Cultural Center** (250 W. Park Ave.; www.nps.gov/jela/prairie-acadian-cultural-center-eunice.htm; ✆ **337/457-8499;** free admission, donations accepted;

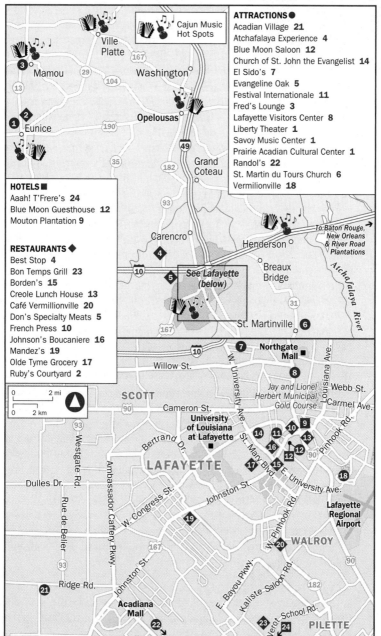

Cajun Music Hot Spots

ATTRACTIONS ●
Acadian Village **21**
Atchafalaya Experience **4**
Blue Moon Saloon **12**
Church of St. John the Evangelist **14**
El Sido's **7**
Evangeline Oak **5**
Festival Internationale **11**
Fred's Lounge **3**
Lafayette Visitors Center **8**
Liberty Theater **1**
Savoy Music Center **1**
Prairie Acadian Cultural Center **1**
Randol's **22**
St. Martin du Tours Church **6**
Vermilionville **18**

HOTELS ■
Aaah! T'Frere's **24**
Blue Moon Guesthouse **12**
Mouton Plantation **9**

RESTAURANTS ◆
Best Stop **4**
Bon Temps Grill **23**
Borden's **15**
Creole Lunch House **13**
Café Vermillionville **20**
Don's Specialty Meats **5**
French Press **10**
Johnson's Boucaniere **16**
Mandez's **19**
Olde Tyme Grocery **17**
Ruby's Courtyard **2**

Wed–Fri 9:30am–4:30pm, Sat 9:30am–6pm), a terrific small collection. Most objects on display were acquired from local families who had owned them for generations, and craft demonstrations, cooking demos, or dance lessons may be in the offing. The most worthy attraction may help dispel the myths and patronizing stereotypes perpetuated by the recent rash of Louisiana-based reality shows.

Each Saturday, when the Cultural Center shuts down, visitors—well, the entire town—migrate next door to the 1924 **Liberty Theater** (2nd St. and Park Ave.; www.eunice-la.com; ℭ 337/457-7389; $5; doors open at 4pm, show 6:30–7:30pm), where the all-French show "Rendez-vous des Cajuns" kicks off with live music, dancing, and jokey storytelling. Even if you speak *non* French, you'll get it. *Note:* Tickets go on sale at 4pm, so you may need to take a break from the Cultural Center to buy them lest they sell out. If you can't make it (big mistake), tune in to KRVS 88.7 on your FM dial (locally) or krvs.org for the stream.

Your dinner bell is probably ringing loudly, and Cajun and Creole specialties await you back in Lafayette at the **Bon Temps Grill** (1312 Verot School Rd., Lafayette; www.bontempsgrill.com; ℭ 337/706-8850; (Sun–Thurs 11am–9:30pm, Fri–Sat 11am–10pm). The barnlike structure belies a comfortable, traditional interior, and the rich crawfish pot pie or shrimp and tasso pasta are worth seeking out. Standard American fare is also plentiful for those who've had their fill of the local stuff.

Still up for more? Check out what's on at the **Blue Moon Saloon** (215 E. Convent St., Lafayette; www.bluemoonpresents.com; ℭ 337/234-2422; cover free (midweek, often) to $20; Wed–Sat 6pm–close), the city's premier live-music venue. Cajun, zydeco, and all forms of modern alternative roots music bring in the LSU student body and others. For more traditional Cajun music and dancing, two-step over to **Randol's** (2320 Kaliste Saloom Rd.; www.randols.com; ℭ 337/981-7080; Sun–Thurs 5–10pm, Fri–Sat 5–10:30pm). You may be joined by fellow tourists on the dance floor, but on Saturday nights you'll certainly find an easygoing, accessible scene (you can dine here as well, but the dance scene trumps the cuisine). For the adventurous night owl, find your way to the outskirts of town to **El Sido's** (1523 N. St. Antoine St., Lafayette; www.facebook.com/ElSidos; ℭ 337/235-0647; cover $7–$15; Fri–Sat 9pm–2am, occasionally other nights). It's not always easy to find out what's on at the gritty, long-standing roadhouse, but on Saturday night it's a good bet it's zydeco, often with a bluesy or urban edge, and some astoundingly good dancing. It gets going around 10pm.

Sunday, Day 3: Lafayette & St. Martinville ★★

After a relaxing breakfast at your B&B, visit **Vermilionville** ★★ (300 Fisher Rd., off Surrey St.; www.vermilionville.org; ℭ 337/233-4077; $10 adults, $8 seniors, $6 students, free for children 5 and under; Tues–Sun 10am–4pm; admission desk closes at 3pm), a Cajun-Creole settlement reconstructed on the bayou's banks, where costumed staff and craftspeople demonstrate activities of 18th- to 19th-century daily life and musicians jam. While it sounds like a kitschy "Cajunland" theme park, it's actually quite a good introduction to the culture. Live music is offered regularly; check the website for schedule. Nearby **Café Vermillionville** ★★, an upscale restaurant in a historic inn, is an alternate dining option during your stay (1304 W. Pinhook Ave.; www.cafev.com; ✆ **337/237-0100**).

Or take the **Atchafalaya Experience,** Lafayette (www.theatchafalaya experience.com; ✆ **337/735-1911** or 337/233-7816; $50 ages 13 and up, $25 children 8–12, free for 7 and under [1 per family]; call for times and reservations), an outstanding swamp, bird, and wildlife tour led by virtuoso naturalists who were raised on these bayous. If you have not yet taken to the waters of the Louisiana swamps, seeing this stunning, primeval, vital ecosystem is a must-do, and these guides are as good as it gets. Bring a hat, sunscreen, water, and insect repellent.

Lunch returns you to downtown Lafayette to the **French Press** (214 E. Vermilion St.; www.thefrenchpresslafayette.com; ✆ **337/233-9449;** Mon–Fri 7am–2pm, Sat–Sun 9am–2pm), a casual but refined spot on the higher end of the hipness scale. The biscuit sliders with boudin balls and sugarcane syrup are to kill for; the chicken and waffles aren't far behind. If you're ready for lighter fare, the winning shrimp salad boasts a kicking rémoulade.

To further experience the history, legend, and romance of this region, take a leisurely drive to the lovely, historic burg of **St. Martinville.** Get there by taking U.S. 90 East heading south out of Lafayette, to Louisiana 182 exit. Turn left onto East Main St., and left again onto LA-96 East for 7.3 miles to reach the peaceful town square. St. Martinville dates from 1765, when it was a military station. It was once known as "la Petite Paris" for the many French aristocrats who settled here after fleeing the French Revolution.

The town centers around **St. Martin du Tours Church,** constructed in 1836—the fourth-oldest Roman Catholic church in Louisiana—and poetry. Besides its natural and historic charm, the town is the home of Evangeline Emmeline, the (debatably) fictional heroine of Longfellow's tragic poem. A statue of her next to the church was donated to the town in 1929 by a movie company that filmed the epic here; star Dolores del Rio supposedly posed for the sculptor. At Port Street and Bayou Teche is the ancient **Evangeline Oak** and commemorative mural, where self-proclaimed descendants claim Emmeline's boat landed after her arduous journey from Nova Scotia.

From St. Martinville, make your way to I-10 again to return to New Orleans, or alternately, via U.S. 90 for a different view. It's slightly longer and moderately more interesting.

PLANNING YOUR TRIP

No matter what your idea of the perfect New Orleans trip is, this chapter will give you the information to make informed plans about getting here, getting around, and the essentials for an easy Big Easy vacation. We'll also point you toward additional resources, so you can let the *bons temps* begin even before you arrive.

GETTING THERE

By Plane

Most major domestic airlines serve the city's **Louis Armstrong New Orleans International Airport (MSY)** (http://flymsy.com), along with several smaller regional lines. British Airways flies in from London, and Condor Air from Frankfurt. The airport is 15 miles west of New Orleans in the town of Kenner. Information booths are scattered around the airport and in the baggage claim area. Private planes often use Lakefront Airport, 9 miles from downtown. *Note:* New Orleans' all-new, $990-million, Cesar Pelli–designed Louis Armstrong Airport is scheduled to open in February 2019. Directional instructions in this section are based on preliminary information about the new airport.

Getting into Town from the Airport

Depending on the traffic and your mode of transportation, it takes approximately 30 to 45 minutes to get from the airport to the French Quarter or the Central Business District.

Most major **rental car** companies operate out of a unified facility that is accessed by a shuttle bus outside baggage claim. Follow the signs.

For $24 per person (one-way), the official **Airport Shuttle New Orleans** van (www.airportshuttleneworleans.com; © **866/596-2699** or 504/522-3500) will take you directly from the airport to your hotel in the French Quarter, Garden District, Central Business District, or Faubourg Marigny. There are Airport Shuttle information desks (staffed 24 hr.) in the airport. *Note:* If you plan to take the Airport Shuttle *to* the airport when you depart, you can also book and pay for a round-trip ($44) in advance via phone or online. For the return, you must call 24 hours in advance to arrange a pickup time. It's free for kids 5 and under and operates daily from 3:30am to 2am year-round.

Airport Limousine also operates from the desks in the baggage claim area. Sedans to hotels start at $61 (www.airportlimousineneworleans.com; ✆ **855/735-5466** or 504/305-2450). Alternately, arrange limo service via **Bonomolo Limousine Service** (www.bonolimo.com; ✆ **800/451-9258** or 504/522-0892). Airport transfer service in a Lincoln MKS runs about $99; ask about in-town hourly rates.

If two or more passengers are traveling, **taxis** are a better, more direct deal than the shuttle. A taxi from the airport to most hotels costs $36 for one to two people; $15 per person for three or more passengers per person. Follow signs to taxi and rideshare stands outside the baggage-claim area. **Uber** & **Lyft** rates run about $37 to $39.

The cheapest option is by **public bus.** The **New Orleans Regional Transit Authority** (NORTA) express line No. 202 runs directly from the airport to Canal St. and Elk Place in the Central Business District eight times daily between 6am and 7pm. Other options: the **Jefferson Transit public bus No. E-2** for $2. It goes to Tulane Avenue and Loyola Street in the **Central Business District** Monday to Friday; on weekends it goes as far as Tulane and Carrollton in Mid-City, where riders can transfer to the Regional Transit Authority lines for an additional $1.25. Buses run from 5:20am weekdays (6:30am weekends). The Tulane/Carrollton line runs until around 9pm daily; the line to Loyola runs until 6:14pm Monday to Friday only. Follow signs outside baggage claim to the NORTA and RTA public bus stop. For more information, call **Jefferson Transit** (www.jeffersontransit.org; ✆ **504/818-1077**) or the **Regional Transit Authority** (www.norta.com; ✆ **504/248-3900**).

By Car

You can drive to New Orleans via **I-10, I-55, U.S. 90, U.S. 61,** or across the Lake Pontchartrain Causeway on **LA 25,** then **US 190.** If possible, drive in during daylight to allow time to enjoy the distinctive swampy scenery. U.S. 61 or La. 25 offer the best views, but the larger roads are considerably faster.

Approximate drive time to New Orleans from Atlanta is 6½ hours; from Houston it's 5 hours; Chicago, 14 hours; Baton Rouge is an hour and a half away. For info on driving while you're in the city, including rental cars, see "Getting Around" later in this chapter.

By Bus

Greyhound buses service New Orleans from **Union Passenger Terminal (UPT)** at 1001 Loyola Ave. (www.greyhound.com; ✆ **504/524-7571**), as does **Megabus** (us.megabus.com; ✆ **877/462-6342**), which has cheap fares to/from select Southern cities where they connect to many others.

By Train

Passenger rail lines pass through some beautiful scenery. **Amtrak** (www.amtrak.com; ✆ **800/872-7245**) trains serve the city's **Union Passenger**

Terminal, 1001 Loyola Ave., in the Central Business District. The station is on the recently completed Loyola streetcar line, and plenty of taxis wait outside the passenger terminal. Hotels in the French Quarter and the Central Business District are a short ride or a healthy walk away.

By Ship

It's not usually considered "transportation," but cruising to or from the Port of New Orleans is increasingly popular. Many passengers add a visit to the Crescent City before or after their voyage—a right fine vacation. Ocean cruises include **Crystal Cruises** (www.crystalcruises.com; ✆ **888/722-0021**), **Carnival Cruises** (www.carnival.com; ✆ **800/764-7419**), **Norwegian Cruise Line** (www.ncl.com; ✆ **866/234-7350**), and **Royal Caribbean** (www.royalcaribbean.com; ✆ **866/562-7625**). Plying the Mississippi River are **American Cruise Lines** (www.americancruiselines.com; ✆ **800/460-4518**), the luxe **French America Line** (www.frenchamericaline.com; ✆ **888/387-1140**), and the **American Queen Steamboat Company** (www.americanqueensteamboatcompany.com; ✆ **888/749-5280**).

Taxi fare from the cruise terminal to most hotels is about $10 for the first person and $7 for each additional person. Parking at the terminal is $20 per day.

GETTING AROUND

By Car

Unless you're planning extensive or far-flung explorations outside the major tourist zones (and, okay, this book does recommend a few outlying destinations), you really don't need to rent a car during your stay in New Orleans. The town is flat, ultra-picturesque, and made for walking; there are plenty of taxis (also **Uber, Lyft,** and **pedicabs**) and decent public transportation. Indeed, a streetcar ride is as much entertainment as a practical means of getting around. Meanwhile, driving and parking in the French Quarter can be a hassle. Many streets are narrow, potholed, crowded, and one-way. Outside the gridded Quarter, streets angle in logic-defying directions in attempt to align around the curvy Mississippi. Street parking is minimal in the Quarter and CBD, and parking lots, including those at hotels, are fiendishly expensive.

That said, all the major **car-rental agencies** have a presence in New Orleans, at the airport and scattered around town. Rates vary widely according to company, demand, and when you book your reservation. Plan in advance, and shop around. You'll pay a premium to pick up a rental at the airport, but it may be worth the convenience. If your stay is lengthy, weigh the difference between renting from a lower-cost, in-town location vs. transfer costs to and from that cheaper locale.

If you're visiting from abroad and plan to rent a car in the United States, foreign driver's licenses are usually recognized, but it's probably wise to get an international one if your home license is not in English. Insurance and taxes are almost never included in quoted rental-car rates in the U.S., and they can be significant.

To rent a car in the United States, you need a valid driver's license and a major credit card (and a passport for foreign visitors). Some will accept a debit card with a cash deposit. The minimum age is usually 25, but Enterprise and Budget will rent to younger people for an added surcharge; they may also require proof of ability to pay (check with them, but it's often paycheck stubs and utility bills). It's a good idea to buy insurance coverage unless you're certain your own auto or credit card insurance is sufficient.

If you're in town for a while or drive in often, download the **Parkmobile app.** Once you complete the annoying set-up, you can conveniently pay for most street meters via smartphone (and add meter time from afar—a huge plus).

At press time in New Orleans, the **cost of gasoline** was about $2.40 a gallon including tax, but we all know how that can fluctuate. Generally, gas costs in New Orleans tends to be at or slightly below the U.S. average. Gas stations are readily available on major streets, but none are located within the French Quarter. When driving in New Orleans, **right turns on a red light** are legal except where NO RIGHT TURN ON RED signs are posted, so keep your eyes open for those. Sneaky red-light cameras abound (as do **speed cameras,** especially in school zones). Similarly, many major intersections restrict left turns. Drive past the intersection, make a U-turn at the next allowable place, then double back and turn right (a maneuver sometimes called the "Louisiana left").

Streetcars run down the center of Canal Street and St. Charles, Rampart, Carrollton, and Loyola avenues, requiring motorists to cross their paths frequently. **Look *both* ways for streetcars,** yield the right of way to them, and allow ample time to complete track crossings. They'll brake if you're in their way, of course, but it's best not to get stuck on the tracks and impede their progress.

It is illegal to have an open container of alcohol, including "go cups," in a moving car, and, of course, driving while under the influence of alcohol is a serious offense.

Keep doors locked and never leave belongings, packages, or gadgets visible in parked cars.

By Taxi or Rideshare

Taxis are plentiful in New Orleans, and except during the busiest times (Mardi Gras and Jazz Fest) they can be hailed easily on the street in the French Quarter and in some parts of the Central Business District. They also usually line up at taxi stands at larger hotels. Otherwise, call and expect a cab to appear in about 5 to 15 minutes; much longer during peak times, events, and in residential areas. The rate is $3.50 when you enter the taxi and $2.40 per mile thereafter. During special events, the rate is $7 per person (or the meter rate if it's greater) to the event site. From the French Quarter to an uptown restaurant or club, expect to spend $12 to $25 depending on traffic and distance; cash or credit cards accepted.

The cab behemoth is **United Cabs;** book by phone or United Cab Passenger app (www.unitedcabs.com; ✆ **504/524-9606**). There's also **Carriage Cab,** the slightly upscale sister to Checker and Yellow Cabs (www.

neworleanscarriagecab.com; ☏ **504/207-7777**). You can even hire a taxi for a few hours or day at negotiable hourly rates (usually around $30/hour), a hassle-free way to tour far-flung areas of the city.

Uber and **Lyft** (available only by app) are usually readily available, but can be slow to show in the midst of big events. Expect the fare to be slightly less than standard taxis till surge prices kick in (which is often).

On Foot

We can't stress this enough: Walking is by far the best way to see New Orleans (besides, you need to walk off all those calories!). You'll miss the many unique and sometimes glorious sights if you whiz past them. Slow down, stroll, and take it in. If it's just too hot, humid, or rainy, seek the shade or shelter of balconies and galleries, and there's always a cab or bus nearby.

By Bike & Scooter

One of the best ways to see the city is by bike. The terrain is flat, the breeze feels good, there are new bike paths and improved driver awareness, and you can cover ground pretty swiftly on two wheels. But streets can be busy, bumpy, and potholed, so experience and comfort with city riding is a plus. **Bicycle Michael's,** 622 Frenchmen St. (www.bicyclemichaels.com; ☏ **504/945-9505**), is the oldest shop and has good-quality, multigear hybrids and mountain bikes (most other rentals are cruisers) starting at $25 for a half-day (4 hr.), $35 a day. **A Bicycle Named Desire,** 632 Elysian Fields in the Marigny (https://abicyclenameddesire.com; ☏ **504/345 8966**), offers 4-hour rentals for $30, 24 hours for $35. At the other end of the French Quarter, **American Bicycle Rentals,** 318 N. Rampart St.(www.bikerentalneworleans. com; ☏ **504/324-8257**), has super-sturdy, well-maintained, cushy-seated single-speed bikes with coaster brakes for $10 an hour, $30 for 8 hours, $40 for 24. If you're staying uptown, hit **Mike the Bike Guy,** $30 per day (open to close) (4411 Magazine St.; www.mikethebikeguy.com; ☏ **504/899-1344**). Rates cited above usually include a lock and optional helmet. All offer longer-term rentals; multi-day minimums may apply during Mardi Gras or Jazz Fest. Also see "Bicycle and Other Wheeled Tours," p. 180 (Desire and American offer tours).

Launched in 2018, the convenient **Blue Bikes** bike-sharing system has more than 500 bikes available to rent by the hour at 60+ "hubs" around the city. After creating an account tied to a credit card, you can grab and go at leisure for $8/hour, pro-rated (use the 60 min. over any length of time). Park the bike back at a hub or at any rack (within the system) for an extra $1. Bikes have lights and a lock but no helmets (not required but recommended in NOLA). Maps and details on the website and app. (www.bluebikesnola.com; ☏ **504/608-0603**).

Avenue Scooters, 1134 St. Charles Ave. (www.avenuescooters.com; ☏ **504/609-3838**), will fix you up with a Lance PCH50. It's a fun, easy way to get around. Rates start at $60 for 3 hours; $80 per full day including helmet and lock. They get up to about 35mph so you ride in car lanes (and get no love from four-wheeled drivers) and follow all traffic rules. Watch those potholes.

By Pedicab

These rickshaw-like tricycles will get two people from A to B via pedal power (a driver's, not yours). They're easy to hail in the French Quarter and occasionally seen in other tourist parts, or you can call to request one—try **Bike Taxi Unlimited** (✆ **504/891-3441**) or **NOLA Pedicabs** (✆ **504/274-1300**). Rates are $5 for the first 6 blocks, $1 per block per person after that (plus tip for your hard-riding driver). It's a great option for fatigued feet or short hops; longer jaunts can add up fast so ask for the rate when you board.

By Ferry

The **Canal Street/Algiers Ferry** (www.norta.com/Maps-Schedules/New-Orleans-Ferry; ✆ **504/309-9789**) is one of the city's great assets, for transportation to the old Algiers Point neighborhood and views of the city from the Mississippi River. It's a down-and-dirty, working ferry, but it's more than that at night when the city's glowing skyline reflects on the water. The 25-minute ride from the foot of Canal Street costs $2 each way, cash only. The ferry leaves New Orleans every 30 minutes Monday to Thursday from 6:15am to 9:45pm; Friday 6:15am to 11:45pm; Saturday 10:45am to 11:45pm, and Sunday 10:45am to 9:45pm. Check for schedule changes on holidays, events, and generally. It's pedestrians and bikes only, no cars. *Note:* A much-needed new ferry terminal and snazzy new boats are in the works, pending a 2020 launch. When you read this, a temporary, ADA-accessible terminal barge will be in use at the wharf just behind Audubon Aquarium at 1 Canal St.

By City Bus

New Orleans has a good public bus system that many locals rely on, so chances are there's a bus that runs exactly where you want to go. The fare is $1.50; transfers are an extra 25¢. You must have exact change in bills or coins, or you can use a **JazzyPass** (see box). For route information, contact the **RTA** (www.norta.com; ✆ **504/248-3900**) or pick up one of the excellent city maps at the **Louisiana Office of Tourism New Orleans Welcome Center,** 529 St. Ann St., in the French Quarter.

Discounted Rides with the JazzyPass

If you don't have a car in New Orleans, invest in a **JazzyPass,** which allows unlimited rides on all streetcar and bus lines. It's a bargain and a convenience at $3 for 1 day, $9 for 3 days, $15 for 5 days. Single-day passes can be purchased when boarding. Get multiday passes at vending machines at the streetcar stops at Canal at Bourbon; N. Peters; White, or City Park streets. You can order them online, but you'll need to allow a week for the physical card to be mailed to you. More info at **Regional Transit Authority** (www.norta.com; ✆ **504/248-3900**).

By Streetcar

Besides being a National Historic Landmark, the **St. Charles Avenue streetcar** is also a convenient, scenic, and fun way to get from downtown to uptown and back. The iconic green cars click and clack for 6½ miles, 24 hours a day at frequent intervals and get crowded at school and business rush hours. Board at Canal and Carondelet streets (directly across Canal from Bourbon St. in the French Quarter) or anywhere along the line.

The tracks wind beyond the point where St. Charles Avenue bends into Carrollton Avenue, ending at Palmer Park (Claiborne Ave.). The original cars run on the St. Charles line, and are neither air-conditioned nor wheelchair-accessible (and it's a big step up). All other lines have A/C and lifts.

The **Riverfront streetcar** line runs the length of the French Quarter, from the Old Mint at Esplanade to Julia Street, with stops along the way. It runs daily 5:30am to 11:30pm and is a great foot saver as you explore the riverfront. The spiffy, bright-red cars on the **Canal Street** line service two destinations. Check the sign on the front of the car: "Cemeteries" goes to several of the older cemeteries and runs daily 5:30am to 4am; "City Park" goes along Carrollton Avenue through Mid-City, to City Park/the New Orleans Museum of Art and Jazz Fest (expect jammed streetcars during Jazz Fest). The City Park route runs between 6:15am and 11:35pm.

The **Loyola line** runs along Loyola Street, connecting the Union Passenger Terminal (and Amtrak and Greyhound passengers) with the Canal Street line, and continues to the French Market on weekends (Sat–Sun 6:30am–9:30pm).

The **N. Rampart Street/St. Claude line** runs from Elysian Fields in the Marigny past Canal Street to the Union Passenger Terminal on Calliope Street every 20 minutes.

The **fare** for any streetcar line is $1.25 each way. Add 25¢ to transfer to or from a city bus. All streetcars take exact change in bills or coins only, or **JazzyPasses.**

[FastFACTS]

African-American Travelers New Orleans' African-American history is rich with important milestones, from the joyous nascence of jazz to the horrors of the slave trade to crucial civil rights achievements (to say nothing of the essential contributions to the city's culture, cuisine, politics, and literature). The **historic Tremé neighborhood** is a touchstone in itself, with a number of worthy sights within its bounds (see p. 31) including the **Backstreet Cultural Museum** (p. 149); the nearby **African-American Museum** remains closed for restoration, but the statewide **African American Heritage Trail** is an excellent network of cultural and historic points; information and maps are available at www.astorylikenoother.com. A visit to the **9th Ward** may be of interest (see "Organized Tours," p. 170). Here, the **9th Ward Living Museum** (p. 152) and **House of Dance and Feathers** (1317 Tupelo St.; www.houseofdance andfeathers.org; © **504/ 957-2678,** open by appointment) are essential for anyone interested in this area or in the Mardi Gras Indian tradition. The

***Essence* Festival** is a huge draw (p. 26), and the restaurant and music options relevant to black heritage could fill a weeklong vacation.

Area Codes   The area code for New Orleans is 504.

Business Hours   They vary, but most stores are open from at least 10am to 5pm; bars can stay open until the wee hours, even 24/7, and restaurants' hours vary depending on the types of meals they serve. Expect breakfast to start around 8am, lunch around 11am, and dinner at 6pm.

Cellphones   See "Mobile Phones," later in this section.

Crime   See "Safety," later in this section.

Customs   For U.S. Customs details and information on what you're allowed to bring home, consult your home country's customs services agency. In the U.S., consult **U.S. Customs** at **U.S. Customs & Border Protection (CBP),** 1300 Pennsylvania Ave. NW, Washington, DC 20229 (www.cbp.gov; ✆ **877/227-5511**).

Doctors   See "Health."

Drinking Laws   The legal age for purchase and consumption of alcoholic beverages is 21; proof of age is required and often requested at bars, nightclubs, and restaurants, so bring ID when you go out. Due to recent crackdowns, nowadays pretty much everyone—even senior citizens—may get carded.

Alcoholic beverages are available round-the-clock, 7 days a week. Bars can stay open all night in New Orleans, and liquor is sold in grocery and liquor stores. You're allowed to drink in public, but not from a glass or bottle. Bars will provide a plastic "go cup" into which you can transfer your drink as you leave (and some have walk-up windows for quick and easy refills).

Warning: Although New Orleans has a reputation for tolerance, make no mistake: Public intoxication and "drunk and disorderly" are most definitely illegal, as many a jailed tourist can testify. Practice moderation and make smart decisions. And don't even think about driving (car, motorcycle, *or* bicycle) while intoxicated: This is a zero-tolerance crime. Do not carry open containers of alcohol in your car or any public area that isn't zoned for alcohol consumption. The police can fine you on the spot.

Electricity   Like Canada, the United States uses 110 to 120 volts AC (60 cycles), compared to 220 to 240 volts AC (50 cycles) in most of Europe, Australia, and New Zealand. Downward converters that change 220–240 volts to 110–120 volts are difficult to find in the United States, so bring one with you.

Embassies & Consulates   All embassies are in the nation's capital, Washington, D.C. Some have consulate offices in major U.S. cities, including a few

in New Orleans. To find a consulate for your home country, call for directory information in Washington, D.C. (✆ **202/555-1212**), or check www.embassy.org/embassies. It's always a good idea to enter this information in your contacts before you leave your home country.

Emergencies   For fire, ambulance, and police, dial ✆ **911** from any phone (it is a free call). Calls from landlines (hard-wired phones) will route to the local emergency dispatch center. From mobile phones, immediately tell the operator your location and the nature of the emergency.

Family Travel   New Orleans doesn't spring to mind as the first place to take a child, but it offers plenty of activities and sights appropriate for children, who often get a real kick out of the city (and love Mardi Gras!). Summer months bring the heat but also the bargains, so weigh your family's tolerance levels for a visit during school vacation. See "Especially for Kids," in chapter 7 on p. 182.

Gyms   Most hotels have at least a nominal fitness center. Some offer day passes to local gyms. Otherwise, workout day passes can be had at two **Downtown Fitness** (www.downtownfitnesscenter.com) locations convenient to the French Quarter and Bywater (333 Canal Place, 3rd floor, ✆ **504/525-2956;** or 2372 St. Claude Ave,

504/754-1101). The storied **New Orleans Athletic Club** has a fabulous indoor pool, library, and (yup) bar (222 N. Rampart St.; www. neworleansathleticclub.com; 504/525-2375). The enormous Health Club at the **Hilton New Orleans Riverside** has two pools plus tennis, squash, and racquetball for additional costs (2 Poydras St.; www.the healthclub.us; 504/556-3742). Members of the **Anytime Fitness** chain can find multiple locations around town. There are also lots of free or inexpensive drop-in workouts around town: The **Cabildo** museum (p. 142) and **Besthoff Sculpture Garden** (p. 152) offer yoga classes. **Move Ya Brass** (www.moveyabrass. com) gives stretch, hip-hop, and twerk workouts in in **Crescent Park** (p. 161). The international free workout group **November Project** has 5:15am and 6am workouts Wednesdays at Champions Square; Mondays at rotating locations (www.facebook.com/ NovProjectNO).

Health If you have a medical condition that may require care, make appropriate arrangements before traveling to New Orleans. **Pollen, sun, uneven sidewalks, overindulgence,** and **mosquitoes** (especially near swamps and bayous) are the most common medical annoyances. Packing insect repellent, sunscreen, protective clothing, digestive aids, and antihistamines may help prevent minor

health annoyances. For "Hospitals," see below. If you need a doctor for less urgent health concerns, try **Ochsner On Call** (www. ochsner.org; 504/842-3155 or 800/231-5257) or visit a **New Orleans Urgent Care** clinic (www.new orleansurgentcare.com): 201 Decatur St. in the French Quarter (504/609-3833; Mon–Sat 9am–5:30pm); the Warehouse District (900 Magazine St.; 504/552-2433; Mon–Fri 9am–7pm, Sat–Sun 9am–5pm); or Mid-City (4100 Canal St.; 504/218-4853; Mon–Fri 8am–7pm; Sat–Sun 9am–5pm). Also see "Pharmacies," in this section.

Hospitals In an emergency, dial 911 from any phone to summon paramedics. Nearby emergency rooms are at **Ochsner Baptist Medical Center,** 2700 Napoleon Ave. (504/899-9311); and **Tulane University Medical Center,** 1415 Tulane Ave. (504/988-5263).

Insurance Travel insurance is a good safety net if you think for some reason you may need to cancel or postpone your trip (or even if you don't). Most medical insurance policies cover you if you are on vacation, but check yours before you depart.

Internet, Wi-Fi & Computer Rentals New Orleans is a pretty well-wired city. Nearly all major hotels have free Wi-Fi in their lobbies, as do many cafes, bars, and all Starbucks (there's one in the

French Quarter in the Canal Place Mall, 333 Canal St.; 504/566-1223). The vast majority of hotels also offer some form of in-room Internet access, usually highspeed, often wireless. Many now include the cost in the room charge; some add a daily surcharge of $10 to $20. Barring that, the easiest option is simply to boot up and see what signals you get; or walk down any commercial street and look for "Free Wi-Fi" signs. Alternately, a concierge or front desk attendant should be able to direct you to nearby public Wi-Fi locations.

Most larger hotels have business centers with computers for rent. Convenient **FedEx Office** locations with fully loaded rental computer stations are at 555 Canal St. (504/654-1057) and 762 St. Charles Ave. (504/581-2541). **Louis Armstrong International Airport** has free (so-so) Wi-Fi coverage in all passenger areas.

Language English is spoken everywhere, while French and Spanish are heard occasionally in New Orleans.

Legal Aid If you are pulled over by the police for a minor infraction (such as speeding), never attempt to pay the fine directly to an officer; this could be construed as attempted bribery, a much more serious crime. Pay fines by mail or directly into the hands of the clerk of the court. If accused of a more serious offense, say and do nothing before consulting a lawyer. Here in the U.S., the burden is on the state to prove a person's guilt beyond a reasonable doubt, and everyone has the right to remain silent, whether he or she is suspected of a crime or actually arrested. Once arrested, a person can make one telephone call to a party of his or her choice. The international visitor should call his or her embassy or consulate.

LGBTQ Travelers New Orleans is a very welcoming town with an extensive and active LGBTQ community and many events specific to or attended by the community. For resources, start with **Ambush Magazine,** 828-A Bourbon St. (www.ambushmag.com). The **Metropolitan Community Church of New Orleans,** 5401 S. Claiborne Ave. (www.MCCNewOrleans.org; ℂ **504/270-1622**), serves a primarily gay and lesbian congregation. The website **www.gayneworleans.com** provides information on hotels, restaurants, arts, and nightlife. The local **LGBT Gay Community Center** (www.facebook.com/lgbtccno; www.lgbtccneworleans.org) lists events and info on its websites. More resources are listed at www.neworleansonline.com/neworleans/lgbt/lgbt_organizations. "The Twirl," a gay-history walking tour of the French Quarter from **G L-f de Villiers Tours** (p. 172), is highly recommended. Also see p. 208 for suggested night (and day) clubbing.

Mail & Shipping At press time, domestic postage rates were 35¢ for a postcard and 50¢ for a letter up to 1 ounce. For international mail, a first-class postcard or letter stamp costs $1.15. For more information, go to **www.usps.com**. Always include ZIP codes when mailing items in the U.S. Use the lookup tool at www.usps.com/zip4.

If you aren't sure what your address will be while in the U.S., mail can be sent to you, in your name, c/o General Delivery at the main post office of the city or region where you expect to be. (Call ℂ **800/275-8777** for info on the nearest post office.) The addressee must pick up mail in person, with proof of identity (i.e., driver's license, passport). Most post offices will hold mail for up to 1 month and are open weekdays 8am to 4pm (Sat 9am–noon). New Orleans' main post office (701 Loyola Ave. in the CBD) has longer hours. Private mailing services include **French Quarter Postal Emporium** (1000 Bourbon St.; ℂ **504/525-6651;** frenchquarterpostal.net).

Medical Care See "Health."

Medical Requirements Unless you're arriving from an area known to have rates of certain illnesses (particularly cholera, yellow fever, and now measles and Ebola), inoculations or vaccinations are not usually required for short-term visitors to the U.S.

Mobile Phones Mobile (cell) phone and texting service in New Orleans is generally good, with the larger carriers all getting excellent coverage. Some dead zones still exist around the city and inside old brick buildings. International mobile phone service can be hit-or-miss (despite what you may have been told before you began your trip). If you plan to use your phone a lot while in New Orleans, it may be worthwhile to purchase a prepaid, no-contract phone locally. You can get hooked up at most drugstores or **Walmart** (1901 Tchoupitoulas St., ℂ **504/522-4142**). Compare the plans' sign-on offers, roaming and data use charges, usage requirements, and limitations to make sure you're not purchasing more extensive or longer-term services than you need.

If you have a computer and Internet service, consider using a broadband-based telephone service such as **Skype** (www.skype.com) or **Vonage** (www.vonage.com), which allow you to make free international calls from your computer. Neither service requires that the people you're calling also have the service (though there are fees if they do not).

Money & Costs Frommer's lists prices in U.S. dollars. The currency conversions quoted below were correct at press time. However, rates fluctuate, so before departing consult a currency exchange website such as **www.xe.com**.

Costs in New Orleans are generally right in the middle of, and sometimes lower than, that in other midsize U.S. "destination" cities—less than New York, for example, but more than Phoenix. Prices have crept up over the last few years, so it's no longer the great value it once was, and costs vary greatly by season. You can often find good hotel deals in the heat of summer, while prices often soar during big events. December's **prix-fixe Réveillon deals** can get you into restaurants for dinners that might otherwise be prohibitive.

With a few cash-only exceptions, **major credit cards** are accepted everywhere (some don't accept American Express, Discover, or Diner's Club). Cash is king anywhere, and ATMs are plentiful throughout the city (including inside many bars and souvenir shops). Expect a $2.50 to $4 charge to use an ATM outside your network. To avoid the fee, most grocery and convenience stores will allow you to get a small amount of cash back with your purchase (from $10–$100, depending on store policy).

Beware hidden credit-card fees while traveling. Check with your credit or debit card issuer to see what fees, if any, will be charged for overseas

transactions, even if those charges were made in U.S. dollars. Check with your bank before departing to avoid surprise charges on your statement.

Newspapers & Magazines The city has two local papers: Baton Rouge-based **The Advocate** (www.theadvocate.com/neworleans) and the **Times-Picayune** (www.nola.com). **Offbeat** (www.offbeat.com) and **Where Y'at** (www.whereyat.com) are monthly entertainment guides with live music, art, and special event listings. Both can usually be found in hotels and clubs, and get scarce toward the end of the month. **Gambit Weekly** (www.bestofneworleans.com), which comes out every Sunday, is the city's free alternative paper and has a good mix of local news and entertainment.

Packing What to pack depends largely on what you plan to do while visiting New Orleans. But comfortable walking shoes are a must year-round. A compact umbrella will often be put to use, as will other raingear during the wetter months (and a sun hat for much of the year). A light sweater or jacket is needed even in the hottest weather, when the indoor A.C. can get frigid. Casual wear is the daytime

norm, but cocktail wear is appropriate in nicer restaurants, and some of the old-liners require jackets for gentlemen. Also see the suggestions under "Health" and "Safety" in this section.

Passports Every air traveler entering the U.S. is required to show a valid passport (including U.S. citizens). Those entering by land and sea must also present a passport or other appropriate documentation. See www.dhs.gov/crossing-us-borders for details. For more on passport requirements, contact the Passport Office of your home country. If you need to obtain or renew a passport, do so at least 6 months before your departure.

Pharmacies Pharmacies (aka chemists or druggists) are easily found. Large chain pharmacies, including **Rite Aid, CVS,** and **Walgreens,** operate throughout the city, including several in the French Quarter. There is a 24-hour pharmacy at the Uptown **CVS** at 4901 Prytania St. (℃ **504/891-6307).**

Police Dial ℃ **911** for emergencies. This is a free call from any phone. Calls from landlines will route to the local emergency dispatch agency. From mobile phones, immediately tell the operator your location and the nature of the emergency.

THE VALUE OF THE U.S. DOLLAR VS. OTHER POPULAR CURRENCIES

US$	C$	£	€	A$	NZ$
1.00	1.26	0.70	0.81	1.29	1.36

WHAT THINGS COST IN NEW ORLEANS

	US$
Taxi from airport to the Quarter	36.00 (for 2 people)
Shuttle from airport to the Quarter	24.00 (per person)
Cost of bus/streetcar one-way	1.25
Day pass for bus/streetcar	3.00
Standard room at Ritz-Carlton	269.00–599.00
Standard room at The Chimes Bed & Breakfast	138.00–244.00
Standard room at Drury Inn	149.00–289.00
Order of 3 beignets or cup of café au lait at Café du Monde	2.42
Dinner at Commander's Palace (3 courses)	51.00 (per person)
Dinner at Meauxbar (3 courses)	49.00 (per person)
Muffuletta sandwich at Central Grocery	22.14
Ticket to a show at Tipitina's	10.00–45.00
Cost of a Hurricane at Pat O' Brien's with souvenir glass	12.00
Cost of a Pimm's Cup at Napoleon House	7.00

Safety It's true that New Orleans has a high crime rate. But most (not all) of the serious crime is drug-related and confined to areas where tourists do not go. Still, we urge you to be very cautious about where you go, what you do, and with whom—particularly at night. In short, behave with the same savvy and street smarts you would demonstrate in any big city: Travel in groups or pairs, take cabs if you're not sure of an area, stay in well-lighted areas with plenty of street and pedestrian traffic, and follow your instincts if something seems "off." Stay alert and walk with confidence; avoid looking distracted, confused, or (sorry) drunk. In fact, avoid *being* drunk—that's just a general good

rule. Speaking of which, one way to ensure you will look like a tourist—and thus, a target—is to wear Mardi Gras beads at any time other than Mardi Gras.

iPhones have become a target of grab-and-run thieves, especially since users, like those who text while walking, are frequently distracted. If you must check something on your phone, stop into a hotel lobby, bar, or shop.

When it's not in use, put that expensive camera out of sight. Use camera cases and purses with a shoulder strap, carried diagonally over the shoulder so a simple tug won't dislodge them. Consider using a money belt or other hidden travel wallet. Ditch the trendy enormous bag and

invest in a cute little shoulder-strappy thing for clubbing, one you can dance with rather than leave on your seat (better yet, go purse-free). Never leave valuables in the outside pocket of a backpack, and if you must store belongings in a car, store them in the trunk. Leave expensive-looking jewelry and other conspicuous valuables at home. And by all means, **don't look for or buy drugs or engage in any illegal activity.**

On **Bourbon Street,** be careful when socializing with strangers, and be alert to distractions by potential pickpocket teams. Use busy Decatur Street to walk from the French Quarter to Frenchmen Street.

Scattered sections of the **Tremé, Bywater,** and the **Irish Channel** section of the Lower Garden District are transitional and may be considered sketchy. This shouldn't dissuade you from visiting, but you should keep on your toes.

Single Travelers Single travelers, both male and female, should feel comfortable in New Orleans. People are generally friendly, and many restaurants, including some of the city's finest, serve meals at the bar—a personal favorite spot when dining solo (Emeril's, Coquette, Cochon, and Acme come to mind). Still, single women travelers in particular should heed the warnings in the "Safety" section, above.

Smoking The city council instituted a broad-reaching law in 2015, banning smoking indoors almost everywhere including hotels, restaurants, casinos, nightclubs, and bars (cigar and vape bars are excepted). Places with patios or courtyards can designate them as smoking areas, but not all do. It's okay on the street a few feet from restaurant or shop entrances, and in most parks. **Marijuana** use in all forms is still illegal. For now.

Taxes The United States has no value-added tax (VAT) or other indirect tax at the national level. Every state, county, and city may levy its own local tax on all purchases, including hotel and restaurant checks and airline tickets. These taxes will not appear on price

tags. The **sales tax** in New Orleans is 10%; **hotel room tax** is 14% plus US$1 to $2 per room per night.

On the upside, international travelers who purchase goods in Louisiana to take to their home countries can often get the sales tax refunded in full. When you make your purchase, keep your receipt and also request a "tax back" voucher (you'll be asked to show your passport). Before you leave the state, bring your receipts and vouchers to the **Refund Center** in the Outlet Collection at Riverwalk mall (p. 213) or New Orleans Airport (location in new airport had not been finalized at press time; check at airport information booth; allow time before your flight). You'll be rebated in cash up to US$500. Larger rebates are mailed; see **www.louisiana taxfree.com** for instructions and more information. Not all stores participate, so ask first.

Also, many original works of art purchased in New Orleans are tax-exempt. Do inquire, as this applies in designated cultural districts only.

Telephones Hotel costs for long-distance and local calls made from guest rooms vary widely. Local calls range from complimentary to astronomically expensive; long-distance calls typically fall into the latter category. Calls to area codes **800, 888, 877,** and **866** are free. If you intend to use the room phone,

definitely inquire about phone charges. You may be better off using a mobile phone or a prepaid calling card. Public payphones are rare, but some (for example, at airports) accept credit cards. Most long-distance and international calls can be dialed directly from any phone. **To make calls within the United States and to Canada,** dial **1** followed by the area code and the seven-digit number. **For other international calls,** dial **011** followed by the country code, city code, and the number you are calling. For **directory assistance** (help finding numbers, aka "Information") in the U.S. and Canada, dial **411.** For other phone services, dial **0** to reach an operator for phone services within the U.S.; dial **00** for assistance with international calls. Also see "Mobile Phones," earlier in this section.

Time New Orleans is in the Central Time Zone (CST), which is 6 hours earlier than Greenwich Mean Time. When it's noon in New Orleans, it's 10am in Los Angeles (PST); 1pm in New York City; 6pm in London (GMT); and 5am the next day in Sydney.

Daylight saving time (summer time) is in effect from 1am on the second Sunday in March to 1am on the first Sunday in November, except in Arizona, Hawaii, the U.S. Virgin Islands, and Puerto Rico. Daylight saving time moves the clock 1 hour ahead of standard time.

Tipping   Tips are a very important part of certain workers' income and the standard way of showing appreciation for services provided (it's not compulsory if the service is poor, but most people leave a smaller tip rather than none at all). In hotels, tip **bellhops** $1 to $2 per bag ($3 if you have a lot of luggage) and tip the **chamber staff** $5 and up per night (more if you've been extra messy). Tip the **doorman** or **concierge** if he or she has provided you with some specific service (for example, calling a cab for you or obtaining tickets or reservations), $5 to $20 or more depending on complexity. Tip the **valet-parking attendant** $2 to $5 every time you get your car; more if you're driving something you need to protect.

In restaurants, bars, and nightclubs, tip **service staff** and **bartenders** 15% to 20% of the check, tip **checkroom attendants** $2 per garment, and tip **valet-parking attendants** $2 to $5 per vehicle. Some restaurants will automatically add a tip to the bill for larger parties (typically 18% for six or more guests, but this can vary). Check your bill or ask your server if gratuity has been included in your bill.

As for other service personnel, tip **cab drivers** 15% to 20% of the fare, tip **skycaps** at airports at least $2 per bag (more if you have a lot of luggage), and tip

hairdressers and **barbers** 15% to 20%.

Toilets   You won't find public toilets or "restrooms" on the streets in most U.S. cities, but they can be found in hotel lobbies, bars, restaurants, museums, department stores, railway and bus stations, and service stations. Large hotels are often the best bet for clean facilities. Restaurants and bars may restrict their restrooms to paying patrons, but it never hurts to ask.

Tours   New Orleans offers tours geared toward antiquing, literature, history, gay and lesbian culture, ghosts, and Voodoo, along with tours of the fabled, stunning swamps, plantation homes, cemeteries, and various areas of New Orleans. For more on tours, see chapters 7 and 11; see chapter 10 for self-guided walking tours.

Travelers with Disabilities

Most disabilities shouldn't stop anyone from traveling in New Orleans. Most public places are required to comply with disability-friendly regulations. Almost all public establishments (except a few National Historic Landmarks) and at least some modes of public transportation provide accessible entrances and facilities.

Still, a few places may be inaccessible, with regulatory allowances due to their historic nature. Before you book a reservation, call and inquire based on your needs. The city's newer hotels, restaurants, and

shops are fully accommodating, and many older ones have undergone excellent retrofitting.

The city's bumpy and uneven sidewalks (and sometimes potholed or cobblestoned streets) can be challenging for wheelchairs and walkers, though most have curb cuts. The St. Charles streetcar requires a big step up and does not have a lift; all other streetcar lines do.

For paratransit information and reservations, call **RTA Paratransit** (www. norta.com/accessiblity; ℂ **504/827-7433**).

Visas   The U.S. State Department has a **Visa Waiver Program (VWP)** allowing citizens from a long list of countries to enter the United States without a visa for stays of up to 90 days. Even for visitors from VWP countries and others for whom a visa is not necessary, an e-passport, online registration through the Electronic System for Travel Authorization (ESTA), and an electronic application are required before departing the U.S. Travelers not eligible for VWP are required to get a visa. Some travelers may also be required to present a round-trip air or cruise ticket upon arrival in the U.S. Canadian citizens may enter the United States without visas, but will need to show passports and proof of residence. Citizens of all other countries must have: (1) a valid passport that expires at least 6 months later than the scheduled end of their visit to the U.S., and (2) a tourist visa. All visa and passport information is subject to change. Check with the American Embassy in your home country at least 6 months before your planned departure and read up at http://travel.state.gov/content/visas/english/visit/visa-waiver-program.html.

Visitor Information

Even a seasoned traveler should consider writing or calling ahead to the **New Orleans Convention & Visitors Bureau,** 2020 St. Charles Ave., New Orleans, LA 70130 (www.neworleans.com; © **800/672-6124** or 504/566-5011; Mon–Fri

8:30am–5pm). The friendly staff can offer advice and help with decision-making; if you have a special interest, they'll help you plan your visit around it—this is definitely one of the most helpful tourist centers in any major city.

The **Louisiana Office of Tourism New Orleans Welcome Center,** 529 St. Ann St. (© **504/568-5661;** daily 8:30am–5pm), has walking- and driving-tour maps; booklets on restaurants, accommodations, sightseeing, special tours; and more.

Be aware: Many of the **concierges, tour offices,** and **visitors centers** scattered around the city are

for-profit offices operated by tourism businesses hawking their own wares. Rather than unbiased services that will recommend the best tour for you, these are commissioned sales offices. If you feel you're getting sold something that's not exactly right, you can always contact any tour company directly to buy tours. Or just use *Frommer's* unbiased recommendations!

Water Tap water is safe to drink in New Orleans, although bottled water is still popular. Treated water from the Mississippi River is the main source of tap water, as is true for most cities along the Mississippi.

Index

See also Accommodations and Restaurant indexes, below.

Accommodations

Map List

Photo Credits

Frommer's EasyGuide to New Orleans 2019, 6th Edition

Published by
FROMMER MEDIA LLC

ISBN 978-1-62887-424-2 (paper), 978-1-62887-425-9 (e-book)

Editorial Director: Pauline Frommer
Editor: Alexis Lipsitz Flippin
Production Editor: Lindsay Conner
Photo Editor: Meghan Lamb
Cartographer: Roberta Stockwell
Cover Design: Dave Riedy

Front cover photo © GTS Productions / Shutterstock.com

For information on our other products or services, see www.frommers.com.

FrommerMedia LLC also publishes its books in a variety of electronic formats. Some content that appears in print may not be available in electronic formats.

Manufactured in the United States of America

5 4 3 2 1

ABOUT THE AUTHOR

Diana K. Schwam, writer and strategic communications consultant, has authored seven books, numerous articles, and scads of content about New Orleans. She followed a familiar path to the city: vacation; enrapture; home ownership; insurance claim; weight gain; Saints fanaticism; contentment; inspiration. She can often be seen in the local clubs, eateries, and cultural havens, or exploring the city's lesser-known or unfolding corners on Miss Gulch, her green, two-wheeled pothole-dodger. Diana continues to have infinite love for the city, the people, and the ghosts of New Orleans; its eccentric elegance and eternal mysteries; its tellers of tales and truths: They are as warm and essential to her as its air. She claps on the twos and fours. Usually.

ACKNOWLEDGMENTS

Ms. Schwam would like to thank Arthur Frommer, Pauline Frommer, and Alexis Lipsitz. She sends love to the original and ever-expanding Fat Pack; the Schwams; Beers; Dileos; Zuckerbergs; Harch; Scot; Alvin Kamara; and Dave and Mary of course. NRAS4EVR.

ABOUT THE FROMMER TRAVEL GUIDES

For most of the past 50 years, Frommer's has been the leading series of travel guides in North America, accounting for as many as 24% of all guidebooks sold. I think I know why.

Though we hope our books are entertaining, we nevertheless deal with travel in a serious fashion. Our guidebooks have never looked on such journeys as a mere recreation, but as a far more important human function, a time of learning and introspection, an essential part of a civilized life. We stress the culture, lifestyle, history, and beliefs of the destinations we cover, and urge our readers to seek out people and new ideas as the chief rewards of travel.

We have never shied from controversy. We have, from the beginning, encouraged our authors to be intensely judgmental, critical—both pro and con—in their comments, and wholly independent. Our only clients are our readers, and we have triggered the ire of countless prominent sorts, from a tourist newspaper we called "practically worthless" (it unsuccessfully sued us) to the many rip-offs we've condemned.

And because we believe that travel should be available to everyone regardless of their incomes, we have always been cost-conscious at every level of expenditure. Though we have broadened our recommendations beyond the budget category, we insist that every lodging we include be sensibly priced. We use every form of media to assist our readers, and are particularly proud of our feisty daily website, the award-winning Frommers.com.

I have high hopes for the future of Frommer's. May these guidebooks, in all the years ahead, continue to reflect the joy of travel and the freedom that travel represents. May they always pursue a cost-conscious path, so that people of all incomes can enjoy the rewards of travel. And may they create, for both the traveler and the persons among whom we travel, a community of friends, where all human beings live in harmony and peace.

Arthur Frommer